Early Praise for *Become a Great Engineering Leader*

James has done it again with a stellar view into the complicated world of leadership in the tech world. Having something that lays out the fundamentals of leadership at the next level has given me the advice and confidence to strive towards what originally felt like an impossible goal. Before this book I was unsure if I wanted to take that next step in my career, and now I am certain that not only do I want to but that I can.

> ➤ **Michael Tempest**
> Senior Engineering Team Lead at Spendesk and Founder of ThinkAsync

As a CTO/VP Engineering Coach, many of my clients struggle with the topics covered by this book. James does an excellent job covering the broad responsibilities of a senior engineering leader and offers many pragmatic tips on how to do them well. This book will be a solid recommendation for many of my current and future clients.

> ➤ **Patrick Kua**
> Founder, patkua.com

Become a Great Engineering Leader is an invaluable field guide for anyone who wants to grow and make a real impact within engineering leadership. It provides the tools you need to help build your confidence and navigate the challenges you will inevitably face as you progress in your career to become an intelligent, empathetic, and visionary leader.

> ➤ **Christopher Butler**
> Director of Engineering, Aidn

This is the guidebook to understanding what's next in your career as a manager and a natural progression in James's series. From strategy to budgeting passing through team formations, James will open a world to you as he explains in detail all the things you need to know to help you build your career. If you are a manager, no matter your intentions of growth, this is your book to learn more about the next level.

➤ **Juan Miguel García Mesa**
  Engineering Manager, Shopify

Become a Great Engineering Leader
Build Effective Skills to Lead and Grow

James Stanier

The Pragmatic Bookshelf

Dallas, Texas

For our complete catalog of hands-on, practical, and Pragmatic content for software developers, please visit *https://pragprog.com*.

Contact *support@pragprog.com* for sales, volume licensing, and support.

For international rights, please contact *rights@pragprog.com*.

The team that produced this book includes:

Publisher:	Dave Thomas
COO:	Janet Furlow
Executive Editor:	Susannah Davidson
Development Editor:	Adaobi Obi Tulton
Copy Editor:	Karen Galle
Indexing:	Potomac Indexing, LLC
Layout:	Gilson Graphics

Copyright © 2024 The Pragmatic Programmers, LLC.

All rights reserved. No part of this publication may be reproduced, stored in a retrieval system, or transmitted, in any form, or by any means, electronic, mechanical, photocopying, recording, or otherwise, without the prior consent of the publisher.

When we are aware that a term used in this book is claimed as a trademark, the designation is printed with an initial capital letter or in all capitals.

The Pragmatic Starter Kit, The Pragmatic Programmer, Pragmatic Programming, Pragmatic Bookshelf, PragProg and the linking *g* device are trademarks of The Pragmatic Programmers, LLC.

Every precaution was taken in the preparation of this book. However, the publisher assumes no responsibility for errors or omissions, or for damages that may result from the use of information (including program listings) contained herein.

ISBN-13: 979-8-88865-066-0
Book version: P1.0—September 2024

Contents

Acknowledgments ix
Introduction xi

Part I — The Role Defined

1. **VP, Director, What?** 3
   Laying Out the Career Tracks 5
   Scope and Impact 14
   Competencies 16
   Getting the Gig 17
   To the Org Chart! 20

2. **Your Place in the Org Chart** 23
   The Division of Labor 25
   The Shape of My Chart: Structures and Patterns 30
   Structural Antipatterns and How to Avoid Them 36
   Flows of Communication and Collaboration 41
   Time Flies… 52

Part II — Tools, Techniques and Time

3. **Time: Observed, Spent, and Allocated** 55
   A Lens of Longtermism 57
   Your Capacity: Your Most Important Resource 64
   Time Management: Models, Tools, and Techniques 69
   Your Calendar: Wielding a Double-Edged Sword 76
   Now, You've Got People to Manage 89

4. **The Games We Play and How to Win Them** 91
   Management 101: The Fundamentals 93
   It's All Just Leadership After All 103
   From the Swamp to Infinity: Achieving Together 107
   Leading Without Authority 118

5. **The Sharpest Tool in Your Toolbelt** **119**
   Individual Contributors: The Higher Rungs   121
   The Four Archetypes: Pieces of Your Puzzle   123
   Deploying Senior Individual Contributors   125
   The Technical Shadow Organization   129
   Looking Sideways   133

6. **The Tragedy of the Common Leader** **135**
   But We Didn't Want This to Become a Dumpster Fire 137
   Magnetism and Polarity: Pulling Peers Together   139
   Actually, It's All on You: Do It Yourself   146

7. **Of Clownfish and Anemones** **153**
   Teenage Rebellion: Raging Against the Machine   156
   Prescriptions Don't Work: Tools Do   158
   Symbiosis: Defined, Observed, and Applied   160
   Skip to the End: Defining the Relationship   161
   When the Stuff Hits the Fan   165
   Three Is a Magic Number   171

8. **Trifectas, Multifectas, and Allies** **173**
   Omne Trium Perfectum   175
   Trifectas: Your Own Perfect Triplet   176
   Extending to Multifectas   184
   Snow Melts at the Periphery   186
   And Now for Something Completely Different   189

9. **Communication at Scale** **191**
   Standing on the Shoulders of Scribbles   194
   Patterns of Communication   195
   Leadership Is Writing   204
   The Grand Commit Log of History   209
   And Now for Our Favorite Parts of the Job   221

10. **Performance Management: Raising the Bar** . . . **223**
    The Rising Tide: Why We're Doing This   225
    Performance Management of Senior Staff   228
    Calibrations: Converging on Fairness   237
    Debugging Common Performance Management Issues   244
    Let's Get Strategic   249

Part III — Strategy, Planning, and Execution

11. Strategy 101 253
    What on Earth Is a Strategy, Anyway?   255
    Engineering Strategy: Your Piece of the Puzzle   258
    Let's Build an Engineering Strategy Together   261
    Cycling Through the Year   270

12. Company Cycles 271
    The Calendar Is Dead, Long Live the Calendar   274
    Sales: Can't Live with Them, Can't Live Without Them   277
    Marketing: Big Bangs Without the Bang   284
    Two Worlds Collide: Troubleshooting and Solutions   287
    Dollars, Pound, Euros, and Yen   292

13. Money Makes the World Go Round 295
    Finance 101: The Basics of Company Finance   297
    Managing a Large Budget: Levers and Dials   305
    Common Dilemmas: Patterns to Follow   314
    Good Times and Bad Times Ahead   318

14. Boom and Bust 319
    Spend! Invest! Grow! Crash! Burn! Rebuild!   321
    Peacetime and Wartime: A Spectrum   326
    Concentric Circles of Trust   328
    Leading Through Peacetime: Invest, Spend, Grow   330
    Leading Through Wartime: Cut, Save, Rebuild   337
    So, Where Are You Going?   345

15. Tarzan Swings from Vine to Vine 347
    The Fallacy of the Straight Line   349
    The Tarzan Method   351
    The Trajectory of Your Swing   352
    Earn, Learn, or Quit   354
    Putting It All Together   356
    Once Again, It's Been a Pleasure   360

Bibliography 363
Index 365

Acknowledgments

Leaders are nothing without their teams, and this book has truly been a team effort.

I would like to thank absolutely *everyone* that I have worked with over the years. You have helped me learn, grow, and crucially, get to a point where I can commit it to paper to help those that are following the same path.

I am exceptionally lucky to work with such smart people at Shopify. They introduce me to new challenges every single day: from technical problems to organizational puzzles and everything in between. A special thank you goes out to those that have managed me over the last few years: Daniel Cotnoir, Sophie Roberts, and most recently Farhan Thawar. Whenever I get stuck I always think, "What would *they* do here?"

My direct team keeps me on my toes and often challenges me to think about the world differently. Thank you to Lyne Champagne, Jon Burns, Oliver Tabay, Sebastien Menard, Joshua McClymont, Graham Scott, Patrick Donovan, Richard Poirier, and Robert Paulsen for all the great work we have done together.

I would also like to thank everyone who gave me in-depth feedback on the book during technical reviews. All your ideas and input have made the finished product far, far better. That's Pat Kua, Nik Bhattacharya, Michael Tempest, Christopher Butler, Juan Miguel, Reuben Sutton, Mike Dalessio, and Andy Polhill: thank you all so much. I appreciate the fact that you took the time for me.

Once again, my publisher, The Pragmatic Bookshelf, has been amazing. I wouldn't have gone through the ordeal of writing a book for the third time if I didn't love working with you. I have had brilliant editorial support from Adaobi Obi Tulton, who has once again kept me on the straight and narrow, helping me express myself better and making sure that the book is as good as it can be.

The last acknowledgment goes to my partner, Rebecca. Not only has she been gracious as I repeatedly disappeared into a writing hole late at night or on weekends, but she has once again created all of the beautiful illustrations that you see throughout the book. I am looking forward to our next big project, which will have already begun by the time you read this.

The last acknowledgment goes to *you*. I appreciate the fact that you have trusted me to help guide you on this next part of your career journey. Once again, I hope that this book opens doors that you didn't even know existed.

Introduction

Often, readers skip past the introduction of a book because they are eager to get right into the first chapter. However, I dare you to be a little different. Take a moment to pause and reflect on what brought you to this moment in time. What led you to be reading this specific sentence in this specific book? *Why* exactly are you here?

Think about it for a second. In fact, in true British fashion, I am encouraging you to put the kettle on, make a cup of tea, and mentally rewind through your career journey so far. How did you get into technology in the first place? What was your first job? Where are you *now*?

Perhaps you are looking to this book to act as a map to guide you through your onward adventure. You may have recently been promoted into a senior management role. You might be managing multiple teams for the first time, wondering just *what it actually is* that you should be doing to be successful. We can help you with that. Maybe you are a seasoned manager, but you are looking to sharpen the tools in your toolbox. We can help you with that, too. Or perhaps you have seen that headhunting email saying that you'd be a perfect fit for a VP engineering role at a new startup, and you want to know what you are getting yourself into. Guess what? We've got you covered. Always.

And get this: even if you are an individual contributor trying to understand how to progress to staff engineer and beyond, there is a *lot* to be gained from gaining deep knowledge of those who are above you in the org chart. Understanding *what* they do, *how* they do it, and *why* they do it can unlock your potential to be even more impactful in your role. After all, you need to understand the playing field to be able to master the game.

No Improvisation, No Gatekeeping

Some history. Nearly four years have passed since I wrote my first book, *Become an Effective Software Engineering Manager [Sta20]*. It was a book that materialized from writing a weekly blog, starting way back in 2017. I started the blog a few years into my first management role as a way of better understanding the challenges that I was facing and what I was learning along the way. After all, as we'll cover later in this book, *writing is thinking*.

I was grateful and surprised that so many people found what I wrote to be practical and useful to them. I would receive emails from readers saying something that I wrote deeply resonated with their own thinking or helped them analyze a specific problem that they were facing. It felt like there was a community of engineering managers out there who were all trying their best to apply the same scrutiny, best practices, and care to their craft as individual contributors do to their code, but comparatively, there was a lack of resources to help them do so.

As a result of these interactions with readers of my blog, the first book was born. It is a complete hands-on guide to running a team, designed from the bottom up to assume no prior knowledge of management and to take the reader on a journey from the first day of their new role through to being confident and successful. As of the time of writing, more people have read that book than I will likely ever meet in my lifetime, which is both humbling and awesome. It's probably one of the most rewarding things I've accomplished. I think that it, along with other great books in our collective canon, has helped lift the floor of our profession, leaving it in a better place than when we joined it. The Boy Scout rule applies here, too: we should leave the campsite in a better condition than when we found it.

There was a principle that I kept in mind when writing that book, and it's one that I've kept in mind when writing this one too: *no improvisation, and no gatekeeping*. Back then I wrote that the problem with management, especially in the technology industry, is that many of us who become managers and leaders haven't been planning to do so for our whole lives.

Often we got into technology through our passions and interests, whether they were realized by building our first ever website or by working out how to build simple applications on our home computers. We were drawn to the craft of software engineering, and we honed that craft either through formal education, or hands-on apprenticeship, or both.

Then, through a combination of preparation, opportunity, and a unique talent, we realized that we could also be good at leading people, and we took the leap. But, unlike our path into software engineering, we found far fewer resources to help us learn how to be good at it. Perhaps we even struggled to get on with our own managers, and we had no role models to look up to. Yet, despite all of this, we *don't need to improvise*. Many of the generalized frameworks and tools that we need to be successful are easy to learn and understand and can, therefore, be applied to our own unique situations. This book, like the last, is full of them.

And let's face it, some people may have said that management wasn't for people like *us*. Perhaps they said that it was for people who were a "different shape," or those who were more extroverted, or those who better fit the stereotype of the hot-blooded corporate executive. But that's not true *at all*. Management and leadership *are* for people like us. *There is no gatekeeping here*. Directors and VPs of engineering are not a special breed of human that you cannot ever become. They are just people who have had a unique mixture of preparation, opportunity, and raw talent that has been honed over time. They come from all walks of life and through many different career paths. And if you're aiming for one of those roles as you go on your journey, we'll help you align the crosshairs.

Random Walks

Getting a senior management role in the technology industry isn't entirely predictable. You can't necessarily preempt the opportunities that are going to come your way or know whether you're going to be ready for them when they arrive. When I joined a small startup in 2011, I had no idea that I was going to be VP of engineering by the time I left. I was far more focused at the beginning on just *building* the product and making sure that it didn't blow up as we scaled. My executive position materialized over many years from a combination of growth, opportunity, a desire to push myself and learn new things, and, of course, a lot of hard work. Moving toward that role was a *random walk*. Each year, the company evolved, and so did I. Metaphorically, when the student was ready, the master appeared.

You, too, are in the middle of the random walk of your career. Could you have really predicted that you would be where you are now? Did you even know that your current company existed when you got your first job? Maybe it didn't exist at all. This isn't a bad thing. In fact, it's pretty rad. You have absolutely no idea where you are going to end up. Maybe an executive role is in your future, and maybe that future is only next year. It only takes one email to change *everything*.

Perhaps your company is going to become a growth rocket ship, and you will be in the cockpit when it happens. Maybe you'll be headhunted by a company that you've never heard of, and it will be an unbounded success and the best decision that you've ever made. Or maybe that will be the *next* one after that. You just don't know: that's the joy of random walks.

However, we know that you aren't roaming aimlessly. The fact that you picked up this book means that you are interested in honing your craft of leadership so that if your random walk stumbles upon a new opportunity, you'll have the confidence and the skills to take it on. That might be at your current company after a reorg lands you with multiple engineering teams to manage for the first time, or it might be a role at a smaller company with a far larger scope and responsibility. Who knows? It's exciting.

Arming yourself with the tools and awareness of what is to come is the best way to prepare for the future. When you're ringing the bell at the New York Stock Exchange as VP of engineering of the hottest technology startup in the world, do cast your mind back to this sentence and spare a thought for the randomness of the walk that got you there.

Your Journey

You could be at numerous places in your journey right now. You could be an engineering manager running a team of individual contributors, wondering what the next step is for you on the management career track. After all, what is a senior engineering manager doing that you're *not*? Perhaps that step has already happened: you're now managing multiple teams, and you're wondering how exactly to split your time and what to focus on. Perhaps you're interested in where you could be going in the years to come. What does it mean to be a VP of engineering, and how can you start learning those skills now so that you're prepared when your random walk takes you there?

In this book, we're going to strip everything back and build our foundations from the bottom up. Forget the specifics of your company and the minutiae of your day-to-day life; this is bigger and more meaningful than that. This is a book about understanding how to be a great leader, which is built upon a solid understanding of organizations, management, people, and most importantly, *yourself*. After all, the leader that you are and will continue to be is something that this book will never be able to teach you since it *is* you. We can't give you ten rules to follow to solve all of your problems; prescriptions are doomed to failure. However, we can help equip that future star (that's you) with all of the tools and insight that they need to forge their own path.

The book is written in such a way that it can be read from beginning to end, but you don't have to do that if you don't want to. Each chapter is a standalone piece of the whole spectrum of senior leadership, and you are more than welcome to jump around to the parts that interest you most. Generally speaking, the further the discussion is in the book, the more senior the role that it is aimed at. However, *all* of it can be useful to you, no matter where you are in your journey. We hope that you keep your copy close to hand and dip into it again and again as you progress through your career.

The Outline of This Book

The first part of the book is Part I, The Role Defined, on page 1, where we are going to lay out the scaffolding for everything that follows. In Chapter 1, VP, Director, What?, on page 3, we'll define the senior roles to help you understand both the scope and what is expected of you as you progress in your management career. Then, in Chapter 2, Your Place in the Org Chart, on page 23, we'll look at common structures of organizations and how those roles operate within them.

We'll move on to the second part of the book, which will fill up your toolbox with ideas. It's called Part II, Tools, Techniques and Time, on page 53. Starting with Chapter 3, Time: Observed, Spent, and Allocated, on page 55, we'll orient your view toward the long term and help you understand how to use your time and energy efficiently and effectively. Building on our long-term view, in Chapter 4, The Games We Play and How to Win Them, on page 91, we'll explore finite and infinite games and how they apply to you, your team, and your company.

No managers are effective without key individual contributors to partner with, and we'll explore how to get the most out of this relationship in Chapter 5, The Sharpest Tool in Your Toolbelt, on page 119. Another key relationship is the one that you have with your peers, and Chapter 6, The Tragedy of the Common Leader, on page 135 looks at why this can be a tragedy of the commons and how to mitigate it.

Managing upward is also key, and we explore the creation of a symbiotic relationship with your manager in Chapter 7, Of Clownfish and Anemones, on page 153 that benefits both of you. Symbiotic relationships aren't limited to the engineering org chart, so we'll explore Chapter 8, Trifectas, Multifectas, and Allies, on page 173 and see why collaboration and accountability are not just limited to front-line teams.

Being an effective leader is also about being heard and understood, and in Chapter 9, Communication at Scale, on page 191, we set up a communication architecture for your organization and help you understand how to use it effectively. The final chapter in this part, Chapter 10, Performance Management: Raising the Bar, on page 223, hones in on the performance management of senior staff.

In the final part of the book, Part III, Strategy, Planning, and Execution, on page 251, we'll sit atop the strategic mountain and look around at the landscape. We'll start with Chapter 11, Strategy 101, on page 253, where we'll dive deep into the creation of a strategy and how to communicate it. Then, in Chapter 12, Company Cycles, on page 271, we'll look at the repeating cycles that companies loop through in order to implement their strategies and how to line engineering up with them. Next, in Chapter 13, Money Makes the World Go Round, on page 295, we'll look at everything to do with money: how to manage large budgets, how it fits into the wider financial picture of a company, and how to wield money confidently and effectively.

The technology industry goes through periods of difficulty. Chapter 14, Boom and Bust, on page 319 will help you understand what it means to lead through peacetime and wartime. Finally, in Chapter 15, Tarzan Swings from Vine to Vine, on page 347, we'll come right back to what we just mentioned in this introduction: how to navigate the random walk of your career and how you might need to go down a few vines to get to where you want to be in the end.

So, What's Next?

Okay! That's it. Time to start. I'm really excited to be on this journey with you. Thank you for deciding to come along with me. I sincerely hope that this stack of physical or digital paper is insightful, entertaining, and helps you to be the best leader that you can be.

Similar to the first book, I wish I'd had all of this information when I started moving up the management ladder. Often, it's a lonely place with fairly weak feedback on what it means to do a good job. The pages ahead are the culmination of taking notes all the way along my own random walk, and I hope that it helps make your walk that much better.

It's time to get going. There's a video call that you're late for, so hurry up and join!

Part I

The Role Defined

So, where exactly are you now? And where are you trying to go?

No company is identical, but the patterns they use to define roles and responsibilities often have many similarities. And it turns out that these similarities have been around since long before computers graced the earth.

What does a VP of engineering do that a director doesn't? And what can the military teach us about the focus in each of these roles?

We're also going deep on one of the most powerful tools that you will wield in the upper levels of management: the org chart.

So, let's lay out the map and see where we're headed.

CHAPTER **1**

VP, Director, What?

Bing! You join the video call. You're the only one there.

You're a little early, but it's unlike your manager to want to chat with you in confidence at such short notice. In fact, you're a little nervous. Your mind begins to cycle through the possible direction that this conversation could take. Is she leaving? Is she unhappy about something? What could it be?

Bing! It's Lisa, your manager.

"Hey! Sorry for being a little late. Lots of last minute stuff to get through. How are you doing?"

"Yeah, I'm alright," you reply. "What did you want to speak about?"

Lisa leans in closer to her camera. "I've got some news."

"Okay..."

"Don't worry, it's good news. But it's important for us to talk about it in confidence, just for the next few days."

You nod, feeling relieved. "Of course. What's happening?"

"It's been a long time coming, but we've just closed our latest investment round. The existing investors *love* what we're doing here and want us to go even faster. They're giving us a *ton* of money."

You keep nodding. "Okay, that's great... But what does that mean for my team?"

Lisa smiles. "You mean your *teams*. Plural."

"Teams?"

"They're growing my role and making me VP of engineering! And, most importantly for you, they want to invest heavily in what you're building. They want a whole department on it. About fifty people."

You sit back and look off to the side of the camera. "Whoa."

"I'd like you to be my director of engineering. We've got a lot of people to hire."

You look back at Lisa. "Am I ready for that?"

She nods. "You've been ready for a while."

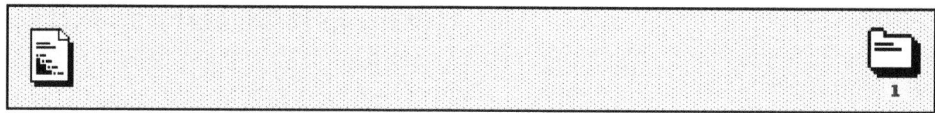

Hello. It's nice to see you here.

We're about to embark on a journey together. We're going to travel to the place where the senior managers live. Yep, *those* people.

They're the ones with the enviable job titles like "director" and "vice president." The ones with the impenetrable calendars stuffed full of back-to-back meetings that clash with each other like some kind of time salad. Most importantly, they're the ones who get to decide what the department is working on today, next month, and next year. And now it's time for *you* to become one of them. But don't worry: this book will be your guide through uncharted territory.

There are typically two giant leaps that you take in your career as a manager. The first is when you go from being an individual contributor to managing others for the first time. This is often a shock to new managers because it is a completely different role they have had no training for. All of a sudden, you are responsible for the output of a whole team of people rather than just your own output. This takes some getting used to.

Despite having many years of experience getting in the zone and carving ahead as an individual contributor, a new manager has to learn a whole new set of skills to be successful. These skills range from delegation, to coaching, to giving feedback and managing performance. In fact, you could say there is enough material to fill *a whole book [Sta20]*.

The second giant leap is where you are right now. It's when a skilled manager of a *single* team of individual contributors gets the opportunity to move up the chain of command to manage *multiple* teams, sometimes forming a whole division or department for which they are accountable. This kicks off another process of relearning your role from scratch.

It involves *managing managers* for the first time, and you are typically responsible for *multiple* features, projects, or products. It can often be daunting. Where do you start? You've likely had no training. Because of your seniority, others look up to you for guidance and direction, even though you may feel like *you're* the one who needs it.

But don't worry, because help is *most definitely* at hand. This book is going to be your guide as you begin to experience and understand what it takes to be effective at the upper levels of management. We're going to cover everything that you need to be successful in a practical and implementable way. This is not a typical leadership book full of waffle and anecdotes. This is an *actionable* field guide that we hope you will keep close to your desk and refer to often as your career unfolds.

We're going to begin by getting ourselves oriented. This chapter is going to dig into how the management career track is defined and how it is interlinked with career progression as an individual contributor.

Here's what we're going to cover:

- *We'll start by outlining the typical job titles for managers in technology companies.* What are they called, and how do they relate to each other in terms of seniority? We'll lean on a military analogy to help us understand the different levels of management and what might be expected of someone performing those roles.

- *Then, we'll expand our definitions to include scope, impact, and competencies to better understand how progression works.* We'll see how scope and impact are used to define the size of a role and how competencies are used to define the skills that are required to be successful.

- *Finally, we'll build on the concepts of scope and impact to understand some of the typical paths to move up the management career track.* We'll see it's not always easy to guarantee progression, so how can you ensure that you're ready when a new opportunity arises?

Let's find out together. It's time to get started.

Laying Out the Career Tracks

Since long before we were building technology, we assigned job titles to people in order to make it clear to them and to others what they do. For example, consider the medical profession. There are many doctors that have specific, differently named specialties.

For example, a general practitioner is a doctor who works in their local community as a first point of contact for people who are unwell and are seeking medical advice. A surgeon is a doctor who performs operations in order to treat a specific illness or injury. A pediatrician is a doctor who specializes in treating children. Different roles, different names. After all, if everyone was just called a doctor, it would be much harder to understand what they do and what is expected of them. It would also be inconvenient if you were seeking treatment for regular migraines and ended up with your leg being amputated!

We follow exactly the same pattern in technology companies. We don't just call everyone a technologist. Instead we have a range of job titles that make it clear what an individual's specialty is and how senior they are. This both helps the individual know what is expected of them and helps others understand what they are responsible for.

In order to help with the definition of roles and responsibilities in companies, we often use the concept of a *career track*. This is a grouping of job titles within the same specialty that increases in seniority in a linear manner.

For example, a career track for an individual contributor might look like this:

- Software engineer
- Senior engineer
- Staff engineer
- Principal engineer

An individual contributor at the beginning of their career would likely have the software engineer job title. As they gain experience and demonstrate they can operate at the next level, they may get promoted to the subsequent step on the career track, which is senior engineer. Typically, this would involve an expansion in their responsibilities, scope, and impact. This continues all the way up the track to the top. For example, a principal engineer would be expected to have a greater impact than a staff engineer and would be expected to have a wider scope of responsibilities.

It turns out we can also define a similar career track in order of seniority for managers, like this:

- Engineering manager
- Senior engineering manager
- Director of engineering
- Vice president (VP) of engineering
- Chief technology officer (CTO)

After starting at the bottom, an individual being promoted to a management position for the first time would likely be given the engineering manager job title. That's usually someone's first foray into management, and they would be managing a single team of individual contributors. At the top of the track, a CTO would be running the entire engineering department. Much like the individual contributor track, each progressive step up the management career track involves more responsibility through an incremental expansion of their scope and impact.

Now, it's worth noting that there are many other roles and specialties in technology companies. However, in order to keep the discussion in this chapter crisply focused, we're going to stick to broad definitions of managers and individual contributors, rather than dividing them up further into subspecialties. For example, you can imagine that this career track concept could work equally well for QA engineers, product managers, designers, and so on.

Parallel Progression

Even though the individual contributor and management career tracks are separate, when they are defined well, they are deeply interlinked:

- *There are many skills that are common to both tracks.* This is especially true at the most senior levels. For example, we would expect senior managers and senior individual contributors to be able to communicate effectively, to be able to influence others, and to be able to make impactful decisions.

- *There are many skills that are shared between levels.* For example, we might expect a similar demonstration of leadership from a principal engineer and a director of engineering, albeit in different contexts.

- *Both tracks are viable growth options for individuals.* A software engineer starting out in their career might aspire to hone their technical craft to become a principal engineer, or they might aspire to hone their management craft to become a director of engineering. Both are valid and possible choices they could work toward achieving over time. The individual chooses their path accordingly based on their interests and strengths.

In fact, we can visualize this interlinking by putting both tracks side by side. The table on page 8 is representative of the dual career tracks at many large technology companies. It shows the individual contributor track on the left and the management track on the right. The level of seniority increases as we go down the table.

Individual Contributor	Manager
Software engineer	
Senior engineer	
Staff engineer	Engineering manager
Senior staff engineer	Senior engineering manager
Principal engineer	Director of engineering
Distinguished engineer	VP of engineering
	CTO

There are some observations that we can make when the tracks are placed side by side:

- *The individual contributor track begins before the management track.* For example, the software engineer role has no equivalent level of management role. This is because an individual contributor will have to demonstrate their technical craft to a senior level before they're given the opportunity to manage others. Only when they reach this level can they choose their track by specializing.

- *The management track ends after the individual contributor track ends.* This is because the CTO role is the most senior role in the department. In most cases, there is no equivalent individual contributor. After all, the buck has to stop somewhere.

- *Roles with the same level should have a similar impact on the company.* From the tracks, it follows that we could expect a similar impact from a staff engineer as we would from an engineering manager. Although difficult to quantify exactly, this definition acts as a useful input into deciding responsibilities, scope, and compensation.

Before we start diving into the specific competencies and behaviors that are expected of managers at each level, we should first acknowledge that staring at the previous table can feel a bit overwhelming. What does it all mean? There are a *lot* of roles, and some look incredibly similar. In fact, a cynical person might even say that these roles and progression paths are no more than a silly game—a trick that is played in order to satiate an individual's need for loftier titles and bigger salaries so they don't ultimately get bored and leave the company.

However, before we get *too* cynical, let's give ourselves some perspective by looking at level definitions that have been around for far, far longer than technology companies have. We can then map these definitions back to our career tracks to see how they relate. This will make things a lot clearer.

The Three Levels of Warfare

There is a huge global organization that has thought a lot about career tracks and progression: the military. As such, there has been a significant amount of work that has gone into defining, grouping, and distributing roles and responsibilities amongst millions of individuals that are deployed across the world in autonomous teams. Clear definitions are crucial since these teams need to work together toward a common goal with a clear chain of command, often in life-or-death situations.

Let's do what all good engineers do: let's read the manual. If we consult the Doctrine for the Armed Forces of the United States,[1] we can see that they define three levels of warfare:

- *Strategic*. This is concerned with the overall goals that the military is trying to achieve. This may mean ensuring that peace is maintained in a destabilized region or that a humanitarian crisis is averted.

- *Operational*: The focus here is on planning and executing broad operations that, when combined, will achieve the strategic goals. For example, this could be a military operation to take control of a specific region that consists of multiple towns and villages.

- *Tactical*: This is the level where individual engagements are implemented. For example, a tactic could be how a specific platoon aims to take a particular building that represents a key vantage point.

When reading these definitions, we can imagine the types of people that would be involved at each level. Let's use the United States as an example. The highest level of strategy may be defined by the president in collaboration with the Joint Chiefs of Staff, who run each branch of the military. Here, a decision is made that a foreign country is now no longer a safe place for U.S. civilians. This means that all U.S. civilians need to be evacuated. From the strategy, operational goals will be defined. Senior managers in the military will be responsible for the planning and execution of the evacuation. This planning involves specifying where the civilians are and how to get them out by dividing the work into distinct operations. Then, following these operations, tactical engagements by numerous teams will be deployed in different locations to reach and evacuate the civilians.

We can use these definitions of strategic, operational, and tactical levels to bring more clarity to the scopes of management in technology companies,

---

1. https://irp.fas.org/doddir/dod/jp1.pdf

although we won't be rescuing any civilians with helicopters. This will greatly assist in helping us understand what is expected of a manager as they progress up the career track. We can use a diagram to visualize this:

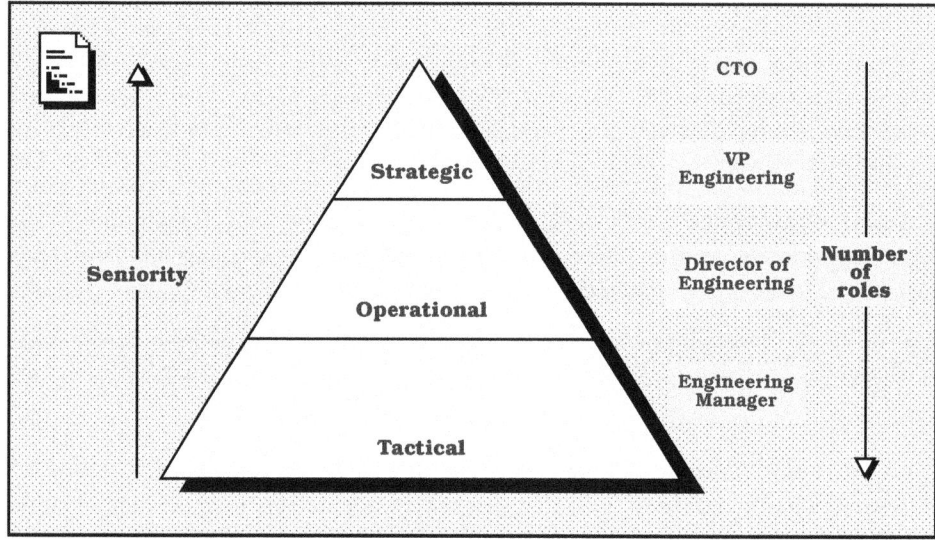

In the diagram, we represent the levels as a pyramid because the number of people involved at each level decreases as we go from the bottom to the top. After all, there is only one CTO. We can also see that an engineering manager is tactical, a director of engineering is operational, and a VP of engineering and CTO are strategic. Seniority increases as we go up the pyramid.

We'll now explore the mapping between the three levels of warfare and the job titles in more detail. We'll start with the tactical layer, and then address the operational and strategic layers. We'll also look at the interesting case of the senior engineering manager, which is a unique artifact of larger technology companies, and consider less common job titles that might be found in industry.

Tactical: Engineering Manager

Let's start at the bottom of the pyramid.

An engineering manager typically manages one team of around five to ten individual contributors. They represent the *tactical* level of management since they are responsible for the day-to-day operations of their team. This team will typically be working on one specific project or feature at a time.

While it is true that there is often a greater level of autonomy in technology companies when compared to other organizations, teams can't just do what they want without asking. The direction of an individual team is typically scoped within a greater operational constraint. For example, a team that owns user authentication flows is unlikely to be able to decide to pivot on to building a brand-new product without alignment at the operational level first. This is because other changes at the tactical level would be required to ensure that the user authentication flows are still maintained. Also, the new product may not even fit into the operational structure the team is currently part of!

Success as an engineering manager is typically measured by the output of the team. Questions that could be asked are: is the team getting the committed work done on time? Are they ensuring that their tactical area is of high quality and is also well maintained? Are they able to respond to incidents and outages in a timely manner? Are they able to coach, mentor, and develop their team members? This book concerns itself with the upper levels of management, so we won't go into detail on what is required to be a successful engineering manager. We'll assume you're already a tenured pro. However, *help is at hand [Sta20]* if you want to refine those skills or if you are looking to refresh your knowledge to better coach others in that role. You may even recognize the author.

Despite the tactical level being at the bottom of the hierarchy, it is essential. Without strong individual teams, the greatest strategies and operational plans will fail. Wars are won by the soldiers on the ground, not by the generals in the war room.

Operational: Director of Engineering

Now, we'll move to the middle of the pyramid: the operational level.

A director of engineering typically manages many teams. This role is considered operational since directors coordinate and execute multiple tactical efforts in order to achieve an operational goal. This means that they influence more control over the *how* of the work, but the *why* has already been decided at the strategic level, although that doesn't mean that they can't influence it.

These are some unique traits of the director of engineering role compared to the engineering manager:

- *They manage other managers.* This means they are accountable for the output of multiple teams, including teams of teams. If a single team consists of five to ten people, then at a large company, a director of engineering might be accountable for the output of 50 to 200 people or more. That's a lot of people to consider, steer, and grow, so delegation is essential.

- *They are accountable for an operational area.* Most directors can succinctly state what their area of accountability is. They may own a product line or a significant area of functionality. For example, if the operational goal is to build a new product, then the director of engineering will be responsible for ensuring the teams under their control are able to build it and deliver it. If they own an existing area, then they will be responsible for ensuring it is maintained and improved and it meets Key Performance Indicators (KPIs) such as uptime and response time.

- *They have likely stepped away fully from any individual contributor work.* While some engineering managers may still be able to contribute some code for their team, the size of the organization that a director of engineering is responsible for means that they are unlikely to be able to contribute code in a meaningful way. Even if they had some time, how would they choose a team to work for? Instead, they are likely to be spending most of their time planning, coordinating the work of their teams, resolving blockers and dependencies, and coaching their staff.

The director of engineering role is a significant step up from the engineering manager role in larger technology companies. It is often considered "executive" even though the individual doesn't form part of the company's executive team. What this means is that directors are expected to be able to operate autonomously, spend the company's money wisely, and run their organization in the way that they see fit; they are typically not told explicitly what to do. Directors at the largest technology companies have often been bona fide C-level or VP-level executives at smaller companies before; after all, they have similar amounts of resources and people to manage.

Strategic: VP of Engineering

At the top of the pyramid, we have the strategic level.

We'll focus on the VP of engineering role here since the CTO role can vary depending on the company and its culture. Also, for the purpose of our definitions at this stage of the book, we can group them together. At some technical founder-led companies, there may not even be a CTO role since the chief executive officer (CEO) founder still has their hands firmly on the technological wheel. We'll touch on this more in the next chapter when we look at typical org chart patterns.

VPs help define the *why* and *with what* we will achieve. These are some unique traits of the VP of engineering role when compared to the director of engineering role:

- *Accountability for some or all of the engineering strategy.* For example, a VP of engineering may run the engineering department as a whole, or they may be responsible for a broad strategic area of the department. Examples of strategic areas can be a flagship product, the developer platform, or the technology infrastructure. Depending on the size of the company, a strategic area could even be a whole *suite* of products that are successful enough to be individual companies in their own right. Often, you can tell something is of VP-level importance if it is true that if it ceased to exist, there would be a catastrophic outcome for the company.

- *Accountability for budgets and headcount.* VP roles are typically where senior managers are much closer to money and what gets done with it. This covers investment in infrastructure, headcount, and definition of the compensation bands and remuneration schemes for staff. This also extends to strategies for hiring, retention, and growth of the department.

- *A focus on the* why *of the work rather than the* how. Whereas directors may be spending their time coordinating projects between teams and running their area operationally, VPs are more likely to be spending their time on what those projects and objectives should be in the first place and whether they are a meaningful investment of time and capital. They may spend their time more on metrics than project planning.

- *A long-term future focus.* If directors are looking ahead to the next year or so in their operational thinking, VPs are looking ahead to the next two to three years of strategy. Questions they are expected to answer include what department growth will look like, how investments in different areas will change based on product and engineering strategy, and what the market and competitors will look like in the future.

- *Reporting to a senior executive.* VPs have one of the hardest jobs to do when managing upward. They need to be self-starting, able to prove that they are making the right decisions, and be able to report on progress in a way that is meaningful to the executive team, who are often not technical. Sometimes, it's lonely at the top.

The Blurry In-Between

The astute reader will have noticed that one of the managerial job titles that we mentioned earlier was missing: the senior engineering manager, which is above engineering manager and below director of engineering. Even more discerning readers will have noticed that senior director of engineering is also missing, which sits above director and below VP.

A senior engineering manager is typically an artifact of larger technology companies. The position is different from an engineering manager insofar that they have multiple teams reporting to them and, therefore, will be managing managers. However, typically, this role is _not always_ accountable for an operational area. That responsibility still sits with a director. Instead, a senior engineering manager is usually accountable for a tactical portfolio that is larger than one team. This means that they are still broadly tactical in their focus, but they have a greater scope of responsibility than an engineering manager. They are also likely to be more senior in terms of experience and compensation.

The senior director of engineering job title may or may not be used at larger companies. Often, the director of engineering role is considered senior enough at the operational layer. For very large organizations, it is normal for directors to have other directors reporting to them. The same is sometimes true of VPs and other VPs. If you're in one of these roles at the largest and most impactful companies on the planet, the senior prefix doesn't really matter all that much in terms of your prestige. The base title goes a long way.

Do note that there are also variants of most of our job titles, such as head of engineering, team lead, and engineering lead. In order to keep the book simple, we're going to use the roles and career tracks that we've defined here. You'll find these tracks at Google, Meta, Netflix, Amazon, Shopify, and many other notable companies. Check it out for yourself: you can see self-submitted data about job titles, levels, and pay at levels.fyi.[2]

If you've seen differently named roles, then they are usually straightforward to map into the job titles we're using here. Just see whether they are tactical, operational, or strategic and choose acordingly.

Scope and Impact

Having the management job titles map to either strategic, operational, or tactical levels is a good way of delineating the tiers of management within a company. However, not all companies are of the same size. A VP of engineering role at a startup is likely to be very different from a VP of engineering role at a large public company. In order to understand how these roles differ from company to company, we can use the concepts of *scope* and *impact*.

- *Scope* is used to describe the boundary of responsibilities that a role has. Typically, these are the responsibilities that you would see in a job advert. For example, the scope of an engineering manager's role would be to manage

---

2. https://levels.fyi

> **Your Turn: Job Title Safari**
>
> Now that we've looked a little deeper into the different job titles that are commonly used in the management career track, it's time to do some research.
>
> - Take a look at the job titles that are used at your company. Based on what you know about the people doing them, how well do they map to the tactical, operational, or strategic levels? How do you think this manifests in how someone in that role spends their time?
> - Think about the kind of role that you aspire to have in the future. What is the job title? Do you have a particular company in mind? Search online or use LinkedIn to find individuals who are currently doing that role. How do they describe what they do? How does it line up with our job title definitions?
> - Are there any other job titles that you've seen that don't fit into the career track that we have defined here? If so, why do you think that they differ?
> - If you haven't already, go to the levels.fyi website and look at the managerial career tracks from the largest and most-known companies in our industry. How do they compare with each other? Which companies have similar tracks, and which ones are notably different?
>
> Keep some of the companies that you've looked at during your research in mind, as we'll be revisiting them for a further exercise soon.

a team of individual contributors and to be responsible for the output of that team. The scope of a VP of engineering role could be responsibility for the output of a whole department consisting of thousands of people.

- *Impact* is used to describe the effect that the person doing that role is having. For example, a high-impact engineering manager would be one who has a high-performing team that is delivering a lot of measurable value to the company. There are direct links between impact and someone's performance in their role.

The interplay between scope and impact is what unlocks progression for managers as shown in the diagram on page 16.

When you get your first managerial role, you're likely to have a small scope and a small impact. After all, you're still learning the skills that you need and gaining experience. As you progress and perform well, your impact will increase as you become a more effective manager. This then unlocks opportunities for you to increase your scope. For example, you may be able to grow the size of your team, contribute by mentoring and coaching others, or take on more responsibilities. This subsequently grows your scope, and then the cycle begins again.

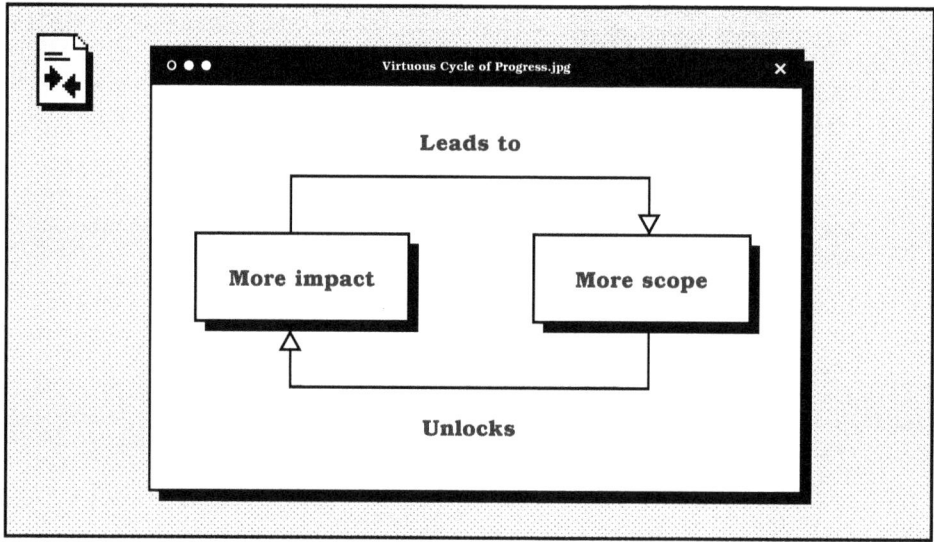

We'll revisit how scope and impact can be used to gauge the relative size and difficulty of roles later in the chapter.

Competencies

Another factor to consider when exploring how a company thinks of their managerial roles is the concept of *competencies*. Competencies are the definitions of the skills that are required to be successful in a particular role. They should be defined in a way that makes them applicable to *all* roles on the career track by scaling them up accordingly. That way, it's easy to understand what is expected at each scope and how to progress to the next one.

Here are some examples of competencies that could be common to individual contributors and managers alike:

- *Professional experience.* How long has the individual been working in the industry? How long have they been in their current role and in similarly scoped roles at different companies?
- *Technical knowledge.* Are they a domain expert in the technologies that they use, or do they still require pairing and guidance from others? Do they lead technical thinking in their team, or do they require their colleagues to take the lead?
- *Mentorship.* Are they receiving mentorship in order to continue to grow into their role, or are they the go-to mentor for their domain?

- *Conflict resolution.* How experienced are they at unblocking decisions and resolving conflicts? Do they often require escalation to their manager, or are they able to resolve most issues themselves?

- *Communication.* How are their technical and nontechnical communication? Can they clearly communicate to other engineers how to solve technical problems and also explain those solutions to nontechnical stakeholders? Do they communicate effectively with their manager and peers?

- *Influence.* Do they have an impact outside of their team? Do other individuals want to be more like them? Do they have a positive impact on the culture of the company?

With a list of competencies and job titles, we can build a competency grid. This consists of *job titles* across the top and *competencies* down the side. A competency grid is a great way to visualize the career track. It can act as a reference for individuals as they understand where they are now and where they want to be in the future in their career progression. It can also be used by managers to help their staff understand what is expected of them and how they can progress.

The table on page 18 shows what the grid could look like for the management track of a hypothetical company using three of these competencies as an example.

Much like job title and levels data, you can also find many examples of real competency grids online: over 75 companies have submitted theirs on progression.fyi.[3]

Remember this handy formula: *your impact in your role is a function of your scope and competencies.* You can theoretically increase both, but only the latter is firmly within your control. You can't promote yourself.

Getting the Gig

Before we end the chapter, we should acknowledge the fact you picked up this book for a reason: it's likely you're a driven individual who wants to progress in their career. You want to invest in yourself in order to give yourself the best chance of achieving your goals. And you're not alone: we believe in you! However, we also know that progression to senior levels, whether as a manager or individual contributor, can be difficult. That's why we spend a whole chapter on it at the end of the book: Chapter 15, Tarzan Swings from Vine to Vine, on page 347.

---

3. https://progression.fyi

Engineering Manager	Director of Engineering	VP of Engineering
Competency: Technical knowledge		
Proficient in the technologies used by their team. Able to lead technical discussions and decisions. Able to mentor others in their team to contribute to a high standard. May still write code depending on the size of their team.	Understands and can drive technical decisions and approaches at a high level across an operational area. May still be a code mergerer. Makes technical decisions with input from others and contributes toward the longer-term technical direction for their teams.	Understands and can evaluate technical decisions and approaches for a whole strategic area, including the department. Typically delegates the details to senior individual contributors while maintaining a clear understanding of the impact of those decisions on strategy and budget.
Competency: Conflict resolution		
Able to work through conflicts with their team and counterparts in other disciplines. Typical conflicts are around prioritization of work, technical decisions, and interpersonal issues.	Is able to resolve conflict within their division and across the department. Typically, these are the same types of conflict as the level below, but at a wider scope. May also be involved in resolving conflicts with external partners and stakeholders.	Resolves conflicts where the stakes are highest. Usually, this is within the executive team and with key external partners and stakeholders. Typically, the buck stops with them.
Competency: Communication		
Able to navigate multiple forms of communication: technical discussion, mentorship, roadmap prioritization, and motivating others. Able to communicate effectively with their manager and peers.	Able to communicate effectively within their division and across the department. Also communicates effectively upward to executive stakeholders and to external partners.	Able to communicate effectively with the department, company, leadership team, and board.

> **Your Turn: Investigate Competency Grids**
>
> Because real competency grids are large and would easily span tens of pages of this book, it's time to get online and do some research.
>
> - If you didn't look at it earlier, go to the progression.fyi website. Browse through the ones that are there, digging into three to five from companies that you know well. How have they defined their competencies? Are there similarities from company to company? Are there any particular formats that work better than others? Why is that?
> - See whether your company has its own competency grid. If so, how does it compare to the others that you've looked at previously in this exercise? If it doesn't, why do you think that is?
> - If you are already a manager, how do you think that you line up with the competencies for your current role? Are there any areas that you need to work on? Are you perhaps even already performing at the next level?
> - Next time you meet your manager, have a conversation about competency grids. If your company doesn't have them, could you help start an initiative to define them? If they do, how can you use them to help you begin a conversation about your career progression?

However, that doesn't mean that you should feel powerless in the process of making the ideal opportunities open up for you. In fact, you always have opportunities to work on your impact by honing your competencies, demonstrating and improving your skills, and finding ways to provably stretch into the *next* level of scope. This is a great way to ensure that you are ready when the right opportunity comes along.

So, how do these opportunities come along? Typically, there are a few ways:

- *Somebody leaves!* A tenured manager leaves the company, and there is a gap in the organization that needs to be filled. Often, it is easier to promote from within than to hire externally, and it may be your opportunity to move upward as a trusted and high-performing member of staff. This is why you should *always* ensure your manager knows where you want to progress to in the long term. You want to be on their mind when these moments arise, and ensuring that you are having a high impact at the top of your scope shows that you are ready.

- *Your company grows in size, opening up more slots in the org chart.* For example, your company may set some ambitious hiring targets after a successful year or after it receives external investment. All those new people need managers! This could mean that your team grows to the point of splitting into multiple teams, or if you are performing well, you could be picked to run a bigger area. Again, ensuring your impact is high is the key here.
- *Alternatively, you move to a smaller company where your current scope and impact map higher.* Sometimes, your current company can't offer you the opportunities that you want within the timeframe that you want them. However, by knowing your scope and impact and being able to quantify it, you can consider moving to a smaller company where you can command a role that is bigger in relative terms.

These three paths are possible because scope and impact translate across our industry as a whole. They are global identifiers. It explains why a VP of engineering at a medium-sized company may be a CTO of a smaller startup as part of their next move. It also explains why they might instead move to become a director of engineering at a large public company. It's all about someone's global scope and impact and how they map to the local job title variables of the company that they are considering.

When you think about where you want to go in your career, remember that *exact job titles are less important than your scope and your impact.* Think about how to quantify them, and then you can better write the narrative of where you've come from, where you are, and where you're going in the future.

> **Your Turn: The Scope and Impact Narrative**
>
> Let's do one more little exercise before we move on. Take a look at the LinkedIn profiles of senior leaders in the industry that you respect, and see what roles they've had over the years. When you think about their scope and impact, does their career progression make more sense? What can you learn from their journey?

To the Org Chart!

That concludes our initial orientation to the management career track. Whew! We've covered a lot of ground in this chapter, so let's recap:

- We began by *outlining the typical job titles for managers in technology companies.* We saw how they were ordered in terms of seniority and how they lined up with increasingly senior individual contributor roles. Then, we saw how they mapped to the three levels of warfare: tactical, operational, and strategic.

- Next, we *expanded our definitions to include scope, impact, and competencies to better understand expectations and career progression.* We saw how scope and impact are used to define the size of a role and how competencies are used to define the skills that are required to be successful. The impact that someone has is a function of their competencies and their scope.

- Finally, *we touched upon some of the typical paths to progress on the management career track.* The key here is that although many opportunities are subject to forces outside of your control, you can focus on continually growing your scope and impact to ensure that you are stretching outside of your comfort zone. This means that you are ready when the right opportunity comes along.

In the next chapter, we'll continue our exploration of management roles by taking a look at typical organizational structures and the effect that they have on what you'll get up to as a manager. We'll also look at ways of shaping your organization for success and avoiding common pitfalls.

CHAPTER 2

Your Place in the Org Chart

Bing! You join the call with your team.

"How did the meeting go?" asks Tara.

Ben chimes in. "Yeah, how did it go? Is everything alright?"

You raise your finger. "I bring good news! Once again, the rumor mill was right. We've raised a whole bunch of new money."

"Wow, that's great!" says Tara. "What does that mean for us?"

"Well, we're growing," you reply. "Quite a lot, actually. Our team is going to be fifty people by the end of the year."

"Fifty?" says Ben. "How are you meant to manage fifty people? That's a lot of one-to-one meetings…"

"There's going to be multiple teams supporting our area," you say. "And here's the thing: they want me to be director of engineering."

"Oh wow! Congratulations!" says Tara. "I'm so happy for you. But who is going to manage *us*?"

"That's a good question," you reply. "There's going to be multiple teams. Like, five or six. I'll need to work that out."

"And what are those teams going to be doing? What are they called?" asks Ben.

"I haven't really thought about that yet," you reply. "I guess we'll have to come up with some ideas."

"Can we call them colors?" asks Tara. "Like, the red team, the blue team, the green team…"

"Why colors?" you ask.

"Well, then it doesn't matter what project they do, they can just be flexible. I read about this start-up that was doing something like…"

Ben interrupts. "That's a great idea. But we should have teams named after animals. Animals are cool. I want to be on the *panther* team. I'm thinking nimble, fast, agile…"

"I think you belong on the sloth team," says Tara. "How were you late to stand-up when your computer is literally next to your bed?"

Ben sighs and rolls his eyes.

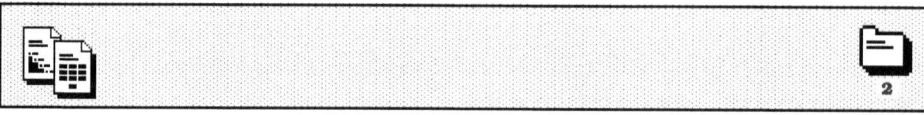

Okay, alright, hang on a second…I can hear what you're thinking. Org charts? *Org charts?*

In the first chapter of this book, we promised that this whole tome would be about the skills, tools, and techniques that you will need to be a successful senior manager. And now we're talking about *org charts*? What gives?

Well, the thing is, org charts aren't boring. They're actually exciting. Important, even. They're not just an indicator of who reports to who, and which poor souls have to do performance reviews twice a year. They're important because they determine the delineation of teams, divisions, and departments. They bring people together on shared missions. They determine clear paths for conflict resolution and escalation. They are a key part of the identity and culture of an organization.

Here's the even cooler bit: they are an essential tool that you wield as a senior manager. Yes, they are a *tool*. You get to design what your organization looks like and which people are working where. If you design an org chart well, you create the right conditions for teams to do their best work, often completely autonomously. If you design an org chart poorly, you can create a political environment where more energy is spent on fighting fires and resolving inner turmoil than is spent on actually getting the work done.

In this chapter, we're going to go deep on org charts. Even if you're skeptical about their importance, we can guarantee that you'll be reevaluating them with a fresh perspective once we're through.

Here's what we're going to cover:

- *We'll start by taking a brief look at the history of the org chart.* Did companies always have them? When did they become a fundamental part of the ways that businesses are structured? And what are some of the more radical alternatives that have been proposed?

- *Next, we'll look at some of the typical org chart shapes that you might see at a technology company.* We'll revisit our role definitions from the previous chapter and see what kind of shapes they fit into, including how to utilize managers and individual contributors effectively.

- *Then, we'll observe some of the antipatterns that arise from how the org chart functions.* We'll look at how to avoid common pitfalls such as too many or too few direct reports and how to avoid making yourself redundant when splitting teams.

- *Finally, we'll look at how you might go about designing your own org chart by modeling different types of teams and interaction modes.* How should you decide what teams to create and what they should be responsible for? How do you balance long-term ownership of infrastructure with the short-term flexibility needed for agile product work? We'll go through a worked example together.

We promise: you're going to love org charts once you're done with this chapter. So let's get started.

The Division of Labor

The reason that humans have become the dominant species is because we are able to collaborate together in large groups toward goals that would be impossible for us to achieve on our own. The complexity and scale of our achievements have increased dramatically over time, *beginning with the first hunter-gatherer tribes roaming the planet through to modern nation-states and global economies. [Har15]*.

This ability to collaborate outside of our immediate social sphere is what has set humans apart from every other species on the planet. Although our ancestors were not the fastest or the strongest, their cognitive abilities meant that they could work together to achieve things that no other species could. Two million years ago, we were able to team up to hunt animals that would have otherwise overpowered individual humans. Around twelve thousand years ago, we were able to form permanent settlements, grow crops, and domesticate animals. As production became more efficient and specialized, humans were able to produce goods for trade and commerce. Small interconnected settlements would grow into larger towns and cities. Inventions such as mathematics, writing, and money formed the scaffolding of the interconnected societies that we live in today.

The evidence of human collaboration is everywhere. In fact, take a look around you right now. Consider the clothes that you are wearing, the items within your immediate reach, and the food inside your refrigerator. It's likely you didn't make any of these items yourself, nor did you bargain directly with the farmers who produced the fruit and vegetables in the crisper drawer. Everything that surrounds you is the result of the work of thousands of people, working for themselves or for larger companies, each with specialized roles and tasks. Farmers, factory workers, designers, engineers, retail assistants, truck drivers, and countless other workers collaborated together, often unknowingly, to allow your surroundings to exist. Neat, isn't it?

This remarkable feat is the result of the *division of labor*. Much like our tribal hunter-gatherer ancestors were able to divide tasks between them so that they could hunt, prepare, and cook a bison, thousands of modern humans are able to perform specialized tasks as part of a larger system. This system can be a team, a company, or even a nation-state. It's this division of labor that means you haven't had to engineer your own refrigerator, grow your own carrots, or sew your own clothes.

The division of labor allows for results that are far greater than the sum of their parts. And it's *exactly* how companies work. By having individuals collaborate together while performing specialized roles, we get iPhones, Teslas, and Netflix. In order to create these complex products, we need to have a way of organizing people into teams, groups, and departments so that each specialized individual knows exactly what they need to do and who they need to collaborate with to produce the final product.

Enter the Org Chart

An *organizational chart*, usually referred to as an *org chart*, is a diagram that shows the structure of an organization. The nodes in the diagram are people, and the edges are the management relationships between them. The org chart is a *visual representation of the division of labor* within an organization.

One of the first recorded org charts was created by Daniel McCallum, the general superintendent of the New York and Erie Railroad in 1855.[1] In order to make sense of the growing structure of the railroad, McCallum drew an

---

1. https://www.organimi.com/the-evolution-of-org-charts/

intricate diagram showing the departments and responsibilities. The following image is from the Library of Congress:

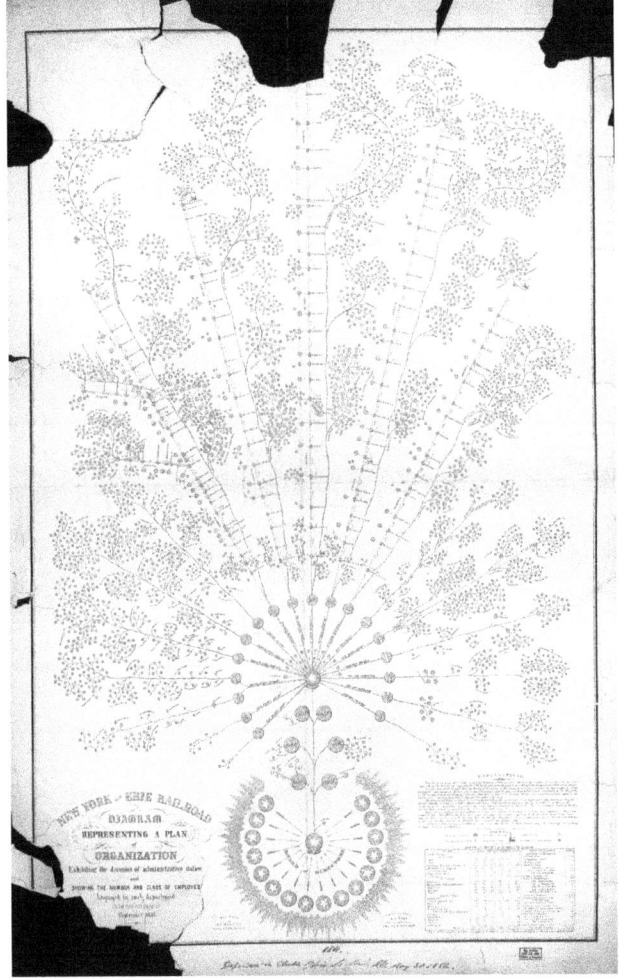

It was a far cry from the neat, tree-like org charts that we see today. It looks more akin to microscopic organisms under a microscope, perhaps because the railroad in 1855 was a complex, evolving, distributed system, created in a time before mass communication and the Internet.

Org charts don't always need to show people, either. They can also be presented at a higher level of granularity, showing the different teams, divisions, or departments instead. This is useful for showing where particular responsibilities lie within an organization, such as engineering, sales, or marketing, or for understanding which teams are adjacent to each other, signifying a higher need for collaboration. See the image on page 28.

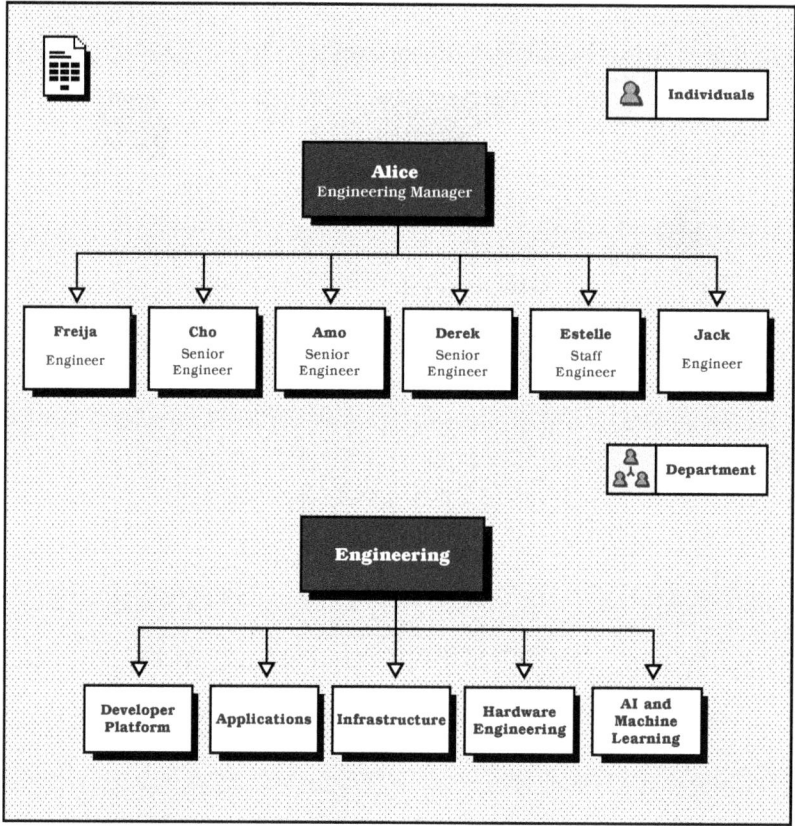

The Org Chart Is a Tool

As a senior manager, the org chart is one of your greatest tools. For example, a good org chart design can help you:

- *Clarify who is accountable and responsible for what.* The grouping of people into teams, groups, and departments makes it clear who owns which projects and parts of the products that the company develops.

- *Understand who manages who.* The edges between the nodes in the org chart make it clear who is accountable for the performance of others and allow for clear lines of escalation.

- *See relative levels of investment in different areas.* It is important to understand the relative size of different teams in order to understand the current investment of resources and to plan for future investment.

- *Encourage collaboration between teams and avoid siloing.* By assigning a collection of related responsibilities to a group of teams, you can encourage collaboration between them. Conversely, you can purposely keep teams separate to encourage them to act autonomously.

- *Avoid duplication or inefficiency.* Having a high-level view of teams and responsibilities can help you avoid duplication of effort when planning and executing projects.

And unlike the evolutionary railroad org chart, you have the power to design your org chart in a way that makes sense for you, your teams, and what you are trying to achieve. They do not need to stay the same forever. In fact, it is healthy for org charts to change and evolve over time as your priorities and goals change.

Sometimes the Old Ways Work Well Enough

Before we begin to look at common org chart shapes and patterns that you will encounter at the tactical, operational, and strategic levels, it's worth noting that over recent decades, there have been some notable, albeit less successful, attempts to reinvent the approach to structuring companies by moving away from the traditional top-down, command-and-control, hierarchical org chart.

Online footwear retailer *Zappos famously adopted holacracy [Har15]*, which is a system of self-organizing managerless teams called *circles* that also separates roles from the people that fill them. People can freely move between, and also perform, multiple roles.

Circles are self-governed and maintain their own roles and policies. The idea is that this maximizes the autonomy and power of individuals; it is a form of extreme decentralization akin to how cities evolve over time. After all, why do we need managers to tell us what to do? However, in 2020, it was reported that managers were reinstated, and the organization had quietly backed away from the holacratic structure in order to make it clearer who had accountability over key areas.[2]

Likewise, online publisher Medium had also experimented with holacracy, but several years later, it reverted back after a period of growth.[3] While it's true that smaller organizations can more easily be structured without managers, as they grow, it appears that the need for managers is more apparent.

In 2014, social media marketing company Buffer published a blog post announcing that they were going to be a managerless company, but they also

---

2. https://qz.com/work/1776841/zappos-has-quietly-backed-away-from-holacracy
3. https://blog.medium.com/management-and-organization-at-medium-2228cc9d93e9?#.ukg1xag8n

reverted later.[4] The video game studio Valve still operates without managers,[5] but they are still relatively small compared to typical technology companies.

Although alternative approaches gain publicity for their radicalism, in reality, they are still the exception rather than the rule. Also, structureless companies often evolve a shadow hierarchy *regardless*, based on power and influence. It seems that for most companies, especially large ones, the traditional org chart is here to stay, and learning how to best use it is, therefore, a key skill for you to wield as a senior manager. In fact, we reckon that you're going to start to love organization design.

The Shape of My Chart: Structures and Patterns

As you spend more time in industry, you'll notice that there are common org chart shapes that you will encounter time and time again. In this section, we'll look at some of these shapes at the tactical, operational, and strategic levels. This will pave the way for you to learn best practices that you can then use to design your own organizations.

Span of Control

Let's start with the most common question: how many people should a manager manage? This number is known as their *span of control*, which is the number of people that report to a manager. Other terms used include *span of management* or *wingspan*. Deciding an optimal span of control is a key part of organization design since it determines the relationship between the overall size of the organization and the number of managers required to support it.

There is no hard-and-fast rule for the ideal span of control. Many organizations aim for around eight to ten direct reports per manager, but a number of factors can nudge this up or down.

At the lower end of the range, you want managers to have at least as many direct reports as needed so that they constitute a meaningful team size and output and the manager has enough management work to do. At the upper end of the range, you want to avoid managers having too many direct reports, which can result in them being unable to provide the support and guidance required because they are overloaded. Given that this may change from manager to manager, you should keep track of the average span of control for your department and aim to keep it within a certain range.

---

4. https://buffer.com/resources/decision-maker-no-managers-experiment/
5. https://steamcdn-a.akamaihd.net/apps/valve/Valve_NewEmployeeHandbook.pdf

Here are some considerations for determining the span of control for individual managers:

- *Practical limits.* If we expect managers to do their job effectively, then there are practical limits to how many people they can manage. For example, ten direct reports could mean ten one-to-one meetings per week in addition to team meetings, individual work, coaching, and mentorship, and having the flexibility to deal with unexpected issues. It's highly unlikely that a manager could do all of this effectively with twenty direct reports. Something has to give.

- *The seniority of the manager.* Typically speaking, the more senior a manager is, the larger their span of control can be. This purely comes down to their experience.

- *The seniority of the reports.* Managing a team of senior individuals is typically less overhead than managing a team of inexperienced individuals. The former will be more self-sufficient and require less guidance, whereas new or inexperienced staff will need more hands-on coaching and mentorship.

- *A manager's level of individual contribution.* Some managers still contribute code meaningfully to their projects, and therefore, they may benefit from a lower span of control. Conversely, managers who delegate most individual contributor work and focus on strategy and planning are able to manage a larger team.

- *The type of work that the team does.* Highly collaborative teams work better with a lower span of control since more inter-team communication and coordination are required. Teams that manage many smaller streams of work can be bigger as they work more independently.

Span of control was a hot topic in the industry during the economic downturn following the COVID-19 pandemic.[6] After companies put the brakes on the rapid hiring of the previous years, many companies were left with managers who had too few direct reports. This resulted in a number of companies flattening their organizations during layoffs in order to increase the average span of control of their managers. Many of the lower-span managers were let go or had to convert into performing individual contributor roles; clearly, neither option is ideal for someone invested in their craft.[7] The lesson here is that if an organization's span of control isn't kept within an ideal range, then there

---

6. https://www.ft.com/content/21ccfe54-88f2-4360-a67e-d3fe1e7df1e5
7. https://about.fb.com/news/2023/03/mark-zuckerberg-meta-year-of-efficiency/

can be a cascade of highly negative outcomes for individuals when times are tough.

Tactical: The Engineering Manager

Knowing that we need to keep a manager's span of control within a reasonable range, let's look at some common org chart patterns that incorporate this.

We'll start at the tactical level, focusing on the place where the span of control is most evident: the engineering manager. A diagram of a typical engineering manager org chart is shown here, including some less common sub-patterns:

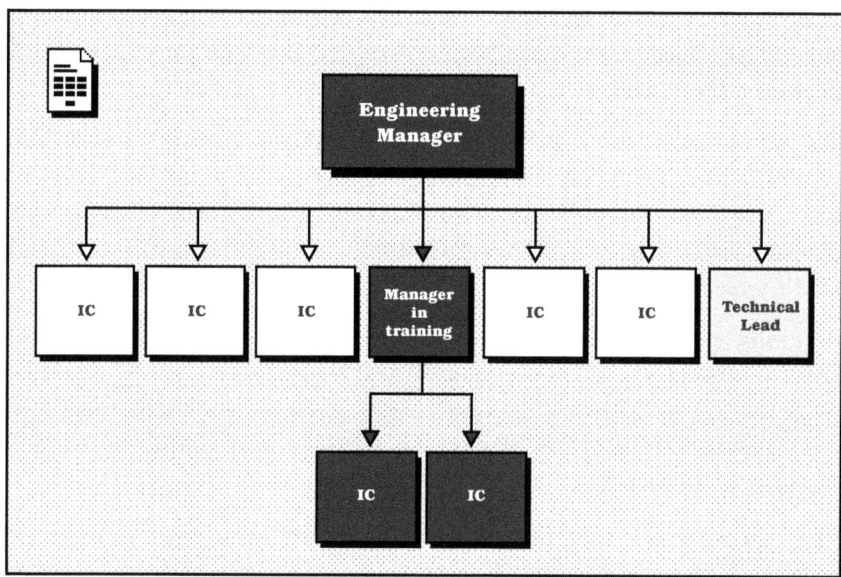

Looking at the diagram, we can see that an engineering manager typically has five to ten direct reports, all of which are individual contributors. This collection of individual contributors is a team, and the engineering manager is responsible for the performance of that team.

Sometimes, there may be some slight variations. For example, in the diagram, we have labeled one individual contributor as the *technical lead*. This is a common pattern where a senior individual contributor takes on responsibility for the technical direction of the team. This can be a good way to provide career progression to high-growth engineers.

Another variation included in the diagram is a *manager in training*. Sometimes, this pattern is used as a way for an individual contributor to try out management in a smaller, safer environment. During times of growth, this can be a great way of systematically incubating new managers. However, this pattern should be used with caution; it can be a dead end for the manager in training if company growth halts, resulting in junior managers with low spans of control that are often first in line when any organization flattening is applied. In the best case scenario, they can revert back to an individual contributor role with their direct reports folding into their manager. However, in the worst case, they may find themselves without a role altogether.

Senior Engineering Manager

The next org chart shape belongs to the senior engineering manager. It is the first shape where we encounter somebody managing managers. A diagram of a typical senior engineering manager org chart is shown as follows:

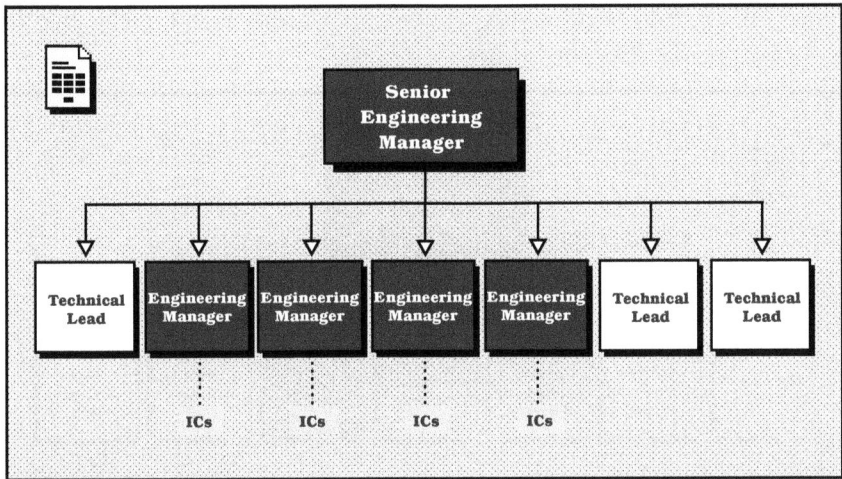

Looking at the diagram, we can see that a senior engineering manager typically has five to ten direct reports. The direct reports are usually engineering managers, with each running a team of five to ten individual contributors following the previous org chart pattern. The senior engineering manager is responsible for the performance of the teams as a whole, and these teams are often responsible for a larger product or service. At a big company, this org chart size could be 40 to 100 people.

Although a senior engineering manager isn't squarely pegged at the operational level, they are an extremely important interface for directors. Organizationally, they wrap a layer of management around a group of related tactical teams, giving them the close support that they need to be successful.

A variation is also shown where the senior engineering manager may have a number of senior individual contributors reporting to them. These are often the leads that are responsible for the technical direction of individual aspects of the area spanned by the org chart. It is an expansion of the technical lead pattern that we saw for the engineering manager.

Having technical leads report directly to the senior engineering manager can be a good way to provide career progression for senior individual contributors and for the senior engineering manager to have a better understanding, and ability to influence, the direction of each of their teams. We'll see this pattern of senior individual contributors reporting to senior managers repeat as we go up the org chart.

Operational: The Director of Engineering

A director of engineering is responsible for a larger operational area that is composed of multiple underlying teams. A diagram of a typical director of engineering org chart is shown here:

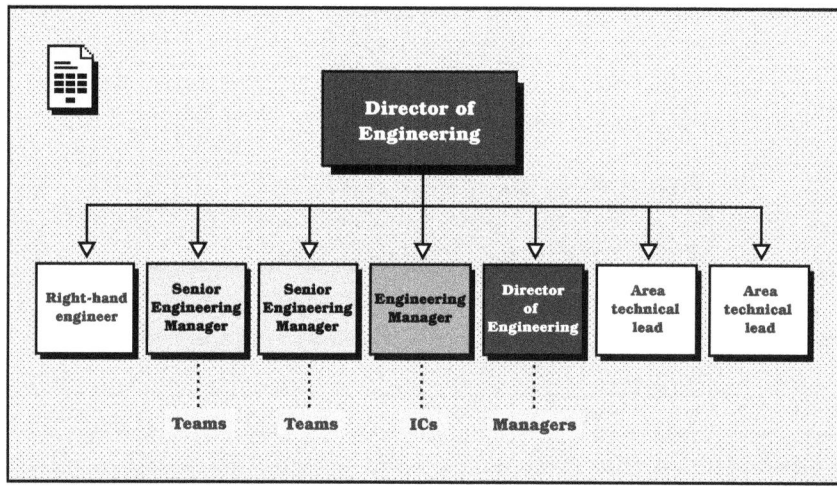

A director of engineering typically has five to ten direct reports. Their management reports can vary in seniority depending on the size of their org. In the diagram, we see multiple senior engineering managers, an engineering manager, and even another director. This is because a director can, in theory, be a *terminal* position (no further natural progression is possible) that is bounded by the strategic and operational needs of the company, and those in director roles can be experienced enough to manage people at the same level as them. At a larger company, an organization size could be one hundred to five hundred or more people.

Directors wrap a layer of management around an operational area, allowing VPs to define a clear interface between themselves and the group of operational teams. This is a key part of the org chart design: it allows VPs to focus on the strategic direction of the company while directors focus on the operational matters needed to travel in that direction.

In our diagram we also highlight two options for senior individual contributors. The first is an *area technical lead*, which is an extension of the pattern we saw for the senior engineering manager. We also introduce a new concept, the *right-hand engineer*. This is a senior individual contributor that's responsible for the technical direction of the *whole* operational area. They form a close partnership with the director.

Both of these patterns provide career progression for senior individual contributors and allow the director to have a better understanding and ability to influence the direction of each team. We even spend a whole chapter on this subject in Chapter 5, The Sharpest Tool in Your Toolbelt, on page 119.

Strategic: The VP of Engineering and CTO

Our final pattern is that of the VP of engineering. A diagram of a typical VP of engineering org chart is shown as follows:

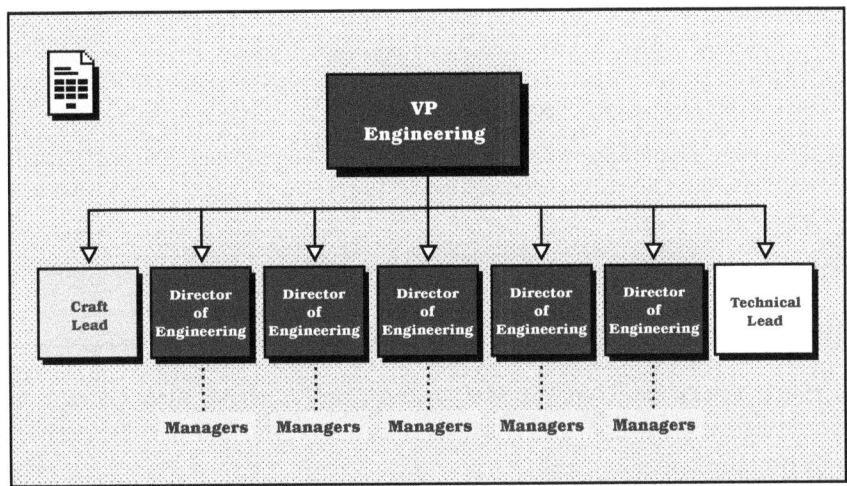

We can see that, like other managers, a VP of engineering typically has five to ten direct reports. However, their direct reports are usually directors. Each of these directors provides an interface into the operational levels that they manage. Collectively, these directors form the implementation of the strategy that the VP defines. Sometimes, a VP can manage other VPs. They may possibly also manage high-growth senior engineering managers who are soon progressing into a director role. At a larger company, a VP's organization size could be five hundred to one thousand or more people.

In terms of individual contributors, we see patterns similar to those in the director org chart. There may be area technical leads, although this is less common, as they usually map better to directors. However, there may be one or more *craft leads*. These are senior individual contributors who are responsible for the technical direction of a particular discipline, such as front end, back end, or mobile. They form a close partnership with the VP and set the technical strategy for the area for which the VP is responsible. Again, we'll dig deeper into the implementation of these roles in a later chapter.

For the sake of brevity, we won't show the CTO org chart here, but it is similar to the VP org chart. The main difference is that the CTO is responsible for the entire engineering organization and, therefore, has a larger potential organization size, with one or more VPs reporting to them.

> **Your Turn: Your Own Org Patterns**
>
> We've looked at some common patterns in theory, but what have you seen in practice?
>
> - Take a look at the org chart at your current company. Does it fit into one of the patterns that we've described here? If not, how does it differ?
> - Are there any parts of your company's org chart that you feel are suboptimal? Why is that? What kind of refactoring would you do based on the patterns here that could make things better?
> - Does your organization utilize senior individual contributors in a similar way to the patterns that we've described here? Do you think that this is a good idea? Why or why not?

Structural Antipatterns and How to Avoid Them

Even though it seems that the shape of an org chart is fairly benign, there are, in practice, a number of structural antipatterns that can arise that you need to be mindful of.

But what do we mean by *structural*? Quite simply, these are issues with the shape and balance of the org chart: too few people here, too many people there, and what happens because of that. It's a bit like having the right types of ingredients for the recipe but not having the right quantities. You can still make a cake, but it's not going to be a good one.

While we explore these antipatterns, let us assume that we have the rough shape of the org chart in an acceptable state; that is, we have the right teams that are doing the right things. We'll look at a more significant org chart problem and the subsequent refactor in the next section. That'll be like a situation where you just have the wrong ingredients for the cake altogether.

Let's start by revisiting spans of control.

Spans and Modes of Operation

We mentioned earlier that an ideal span of control is somewhere around five to ten people, depending on the manager, their seniority, and the type of work that the team does. Antipatterns arise when the size of the team does not suit the manager's strengths. Teams *can* be larger or smaller than the ideal range, but they require a manager to perform in a particular *mode of operation*, although extremes are still problematic.

A mode of operation is a blueprint for how a manager will typically act and spend their time as a function of how many direct reports they have. We can show this visually with a scale that shows the number of direct reports and the resulting mode of operation. The scale is shown as follows:

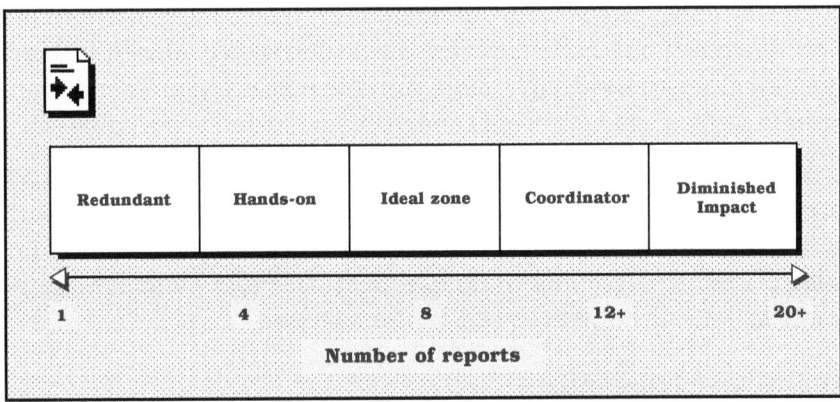

Let's look at the diagram in more detail, from left to right:

- *A manager with one or two direct reports is effectively redundant in their role.* There isn't enough management work to do to keep them utilized and growing as a manager. Ideally, managers with spans of control this small should convert to individual contributor roles and have their reports fold into their manager, or they should be given a larger team to run.

- *A team that is on the lower end of the ideal range (three to six) is suited to hands-on managers.* If a manager is still a strong individual contributor, then with a small team, they can still contribute meaningfully to the team's output. This configuration can work well for those who are beginning in management (they have fewer people while they learn their craft) and for those who are able to perform as technical leads (they have more time to contribute individually).

- *The ideal mix falls in the middle of the range (five to ten).* This is the sweet spot for most managers. They have enough direct reports to be able to delegate work and provide support and guidance, but not so many that they are unable to do their job effectively. This span of control should constitute the majority of teams in your organization.

- *A team that is on the large side (12 to 15) is where management and coordination tasks dominate.* A manager with a team this large becomes effectively a coordinator and gets everything done through delegation. This configuration is sustainable for temporary periods of time, but you should find a solution to this as soon as you can by splitting the team.

- *At the extreme end of the range (15 or more) is where managers become ineffective and their impact diminishes.* There is simply too much going on to keep on top of. Just imagine what it's like to do fifteen or more one-to-one meetings per week, in addition to team meetings, individual work, coaching, mentorship, and having the flexibility to deal with unexpected issues. It's not sustainable, and you are not giving your manager the chance to do a good job. This configuration is a recipe for attrition.

With this scale in mind, you should revisit your org chart periodically to ensure that managers are performing in the right mode of operation for them, including addressing those at the extreme ends of the scale by folding or splitting teams. It's essential to do this to ensure that your managers and your individual contributors are set up for success.

Making Yourself Redundant

Here's an antipattern that can result from trying to make things better. In the previous section on spans of control, we identified low-span managers as *redundant* in the sense that those managers don't have enough managerial work to do. But how does this actually happen? Is it only the case that when people leave a team that the manager is left with too few direct reports? Well, actually, and ironically, it happens during periods of *expansion*.

When a company is growing, it may often begin by hiring more individual contributors to work in the existing teams. This is a good way to scale up quickly, as the existing teams are already working well together and can provide a good environment for new hires to be onboarded. However, as this continues, the span of control of the existing managers begins to get too large. This then presents an opportunity to split teams up, giving individual contributors who want to get into management a chance to do so; they can hop into the newly created management roles.

Operating with the progression of others in mind and the desire to progress their own careers by managing multiple managers, a manager may split their team into two or more teams, each with a newly promoted engineering manager at the helm. These teams then report to them.

However, this can effectively make the manager redundant by going from managing too many people to managing just two or three; they have delegated all of their responsibilities away, effectively retiring on the job. This is not a good place to be if growth slows, or if the company needs to flatten the organization.

Instead, a far better solution that avoids this antipattern is to promote or hire one engineering manager to run *one* of the sub-teams and then *run the other team themselves*. This ensures that the manager has enough direct reports to remain effective and impactful. It also maintains the ideal span of control in the org chart at both levels.

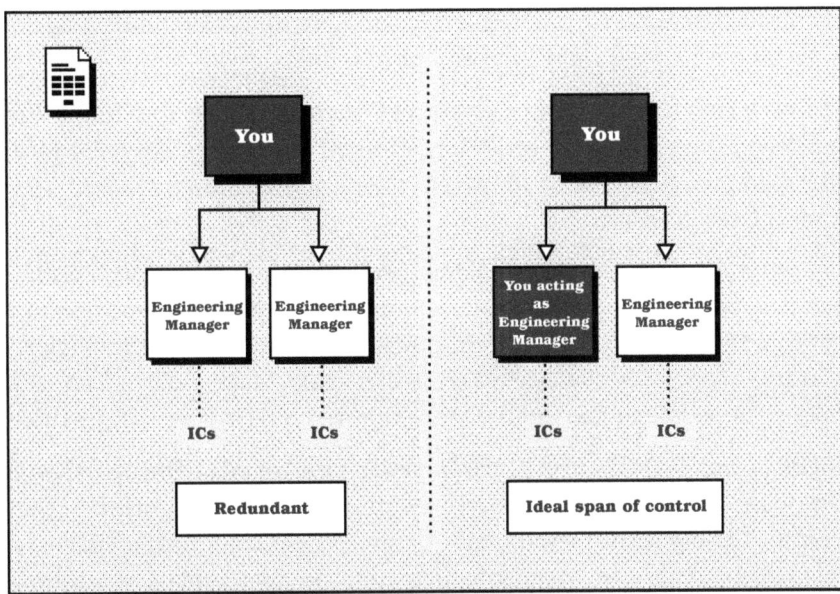

Rigidity and Self-Selection

Another antipattern can arise when org charts are not periodically updated in order to match the current investment that the company wants to make in individual areas. While it is true that teams should ideally be long-lived so that people can build deep trust with their manager and their peers, it is *also* true that *organizations benefit from people moving around [Hel20]*. Movement enables the spread of context and the sharing of ideas and prevents people from becoming bored and feeling like they have no progression available to them without a promotion.

You should therefore periodically review your org chart to ensure that it is still fit for the priorities of your organization. A typical cadence for doing this is once per year. This is a good time to review the span of control of your managers and the relative investment in each area.

More excitingly, it also presents an opportunity for you to allow your staff to self-select which team they want to be on. This can be a great way to allow people to move toward what interests them and to give them a sense of ownership over their career progression.

You can run a self-selection exercise by following these steps:

1. *Look at your current organization and work out the percentage investment in each area as determined by the number of people in each team.* For example, four teams of eight people would represent a 25 percent investment in each area. Check with your manager and stakeholders to ensure that this is still the right investment to make.

2. *If this investment is no longer correct, then work out the ideal state by modeling the teams and seats within them that you need going forward.* For example, if you need to invest in a new area, then you may need to split a team into two.

3. *Create a questionnaire that allows people to self-select which team they want to be on.* This should be a simple form that allows people to rank their preferences for working on particular teams and technologies. You can use a tool such as Google Forms to do this. Make sure to lead with the option for people to stay on the team they're on if they are happy there.

4. *Fill the seats in the new org chart based on the results of the questionnaire.* You can do this manually, or you can do so via an algorithm that you create. The algorithm should aim to give people their first choice if a seat is available but also take into account the preferences of others. For example, if two people are destined for the same slot, then there should be clear criteria for picking one over the other, such as performance rating, tenure, or other factors. Ensure that this algorithm is fair and transparent.

Once you've run the algorithm, share the outputs with your managers and stakeholders to ensure that they are happy with the results. Ensure that each member of staff has the opportunity to acknowledge that they are happy with the assignment and perform any manual overrides if they are necessary. When you're done, decide on a date that everyone will swap. Communicate it, then do it.

Giving people the option to move teams, even if a majority stay put, is a great way of giving people more control over their work. Those that want to move will therefore be less likely to leave the company through boredom and attrition than if they stayed on the same team.

Centralizing the process of moving teams also removes the politics that can arise when people try to move teams by themselves. After all, have you ever had to tell your manager you didn't want to work for them anymore? It's not that easy!

Flows of Communication and Collaboration

Now that we've looked at some common org chart shapes and antipatterns, let's look at how you might go about designing your own org chart. With what we've learned so far, we are able to ensure we have the right number of managers at each level and that we have the right number of direct reports for each manager. But what should those teams actually *do* in order to be effective? How should they collaborate together? What rules should we use to guide us when designing our org chart?

We can start by looking at three notable adages that are relevant to organization design: Conway's Law, Dunbar's Number, and Team Topologies.

Conway's Law

In 1967, Melvin E. Conway wrote that "any organization that designs a system (defined broadly) will produce a design whose structure is a copy of the organization's communication structure." This is now known as Conway's Law.

In other words, the software systems that we build are a reflection of the way that communication flows within an organization. What is one of the primary drivers of how communication flows? You guessed it: the org chart. Therefore, it's crucial to design organizations that not only facilitate people working together effectively but also increase the chances that what they build is the best system possible.

You've likely seen the negative effects of Conway's Law manifest. Badly designed teams can make collaboration a complete pain, which drives the need to find workarounds to maintain speed, which then produces technical debt, duplication of effort, and a whole host of other problems, such as finger pointing and calling people rude names.

Thus, in terms of org chart shape, we need a design that facilitates the right collaboration and communication between teams. But how big should each team, division, and department be? How many people should be in each? This is where Dunbar's Number comes in.

Dunbar's Number

In 1992, anthropologist Robin Dunbar proposed that there is a cognitive limit to the number of people with whom an individual can maintain stable social relationships. This limit is known as Dunbar's Number and is estimated to be around 150. There are *subdivisions within the 150 [KM15]*, such as five intimate friends, 15 good friends, 50 friends, 150 meaningful contacts, 500 acquaintances, and 1500 people that you can recognize.

The smaller the group of people, the more intimately you know them, harbor increased levels of trust with them, and have the ability for high-bandwidth communication. From the perspective of work relationships and org chart design, this model works. We want small, high-bandwidth teams at the frontier, clusters of these teams that collaborate together frequently, and groups, divisions, and departments where what they do and how they do it is well understood at a high level.

In fact, we can see this in the org chart shapes that we looked at earlier. The tactical level is where we have the smallest teams, such as an engineering manager with five to ten direct reports. This facilitates high-bandwidth communication and collaboration. At the operational level, we have directors running organization sizes within the ballpark of meaningful contacts and acquaintances (100-500+). At the strategic level, we have VPs with organization sizes in the range of acquaintances and people that you can recognize (500-1000+).

Therefore, we want to structure our teams and our boundaries between them in a way that respects the cognitive limits suggested by Dunbar's Number and also positively exploits the communication patterns that are suggested by Conway's Law. But how do we do this in practice?

While the reality of org chart design in the real world is typically more nuanced and messy than we would like, we can apply a model to how we structure our teams and the types of communication and collaboration that we expect between them. One of the neatest models is that of *Team Topologies [SP19]*.

Team Topologies

Team Topologies is a model for team design that was published by Matthew Skelton and Manuel Pais in 2019. It proposes different types of teams and interaction models that are tools you can wield when you are designing your org chart from scratch, considering refactoring the one you already have in place, or debugging issues with how your teams are working together.

We'll start by introducing the four types of Team Topologies. We'll then look at the three types of interaction models that can occur between teams. Then, we'll look at how we can apply these models to a buggy org chart in order to refactor and improve it.

With an understanding of Conway's Law, Dunbar's Number, and the Team Topologies models, you'll be well equipped to design your org chart in a way that will allow your teams to do their best work.

Team Types

These are the four types of teams in the Team Topologies model:

- *Stream-aligned teams*. Typically called "product teams" in agile nomenclature, these are autonomous, cross-functional teams that are responsible for a continuous flow of work aligned to a business domain or organizational capability. Many such teams exist concurrently, each responsible for their own flow of work.

- *Enabling teams*. These teams support the stream-aligned teams by owning and developing shared platforms, frameworks, and tools. They are typically staffed by specialists in a particular domain and work by cross-cutting the stream-aligned teams to ensure that they are able to work effectively.

- *Platform teams*. These teams enable the stream-aligned teams to work autonomously by reducing the cognitive load of getting work done. For example, a platform team may own the deployment infrastructure and tooling that allows stream-aligned teams to deploy their code to production whenever they need to.

- *Complicated subsystem teams*. These teams own and develop the most complex parts of the system that require specialist knowledge, to the extent that without that specialist knowledge, the system would be unable to function or improve. Like platform teams, they reduce the cognitive load for stream-aligned teams. Examples of complicated subsystems could be distributed storage systems, large language machine-learning models, or complex mathematical algorithms.

> ### Your Turn: Which Topologies Exist in Your Department?
>
> Before we go any further, let's take a look at the teams in your department.
>
> - Which of the four topologies do you see around you? What do they do?
> - Can you spot any teams in your department that don't fit the types mentioned? If so, why do you think that is? Should they instead follow one of the topologies?

Interaction Modes

The second part of the model describes how teams communicate. The model proposes three interaction modes between teams:

- *Collaboration.* This is where two teams work together closely to achieve a shared goal.
- *X-as-a-service.* This is where one team provides a service to another team with minimal interaction, such as an API.
- *Facilitating.* This is where one team helps another team to clear impediments and improve their ways of working.

We have now defined four types of teams and three interaction modes. That might seem like a lot to take in. However, a neat feature of the Team Topologies model is an accompanying visual representation. It brings the concept to life and makes it very easy to understand.

Let's have a look at it. The interaction modes can be represented by the following diagram:

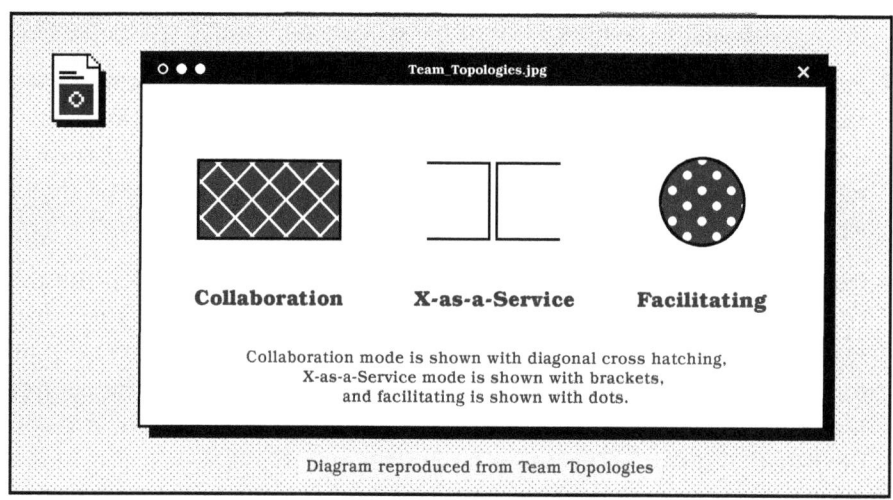

These patterns can be put together with shapes that represent the team types to create a visual depiction of an organization. Here's an example:

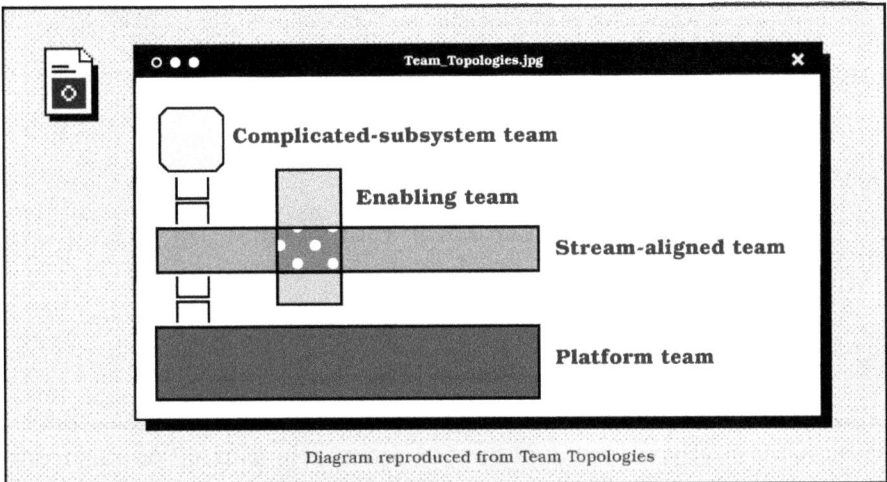

Diagram reproduced from Team Topologies

From the diagram, we can see that:

- There is a *stream-aligned team* responsible for a particular flow of work.
- There is an *enabling team* that interacts with the stream-aligned team via facilitating.
- There is a *complicated subsystem* team that interacts with the stream-aligned team via X-as-a-service.
- There is a *platform team* that interacts with the stream-aligned team also via X-as-a-service.

With these visual aids, we can sketch out different types of organizations and how they interact. This is useful for understanding the current state of the world and whether it has bugs that may need fixing. It's also useful when designing a new org chart from scratch to make sure it works as intended.

Another feature of the Team Topologies model is that it can be fractal. In other words, you can apply the same model at different levels of granularity. The prior example could represent a whole department, or it could represent a subdivision in a larger department. You can have topologies in topologies in topologies and zoom in and out as necessary.

The Team Topologies model makes it clear how teams function and interact, and it helps them set expectations for healthy interactions. Next, we'll look at how we can use this model to investigate a buggy org chart and then make it better.

Applying Team Topologies

Oh, we almost forgot to tell you...

Let's imagine that you have just started a new role as a VP of engineering. You've previously been working as a director of engineering for a public technology company, but now you've decided to move to a smaller start-up to get your first VP role. You are going to be running the entire department. The company has been growing quickly and is in the process of seeking investment to scale up even further. That's why this opportunity was exciting to you: you'll be able to ride a wave of growth and make your mark as a leader.

You are running the engineering department that is responsible for building a software as a service analytics product. This product crawls the Internet, indexes web pages, and provides dashboards that allow users to search for insights and trends over time. For example, your users may want to know how many times a product has been mentioned online in the past year and how that compares to other competing products. They also may want to dig into which of those product mentions are from different types of websites such as news, blogs, and social media. The product is used by a number of large companies to track conversations about their brand and to understand how their products are being perceived by the public.

The rough architecture of the product looks like this. And yes, the Internet is a cloud as shown in the diagram on page 47.

However, when you arrive, despite the success of the product, you find that the department is in a bit of a mess. The engineers are unhappy, the user experience is inconsistent and buggy, and the commercial teams are frustrated with the speed of development. It seems the company has grown quickly and chaotically over the past few years. It seems like this is why they hired you.

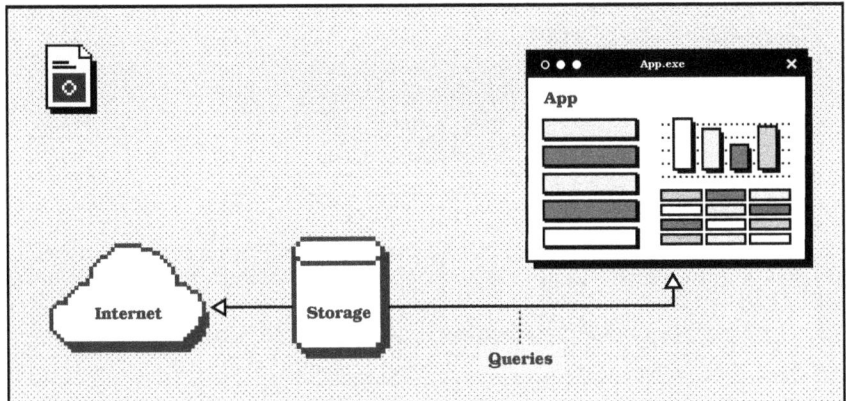

You begin by spending time talking to people across the company and also to your largest clients. These are some of the common complaints you hear:

- *The UX has suffered greatly as the product has grown.* Each new feature feels like it has been added in a silo with no thought to the overall user experience. Nothing feels consistent.
- *The speed of indexing new data is slow.* It can sometimes take days for new data to be available in the product, which is not helpful for clients that want to track mentions of their products in real time, such as when they spend money on television advertising.
- *The speed of the product is inconsistent.* Some components are fast to load, but some are slow. It's not clear why this is the case.
- *Key metadata is sometimes missing.* For example, your largest client, who has an API integration with the product, has noticed that the star ratings for reviews are sometimes missing. This is a key metric for them to track.

With these observations in hand, you start by investigating the way the teams collaborate with each other. As part of trying to understand which teams are which and who reports to whom, you sketch out the org chart to get a better idea of how the department looks. You find that it looks like the diagram on page 48.

The org chart has grown organically and quickly. There are four main teams:

- *Reviews (14 staff).* This team focuses on the collection and display of reviews from across the web. They are full-stack; that is, they work on both the front end and back end, contributing to scraping, indexing, storage, and the user interface.

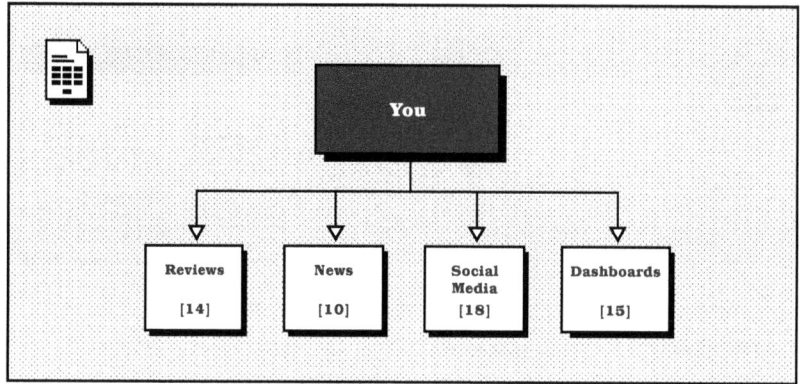

- *News (10 staff)*. Created at the same time as the Reviews team, this team performs the same function but for news articles.
- *Social Media (18 staff)*. Created more recently, the social media team focuses on scraping and indexing social media posts. This includes data collection that requires users to provide credentials to social media platforms in order to collect data in ways that meet the terms of service of the networks.
- *Data (15 staff)*. This was the original team that built the first version of the product, but then specialized into running the web crawlers, the API, and the search index. They work with the other teams to add new data sources and to add functionality to the centralized platform.

Noting the initial observation that all of the managers have large spans of control, you use the team topologies diagram to classify the teams and model the interactions between them.

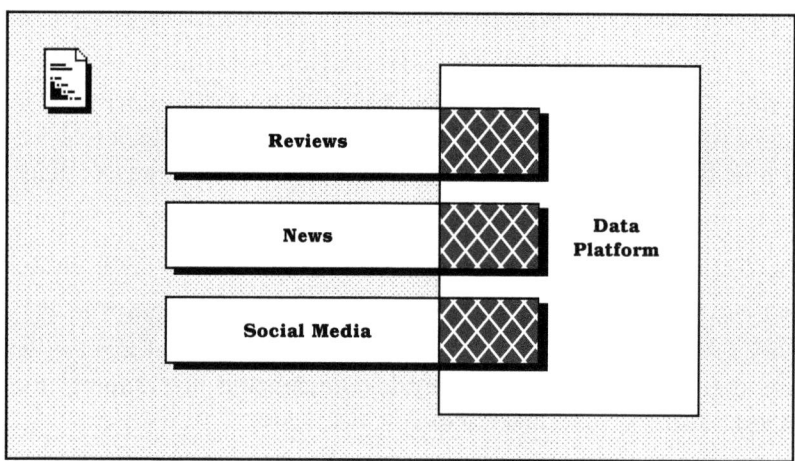

From your diagram, you can see that:

- *There are three stream-aligned teams.* These are Reviews, News, and Social Media. All try to work on improving their own area of the product autonomously, driven by the data that they collect.
- *The Data team collaborates directly with every stream-aligned team.* This means they have to consult across three fronts while having to prioritize and execute their own work. As the product scales and adds more data types, this can only get worse.
- *Additionally, the Data team does many different things, and this makes it hard for them to focus.* For example, crawling speed has been decreasing and needs addressing, but they also have to balance working on data storage and consulting with the three stream-aligned teams.
- *There is no team that owns the holistic experience of the application.* The three stream-aligned teams focus inwardly on their own areas, which means that conflicting priorities in the overall user experience are difficult to resolve since there is nobody keeping tabs on visual consistency.

With these faults in mind, you think about an alternative diagram that could address the problems. Here's what you want from your ideal state:

- *Clear ownership of the visual experience of the product.* You want to have one team accountable for this, ideally creating reusable visual components like charts and tables that all of the other teams can use. This will ensure visual consistency across the product.
- *Clear ownership of the web crawling infrastructure*, implemented in such a way that they can work uninterrupted on the most important issue: speed of data acquisition. This will ensure that pressure from the commercial teams can be addressed.
- *The stream-aligned teams to continue to exist, but have clear interaction modes with other teams.* The two key interaction points are around data collection (for improving data coverage) and dashboards (for ensuring overall product consistency).

With these criteria in mind, you sketch out an ideal state as shown on page 50.

Here's what you've identified in your diagram:

- *Your three stream-aligned teams still exist* so they can work on their areas autonomously.

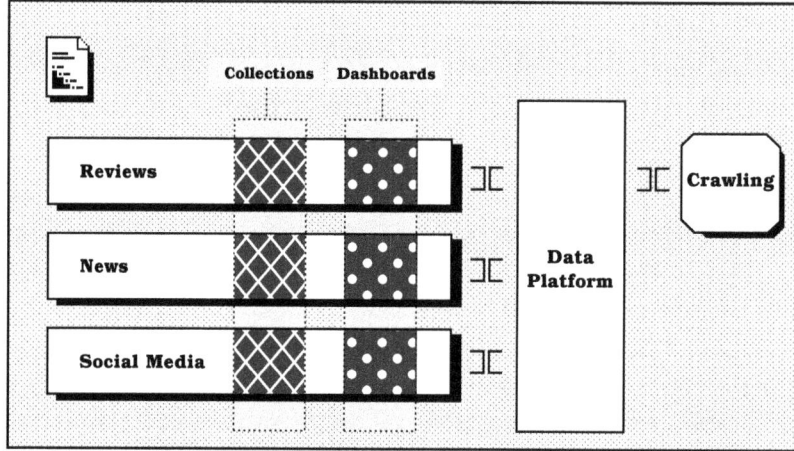

- *You have created a Collection team*, which is an *enabling* team focusing on *collaborating* with the stream-aligned teams. They help them ensure that the crawlers go to the right websites with appropriate revisiting intervals. They also make sure that data is stored correctly and is available for retrieval in the right format with the appropriate metadata.

- *You have created a Dashboards team*, which is an *enabling* team focusing on *facilitation* via reusable visual components for the stream-aligned teams to use. They are accountable for the holistic look and feel of the product. They also review changes to common areas of the product to ensure that the overall user experience is consistent.

- *You split the Data team into the Data Platform team and the Crawling team.* The Data Platform team is responsible for the storage infrastructure and defines clear *X-as-a-service* APIs for the stream-aligned teams and the Crawling team to retrieve and ingest data, respectively. The Crawling team is a *complicated-subsystem team* that focuses solely on the crawling infrastructure, and they maintain a sole focus on their work.

Using the diagram, you then map out a brand new org chart as shown on page 51. You ensure that each team has a clear focus and that the span of control is more reasonable for the manager of each team. You run a self-selection exercise to allow engineers to move between teams if they wish.

It looks like you've done a great job of refactoring the org chart and defining the interactions between the teams. Well done! With everything that you've learned in this chapter, you've just designed a re-org at a Series A company. Not bad for a day's work.

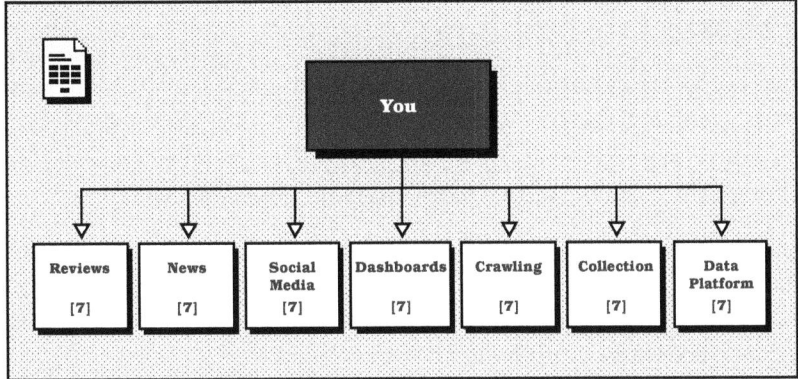

If it isn't already top of your mind when reading this, actually *implementing* this new design via a re-org requires tact, diplomacy, and a lot of good communication, which we'll focus on later in the book. You can't just drop the mic and walk away at this point.

By redesigning the org chart around the team topologies model, you've ensured that the teams are set up for success: they have *clear ownership* of their areas, and they have *clear interaction modes* with other teams. Not only will this make the teams more focused and autonomous, but, as a side effect, it will also ensure that the product is better designed and built.

> ## Your Turn: Refactor Your Department
>
> In the previous exercise, we asked you to look at your own department and identify the team topologies that exist. Now, let's take it a step further.
>
> - Identify the part of your department where you feel that interactions are suboptimal. For example, perhaps there is recurring friction between two or more teams, or perhaps there is a duplication of effort that you think could be avoided.
> - Map out the suboptimality using the team topologies model. What types of teams are involved? How do they interact with each other? What do you think this says about the problem that you identified?
> - Redraw the team topologies model to reflect the ideal state. What types of teams would you introduce or remove? How are you proposing to change the interactions between them?
> - Refactor the org chart to reflect the ideal state. What do you think about the new org chart you've created? Can you solve any span of control issues at the same time?
> - For bonus points, show what you've just done to the people who run those areas. Do they agree with your assessment? What do they think about the proposed changes?

Time Flies...

When we began this chapter, we promised that you'd leave with a newfound appreciation for org charts. We hope that now is the case. After all, you've just done a re-org that was driven by clear principles and models that are guaranteed to help those teams work together more effectively.

You may even find yourself standing in the kitchen while you wait for dinner to cook, moving around the salt and pepper shakers and spice tins, thinking deeply about the teams in your department and how they interact with each other. Just make sure you don't burn the onions.

Here's what we've learned:

- *We looked at the history of the org chart* and how it has evolved over time. We saw that the org chart is a tool that can be used to help us understand the structure of an organization and how it functions and interacts with itself.

- *We looked at some common org chart shapes* that you will encounter at technology companies at the tactical, operational, and strategic levels. You can now use these as a starting point for designing your own org chart.

- *Then, we looked at some of the antipatterns that can arise from how the org chart functions.* We saw how to avoid common pitfalls that occur when teams grow or shrink without care being taken to ensure that the org chart is refactored accordingly.

- *Lastly, we went through an exercise of refactoring an org chart that was in a suboptimal state.* We used the team topologies model to map out what was wrong with it and then designed better interaction patterns between the teams, resulting in a better org chart.

And that's the end of the first part of the book. We've spent two chapters analyzing company structures from afar and learning how and how not to design them.

In the next part of the book, we're going to come much closer, dropping in on what it's *really* like to be a senior manager from day to day. That begins with understanding how to manage your time effectively. What should you be doing? When should you be doing it? How do you find balance within the chaos? We'll answer all of these questions and more.

Part II

Tools, Techniques and Time

More responsibility means more for you to wrap your head around each day. If you thought that context-switching was bad running one team, then wait until you're running a whole department!

This section is all about the tools that you need to be successful in ever more senior management positions. It's going to be like walking into a well-stocked hardware store after spending a whole day trying to cut some wood with your kitchen cutlery.

We'll be covering how to use your time, how to play long-term and infinite games, how to get your staff to work well for you, and how to work best with your manager and your multifectas, and we'll also cover communication at scale and management of senior individuals.

You'll soon be heading back home with a power saw. Metaphorically, of course.

CHAPTER 3

Time: Observed, Spent, and Allocated

Bing!

"Whoa, look who's here!" says Ben. "Nearly sixteen minutes late. That is a brand new record."

"Sorry, sorry, sorry," you say. "Honestly, I'm in so many meetings now, it's getting silly. Sometimes, I end up double-booked. Actually, y'know, yesterday I was triple-booked. Then I have to pick *one*, and then people get annoyed I'm not in the *other* meeting."

"Too popular, you see. You get a promotion, and then you're the coolest person around. I know how it is," says Ben. "Remember us little people when you're rich and famous…"

"If you chopped yourself into three, you could attend them all," says Tara.

"Could we get your head in ours? At least we could talk to you," says Ben.

"Argh," you say. "I'm sorry. I've not even looked at the agenda. What are we talking about today?"

"We're going through our design document ahead of the technical review tomorrow," says Tara. "Did you get a chance to read it?"

You sigh. "No, I'm sorry. I've been so busy. It was my first thing to do today, and then I had to deal with a bunch of fires."

"Okay, well, we'll go through it now," says Tara. "I'll share my screen. Can you see it?"

"Yep," you say.

"Okay, so we've got a bunch of diagrams here," says Tara. "The arrow on the left represents the messages that we're already pulling from the streaming team…"

Your mind wanders. You can see there's a DM that's just popped up on your screen. It's from Lisa. You remember she emailed you earlier but you hadn't read that either. You open your inbox, and there are over thirty unread emails. You feel a little overwhelmed.

"So what do you think?" says Ben.

"Sorry, what?" you say.

"What do you think about the design? Do you feel that what we're asking of the streaming team is reasonable?"

"Uh, yeah, sure. I mean, I don't know," you say, while your eyes dart around the diagram, trying to get some context. "What do *you* think?"

"I think I'll go through it one more time," says Tara. "Let's start with the arrow on the left."

"Thank you. Give me a second," you reply, closing your other applications. "Right, I'm in the room."

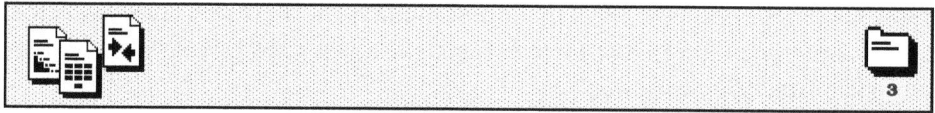

If you had a conversation with any senior manager about what they find most challenging about their job, it's likely that time management would be high up on their list. From meetings to emails to interruptions to a constant stream of requests, senior management can sometimes feel like a juggling act with an infinite stream of inputs.

While it may be the case that you will always find yourself in a battle against all of the things that require your time, it is important to remember that you aren't helpless against them. In fact, with the right framing, techniques, and tools, you can take back control of your time by using it more mindfully, purposefully, and effectively.

Mastering how you spend your time is one of the cornerstones of being successful in your role. The difference between managers who manage their time effectively and those who don't is stark. The former are able to execute on what matters most while finding time to think, plan, and reflect. The latter are constantly fighting fires, managing high stress levels, and struggling to raise their heads above the parapet.

In this chapter, we're going explore in detail how you should think about your capacity and how you should allocate your time. Although many of these techniques are simple, they are not straightforward to implement. The real world has a habit of continually transforming order into disorder. However, with discipline and practice, you can maintain that order more effectively.

Here's what we're going to be covering:

- *We'll start by exploring how you should think about your time.* What does it actually *mean* to spend your time on something as a manager, and what does it mean to push back and say no? We'll help you design a specific lens through which you can view your time and use it to make decisions about how to spend it.
- *Then, we'll move on to your capacity.* This is your most important resource, and we'll cover how to manage it, how to keep it high, and how to replenish it when it's low.
- *Next, we'll walk through a number of tools and frameworks that can help you manage your time.* These techniques, when used in combination with your lens, will allow you to make decisions about what to do now, later, never, or to delegate.
- *Finally, we'll move on to your calendar.* This is both a tool and a representation of how you spend your time, and, as such, it is important to use it correctly. We'll cover time blocking, batching, focus, and doing nothing and dive into the power and pain of meetings. We'll cap off the chapter by performing a quick audit of your time.

So, with that covered, ensure that you've blocked out an hour or so in your calendar, and we can get started.

A Lens of Longtermism

Humans can be extremely short-sighted. On a regular day, we may find ourselves getting frustrated at the smallest inconveniences, such as a three-minute wait at the checkout line in the supermarket or the person in front of us walking too slowly. We find immense grief in these small and inconsequential things despite the fact that in those moments, many aspects of our lives are actually going well. We may have more going right with our health and our bodies than is wrong with them, we may have somewhere safe to live, and we may have a job that we mostly enjoy doing. However, for those three minutes spent in a line or those moments trailing behind a slow walker, we are consumed by a feeling things are immeasurably wrong in the world.

Our short-sightedness also leads to poor decisions. While we are in that supermarket checkout for three minutes, we may get gradually more impatient and irritated to the point that we are rude to the person in front of us who is taking their time packing their bags while talking to the cashier. We may even go so far as to take that frustration out on the cashier themselves, who has done absolutely nothing wrong; in fact, they are offering excellent customer service to the person that they are talking to. Also, when we get outside and find ourselves trailing behind someone walking slowly, the residual annoyance from the checkout line may build to the point that we barge past them on the sidewalk, making them feel threatened by our behavior.

The actions that we take in a moment are a function of the lens that we look through. When we are in that supermarket line or on the sidewalk, we can default to a lens of short-termism. Humanity and society go out of the window because all we can see is bounded by the frame of the immediate self and the temporary inconvenience that we are experiencing. This limiting lens leads to poor decisions and poor behavior.

Instead, if we were able to look through a lens that has a *wider* field of view than just our immediate self and experiences, we would perhaps find ourselves acting differently. We would be able to see that the three minutes in line is a tiny fraction of our day and that the person in front of us is not intentionally trying to make us late. They're just having a nice conversation while packing their shopping. Perhaps this is the first good conversation that the cashier has had today. Also, the person walking slowly in front of us may be simply enjoying their walk home after a long day at work, helping themselves to unwind a little before they see their family.

Despite our short-sightedness, the concerns of the world are *not* limited to our own immediate experience. So, if we reframe them accordingly with a *bigger* field of view, we can make *better* strategic and practical decisions that have a more positive effect on the future.

An ethical stance that gives the long-term future precedence is called *longtermism*. At the core of longtermism is the idea that *influencing the long-term future is a key moral priority of our time [Mac15]*. At present, the majority of humanity will live in the future long after we have lived. There are many more humans to come than have already been. However, we currently make decisions that are not aligned with reducing major risks to our species in the long-term future, such as more aggressively tackling climate change or reducing the risk of nuclear war. We are blinded by our immediate experience.

If we imagine a future where humans continue to exist for another million years, bearing in mind this may be an underestimate since the universe will exist for *trillions*, then the decisions that we make today will have a huge impact on the future of humanity.[1] After all, everything that exists today was built by the previous 200,000 years or so of humanity, which is the product of about 109 billion humans that have since died. For the next hypothetical 800,000 years, there may be a *trillion* more humans to come. The question is, are we doing right by them from moment to moment?

This is why it is important to have a longtermist view. It leads to better strategic priorities and decisions in the here and now.

Longtermism at Work

Longtermism is not just an ethical stance for our personal lives. In fact, it can be used as a guide for how you decide to spend your time each day in your job, even if you don't intend to be at the company for the rest of your working life. Think about it: if the company and your organization were still around long after you were gone, what would you be doing differently today in order to ensure that your software was still running effectively, your staff was still happy, and your customers were continuing to get value from your product?

More importantly, you can use longtermism to help you decide what *not* to do. Without a longtermist lens, it is easy to get dragged in many unimportant directions from day to day that have little value or meaning in the future. Additionally, you may find yourself cutting corners that will leave you in a worse state. A classic engineering example is technical debt. When faced with a challenging, immovable deadline, you implement quick hacks that help you meet your immediate needs but create *more* work in the future because the code is now harder to work with.

> **A 100-Year Company**
>
> 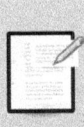 At the company I work for, one of the core values that I come back to as a leader is that we are building a 100-year company. When faced with decisions from how to build infrastructure to how to write documentation, this core value helps us to make decisions that stand the test of time and reduce future toil and technical debt.

The diagram on page 60 shows the potential direction in which decisions move when you spend your time with a longtermist lens vs. the contrarian short-termism approach. Your challenge as a leader is to choose how you spend your time and the time of others to ensure you're moving up and to the right.

---

1. https://ourworldindata.org/the-future-is-vast

Maintaining this longtermist lens helps you achieve your overall strategy, which is what we'll cover later in Chapter 11, Strategy 101, on page 253.

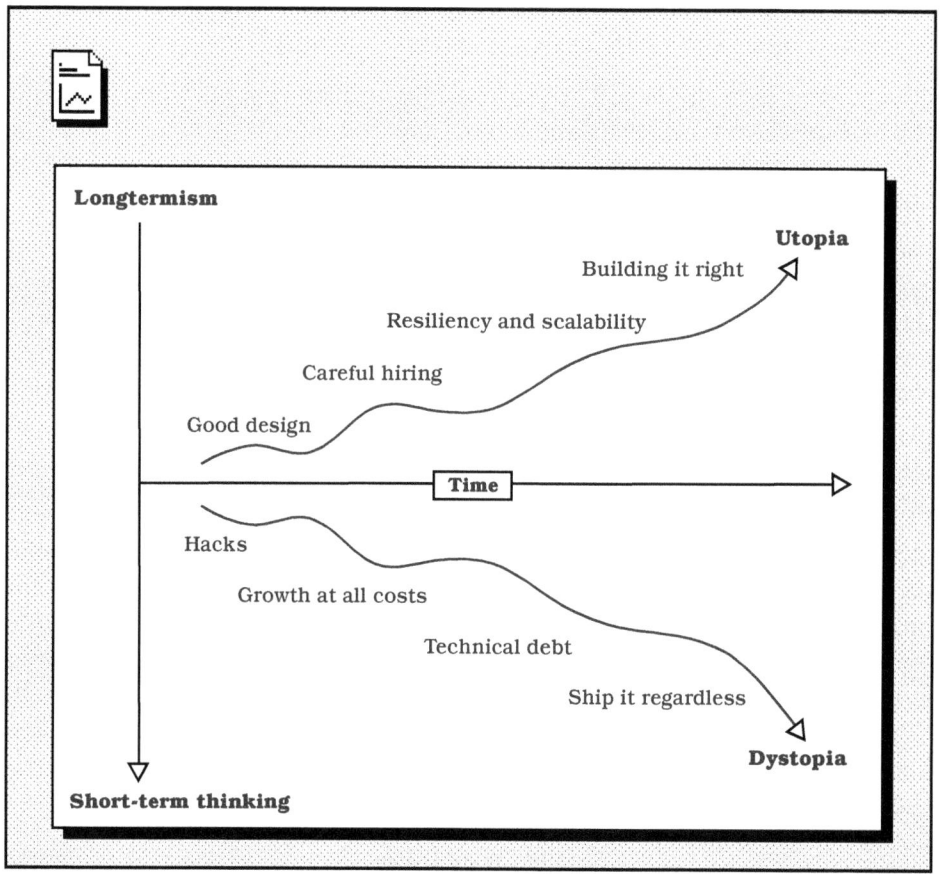

Despite the needs of the present being immediate and visceral, the long term is where you need to focus your attention as a leader. This is not to say that you should ignore the present, but rather, you need to weigh the needs of the present against the needs of the future, with a heavy bias on the latter as the most pressing. What is also important is that you are able to instill this mindset in your teams so that they are also able to make decisions that are aligned with the long-term future of the company.

Application of a longtermist view is not only reserved for big decisions such as whether to prioritize one project over another or whether to hire somebody. It applies equally to small decisions about how you spend your time every single day.

With a longtermist lens, you will naturally turn your attention to the bigger picture in your role: where your organization is headed, what you should build in the coming months and years, and how you can coach your team so that you have a strong bench of talent to accompany you on that journey. With the opposite lens, you may find yourself spending your time on urgent but unimportant activities.

Train yourself to hold up a longtermist lens to every activity you do, from opening a browser window to working out how to spend that hour gap you have between meetings. You'll be surprised at how it can shift your behavior and your decision-making, ultimately progressing your career.

For example, having a longtermist view can help you think of the right outcome for your organization in these ways:

- *Ensuring that you have a clear vision and strategy* for your organization that is aligned with the long-term future of the company

- *Making sure that you are hiring and developing the right people* who will be able to take the company to where it needs to go, including investing in less-experienced staff that could become future stars

- *Developing your bench of successors* so that you have a strong pipeline of talent that can take over from you when you move on to new challenges

- *Working on scalability, resilience, and reliability* as part of your projects rather than as an afterthought, including ensuring that all of your systems are well documented, well understood, and instrumented for observability

- *Slowing down projects that are moving faster than interconnected teams can handle* so that you can ensure that the whole system is moving forward together rather than building up technical debt that will need to be paid off in the future

These are just some of the possible ways that you can apply a longtermist lens to your work, often resulting in a shift in your priorities and the way that you and your teams spend your time. However, the future will thank you for that ability to step back, think, and tend to the long-term health of your organization.

> **Your Turn: Think Long Term**
>
> When you next get a moment, take a look at your to-do list and calendar for the coming week. Armed with what you've just read, hold up a longtermist lens to it.
>
> - Imagine that your team, division, or department is still around in 100 years. In order to ensure that it is functioning well, what would you be prioritizing today that you aren't right now?
>
> - Take a look at your to-do list items. What kind of time horizon do they have? Are they focused on the present, or are they focused on the future? How can you shift your perspective to be more longtermist?
>
> - Next, look at the meetings that you have in your calendar. Are they moving the needle on the long-term future? If not, can you change their focus or just delete them altogether?
>
> - Go through an exercise with your team or peers to discuss what you would be doing differently if you were to take a longtermist view. What would you be doing more of? What would you be doing less of? What would you stop doing altogether? You'll be surprised at the insights you generate.

Your Time Is Not Your Own

In addition to ensuring that you are applying a long-term view to everything that you spend your time on, it is also important to remember that your *time is not your own*. As a senior manager running an organization, you need to spend your time as if it belongs to that organization, rather than yourself. This is because your time is a resource that is used to achieve the organization's goals.

This principle is especially important since senior management does not come with a prescriptive list of tasks that you need to do. Nobody will be explicitly telling you how to spend your time. Instead, with your longtermist lens, you need to decide what to do in the time you have available. This means portioning your time to ensure:

- *You know whether the organization is on track with its goals.* This involves scheduling time to review metrics, projects, and other indicators of progress.

- *You are connecting with and steering your direct reports.* This involves scheduling regular one-to-ones and group meetings and being available for impromptu conversations that keep the organization running.

- *You are attending whichever meetings with your teams that benefit from your presence.* These could be regular project meetings, technical reviews, or performing skip-level meetings.

- *You are connecting and collaborating with your peers and other groups with which your organization is interacting.* Building trust and rapport with these groups enables better alignment, sharing of ideas, and easier resolution when there are conflicts and blockers.

- *You are spending time on your own strategic work.* This can be anything from writing proposals for future directions to dealing with escalations that prevent your progress.

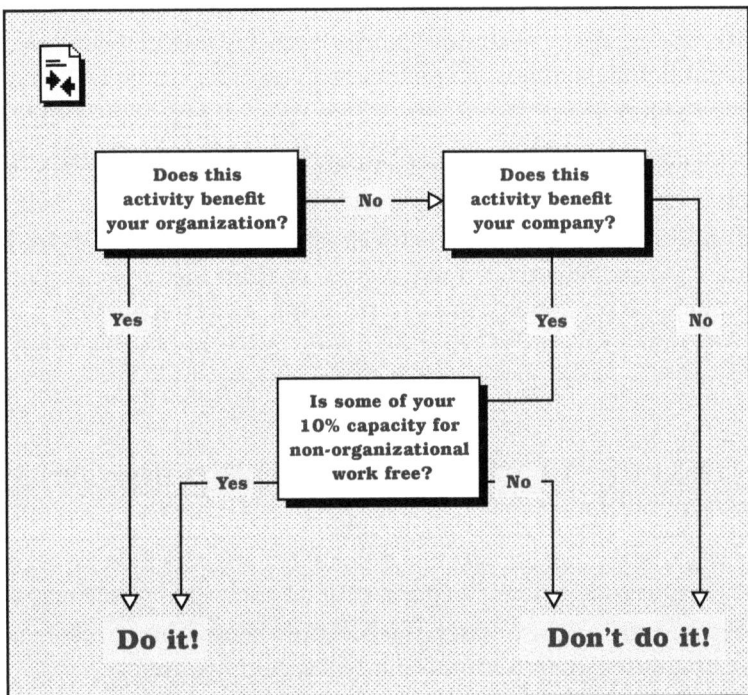

Fundamentally, almost every activity that you are spending your time on should be in service of the organization; it is the litmus test that you apply when you are inevitably asked to do additional things. If they align with the success of your organization, then yes, you do them. If not, then you decline.

There is one exception to this rule, which is that sometimes your time may be requested in a way that benefits the company but not *specifically* your organization. Examples of this include being asked to interview candidates for other teams, speaking at town halls or external events, or helping out with a company-wide initiative. Reserve a small amount of your time for these activities, but be careful not to overcommit. A good rule of thumb is to reserve around 10 percent of your time, and do remember that you always have the option of declining if you are in a pinch.

Your Capacity: Your Most Important Resource

The internet is full of opinions about how to manage your time. There are even whole books written on it. However, they miss an important nuance: it's not the *quantity* of time that you are able to juggle, assign, and manage that matters; it's the *quality* of the time that you are able to spend on your tasks.

Before we talk about time management, we need to talk about your *capacity*. Regardless of where you work or how senior you are, you have a finite amount of capacity. There are only so many hours every day in which you are working effectively, and only so many of those hours that you can spend in a state of productivity and flow.

Everyone typically dedicates the same number of hours to their work. However, everybody is different in finding how and when they work best. Some people are better at finding flow in the morning, while others are better in the afternoon. Some people thrive on long blocks of time spent on a single task, whereas others prefer to work in shorter bursts, switching to new tasks often to avoid repetitiveness. It's likely you already know what works best for you.

However, although you will find that you have a higher degree of self-direction and autonomy as a senior manager, optimal allocation of your capacity is not a box-packing problem where you *must* allocate every single minute of your day. This is an antipattern.

Instead, you should aim to allocate a default workload that is *not* your full capacity, purposefully leaving some portion of your time unallocated. This is because you need to leave space for the unexpected, such as escalations, meetings, and other interruptions that will inevitably arise.

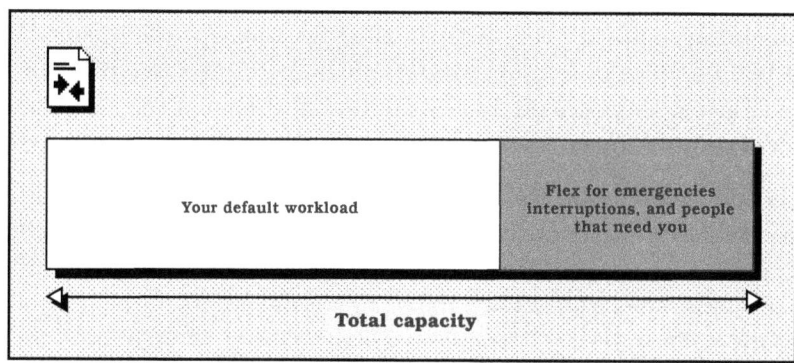

It's likely we've all worked with leaders who are impossible to get hold of when we need them. They are always in meetings or working on something urgent and are otherwise unreachable. This should be seen as a *bug* rather than a feature. These leaders are not managing their capacity effectively. They are not leaving enough unallocated breathing room for the impromptu events that happen every single day. This is bad for the organization since they are not immediately available in times of need. It is also bad for the leader since they are constantly in a state of reactivity.

If we've been lucky enough to work with leaders that manage their capacity *well*, then we may have been surprised that when we reach out with something urgent, they are able to respond quickly and effectively—perhaps they've offered to jump on a call straightaway. This isn't luck. It's just good capacity management. Make sure that you're always available for your team when they need you.

Now, before we move on, it's worth calling out that not everyone may be in the position to be able to leave some of their capacity unallocated. When companies demand that their staff work unreasonably long hours or when they are understaffed during challenging economic times, the advice in this section may be much harder to apply. If you find yourself in this situation, then you should seek to understand whether it is a temporary situation or a permanent one. If it is temporary, then you should do your best to manage your capacity until the situation improves. If it is permanent, then you should consider whether you are in the right role or whether you should be looking for a new job that is more sustainable.

Managing Your Energy

You are only able to allocate as much time to your tasks as your capacity allows. However, your capacity is not a constant, it is a function of your energy levels. On a given morning, if you are well-rested and feeling good, you will likely have a productive and effective day and also be stable in the face of unexpected events. However, if you are tired, overworked, or stressed, you will be unlikely to apply yourself in a measured and effective way.

Your energy levels affect your total capacity:

- *Your capacity has a fixed upper bound, which is the number of hours in a day you're able to work effectively.* In a senior management role, this may manifest as three to four hours you can dedicate to deep work such as writing, reading, or thinking. The rest of your time will be spent in meetings, one-to-ones, and other activities that require your attention.

- *Your capacity depletes when you are spending time on tasks that drain your energy.* Exactly what these tasks are will depend upon the individual, but these are typically tasks such as production incidents, overwhelming input, repetitive toil, conflict, delay, blockers, and overwork. The more you find yourself here, the more your capacity will shrink as the days go by.

- *Your capacity replenishes when you are spending time on tasks that energize you.* Again, this will depend upon the individual, but these are typically things such as finding flow in deep work, making progress on your projects, achieving goals, helping others, and, most importantly, getting good rest and balance outside of work time. The more you find yourself here, the more your capacity will grow until it restores to the upper bound.

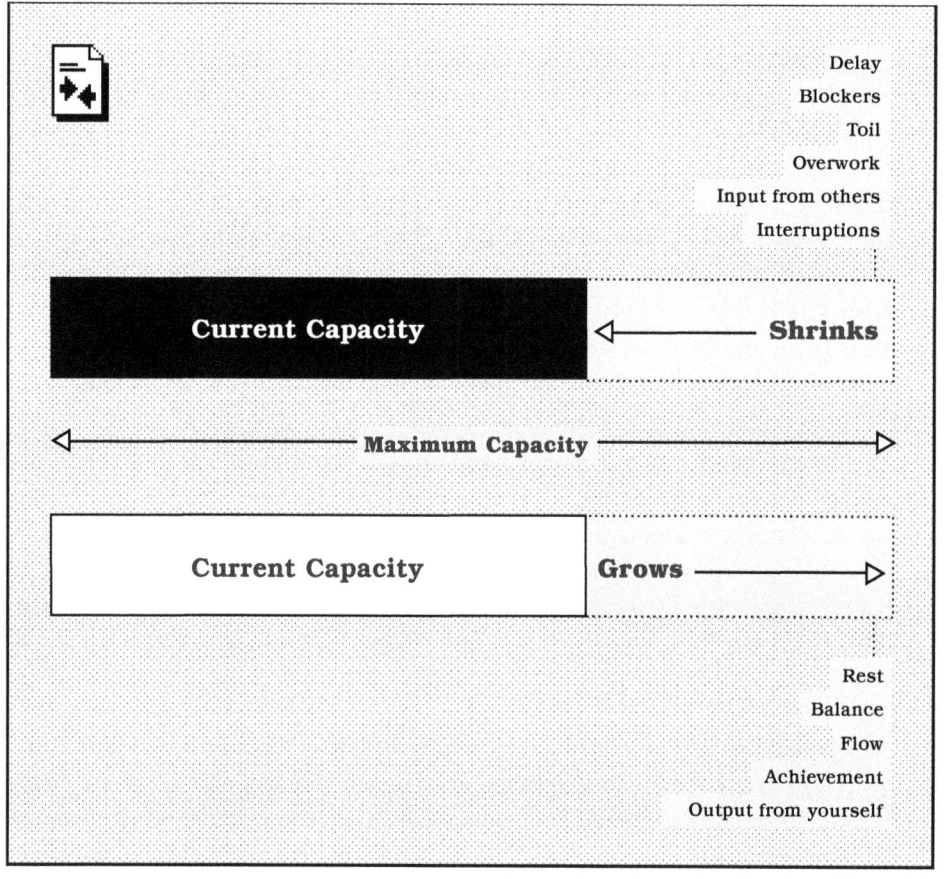

Therefore, it follows that you need to be mindful of your energy levels since they directly affect the quality of your work. This requires introspection and regular reflection on your tasks and activities. In addition to being effective at managing your time and output, you also need to balance hard work with rest, reactive firefighting with deep work, and meetings with focus time. You will know what increases and decreases your energy levels; it's up to you to ensure you're spending your time in a way that keeps your capacity high.

> **Your Turn: Log Your Week**
>
> In order to better understand the relationship between your capacity and your energy levels, it is useful to keep a log of how you are spending your time and how you feel. Although this exercise may seem simplistic, trust in the process. It may be enlightening.
>
> - For the next week, at the beginning, middle, and end of each day, log what you feel your energy level is on a scale of one to ten. One is completely drained, and ten is completely energized. You can use a spreadsheet, a notebook, or whatever works for you.
> - Alongside each log entry, jot down what you have been doing in the last few hours. This could be meetings, one-to-ones, deep work, or anything else.
> - At the end of each day, note how many hours of productive work you did. This can be deep work or meetings where you thought you were effective.
> - At the end of the week, take a look at your log. What patterns do you see? Are there any activities that are consistently draining your energy? Which activities increase it?
> - How did you feel about your capacity by the end of the week? Was Friday an unfocussed slog, or was it a day of high productivity? Can you see a relationship between your energy levels, the type of tasks that you were doing, and your capacity? What can you do next week to improve your capacity?

You owe it to yourself and your team to work on keeping your capacity high. The more capacity you have, the better work you'll do, the less reactive you'll be, and fundamentally, the more output you'll produce.

Don't be the frazzled stress ball that struggles through each day. Understand the tasks you spend your time on, how you work, and how you can look after yourself to keep your capacity in check so you can do your best work. You'll be surprised at the difference it makes.

Input vs. Output: The Tug of War

With a broad scope of responsibilities, you will find yourself subjected to a constant stream of inputs. These inputs can come in many forms, such as emails, messages, meetings, and interruptions. There isn't anything you can do to avoid this; it's just part of your job. It's the entropy that you must deal with on a daily basis.

However, although it's unavoidable, it is manageable. What you *should* do is actively balance the time taken on these inputs with the outputs that you create. Outputs are the things that add value to the organization, such as proactive discussions, nudges, decisions, reviews, and proposals. You have to protect the time to do these; otherwise, entropy will take it from you.

Without keeping the balance between your inputs and outputs in check, you will find yourself in a constant state of reactivity. Unfortunately, this is where many managers find themselves, and not only is it stressful to be out of control, but it is also the breeding ground for ineffectiveness. Anyone can be reactive—just sit in front of email, chat, and other people and see what comes at you. On the other hand, it takes disciplined effort to be proactive and to create outputs that have value to the organization.

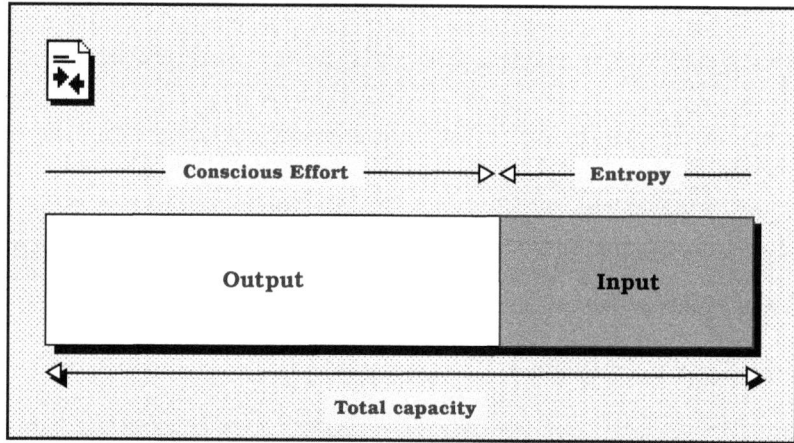

In the diagram, we represent this tug-of-war between inputs and outputs as the way in which your total capacity is being divided. It is rarely in a constant state of balance, as each hour, day, and week is different. However, understanding where you are at any given time is a key skill. Experienced managers can *feel* when they are out of balance and will course-correct without thinking about it. However, if you aren't sure, you can run a simple audit of your time to see where you are spending it.

> **Your Turn: Input vs. Output**
>
> As you go through the week, keep a log of how you are spending your time. Categorize your activities into inputs and outputs. It's up to you to choose which activities are which.
>
> - How much of your time was spent on inputs vs. outputs? What was the ratio? Does this surprise you?
>
> - What were the inputs that you were dealing with? Were they emails, messages, meetings, or something else? Were they expected or unexpected?
>
> - What were the key outputs that you were creating? If you could summarize your week in a few sentences, what would you say you achieved on behalf of the organization?
>
> - If the balance between inputs and outputs was out of whack, what can you do next week in order to make it better? Can you prioritize your tasks better or block out focus time without interruptions? Can you say no to some meetings? Can you delegate to others?

Time Management: Models, Tools, and Techniques

In this section, we're going to cover a number of different models, tools, and techniques you can use to help you manage your time. Your work time exists *within* your capacity, which is why we covered that first. These time management techniques are not prescriptive, but rather, they are a set of tools that you can use to help you make decisions about what matters, what doesn't, and how to prioritize.

We'll start with an old tool but a good one. Even though it's likely that you've seen it before, it's worth revisiting it with a new lens.

The Eisenhower Matrix

The Eisenhower Matrix is a simple tool that helps you prioritize your tasks based on their urgency and importance. It was popularized by Stephen Covey in his book *The 7 Habits of Highly Effective People [Cov94]* but was originally attributed to Dwight D. Eisenhower, the 34th president of the United States.

In a speech in 1954, Eisenhower said, "I have two kinds of problems: the urgent and the important. The urgent are not important, and the important are never urgent." This is the basis of the Eisenhower Matrix as shown in the diagram on page 70.

The Eisenhower Matrix

	Urgent	Not Urgent
Important	Do	Schedule
Not important	Delegate	Delete

The matrix is split into four quadrants, each of which represents a different type of task:

- *Urgent and Important.* These are the tasks that you should have at the top of your list to do as soon as possible.

- *Important but Not Urgent.* These are the tasks that you should schedule to do later, ideally when everything in the first quadrant is done.

- *Urgent but Not Important.* These are the tasks that you should delegate to others or do later if you have time.

- *Not Urgent and Not Important.* These are the tasks that, ideally, you shouldn't have to do at all. Delete them if you can.

Now, the Eisenhower Matrix is a great tool, but it's not perfect. In fact, we could criticize it for being far too general. For example, what does "important" mean? What does "urgent" mean? Are you deciding what is important and urgent, or is somebody else? How do you deal with different contexts and situations that end up clashing in priorities? These are all valid questions.

The reality of senior leadership is that you may be dealing with multiple concurrent priorities that are all equally important or urgent because each exists in a different context. In a sense, you may find yourself in a situation where you have multiple Eisenhower Matrixes that all overlap. Being responsible for many different things at once is a common challenge, and perhaps it is best addressed by introducing an enveloping model that will help you deal with this complexity.

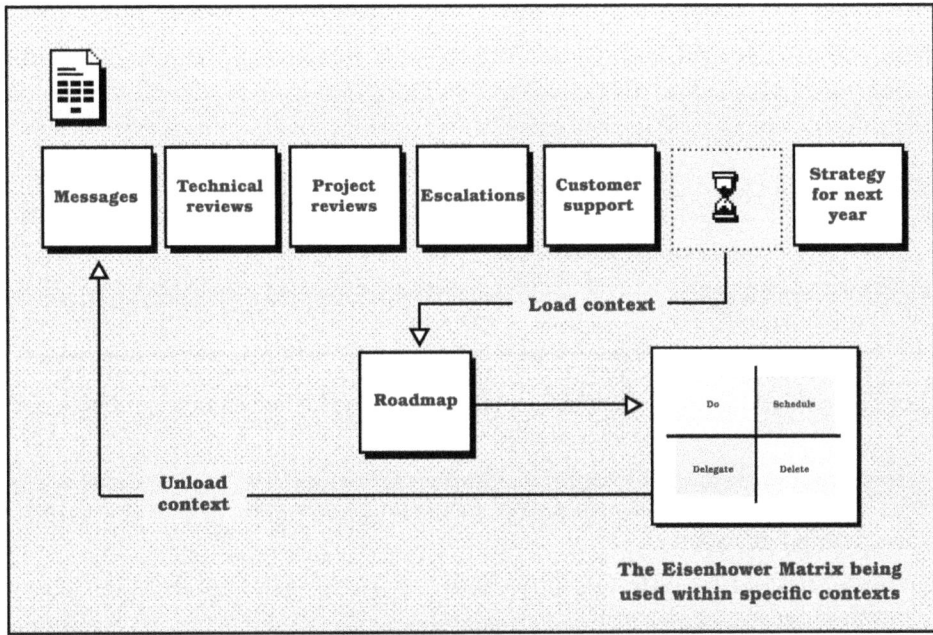

The Eisenhower Matrix being used within specific contexts

Imagine that the Eisenhower Matrix is represented in code as a function that takes in a context that contains a list of tasks and returns that are ordered by priority. For example, you may have a context for a project that you are working on, a context for your emails and messages, and a context for your technical reviews.

Your brain can only run one context at a time; it is single-threaded. So you have to load a context, work on the tasks within it, then unload it into storage. For example, the first thing you might do at the beginning of your work day is check your messages and emails. Your brain loads the context for this task, and you work through it. Then, you unload that context into your brain's memory and load the next context, which might be a project that you are working on. You work through the tasks in that context and then unload it. You then load the next context, and so on.

Each context will have subtle definitions of what important and urgent mean. For example, in the context of your emails, urgent may mean you need to respond to a customer, and important may mean that you need to respond to a colleague who is blocked in their work because of you. In the context of a project, important may mean you need to review a design document, and urgent may mean that you need to make a decision on something shipping later today. It's all relative. However, within each context, it's clear how to proceed, and you can manage the progress of each context relative to the others.

We'll come back to this idea of contexts later in the chapter when we talk about your calendar. It turns out that blocking out time is a fantastic way of creating the space to load contexts and work through them in a state of flow.

> ### Your Turn: The Power of Eisenhower
>
> Take a look at your to-do list. Let's apply some Eisenhower:
>
> - Is your to-do list organized according to the Eisenhower Matrix? If not, can you reorganize it?
>
> - Is it clear what's important and what's urgent? If not, how can you clarify this? Does it get easier if you hold up a longtermist lens? What about if you hold up a lens of your time belonging to the organization?
>
> - If you still struggle to prioritize, can the idea of contexts help? What if you bucketed tasks by the context to which they belong? How would that change your prioritization?
>
> - If you've grouped tasks by context, have you been working on them in the past in a way that lets you load and unload contexts cleanly, giving you the opportunity to work in a state of flow? If not, how can you change your approach to give you more focus time?

Saying No

One of the most powerful tools that you have in your arsenal is the ability to say no. Your capacity is finite, and you need to ensure that you are spending it on the right things.

Saying no is a tool built on top of the previous tools that we've covered. You may need to say no to something because it is not important or urgent, according to the Eisenhower Matrix. Alternatively, you may need to say no because you are already at capacity and you cannot take any more on. Perhaps you may need to say no because when you are holding up your longtermist lens, you can see that it is not aligned with the long-term future of the organization. Remember: you are saying no because you've determined that your other activities are more important to your team, not because you don't want to do it.

However, the tool of saying no is often missing key details. While saying no to something in your personal life is relatively easy (most of the time), saying no to something in your professional life is much harder, as typically, something being asked of you is something that your company needs to do.

Therefore, saying no as a senior leader still requires you to solve the problem for the people who asked you. Assuming that you have decided to say no to something, you should:

- *Explain why you are saying no.* You'll have your reasons, from not having enough time to it being a better fit for somebody else. Explain these reasons to the person who asked you.
- *See whether you can delegate it.* If you can't do it, who can? If there is someone else who can do it, then make the connection and remain accountable for ensuring that it gets done.
- *If you can't delegate it, make it clear when you can do it in the future.* Give the person asking some details about the possible timeframes and see if they can work within those constraints.

Practice saying no, but hold yourself accountable for finding a solution regardless. This way, the organization still gets what it needs.

Getting Executive Assistance

You may be in a role that provides you with an executive assistant to help you organize your time. You may have one assigned to you personally, or you may have a slice of an assistant that is shared with other leaders. If you are lucky enough to have an assistant, then you should use them as an extension of the Eisenhower Matrix technique.

- *Weekly or daily, review your matrix together.* Your assistant can help you to organize your tasks into the matrix and then help you to prioritize them. They can also help you schedule your tasks into your calendar.
- *Allow your assistant to help you to say no.* Your assistant can help you to say no to tasks that are not important or urgent by picking up the communication overhead and ensuring that there are still paths to resolution, either via delegation or scheduling for the future.
- *Work together to manage your energy.* Your assistant can help you manage your energy by ensuring that you have time for rest and balance and by helping you manage your calendar so that you block out time for focus work. Make it clear to your assistant which parts of the day you prefer to use for which purpose, and delegate calendar management to them.

- *Give them control of your inbox.* Your assistant can help you manage your inputs by triaging your inbox, perhaps using a system similar to the Eisenhower Matrix. They can also help you manage your messages and other inputs, ensuring that you are only dealing with the most important and urgent ones personally, helping you context-switch far less.

From experience, those who have an executive assistant available for the first time will dramatically *underutilize* them. This is because they feel that they are burdening them with their work or that they are not important enough to have an assistant. This is a mistake. Your assistant is there to help you to be more effective, and you should use them as much as you can. They are a force multiplier for your capacity, and they can help you to be more effective in your role.

Deadlines and Cadences: The Greatest Trick You Can Play on Yourself

Since much leadership work is self-directed and future-facing, it is easy to fall into the trap of never getting it done. If you ever need proof that long and open-ended projects never seem to finish, just ask any Ph.D. student why they haven't completed their thesis yet. Leadership roles can have many similarities to doing a Ph.D. You are given a broad scope of work, nobody is telling you exactly what to do, and you are expected to make progress despite a world of interruptions and distractions.

One of the most powerful tools that you have at your disposal is the ability to set artificial boundaries that help you progress. Even though it is one of the oldest tricks in the book and one that others hate when you do it to them, it is still one of the most effective ways of getting things done. Think of it like a hack that exploits Parkinson's Law, which is the idea that work expands to fill the time available for its completion. Why not set a deadline that is sooner than you think you can do it and see what happens? You'll be surprised at how much you can get done. And you'll also be annoyed that the trick works again and again and again.

However, abusing this hack repeatedly can start to feel cheap. While it's good to challenge yourself to get work done quickly, if you push yourself too much, then you are going to overwork and reduce your capacity. That isn't sustainable. It works for the occasional important deadline, but you'll tire from false urgency if you do it too much.

This is where you can evolve the trick to work in unison with your capacity by exploiting the natural rhythms of the Gregorian calendar: the day and the week. These recurring synthetic deadlines are *cadences* that you can use to help you make sustainable progress. They are also a great way of keeping your team aligned and accountable over longer periods. We'll look at cadences for teams in Chapter 12, Company Cycles, on page 271. However, for now, let's look at how you can use cadences to help you use your time productively.

Days and weeks have some neat properties for helping you get things done:

- *They are bounded by rest time.* A day has a morning and an evening, and each week is followed by a weekend. Each cadence has a natural start and end with rest in between, which helps you manage your energy levels and, therefore, your capacity. If you push yourself a little, you'll get a break at the end.

- *You often underestimate how much you can get done in each period.* Thus, if you apply a little Parkinson's Law, you'll surprise yourself and others with your productivity.

- *Everyone else at work is using them.* This means that you can use them to your advantage to align with others, such as your team, your peers, and your manager.

Cadences work well if you bookend them with two activities:

- *Setting goals for what you want to achieve in the cadence.* For example, at the beginning of the week, you may want to draft a proposal for a new project, and by the end of the week, you may want to have it ready for review.

- *Sharing it widely with others at the end of the cadence.* For example, at the end of the week, you commit to sharing your proposal with your team, your peers, and your manager. This helps you to be accountable for your goals and also helps you get feedback and input from others.

As we progress through the book, you'll pick up a number of different long-termist activities that you can use as goals for your cadences. Keeping yourself accountable for these activities by setting goals and sharing them with others is a great way of making progress in roles where nobody is really telling you what to do. That's why you have to tell *yourself* instead!

Using Accountability Partners

If keeping yourself accountable is challenging, especially if you are not used to the amount of autonomy that you have in a senior leadership role, then *accountability partners* are a great way of helping you stay on track. Some people can find that sharing their commitments with others makes work much more exciting and motivating. An accountability partner is someone you trust and with whom you can share your goals. Ideally, they will be in a similar role to you, such as one of your peers, and even more ideally, they might want to share their goals with you, too. This way, you can keep each other accountable.

Your accountability partner becomes part of your cadence. At the beginning of the cadence, you share your goals with them, and at the end of the cadence, you share your progress. If you are both participating in sharing with each other, then it's a great chance to learn what somebody else is working on, which gives an insight into their own world; plus, you can give each other feedback, input, and a healthy dose of encouragement at the end of each cadence.

I've had success finding accountability partners by simply asking my peers whether they'd be open to receiving a few messages a week on our chat platform about what I'm working on. Typically, this comes with a get-out clause that if they are too busy, they can just ignore me. However, in practice, this rarely happens; there's a lot of good conversation and encouragement that comes from it, and it helps you push yourself that little bit harder. And, of course, sending what you've been doing to your manager once a week is a great way of keeping them in the loop, too. We'll explore more strategies for communicating with your manager later in Chapter 7, Of Clownfish and Anemones, on page 153.

Another flavor of accountability partner is actually more than one: it's a group! The term *mastermind group* is used to describe a group of people that meet regularly to discuss their goals and progress. The term was coined by Napoleon Hill in his book *Think and Grow Rich [Hil15]* and has been used by many successful people to help them achieve their goals. The simplest implementation of a mastermind group is a private chat channel where you post your goals and progress, and others do the same. However, you can also supplement this with regular meetings to discuss topics in more depth and give each other feedback and input.

Once you've started working to cadences, you'll wonder how you ever tackled open-ended work without them.

Your Calendar: Wielding a Double-Edged Sword

It's impossible to talk about your time without talking about your calendar. Your calendar is the tool that you use to *schedule* your time, and, most importantly, it is the way that *others* do the same. Therefore, it follows that

> **Your Turn: Hold Yourself Accountable!**
>
> See if you can use the techniques that we've just covered to better utilize your time by setting cadences and then holding yourself accountable for your progress in them.
>
> - Start by setting yourself a weekly cadence. At the beginning of each week, write down what you'd like to achieve for the long-term benefit of your organization over the next five working days. Then, at the end of the week, share your progress with either your manager, peers, team, or all three!
> - If you'd like to take it a step further, find an accountability partner. Ask your peers whether they'd be open to receiving a few messages a week about what you're working on. If you'd like to go even further, set up a mastermind group with a few of your peers.

in order to be effective at managing your time, you also need to be effective at managing your calendar. The two go hand in hand.

This section refers to your calendar as a double-edged sword because it can make or break you. If you utilize and control your calendar well, it can be a powerful tool. However, if you don't, it can become a tool that others use to control *you*!

Depending on your company culture, you may find that your calendar is a free-for-all, and anybody can book you at will. What a nightmare! Every unallocated hour is a dice roll for a potential meeting that sucks away your time. In this section, we are going to focus on simple and straightforward techniques you can use to take back control of your calendar and transform it into a powerful tool for managing your capacity and energy and making sure you get stuff done.

Blocking Time

The first and most important technique is to block time out for yourself. Otherwise, how are you expected to drive the future of your organization if you don't know when you have the time to do so? Blocking time is a simple technique that you can use to ensure that you have the space to work on the things that matter. More importantly, it marks out the time that you *don't* have available for others to book.

You know what? Let's start taking back control of your calendar right now. When it comes to getting things done, there's no time like the present (no pun intended).

To begin with, block out the following:

- *The beginning and end of each day.* Make it clear to others when it's too early or too late to book time with you. This is especially important if you are working across time zones. Leave a note on these blocks to indicate how to request time if it is an emergency.
- *Your lunch break.* Yep, book an hour for lunch. Even if you don't eat then, block it anyway to get away from your desk and to give yourself a break.

Okay, this is a great start. Making sure that your non-working hours are blocked out means that you can protect your energy and your capacity.

Next, you need to think about how you are going to spend your working hours. We appreciate that you may already have a busy calendar that you can't immediately refactor, so consider the following to be an ideal north star that you can work toward with time.

Decide the best way to distribute your *recurring meetings*. Building on the context-based loading and unloading that we covered earlier with the Eisenhower Matrix, think about how you work best. For example, some people like to batch similar meetings together, such as one-to-ones or group syncs. This means you can load the context for that type of meeting, get in the right brain space, and then concentrate on them back to back without context switching. Alternatively, you may prefer to spread them out throughout the week. It's up to you: you know how you work best. Get your recurring meetings fitted in.

Next, you need to decide how much of your time you want to block out for your own *deep work*, and when it's best to do so. This is the time you will use to work on your projects, write proposals, read and review the work of others, and generally do the things that move the needle on the long-term future of your organization. Here, a state of *flow* is key. You may be the kind of person who finds blocking out several whole mornings every week as focus time works best for you. Alternatively, you may prefer to work in shorter blocks of time, such as two hours in the morning and two hours in the afternoon. It's up to you. But most importantly, *block them out* as recurring focus time in your calendar so others know you're busy and cannot be booked while they are happening unless it's an emergency.

Finally, you need to decide how much time you want to leave *unallocated*. Think back to the capacity section where we recommended you leave a portion of your time free. This is the time that you can use to deal with escalations, unexpected meetings, and other things that come up. Just leave it unbooked in your calendar. If you don't need it, then you can use it for your own work.

Depending on the calendar software you use, there may be other useful features you can use to help you manage your time. For example, Google Calendar allows you to schedule bookable portions of time for others. This is a great way of making yourself available while still maintaining control of your calendar. Think of it like a professor's office hours. You'll have a metaphorical open door, and while nobody is knocking, you can get on with something else.

Some calendar software also has functionality to set your working hours, meaning that meetings are automatically declined that are in your mornings and evenings. However, do be mindful that auto-declining meetings *can* come across as a bit passive-aggressive depending on the way that you implement it. It's up to you to think of the user experience of others. Make sure you leave a nice message.

With a little bit of pruning and rejigging, you may end up with a blissful calendar like the following example. This is a calendar that is organized around the principles that we've just covered. It's not too dissimilar from my own.

Time	MON	TUE	WED	THUR	FRI
07.00					
08.00	School run 08.00 - 09.00	School run 08.00 - 09.00	School run 08.00 - 09.00	School run 08.00 - 09.00	School run 08.00 - 09.00
09.00	Focus time 09:00 - 12:00	Focus time 09:00 - 12:00	Focus time 09:00 - 12:00	Focus time 09:00 - 12:00	Focus time 09:00 - 12:00
10.00					
11.00					
12.00	Lunch 12.00 - 13.00	Lunch 12.00 - 13.00	Lunch 12.00 - 13.00	Lunch 12.00 - 13.00	Lunch 12.00 - 13.00
13.00	1:1 13.00; 1:1 13.30	1:1 13.00; 1:1 13.30	Focus time 13:00 - 16:00	Office hours: book a slot 13.00 - 15.00	Skip-level 13.00; Skip-level 13.30
14.00	1:1 14.00; 1:1 14.30	1:1 14.00; 1:1 14.30			Skip-level 14.00; Skip-level 14.30
15.00	1:1 15.00; 1:1 15.30	Project review 16.00 - 17.00			
16.00	Project review 16.00 - 17.00			Project review 16.00 - 17.00	Project review 16.00 - 17.00
17.00					
18.00	End of day 18.00 - 20.00	End of day 18.00 - 20.00	End of day 18.00 - 20.00	End of day 18.00 - 20.00	End of day 18.00 - 20.00
19.00					
20.00					
21.00					
22.00					

> **Your Turn: Refactor Your Calendar**
>
> There's never a better time than now to refactor your calendar.
>
> - If you haven't already, follow the previous steps to block out your time, ensuring that you've covered your working hours, breaks, recurring meetings, focus time, and unallocated time. If it's too hard to do it all at once, don't worry. You can chip away at your calendar over time and gradually nudge it into the shape you want. You'll find that the control and predictability that you'll get from an organized calendar is well worth the effort.
>
> - If you can, have a look at the calendars of some of the most senior leaders in your organization. How do they organize their time? What can you learn from them?
>
> - Bring up calendar organization with your peers, manager, or team and see what they do. You may find that you can learn from each other.
>
> - For fun, with this same group, see if you can find the messiest calendar in the organization. You get extra points for anyone who is regularly quadruple-booked!

Getting the Most out of Focus Blocks

So, you've managed to carve out some focus time. Excellent! That's a start. But what exactly do you do with it? How do you make sure you're using it effectively? After all, we're sure you've previously done this only to be interrupted by a colleague or to find your attention wandering to something else.

Creating the Right Environment

The first thing that you need to do in your focus blocks is create the right environment for you to work in. This means:

- *Setting your status to busy on any applications that support it.* If you can leave a status message, let people know that you are head down in focus time and that you'll get back to them later.

- *Closing all unneeded applications and disabling non-essential notifications.* If you don't need it, close it. This includes email, messages, web browser tabs, and anything that might generate inputs that will distract you from your outputs.

- *Setting a goal for what you are going to achieve in the focus block.* This could be a task, a document, or a set of actions. Deciding exactly what you want to do will help you stay focused and will give you a sense of achievement when you complete it.

The Pomodoro Technique

If you are the kind of person who finds themselves easily distracted, especially when you are working over several hours on self-directed work, then a great tool that you can use is the *Pomodoro Technique [Cir06]*. This is a time management technique that was developed by Francesco Cirillo. Based on a tomato-shaped kitchen timer (hence the term "pomodoro"), the technique is simple: you set a timer for 25 minutes and work on a task until the timer rings. You take a short break (typically five to ten minutes) and then repeat. After four pomodoros, you take a longer break.

At the end of each pomodoro, you can take a moment to reflect on what you've just done. If it helps, you can log what you've done in a notebook or a spreadsheet. This is a great way of keeping yourself accountable and also for looking back at what you have achieved over time.

Things to Focus On

There are a lot of things that you can focus on in your focus blocks. You'll know best, but here's a few ideas:

- *Making progress on whatever your goal is for your current cadence.* For example, if you have a goal to write a proposal, you can use your focus blocks to write it carefully and thoughtfully.

- *Reading and reviewing the work of others.* For example, this could include technical designs, project proposals, and pull requests.

- *Producing asynchronous content for broadcast to others.* This could include weekly updates for your team or your manager, research or explainers for your team, or improving onboarding documentation.

- *Any other longtermist activities that you have identified.* For example, you may have a goal to spend time studying competing products or learning a new technology.

Keeping your focus block scoped to one general context or activity is a great way of keeping yourself in a state of flow. As well as being productive, this feels really good. It might remind you of the feeling of being in the zone when you were writing code all day. Bliss.

One obvious item excluded from this list is working on your usual messages and email. Should you be scheduling these in focus blocks? Well, it's up to you, but it depends on how important those messages and emails are. After all, your focus blocks are meant to be the time you're working on the things that drive your organization forward for the long term. Arbitrary messages and emails don't really do that, even when they are wrapped in the task of achieving inbox zero.

A better approach is to timebox your messages a few times a day, say, first thing in the morning, after lunch, and at the end of the day, and apply the Eisenhower Matrix to them. Any messages that *do* require a considered and thoughtful response can be scheduled in your focus blocks. The rest shouldn't eat up time that could be spent on more important things.

The Power of Nothing

You should also never underestimate the power of scheduling nothing at all in your focus blocks. Although this might seem counterintuitive, especially to those that are completer-finisher personality types, you need to give yourself space to think and for your mind to wander. Sometimes these are where you have your best ideas.

For example, if you chose one of your focus blocks every week to be filled with nothing, then you could:

- *Spend time using the product you build.* Too many senior leaders get out of touch with the software their organizations create. Using the product is a great way of getting back in touch with what it means to be a user. You could focus on a particular area of the product, such as the parts your team builds. What is the experience like? What could be improved? What are the pain points? What are the opportunities?

- *Check out the work going on in other teams.* This is a great way of getting a feel for what is going on in other parts of the organization. You could start by reading some of their documentation, pull requests, or design documents, or just try using their functionality.

- *Pick some recent design documents and read them closely.* Depending on the size of your team, you may not get the chance to be close to the details in each area you are responsible for. You can use your focus time to read deeply into the design documents that your team has produced. You can comment and give feedback and share them more widely if they are great examples.

- *Read some of the latest research in your field.* Given that you are meant to be holding up a longtermist lens, you should be keeping up to date with the latest technology and research in your field. What new technologies are worth prototyping with? Are there opportunities to improve your architecture? What about the latest artificial intelligence trends and their applicability to your work?

Choosing *not* to fill some of your focus time is a great way for you to explore, play, and follow your interests. It also provides great material to have further discussions with your team.

Meetings: Crisp, Clear, and with a Purpose

Other than your focus blocks, it's likely that a significant portion of your time will be spent in meetings. They are a necessary evil: synchronous communication is essential for certain types of collaboration and communication. However, they can also be a huge drain on your time and capacity if they are not managed well. Meeting culture varies from company to company and geography to geography, and you may not have much control over changing this culture as a whole. However, you *do* have control over *your* meetings.

We'll be diving deep into different types of meetings as we progress through the book, so we'll stay focused on the *time* aspect here—notably, making sure that they are worth your time and the time of others that are in attendance.

To Meet or Not to Meet: That Is the Question

We are living in an era that has been defined by decades of calendar abuse. We should not be drawn towards meetings as senior leaders; we should be drawn toward measurable outcomes for our organizations. While it is true that achieving those outcomes may need *some* meetings, it is also true that we've become addicted to a false feeling of productivity that comes from being in them. We need to break that addiction. We started this chapter by ensuring that you are prioritizing blocking out time to focus on the *tasks* that matter. Now, we need some guiding principles for which *meetings* matter and which meetings don't.

Let's work backward from first principles. What's unique about meetings compared to individual work? It's the fact that everyone in the meeting is there at the same time—they are present and focused on the same thing. However, we could also imagine that those attendees could just be on chat or email at the same time. What is it about meetings that is unique? Well, it's the fact that being on a call or face-to-face unlocks the ability to use high-bandwidth multi-participant communication by speaking and using body language that gives a greater insight into how people are reacting and feeling. And are there any other unique properties of meetings? Yes—the combination of the previous two answers means that the participants get to actually build trust and rapport with the others on a human-to-human level, which is something that is hard to do over other forms of communication.

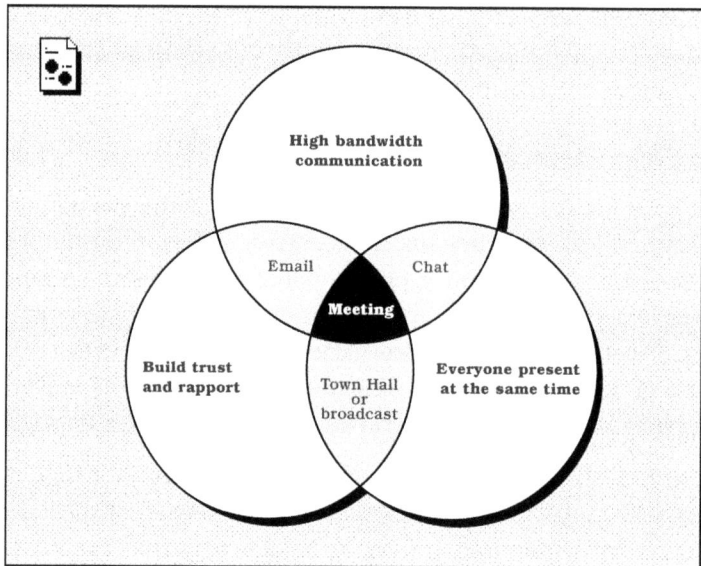

When overlaying these properties as a Venn diagram, we can see the following:

- If you are in a situation that benefits from all three properties—that is, high-bandwidth communication, the need to build trust and rapport, and the need for everyone to be present at the same time—*then you should have a meeting*. Examples of this include one-to-one meetings with your direct reports, resolving high-stakes conflicts, and generating creative ideas with a group of people.

- If you don't need the communication to be multi-participant and high-bandwidth, then a *broadcast of a video or a town hall scenario works well* (*many* attendees but *few* speakers). You can see this pattern in all-hands meetings at companies. Even though only a few people speak, the synchronous nature of the meeting still builds a feeling of camaraderie and trust; you're all in it together.

- If you need high-bandwidth communication and synchronous presence but the nature of the topic is fairly benign, then *chat still works well*. For example, you might be having a quick exchange around a deploy that seems to be a bit slow. Multiple people can input into a chat conversation in a way that is high-bandwidth and mostly synchronous, but it doesn't require a full-blown meeting.

- If you need to discuss something that requires high trust and rapport but physical presence *isn't* required, *then email is a good choice*. For example, you may need to write an in-depth reply explaining why you think a particular project is a bad idea. You want to make sure everyone is able to express themselves succinctly and clearly, but there's no need for that to happen in a meeting room. The lack of synchronous presence means people can take their time to think, draft, and edit their responses carefully.

You should hold up this model to any meetings that you currently have or are thinking of having and see whether you can convert them into the suggested alternatives that give you more flexibility and control over your time. You will also find that as you interact with more senior leaders who have little space in their calendars, it is often better for the organization if you use the alternatives. This is because the *speed of a decision should not be limited by the availability of the person with the busiest calendar.* Progress should not stall because someone isn't available to meet until next Thursday. Instead, be creative in finding other ways to make progress.

Clear Agendas, Clear Outcomes, Clear Actions

If you do need to have a meeting, then you need to make sure that it is crisp, clear, and with a purpose. This means that you need to make sure that you have a clear agenda, clear outcomes, and clear actions. This covers the before, during, and after of the meeting.

A *meeting agenda* should be written before the event and shared with all attendees. Typical ways of doing this are in the description of the calendar invite or in a separate document. The agenda should include:

- *The purpose of the meeting.* Why are you having it? What is the goal?
- *The talking points.* What are the topics that you are going to discuss? What are the questions that you want to answer? What are the decisions that you want to make?

If you are feeling particularly brave or rebellious, you could take the stance that you won't attend any meetings that don't have a clear agenda. However, in the real world, you may find that the rest of the organization will just go ahead without you and wonder why you're being so awkward. However, instead of not going, consider being the person who creates the agenda, setting a clear example to others of what good looks like. You'll find that others will follow.

When the meeting starts, it's worth having the first talking point as a review of the agenda and an agreement on what the *outcomes* would ideally be for the attendees. This is a great way of making sure everyone is on the same page and the meeting is going to be productive. Outcomes may be a deeper understanding of the topic, alignment on what the next steps are, a decision that resolves an outstanding conflict, and so on.

It can also help if one person in the meeting acts as the *chair*. A chair of a meeting is responsible for making sure that the meeting stays on track and that the outcomes are achieved. They can also take notes of the discussion, keep track of time, and nudge the conversation forward if it is getting stuck or going off-topic.

Once you've reached the end of the agenda, or if the meeting is coming to an end, the chair should do a quick review of what was discussed from their notes. Then, the *actions* should be decided. Who needs to do what, and by when? These actions should be read through and assigned, with agreement from the group.

Meeting hygiene is really simple. However, it's so easy to slip back into bad habits that waste your time, others' time, and, most importantly, the time of your organization. Make sure that every meeting you do is crisp, clear, and with a purpose. The more you demonstrate this, the more that others will catch on and follow suit.

Calendar Stagnation: Blowing It All Up

We discussed earlier that your capacity is a tug of war between your output and your input: without effort and attention, noisy inputs will take up all of your time, and you will get nothing done. You have to actively protect your time to make progress. There is a similar dynamic with calendars: like an old bicycle that you never ride, entropy will make it stiff, unworkable, and a pain to use. You have to actively maintain it to make sure it's working for you.

Do you remember the day that you started in your current role? You probably had a clean calendar, and you were able to build it up from scratch. It was a blissful experience of moving your time freely around like an artist on a canvas. What does it look like now? Probably not quite as clear as it once was. As a leader, you should take time to clear down your calendar debt in the same way that you would expect your team to clear down their technical debt.

It is extremely healthy to reset your calendar at various points of the year. Sometimes, there are natural points to do this, such as the start of a new year or the start of a new quarter. The technique is simple: just delete every single recurring meeting that you are able to. Then, start from scratch with the technique that we covered earlier in this section. We cling to recurring meetings like they have been decrees from the gods, but they are not. They're just meetings. If they are not serving you, then get rid of them. If it turns out they were worth it, you can always add them back.

If you happen to be running a large organization, such as the whole department, you can take this one step further: why not delete *everyone's* meetings a few times a year? This is a neat way of resetting the culture of the organization and making sure that everyone is using their time wisely. Shopify has written about using this technique: the chaos monkey comes along and explodes your calendar. Yes, it's inconvenient, but you can hear the organization breathing a sigh of relief.[2]

Fight the entropy of your calendar. Reset it regularly. You'll be surprised at how much better you feel.

Syncs, Status Updates, and Other Ways to Die

The previous advice is reasonable if you either own the meetings you're in or if you're influential enough to change or decline them. However, if you're in middle management, you may not have this control. In this case, you may need to persuade others by offering compelling alternatives to meetings that are a drain on your time.

In the table on page 88, we enumerate some of the worst types of meetings that you may encounter and offer some alternatives that can achieve the same outcomes without the need for a meeting.

Hopefully, these examples, in combination with the previous section, paint a clear picture: your time and your organization's time are *extremely* precious. Synchronous meetings are useful when they are used in the right way, which is when there is a need for high-bandwidth communication, the need to leverage and build trust and rapport, and the need for everyone to be present at the same time. However, without keeping entropic behavior in check, you can end up with a calendar full of meetings that waste your organization's time and deplete your energy and capacity.

Fight the good fight. Protect your time and produce clear outputs instead. You're not paid to look busy—you're paid to make progress.

Auditing Your Time

Let's end this chapter with a quick exercise. In *High Output Management* [Gro95], Andy Grove, the former CEO of Intel, categorizes the activities of a senior manager into four buckets:

- *Information gathering.* This is where you gather information from others to help you to make decisions.

---

2. https://www.bloomberg.com/news/newsletters/2023-02-14/how-shopify-cut-320-000-hours-of-unnecessary-meetings

Type of Meeting	Why It Sucks	A Non-Meeting Alternative
Stand-ups	While often useful, stand-up meetings without focus or during periods of few blockers or interlocking work streams can degrade into an enumeration of what everyone is doing with little interaction or new knowledge being shared.	Consider converting the meeting into a chat channel where people can post their updates asynchronously. This allows people to read and respond to each other's updates and also allows people to post updates at a time that suits them. There are plenty of plugin bots that can help you automate this also.
Group syncs	Teams can often have a weekly sync where everyone gets together to share what is top of mind and what they are working on. This often gets booked because it is felt this is the normal thing to do, but it's often a waste of time if there is no clear agenda or purpose. This isn't just an artifact of individual teams; it can also happen from the middle management level all the way up to the top.	Instead, consider having the team collaborate to produce a weekly update that is shared asynchronously with the wider department. Writing the weekly update is a forcing function for the team to reflect on what they have achieved and what they are working on, which was the original intention of the meeting, but it also increases visibility for the rest of the organization of what the team is doing.
Status update one-to-ones	Entropy also creeps into one-to-one meetings, turning them into status updates. This detracts from the possibility of coaching and mentorship and more interesting, wide-ranging conversations.	Instead, work with your direct reports to encourage them to write weekly updates that they can share asynchronously with you. This gives you the opportunity to read and reflect on their updates and use the one-to-one time to discuss the topics that are most important to them.
Staff meetings	Similar to team syncs, staff meetings, which are regular meetings of a manager and their direct reports higher up in the organization, can be seen as a forum to share and discuss priorities and concerns. However, without a clear agenda and purpose, they can either degrade into status updates or just become a channel for the most extroverted to dominate the conversation.	Instead, consider investing in the staff meeting so there are regular focused topics discussed, such as how to improve the speed of the deployment process or how to speed up interviewing candidates. If you can't invest in an engaging agenda, and you can't delegate this duty to someone else, consider cancelling the meeting and encouraging your direct reports to share their updates asynchronously with you.
Unfacilitated brainstorming	Groups often delay ideation until they can get together synchronously to brainstorm. However, without expert facilitation, these sessions can often be inefficient.	Instead, consider getting participants to write or sketch ideas beforehand and then share them asynchronously with the group. This gives everyone time to think about the ideas and to provide feedback and input. Then, you can use a synchronous meeting if it's needed to discuss the ideas further in a more focused manner.

- *Decision-making.* This is where you are making decisions based on the information that you have gathered.
- *Nudging.* This is where you are influencing others to make better decisions.
- *Being a role model.* This is where you are setting an example for others to follow.

> **Your Turn: Which Activities Do You Spend Time On?**
>
> Open up your calendar and take a look at the last week:
>
> - How much of your time was spent on each of these activities?
> - Work out the percentage split of your time between these activities. What do you think about this split? Is it what you expected?
> - Are there other activities that you take part in that don't fit into these categories? If so, what are they? Andy Grove was the CEO of a public company, so his categories may not fit your role exactly. Would you introduce any new categories for your own work?
> - Reflect on what you've learned and think about whether you are spending your time in the right way. If you aren't, then what can you do to change it?

Now, You've Got People to Manage

How are you feeling about your time now? We hope that you see it as a precious resource that you need to protect and manage, not just for your own sake, but for the sake of your peers, team, and your organization.

We've covered a lot in this chapter, so let's recap:

- *We began by designing a long-term lens for your work.* This lens is a tool that you can use to frame any activity that you are doing and to help you decide whether it is worth your time. A longtermist perspective is essential for senior leaders to have.
- *Next, we looked at your capacity.* We saw how your capacity grows and shrinks with your energy and the types of activities that you are doing, thus making it critical for you to protect your time for the things that generate and maintain your capacity.
- *We then explored a number of tools you can use to manage your time effectively.* We looked at the Eisenhower Matrix with pluggable contexts,

saying no, setting deadlines, and creating cadences, and the power of accountability partners and groups.

- *Lastly, we looked at your calendar.* We saw how your calendar is a double-edged sword that can either help you manage your time or be a source of stress that others use to control you. We looked at how to block out time, how to get the most out of your focus blocks, and how to manage meetings. We finished with a quick audit to categorize the activities that you spend your time on.

Discipline is *key* to managing your time. We encourage you to revisit this chapter periodically to make sure that you are still being proactive about it. It's easy to slip back into bad habits, especially when you are busy and continually interrupted. Revisit these techniques often and nudge yourself back on track.

In the next chapter, we're going to explore the relationship you have with your staff. As you progress up the org chart, your reports become more senior and autonomous and often know more about their domain than you do. How do you make sure that you are still adding value? We'll explore all this and more.

CHAPTER 4

The Games We Play and How to Win Them

"It's cool that we get to work together. Everyone calls me Vic, by the way. Victoria always sounds too formal."

You smile. "Yeah, I'm looking forward to it. I've never had a principal engineer reporting to me before, so I'm excited to learn from you and see what we can build together."

Vic nods. "I've been working on the same part of the product for a long time, and it's going to be refreshing to learn something new. So, what's it like reporting to you?"

You pause. "That's a good question. Erm…"

"I mean, how do I know that I'm going to be successful? What do you expect from me?"

You remain paused. "I've not really thought about this. If I can be honest, you are probably more experienced and senior than I am. How did it work with your previous manager?"

Vic shrugs. "He kinda just let me get on with things. That suits me pretty well from day to day, but I never really had an idea of whether I was doing something meaningful, y'know? I mean, what's the bigger picture? I couldn't tell you."

"That's interesting," you say. "What *could* it be? You know, if you had to decide."

"Hmm. Like, are we building things that are going to scale and last for years? Are we using the right technology that enables us to move fast? And to build features with minimal effort? Are we building a team that's going to be able to do this sustainably without burning out? I don't know. I've not really thought about it in depth before."

You nod. "Nor have I, if I'm honest. Since we started here, it's just been about getting things done and firefighting. Every day has been pretty reactive. I've never thought about strategy or much about where people like you or I will be in a few years."

"Maybe this conversation is coming at the right time. We should keep talking about it."

"One hundred percent," you say. "What was one of the best bits of working with your previous manager?"

"You mean apart from the fact he was never there and didn't really understand what I did?" says Vic, laughing.

"I think I can do better than that," you reply.

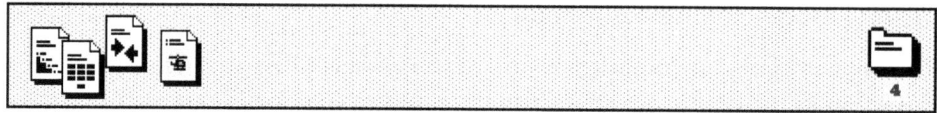

When you became an engineering manager for the first time, it's likely that your role and what was expected of you was relatively clear: your team of individual contributors looked to you for direction and to perform all of the typical managerial duties, thus allowing them to get on with their craft.

The delineation of responsibilities in the front lines of management was easy to wrap your head around. And since you knew what it was like to be an individual contributor yourself, you were also able to manage your staff with the empathy and understanding that comes from direct experience.

Yet, as you progress to ever more senior management positions like the ones that we have covered so far in this book, the delineation can become *less* clear, and the old techniques don't work as well.

First, you will be managing managers, some of whom may have more years of experience in the industry than you have yourself. You will also be managing senior individual contributors, who may have risen to higher levels in their craft than you were ever able to. This means the way that you managed a single team previously may not be appropriate for the new context that you find yourself in.

So what do you do?

This chapter is all about the unique challenges of managing larger organizations through other senior staff, and we'll explore how to frame your collective world in a way that makes sense and enables you to achieve together.

Here's what we're going to cover:

- *We'll begin by covering the fundamentals of managing senior people.* We'll look at coaching vs. directing, delegating vs. micromanagement, and how to run effective one-to-ones. We'll also look at how to use brag docs to help you manage your team and make your life easier.
- *Next, we'll bust a myth.* We'll explore how managing senior managers and senior individual contributors is not a different art; it is the *same* art, just applied in a different context. This will greatly simplify your approach to getting the best from your team.
- *Then, we're going on a journey from the swamp to infinity.* There is so much happening in a large organization that it can be hard to know where to focus your attention and to know whether you are succeeding. We'll look at finite and infinite games as a framework to think about the outcomes that you are all trying to achieve together and how to win them.

When you finish this chapter, you should have a broad toolkit for thinking about how to manage the senior staff that report to you at an interpersonal level and also how to frame and execute all of the work that you will collectively tackle as a team. That's no small feat, so let's get started.

Management 101: The Fundamentals

Regardless of how senior your direct reports are, the fundamentals still matter. This is as true for you as it is for them. In this section, we'll cover the basics of management that you should be applying so that you have the scaffolding in place to build your relationships.

Coaching vs. Directing

As you become more senior and move up the org chart, the way that you manage your team will change. Since you will be managing managers and far more senior individual contributors, it is less likely that you will need to direct them in the same way that you would direct an individual contributor who is less experienced than you. Instead of *directing*, you will be *coaching*.

To those who haven't been coached by a skilled individual before, coaching can seem like a nebulous concept. It can make you think of sports team locker rooms or even highly caffeinated life coaches encouraging you to look in the mirror and scream at your reflection to improve your self-confidence. Fortunately, this is *not* what coaching is about. Instead, coaching is about helping your direct reports to *find the answers themselves*, rather than telling them what to do.

This is important for two reasons. First, it is likely that your direct reports will know more about the domain that they are working on than you do. This means that they are better placed to make decisions about what to do than you are. Second, good coaching encourages others to think for themselves and to take ownership of their work and their decisions. This is a key part of building an autonomous, high-performing team.

The act of coaching is effectively just having a structured conversation with your direct report. You can frame this conversation by using a model called *GROW [Dow14]*. This model can be applied in many different situations and in timeboxes of varying lengths. For example, it could form the basis of a one-to-one, or it could be used within a group setting to help a team solve a problem. It can even be used on your own to help you think.

Here's what GROW stands for:

- *Goal*: What is the goal of this coaching session? What is the problem that we are trying to solve?
- *Reality*: What is the current situation like now? What is the context in which we are operating?
- *Options*: What are all of the ways in which we can tackle this problem?
- *Wrap-up*: What are the next steps? What are the decisions and actions that we are going to take?

You may have noticed that the descriptions of each of the steps within the model are questions. This is because questions are *essential* to coaching. When you are in a coaching conversation, you have *two mutually exclusive modes [Dow14]* of conversation that you use with your staff. These are:

- *Directive*: This is where you are instructing them on what they should do. It is a "push" action, where you are solving the problem for them.
- *Following interests*: This is where you are listening to them, reflecting on what they are saying, and summarizing it back to them. It is the opposite of being directive. It is a "pull" action, where you are helping them to solve the problem themselves.

Following interests is *all* about asking good questions. And it's also where the meat of coaching happens as shown in the diagram on page 95.

The key to coaching is to "keep the thought bubble over their head." You use the two different modes to do that. This is best illustrated by example. Let's say that you are coaching a direct report who is a manager. They have a

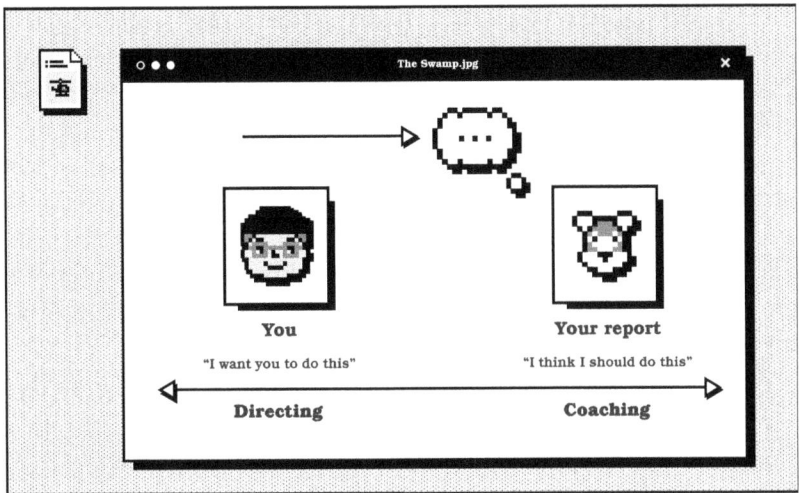

member of staff who is underperforming, and they are not sure what to do. You could have a conversation that goes like this, following the GROW model:

YOU: Okay, so what's the goal of this conversation?

THEM: We need to figure out what to do about Bob. He's not performing well.

YOU: Right. How is he not performing well?

THEM: He hasn't been delivering on his projects, often being the only person on the team who is lagging behind on deadlines. Also, his communication is poor: he sometimes doesn't respond to emails or chat messages, and recently, he has been missing some meetings that he's invited to with no excuse.

YOU: Okay, so he's falling behind and starting to show far less effort than the rest of the team. That definitely sounds like he's disengaged. What have you tried so far?

THEM: I've talked to him about it twice in his one-to-ones and he's said that he's fine, but he's not really given me any concrete reasons as to why he's not performing well. I've said that if he doesn't improve, then we'll have to take more formal action, but he hasn't changed his behavior. What should I do?

YOU: That sounds like he has heard the message but not taken it on board. Tell me, what do we usually do in this situation when someone isn't performing?

THEM: When we've had this in the past, we've put someone on a performance improvement plan (PIP). We've also had to let people go if they don't improve.

YOU: That sounds like a good idea. I'm aligned with that. What do you think you should do next?

THEM: I'll talk to HR and let them know that I'm going to request we put him on a PIP. I'll loop you in on the email.

> **YOU:** Great. Remember that PIPs are a win-win for you as a manager. If they want to improve, they will. If they don't, then sometimes an exit is the best thing for everyone, including the team. They want to work with people who are engaged and doing good work.

In this example, you used questions to follow their interest and to keep the thought bubble over their head. In this situation, you didn't need to lean on being directive because they were able to find the answer themselves. They were able to do so with your reassurance, which was evident in the way that you summarized back to them what they were saying and your statement that you were aligned in the next steps to be taken.

Although this example is management focused, coaching can be used everywhere. It is just as useful for working with senior individual contributors in order to figure out challenging technical problems; you use the same model and the same techniques. Once you've got the hang of it, it's a very powerful tool to have in your toolkit. Think of it as a lightweight wrapper around a conversation that helps you to get the best out of your interactions and, in turn, helps your direct reports to get the best out of *themselves*. If you get really good at coaching, you'll find that you can use it in almost *any* situation.

> **Your Turn: Get Coaching**
>
> In your next one-to-one, try out the coaching techniques that we've covered in this section. You can try to weave it into the conversation naturally, or you can be explicit about it and say that you want to give it a go together.
>
> - When your direct report next brings up a problem, apply the GROW model by asking them what the goal that they want to achieve is.
> - Then, ask them what the current reality is. Keep pushing the thought bubble over their head by asking questions to get to the root of the problem.
> - Get them to enumerate all of the options that they have at their disposal. Are you able to get them to decide without being directive yourself?
> - Agree on the next steps. Finish the conversation by asking them how they felt about your exchange and whether they found it useful.

Delegation

The second fundamental skill to sharpen is delegation. The larger the organization is that you run, the larger the output that you are accountable for. You clearly can't do this all yourself; that's why you have all of these people and teams with specific responsibilities and projects. But have you *really* thought about what it means to delegate work to others?

Delegation is not the act of giving other people tasks to do. Although this forms one of the mechanisms by which delegation works, it completely misses the point. The key maxim is that delegation is the act of giving the *responsibility* of a task to others while still maintaining *accountability* for it being done and to the high standard that you expect. Yes, you are accountable for every single piece of work that is being undertaken in your organization, even if the responsibility for that work is distributed across hundreds or thousands of people. The buck stops with you.

Fundamentally, delegation is about *ownership*, and that ownership goes all the way down the org chart. If you have five teams working on five areas, each owns their area individually, but you own them *all* collectively. It goes all the way up the org chart, too: the CEO owns the output of the entire company and delegates the responsibility for slices of that output to the rest of the organization.

Increasingly and correctly, we strive to build teams that have autonomy. This means that they are able to make decisions about how they work and what they work on. However, this can introduce a management antipattern when managers *abdicate* their responsibility for the work that their teams are doing. This is wrong and is an example of delegation done badly. Your teams can be autonomous, but you are still accountable for the work that they do. This is a subtle but key difference.

Delegation is also a spectrum rather than a Boolean operation. In reality, any act of execution is *not* a choice between delegating it or doing it yourself. Instead, in order to maintain accountability and visibility, you will delegate somewhere along a range depending on the task being done. The diagram illustrates this:

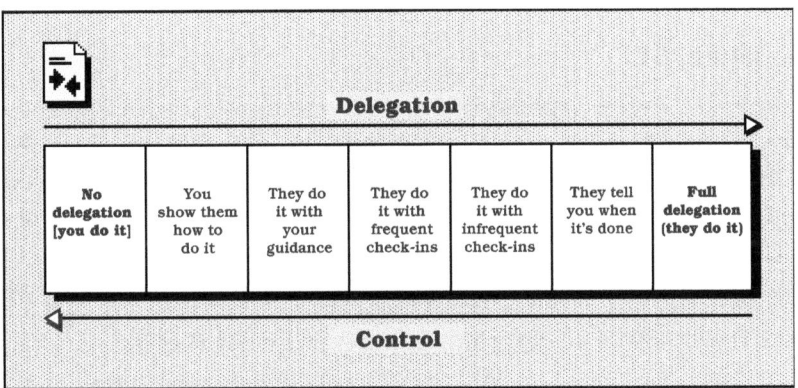

Any task, regardless of the size, will fall somewhere along this spectrum. Where it falls depends on the competency match between the task and the person or team that is doing it. For example, if one of your teams needs to implement some small UX changes to their product as a result of customer feedback, they are likely to be able to do it with little to no input from you. Thus, the delegation of this task is at the far right of the spectrum. They just do it, and they probably don't even need to tell you.

However, if you are working on a large and intricate piece of work, such as defining next year's roadmap for your organization, then it's likely that you will work closely with each of your teams and direct reports, traversing up and down the delegation spectrum, depending upon on the complexity of each individual piece of the whole and the skill of the person or team that is working on it.

The key to delegation is to be explicit about the position on the scale for yourself, who is *accountable*, and the person or team that is *responsible*. In order to ensure the tasks are done to the standard that you expect, set check-in frequencies and formats that are appropriate to the place on the diagram. For example, for teams happily executing on their roadmap, perhaps a written weekly update will suffice. However, during a major production incident, you may want to be on a video call with them every hour. The key is to be explicit about your expectations and to set the check-in frequency and format accordingly.

Getting delegation right can make or break you as a leader. Doing it correctly is the *only* way that you can properly scale yourself and your organization. That isn't to say you can't be hands-on and in the details—you can. That's the left-hand side of the spectrum. However, you need to choose what to engage with closely with your limited time and ensure that everything else is appropriately delegated via the right-hand side.

One-to-Ones 101

If management were a human body, then one-to-ones would be the spine; they are the backbone of your relationship with your direct reports. Without them, the essential relationships, trust, and communication that you need between you, your direct reports, and the organization as a whole will not be there. (This is one of the strangest analogies that I've ever written, but I'm going to stick with it.)

You may have, now or in the past, experienced what it is like to report to a senior member of staff. Thus, you may have experienced a common scenario where you find that your one-to-one meetings keep moving, getting cancelled, or aren't even being booked in the first place. This may have given you the impression that one-to-one meetings are something that just the *front-line* managers do in an organization and that *senior* managers don't need to do them. This is completely false. These meetings are essential. There is no excuse not to do them.

Treat your one-to-ones with the utmost priority. You should do them with your staff every week. If the content is not engaging enough, and your report suggests doing them with less regularity, then guess what? You need to get better at generating engaging content!

Also, if you have something important that gets booked over them in the calendar, then it's on *you* to make sure that you find an alternative time. Ensure that you execute on your one-to-one schedule with the same discipline that you would execute on any other meeting. They don't need to be an hour long. You can start with 30 minutes once a week and see how it goes.

Given that you are reading a book about senior leadership, it's likely that you don't need convincing as to why one-to-ones are important. You already know that they enable you to build trust and rapport and to learn how to get the best out of your direct reports. You also know that they are a chance to coach them and help them to grow.

However, it's worth noting that this is also a chance for the *inverse*: for your reports to get to know and trust *you*. This is especially important if you are new to an organization or if you hold a particularly senior role. Natural imbalances in power dynamics can make you wonder why your reports don't open up to you while you forget that you are a VP who runs their department. That's your problem—it's on you to make sure that you are approachable and can be trusted.

Contracting

If you have staff that either have trouble opening up to you or are new to reporting to you, then you can do an exercise called *contracting [Sta20]*. This is where you kick off your relationship by exploring what you both want to get out of your one-to-ones. You can do this by asking the following questions, which you can prepare in advance. It is important to note that you both ask these questions of *each other*; it is not a one-way exercise.

- *What are the areas that you would like support with?* For you, this is a great way of reinforcing which aspects of your report's role are on which parts of the delegation spectrum. For them, it is a great way of getting clarity on what you expect from them and also highlighting where they may need help—for example, if they are finding a particular aspect of their role challenging.

- *How would you like to receive feedback and support from me?* This is about understanding how each of you operates. For example, you may have different personality types, and so you may need to adapt your style to suit them. Additionally, you may have different preferences for how you receive feedback. Some people prefer to receive it in the moment, whereas others prefer to receive it in a more structured way. This is an opportunity to understand how you can best support each other.

- *What could be a challenge for us working together?* There may be practical limitations here, such as time zones, that will mean you will need to lean heavily on asynchronous communication outside of your one-to-ones. However, there could be other challenges, such as having a domain knowledge gap that you will need to work on closing; this is how you surface all of this early.

- *How might we know if the support I'm offering isn't going well?* Often, one-to-ones can degrade over time when the content becomes stale or the relationship becomes strained. This is a way of declaring up front that you both should call it out if this happens and agree on how you will do so.

- *How confidential is the content of our meetings?* As a senior leader, there will be many topics that you will naturally want to take away, discuss, and resolve outside of the one-to-one. But are any topics off-limits? Do you default to open or closed in how you handle information? Discuss this up front with examples so that you are both aligned.

Even if you've managed your staff for a long time, try this exercise out and see if it can reinvigorate your one-to-ones with more clarity and purpose.

Focus and Format

In order for your one-to-ones to run smoothly, you need to have a clear focus and format. This is the same hygiene that you should apply to any other meeting to ensure that they're effective. Here's what you should do:

- *Create a shared agenda*: You should have a shared document that you both contribute to in order to create an agenda for your one-to-ones. Lead by example by adding your own items ahead of the meeting and encourage your direct report to do the same. You can jot down anything on your mind as the week goes on, ensuring that there is plenty to talk about.

- *Be mindful of time*: All of the most important content in one-to-ones tends to happen in the last five minutes as time pressure forces it to the surface. This seems to happen regardless of how long the meeting is. Therefore, you should be mindful of the time and ensure that you leave enough to cover anything on the agenda. Before you start, review what's on it and reorder it so that you can cover the most important things first.

- *Fight against status updates*: In the same way that entropy eats away at your time and your capacity to do deep work, status updates can eat away at your one-to-ones. You should continually fight against the need to fill your one-to-one time with these and instead push your reports to deliver them to you in other ways, such as a weekly written update that could be broadcast to a wider audience. Not only does this free up your time, but it signals that your one-to-one time is precious and can be used for more important things.

- *Use time to coach*: You should aim to find at least one item to coach your direct report on each week. You can use the GROW model that we covered earlier, or you could simply ask, "what's on your mind?" and see where the conversation goes as you practice active listening and summarization. You can also use this time to give feedback, both positive and constructive.

- *Link topics to career progression*: Try to find hooks within the subjects that you discuss that you can use to link to the career progression of your direct report. For example, if they are in an escalation because of a lack of consensus around a technical direction, you could use this as an opportunity to coach them to improve their stakeholder management skills, which are essential for them to progress to the next level.

- *Summarize and agree to next steps*: At the end of the one-to-one meeting, recap what you covered and what the next steps are, such as actions or decisions that either of you need to take. This is a great way of ensuring that you are both aligned on what was discussed and what needs to happen next.

Simple hygiene can transform your one-to-ones from being a chore to being a highlight of your week. If you're finding it hard to prepare for them, then why not dedicate one of your focus blocks to doing so? You can use this time to review agendas, think about what you want to discuss, and prepare feedback.

Brag Docs: The Greatest Gift You'll Ever Receive

The final essential tool in your toolkit is *brag documents*, or brag docs[1] for short. As the seniority of those who you manage increases, so does the amount of delegation that you exercise with them. At senior levels of companies, those who report to you will be the domain experts in their areas, and more often than not, they will be best placed to direct themselves.

Having highly autonomous staff is a boon—you know that you can turn your attention elsewhere. However, it can also be a hindrance—you may not know the details of what they are doing and the specifics of how they are doing it. This can make it challenging to have enough visibility to be able to manage them effectively, and most importantly, you can find yourself unable to write a detailed and actionable performance review. This is especially true for senior managers who report to you, where their output is a function of those that they manage. What exactly have *they* done?

This is where brag docs come in. Rather than you having to keep track of what your direct reports are doing, they can *keep track of it themselves*. They do this by maintaining a shared document that they update regularly with their achievements, challenges, and goals. Although one could imagine that this could be seen as lazy management on your part, it is actually quite the opposite. Your reports get to take ownership of highlighting their achievements, which means that there is a consistent stream of information that you can use to give them continual feedback and write their performance reviews.

A way to have your staff structure a brag doc is as follows:

- *Choose a period of time*: Pick a cadence that makes sense to you. Often, having a document per review cycle is a reasonable choice, but you can also have a document per quarter or per year. Whatever works best.

- *Frame broad goals at the top*: Have the document outline what they are trying to achieve over the period of time that the document covers. This could be goals or metrics that their team is trying to hit, personal goals that they are trying to achieve, or objectives identified in their previous performance review.

- *Keep it close by and add rough notes continually*: Don't encourage your reports to spend time writing up detailed notes to the point that it becomes a hindrance. Instead, encourage them to keep the document open and to jot down anything they achieve as they go through each day. This could

---

1. https://jvns.ca/blog/brag-documents/

be a new feature that they shipped, a proposal that they wrote, or a new hire that they interviewed. The key is to keep it up to date; it needs to become a habit.

- *Encourage your staff to link achievements to wider goals*: This is important. It's not enough to just list achievements; ideally, they need to be linked to the goals that were set at the top of the document. This helps to provide context and show how the achievements are contributing to the wider goals of the organization. For example, shipping a feature may contribute to the goal of increasing user adoption in an area of the product. Interviewing a new hire may contribute to the goal of growing the size and impact of the team. Having your staff engage in this broader strategic thinking is a great way to help them level up.

- *Review it regularly*: You should review the document between you at periods of time that make sense to you both. This could be every week, month, or quarter. The key is to make sure that you are both aligned on the contents of the document and that you are both happy with the progress that is being made.

Believe me, writing a performance review for a member of staff that has a detailed brag doc is one of the greatest gifts that you can receive. You should keep one for yourself too, because can you really remember exactly what you were doing four months ago? If you can, perhaps you'd be better off counting cards at a casino. And don't worry; we'll dive much deeper into performance management in Chapter 10, Performance Management: Raising the Bar, on page 223.

It's All Just Leadership After All

Once upon a time, in a galaxy far, far, away, when I first got into management, I had mistakenly assumed that progression up the org chart meant only managing *other* managers. I was totally wrong.

Individual contributor career progression grows in parallel with management career progression, and in large organizations that implement these dual tracks, you will see individual contributors with the *same* seniority as managers. This goes all the way up to the top, as we saw in Chapter 2, Your Place in the Org Chart, on page 23.

For example, at large technology companies, you will find principal engineers reporting to directors, and sometimes, you will find distinguished engineers reporting to VPs. Each has a different skill set but the same seniority and scope.

> **Your Turn: Get Bragging**
>
> Introduce the concept of brag docs to your direct reports. You can do so by showing them this part of the book or by sending them a link to Julia Evans' original article.
>
> - Ask each of them to create a brag doc for the current review cycle and share it with you. Ask them to write their goals at the top of the document. If their goals aren't clear, then that's a worthwhile conversation in itself!
> - Ask them to prefill the document with any achievements that they can remember from the past few months. This exercise makes it clear how quickly historical achievements drop out of memory and should encourage them to want to keep a document up to date!
> - Agree on a cadence to review the document with them. Make sure that you use it as a chance to deliver positive feedback and to push them to achieve more.
>
> If some of your staff find it hard to start this habit, why not use your one-to-ones as an opportunity to work on their brag doc together? You can both edit it as you talk to them about what they have been working on. After a while, they'll pick up the habit themselves, yet another reason why regular one-to-one meetings are so important.

We'll study the senior individual contributor relationship in more detail in Chapter 5, The Sharpest Tool in Your Toolbelt, on page 119, but let's begin by focusing on how you manage senior staff using the tools that we've covered in the previous section.

Progression up the managerial track, therefore, isn't just about managing other managers; it's also about *managing senior individual contributors*. This makes senior management doubly challenging because you need to be able to manage both roles effectively, and a new senior manager may now be managing individual contributors that have *far, far* surpassed them in their own craft.

The pertinent question is whether you should *manage senior managers and senior individual contributors differently*. After all, they have different roles and responsibilities, and it would be natural to assume that the way you manage a staff engineer would be different than the way you manage an engineering manager. Right?

Nope, that assumption would also be wrong. Sorry.

You *don't* need special strategies for managing both roles. In fact, you can apply the *same* strategy to both, and not only does this simplify your approach, but it actually encourages the *best* behaviors from both roles.

Let's explore this in more detail.

Control at the Intersection

At the beginning of this chapter, we explored a model for delegation: it's a spectrum that you traverse depending on the competency match between the task and the person or team that is doing it. You may assert *more* control through hands-on involvement or *less* control through delegation.

It turns out we can also use this delegation model to work out how best to manage senior staff that report to you, regardless of their role. The key is to think about the intersection between the two roles. The following Venn diagram illustrates this:

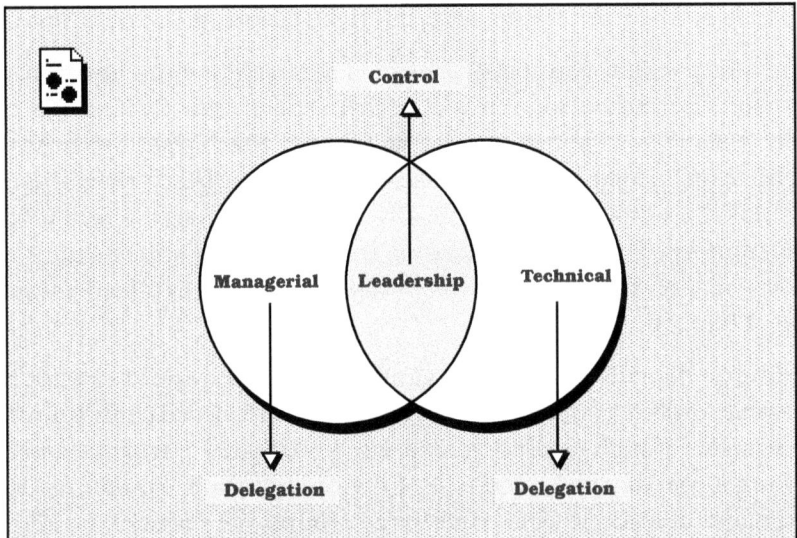

Both circles represent the roles of senior managers and senior individual contributors. The circle on the left is that of the manager (who produces output through *management*), and the circle on the right is that of the individual contributor (who produces output through *technical contribution*). The *intersection* between the two circles is the shared aspect of the two roles: *leadership*.

Yes, leadership is an overloaded and sometimes hand-wavy word that often means nothing. But what do we specifically mean by it? Let's break it down:

- *Managers demonstrate leadership by leading organizations.* Whether it's one team or a whole department, they are accountable for the output of the organization that reports to them. The responsibility of individual tasks is delegated to their direct reports, and the manager leads the organization to achieve its goals by defining the right teams, people, and processes.

- *Senior individual contributors demonstrate leadership by leading technical initiatives.* This may manifest in being the lead developer on a project or being responsible for a technical area of the product. Even though they do not have direct reports, they set technical direction and are accountable for its success.

The key to managing both roles with the same approach is to focus on that intersection between the two circles: *developing their leadership.* This is where you should assert the most control and where you should be most hands-on. This is where you should be coaching them, giving them feedback, and helping them to grow. It's where you should work closely with them to ensure they are working on the right things with the right people at the right time.

What you keep within your close control is ownership of the *target* that your direct reports are aiming for, but you let them choose exactly *how* they choose to hit it. A manager reporting to you will aim at that target by constructing the right team, people, and processes for the job. Then, they'll use their managerial skills to make it happen. Given the same target, a senior individual contributor will aim at it by leading the design and implementation that makes it a reality. The key is that *both disciplines* use their leadership skills to make it happen.

Depending on the culture of your organization, you may need to work harder to encourage *explicit* leadership from your senior individual contributors. This can be framed through exhibiting model behavior other engineers can follow, thus being a role model for the rest of the organization. You do *not* have to be a manager to lead projects, steer large groups, get consensus, and make decisions. Ensure your senior individual contributors are doing this, too.

Example targets are:

- *Building a new feature.* A manager will assemble the right team, people, and processes to build it. A senior individual contributor will help assemble the right technical solution to build it. *Both* lead others via their span of control or their influence to make it happen.

- *Improving the reliability of a system.* The responsibilities of the roles are outlined as we've discussed, but the target will be key metrics to achieve, such as increasing uptime, smoothing the range of latency, and reducing error rates.

- *Improving the speed of a system.* This time, the target could be metrics such as increasing throughput, improving P99 latency, and a reduction in resource usage.

Whether you're managing a manager or a senior individual contributor, the aim is the same: you stay hands-on and control their target. However, how that target is achieved is an implementation of their specific skills.

By utilizing your management fundamentals of coaching, delegation, and one-to-ones, combined with your focus on the target, you can lead both roles in the same way.

The neat corollary of this is it encourages close collaboration between the two roles by default. For example, if an engineering manager and their staff engineer are aiming at exactly the same target and being measured on its success, then collaboration and alignment follow almost effortlessly, making everyone's job easier.

From the Swamp to Infinity: Achieving Together

As we mentioned in the last section, you and your staff are aiming at the same target, but you are trying to hit it in different ways: your individual contributors are aiming at it through technical leadership, and your managers are aiming at it through organizational leadership, and you are accountable for the outcome. Your relationship with your staff needs to be viewed through a lens of *achieving together*—you are all working towards the same goal.

However, the nature of day-to-day work is messy. We can talk about achievement and setting targets together on these pages, but we all know the reality is Monday morning will come around, and you'll be back in the weeds.

On a given day, as you likely know, there is rarely one single task to focus on; it is often a complex web of interrelated tasks that, when described individually, may be an endless list of, well, *stuff*. Conversations to have, decisions to make, tickets to complete, and blockers to resolve.

Without keeping the targets you want to hit front and center, the relationship between you and your direct reports can become a never-ending stream of arbitrary and reactionary tasks that will likely wear you all down. You will be sucked into the details and lose your perspective.

The Swamp

Before we start to introduce some framing, let's look at what happens when there isn't any.

Many new senior managers progress into their role without training or guidance on how to frame the portfolio of work that is being undertaken by themselves and their organization.

As a result, all of the projects they oversee, the conversations they have, and the decisions they make can become a never-ending stream of tasks. The priority, framing, accountability, and meaning of everything become flattened, collective focus and prioritization become unclear, and the guidance of their direct reports becomes reactionary and unstructured. Being in this position is what we call *the swamp*.

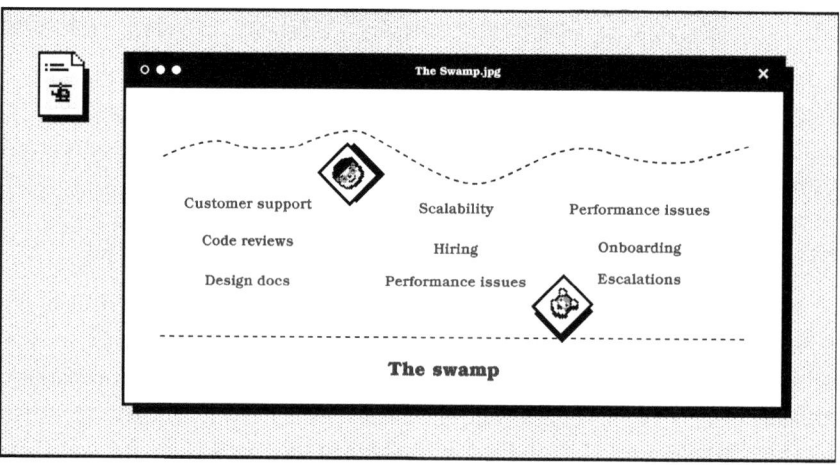

Managers in the swamp spend their days wading through the mess, stumbling across arbitrary tasks, projects, and decisions. At the beginning of the day, they have no idea what they are going to be doing. They roll up their sleeves and trouser legs and dive in.

They bump into issues at random as they wade through the muddy water. There is a technical design to review. Better look at that. Oh, there are also some candidates to review for several open positions. Yep, better do that as well. Actually, isn't that Bob's responsibility? Okay, what's next? Looks like there are some support issues. Better look at that, too. Each task floats to the surface out of nowhere and is covered in goop, so each needs investigation as to what it is and whether it needs completing or delegating.

The one-to-one agendas that they have with their staff become myopic status updates because there is so much floating around them that they need help understanding. The ownership and delegation boundaries become unclear. Topics of conversation become "have you seen that email from the VP?" or "what is happening with this customer request?" or even "what's the status of that bug fix?"

Continually reacting to one thing after another, dipping in and out of one project to the next while wading through mud, is exhausting. And, most importantly, in addition to being inefficient, this random context-switching typically leads to sub-optimal decisions being made in the global context of the organization and the manager and their staff feeling like they are never making any progress.

The issue with the swamp is that it is actually a problem of your own causing. All of the tasks and conversations are floating around in the goop because both you and those that you work with haven't built the required scaffolding to organize, compartmentalize, and frame them.

Thus, you interact with them at random with no clear mental model to help you make sense of them. In order to elevate yourself and your tasks out of the swamp, you need to build that scaffolding together with your staff. Then, both you and they can use it through your one-to-ones and coaching to better understand the work that you and your organization are doing and why you are doing it. Fundamentally, this scaffolding will allow you to make more globally optimal decisions together.

Finite and Infinite Games

The scaffolding we're going to use is that of *finite and infinite games*. This is a model that was introduced by James Carse in his book *of the same title* [Car12]. After learning about this model, I found it incredibly helpful for framing my work and the work of my teams. It maps well into the strategic, operational, and tactical levels that we explored in Chapter 2, Your Place in the Org Chart, on page 23, and it allows for deeper and more longtermist thinking compared to the usual software engineering models of sprints, roadmaps, and backlogs.

The model is simple: there are two types of games that we play in life, and they are defined as follows:

- *Finite games*: These are games that have a defined start and end. They have a set of rules that are agreed upon by all players, and the aim of the game is to win. Examples of finite games are sports, board games, and video games.

- *Infinite games*: These are games that have no defined start or end. The players come and go, and the rules change all of the time. The aim of the game is to keep playing. Examples of infinite games are life, business, and careers.

The key to the model is that finite games can be played *within* infinite games, but not vice versa. And the neat trick is that it also maps to how we run initiatives across the strategic, operational, and tactical levels that we explored in Chapter 2, Your Place in the Org Chart, on page 23. Let's start off by looking at finite games.

Finite Games

You and your teams are continually playing finite games. They can be small, like answering a support ticket or completing a sprint, or large, like shipping a new product or hitting a revenue target. The key is that they have a defined start and end, and the aim is to win.

Success at the tactical level of an organization is defined by identifying, framing, and winning these finite games. This is the level at which you and your staff are operating on a day-to-day basis. If we represented a finite game as a diagram, it would look a little something like this:

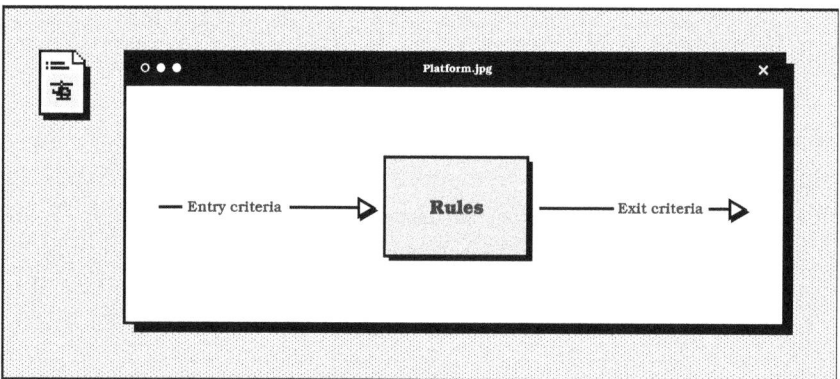

Each finite game has the following:

- *Entry criteria*. What is your current situation? What is the problem that you are trying to solve? What is the opportunity that you are trying to take advantage of? Example entry criteria could be that your biggest customers need a new feature that you lack or that your team needs to hire a new engineer to increase capacity.

- *Rules*. What are the rules of the game? Specifically, what are the constraints that you are operating within? Examples of rules could be that you need to create the feature by the end of the quarter or that you need to hire the engineer within the next month while sticking to a budget.

- *Exit criteria*. What does winning this finite game look like? What will you have achieved to know you have won? Examples of exit criteria could be that you have shipped the feature or you have hired a new engineer.

Finite games are like platforms that have been erected over the swamp that you and your staff can stand on to gain perspective. Instead of wading through a swamp of stuff that is happening all over your organization, you can instead hoist the tasks up, group them, interrogate them, and understand how each of them is contributing to the finite games that you are playing. You can then use this information to make better decisions about what to do next.

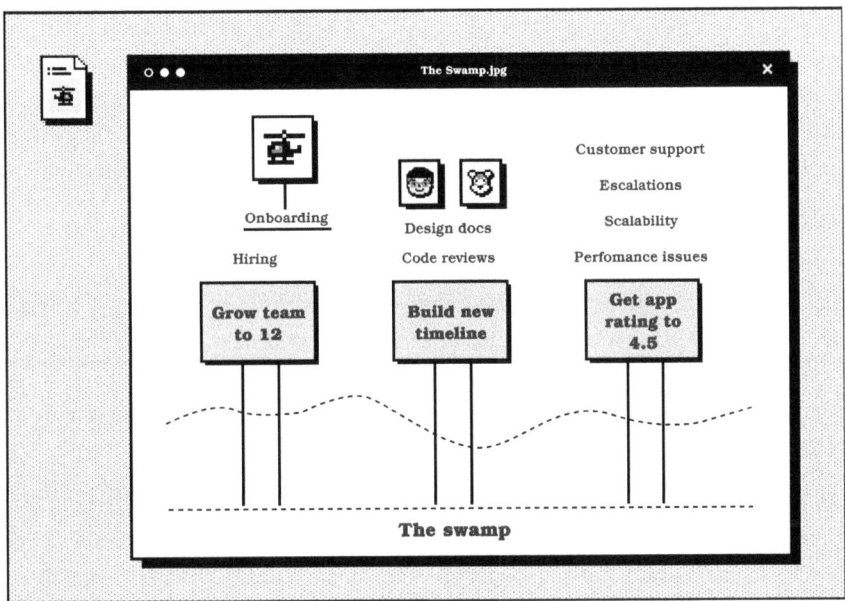

In the diagram, we've taken the contents of the swamp from earlier and constructed finite game platforms out of them. These finite games are:

- *Grow the team to 12.* You know how to do that, and the rules of hiring are well understood. The tasks that contribute to this are working on the onboarding process and spending time hiring. The exit criteria are clear: when the team is 12 people, you have won.

- *Building a new timeline feature.* This is your most requested addition to your software, and the tasks that are contributing to this are working on the design and implementation of the feature. The rules are the team writing code together, and the exit criteria are clear: when the feature is shipped, you're done.

- *Getting an app rating of 4.5 on the app store.* Currently, your app rating is below the threshold that boosts its presence in search results. It also signals to potential customers it has some quality issues. Therefore, customer support, escalations, scalability, and performance issues are all contributing to this finite game. The rules are you need to get your customers to rate it highly. The exit criteria are clear: you've won when the rating of your app is 4.5.

This is transformative: the swamp has been transformed into three finite games with clear players, rules, and exit criteria. This allows you to abstract away the details, meaning that you can delegate more individual tasks while not losing sight of the purpose and meaning of each of them.

In addition to enabling greater delegation, finite games enable far better coaching opportunities. You can frame your conversations around entry criteria, rules, and exit criteria. You can ask questions like, "what is the current situation that we are in?" and "what does winning look like?" This generates far more interesting conversations than, "what are you working on?" and "how is it going?"

Why Now?

As you work with your staff in their one-to-ones, group meetings, and other interactions, it is your job to ensure that the *minimum* number of finite games are being played at any one time. This is because the more finite games are played, the more *context-switching* is happening, and the more the team is being pulled in different directions.

The main form of entropy in organizations is the gradual increase in the number of finite games being played to the point that the organization becomes unable to make meaningful progress on any of them; everyone is stretched too thin to be effective. This is like when your old computer didn't have enough memory, and all of the open applications slow down. Continually paging their data in and out from the hard disk is prohibitively expensive. The same is true for your organization. Continually switching between in-flight finite games will slow you down.

Thus, it's your job as a leader to understand the current capacity of the organization and work with your staff to keep the number of finite games being played at a level that is appropriate for the team. Any time that a new priority emerges, frame it as a finite game and ask the question, *"why now?"* If it is important enough, the answer will be clear, and it will form the entry criteria for a new finite game. If it isn't, then it can be deprioritized until later.

If it's the case that a new finite game needs to be played, then you can work with your staff to understand which of the existing ones can be paused in order to make space. One route to doing this is revisiting the entry criteria of each game that is currently in flight and seeing whether it is still as relevant as it was when you began it.

The Fastest Route to the Exit

Given that there are clear exit criteria in each finite game, you and your staff have the ability to be creative in the way that you achieve them. You should think of the fastest route to the exit that is possible within the rules.

In our prior example, one of the finite games was to get your app rating up to 4.5 so that it would have a better ranking in search results. One way to achieve this could be to continue adding new features and functionality in the hope that people would rate it highly. However, this would be a slow and indirect route to the exit. Instead, a faster route could be to focus on the customer support issues that are causing the low ratings and fix them, then ask the customers who contacted you to re-rate the app. You could also ask customers who have left no rating to give one, which could be as simple as sending a notification to them.

Finding the fastest route to the exit is a key skill in leadership that you can use when coaching. Try it with one of the current projects that your staff are working on. Are they really on the fastest route to win the finite game that they are playing? If not, what could they do differently?

> **Your Turn: Identifying Finite Games**
>
> Identify the finite games that you are currently playing in your organization.
>
> - Share the definition of finite games, including the entry and exit criteria, with your direct reports.
> - Ask them to identify the finite games that they are playing. Specify the entry and exit criteria for each one.
> - Was it easy to identify them? If not, why not? Are there any that had unclear entry or exit criteria? If so, why?

Infinite Games

We mentioned earlier that there are *infinite games* in addition to finite games. Finite games can be played *within* infinite games, and the purpose of playing infinite games is to be able to continue playing.

This can sound a little mysterious. What does it mean to "keep playing"? Isn't managing an organization hard enough without needing to inject highbrow metaphorical concepts into it? Let's build on the finite game model to understand what it means to play infinite games.

In the previous section, we explored how running an organization as a senior leader without careful framing and focus can be hard. We said it can be like wading through a swamp of tasks, decisions, and conversations. We showed that by identifying the finite games that each of your tasks contributes to, you can build platforms that you and your staff can stand on to gain perspective, organize your focus, and make better decisions. These finite games become the scaffolding that you use to build your coaching relationship with your direct reports, regardless of whether they are a manager or an individual contributor. You're all working on a set of finite games, and you want to win them together by using whatever tools you wield.

An efficient company is one that is *continually* identifying, framing, and winning finite games. Think of the product roadmap. It never ends; all of these finite games push a company further toward its goals. If we take our previous diagram and zoom all the way out, perhaps all the way into outer space, we might see something that looks a little like this:

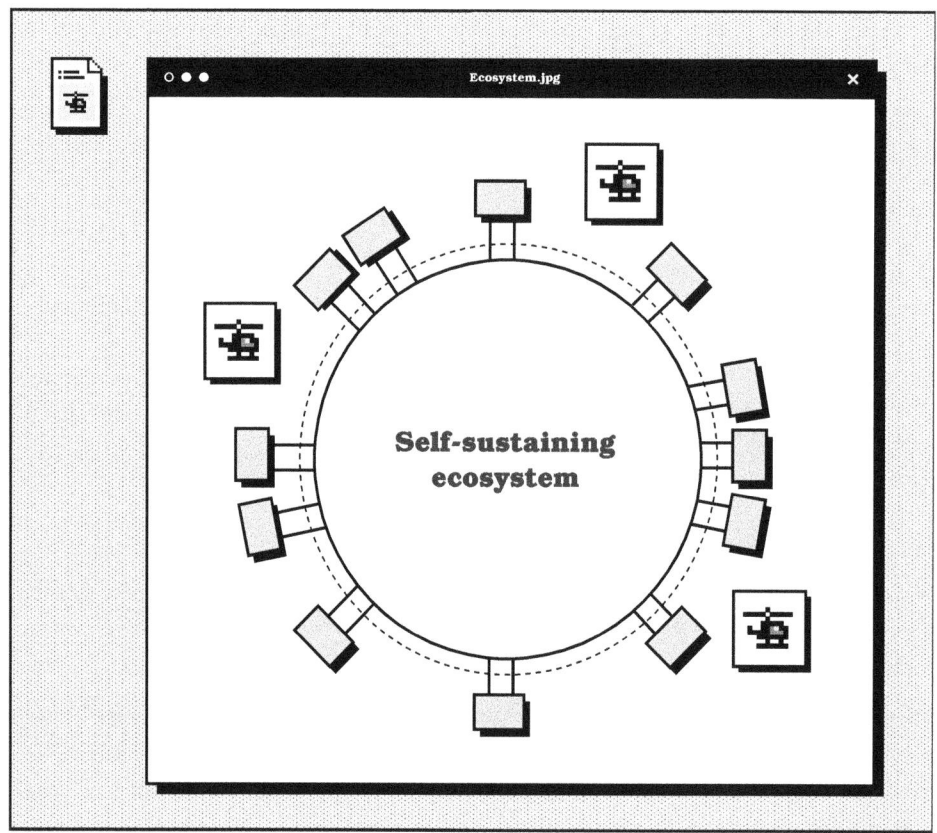

Here, we see an entire world of finite games being played by the organization. Each part of the organization hoists and groups the tasks, decisions, and conversations that are happening inside the swamp and elevates them into the finite games to which they are contributing. In the Engineering department, various features and functionality are being built. Over in Sales, they're trying to hit their target for the quarter. In Marketing, they're trying to grow the number of leads that come to the website by running ad campaigns. In Customer Support, they're trying to complete the backlog of support tickets. None of these activities ever stop. They are all finite games that are being played *within* the infinite game of the organization.

The infinite game is for this organization to exist indefinitely. In order for the company to exist, for the product to be successful, and for everyone to continue to have jobs and meaningful work, the infinite game is to keep building and shipping a product that people want to buy and to grow and sustain a healthy organization that can do this.

Thus, if finite games are *tactical* and collections of finite games are *operational*, the infinite game is *strategic*. It involves defining the purpose of the organization, its culture, and its values. It means putting the right people in the right roles and ensuring that they are working on the right things. It also means working in a sustainable way that ensures staff want to stay for the long term and building products in a high-quality, resilient, and scalable manner. It means building a company that can keep playing. Forever.

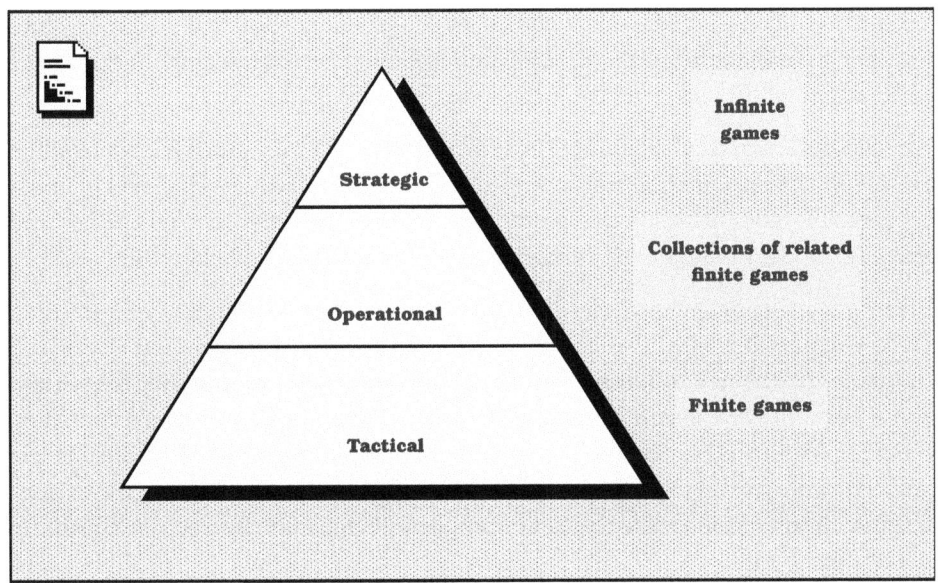

If you had to definite the infinite game that your teams are playing right now, what would it be? What is the purpose of your organization? Will that purpose still make sense in five years' time? And what about 100 years? Knowing the answer to this question is important because it is the north star that will guide you and your staff in choosing which finite games to play.

Consider two start-ups. Both of them are building a similar product: a web application that allows people to manage their personal finances. Both of them are playing the same finite games: shipping features, hiring staff, and hitting targets for active users. Internally, at each company, however, the focus is different. The first company has defined its mission as "enabling the world to make better financial decisions." The second company has defined its mission as "become the first personal finances app to IPO." (IPO stands for initial public offering, which is when a company first sells its shares to the public. It is often seen as a marker of success.)

During the early days of both companies, progress is similar when one is compared to the other. The apps gain more functionality and become more useful, and both grow their user base. Both attract investment and continue to hire staff to do even more of what they were doing before.

However, as time goes on, the differences between the two companies become more apparent. The first company, with its mission to enable the world to make better financial decisions, invests in longer-term initiatives such as producing financial education content and training courses, brokering partnerships with financial institutions to help users link all of their data together to help with financial planning, and also invests heavily in customer support to help users with their financial problems.

The second company, because of its mission to IPO as quickly as possible, invests in shorter-term initiatives, such as building features that will primarily increase the number of users and invests heavily in marketing and advertising campaigns with celebrities to drive traffic to the website.

Over time, the first company becomes the market leader in the personal finance space. It has a loyal user base that trusts it, the largest data sets and connectivity, the best customer support, and the most comprehensive educational content. The second company grows a large user base that eventually becomes frustrated at the pace of product development and the quality of the product, and so they switch to the first company, making it even more successful. In an ironic twist, the first company IPOs, and the second company is acquired by it.

The difference between the two companies is the first company has aligned on playing an *infinite game* that is focused on the long term, and the second company is playing a *finite game*. Finite games steer you toward the exit criteria. Infinite games mean that you can continue playing, forever.

When you are working with your staff and prioritizing the finite games that you are playing, it is even more important to understand the infinite game that you are contributing toward. If you don't, then you may find that competitors that are playing an infinite game will outlast you.

> **Your Turn: Identifying Infinite Games**
>
> Step back and think about the work your team, department, or company is doing.
>
> - What is the infinite game that you are playing? Is it something that is defined by the company's mission, or is it not clear to you?
>
> - Introduce the concept of infinite games to your direct reports. Is it clear to you what your infinite game is? Can you define one for your teams? For example, your infinite game could be to "enable the world to connect better at work" or "make fitness accessible to anyone, anywhere." If you're running a smaller team within a much larger company, it could even be to "make the world's best charting visualizations." Perhaps you might set yourself a higher bar for your work.
>
> - With an infinite game defined, does it make you think differently about the finite games that you are playing? Are you playing the right ones? Test whether the infinite game is fueled by them.

Your job as a leader is to ensure that all of the work that your organization is doing is contributing to the infinite game that you are playing. If it isn't, then you should stop and find finite games that do. If you don't have a strategy, then don't worry; we will work through defining one in detail in Chapter 11, Strategy 101, on page 253.

An important part of this strategy will be ensuring stability for the players. You want to ensure that your staff are happy, motivated, growing, learning, and, most importantly, not burning out. The infinite game of team health, individual happiness, efficiency, and maintaining a high quality standard for your product and codebase are all key metrics that you should be tracking.

Start your day tomorrow by thinking about the finite and infinite games that you are playing and how they are interlinked. If you have one-to-ones with your staff, we think they are about to get *much* more interesting. And we aren't stopping there.

Leading Without Authority

We have covered a lot of ground in this chapter. You're starting to think much more deeply about the organization that you want to run and how you want to run it.

Here's what we covered:

- *We began by looking at the fundamentals of managing people.* We covered coaching vs. directing, delegating vs. micromanagement, and how to run effective one-to-ones. These are the fundamental tools that you will use when interacting with your staff day in and day out. We also covered the concept of brag docs, which will make your life *infinitely* easier when it comes to understanding what your staff are up to.

- *Then, we saw how managing managers and senior individuals can use these techniques, too.* You want to delegate how they do their job to them, but stay firmly in control of what they are aiming for and then develop their leadership skills to help them to get there.

- *Finally, we used the model of finite and infinite games as a way of framing the work that you and your organization do.* We saw how companies are continually playing finite games within the infinite game of the organization. We also saw how the infinite game is the north star that you should use to guide your decision-making.

Next, we are going to look at one of the sharpest tools in your toolbelt: senior individual contributors. We will explore how to get the best from them and how to help them grow and progress in their careers.

It might be time to embark on a finite game of making a cup of tea. We'll see you in the next chapter.

CHAPTER 5

The Sharpest Tool in Your Toolbelt

"Since we talked about it, I keep seeing finite and infinite games everywhere I look. It's becoming an obsession," says Vic.

"What do you mean?" you reply. "As in, you're looking at our projects differently?"

"No, I mean *everywhere*. Last night, I was washing up, and I realized I was partaking in a finite game against dinner inside an infinite game against the entropy of my kitchen."

You laugh. "Oh no, I'm sorry. I hope you recruited more players to help you out."

Vic smiles. "The kids can be hard to persuade. You know, I was also thinking about the contracting exercise we did. I like the idea of us being able to work together to lead the org, but I'm not exactly sure how we make that happen. Aren't we just going to end up effectively doing the same job?"

"The same job? What do you mean?"

"Well, if we are going to partner in this way, aren't we just going to be doing the same things? And being in the same meetings? Where does my role end and yours begin? And given that I report to you, isn't it just going to be you making all the decisions anyway?"

"Yeah, that's a good question. But this time, I might have the answer: you can be my *right-hand engineer*. It's an archetype for your role that I think might be a good fit for us and a good fit for everyone else as well."

"A right-hand engineer? What's that? Some kind of special counsel?"

"Let me tell you all about it."

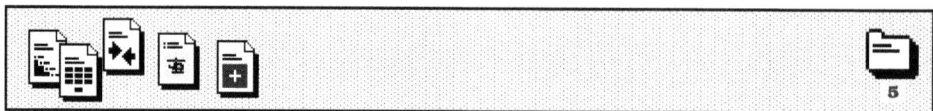

Back in Chapter 1, VP, Director, What?, on page 3, we looked at the career track for individual contributors and saw how it progresses in parallel to the management track. For example, beyond the senior engineer role lies the staff engineer and then the principal engineer. In Chapter 2, Your Place in the Org Chart, on page 23, we also explored some organization configurations for managers as they increase in seniority from engineering manager to director and to VP and beyond.

Notably, we acknowledged there is a world where senior individual contributors can exist at these higher rungs of the org chart, taking a clear *leadership* role in the team, division, or department they are part of. Managers, regardless of their seniority, will always benefit from a close relationship with a partner who can collaborate with them on determining the technical direction of their organization, setting the bar for technical standards and excellence, and also helping to mentor and grow the engineers on the team.

In this chapter, we'll explore how to make this partnership happen in practice. Here's what we're going to cover:

- *We'll revisit the individual career progression paths that run in parallel to management.* We will see that these also map to strategic, tactical, or operational levels of your organization.

- *Next, we'll explore a neat model of archetypes for your most senior engineers.* Not only can it help classify and demystify the types of work that they do, but it can also unlock their thinking about career progression and how to play to their strengths.

- *Then, we'll traverse the org chart from bottom to top and match managers with archetypes.* This gives us a framework for how to deploy them in our organizations.

- *Lastly, we'll think about all of your senior individual contributors as one collective group.* This virtual team is not defined by the org chart, but they are a critical team for you to help connect, grow, and steer, either directly or indirectly.

When you finish this chapter, you should have a good intuition for how best to deploy your growth-oriented senior individual contributors and also how to manage them effectively from where they are situated.

Not only will this intentional deployment help your best staff grow and thrive in your team, it'll also enable you to be more hands-on, directive, and close to the technical work that is happening. This is key to you being successful in highly technical organizations: you can complement any knowledge gaps or weaknesses that you have with the expertise of your right-hand engineer. As a partnership, you can conquer anything.

Individual Contributors: The Higher Rungs

In the last decade, our industry has undergone a culture shift that has, in turn, elevated the craft of managers. The Internet and bookshelves all over the world have welcomed a plethora of resources on how to be effective leaders in technology organizations. In fact, the very existence of this book is a testament to this shift. Managers are now deeply invested in becoming better at their craft. However, as we know, managers are not the only people that we work with.

More recently, the senior levels of individual contribution have been getting more attention, with two books being published that look at *what* it means to be senior and *how* one should be impactful. Both the *Staff Engineer [Lar21]* and *The Staff Engineer's Path [Rei22]* provide complementary perspectives. The former is written by a technology executive who has coached and led many senior individual contributors, and the latter is from a senior individual contributor who has mastered their craft.

In Chapter 1, VP, Director, What?, on page 3, we saw that a growing engineer reaches a fork in their career beyond the senior engineer role. Depending on whether they want to further specialize in their craft or whether they want to take on leadership responsibilities, they can choose to become either a staff engineer or an engineering manager. We also saw in Chapter 4, The Games We Play and How to Win Them, on page 91 that regardless of which path in the fork they select, both tracks share the same principle: *leadership*. And given what you already know about the breadth, depth, and complexity of management roles, it should come as no surprise that the same is true for senior individual contributors.

We can represent this choice visually: just take a look at the fork in the diagram on page 122. It shows how the career tracks run in parallel to each other all the way to the top. For example, we would expect similar scope and impact at the staff engineer and engineering manager levels, and at the principal engineer and director levels, despite them being on different tracks. They just use a different implementation to have the same impact.

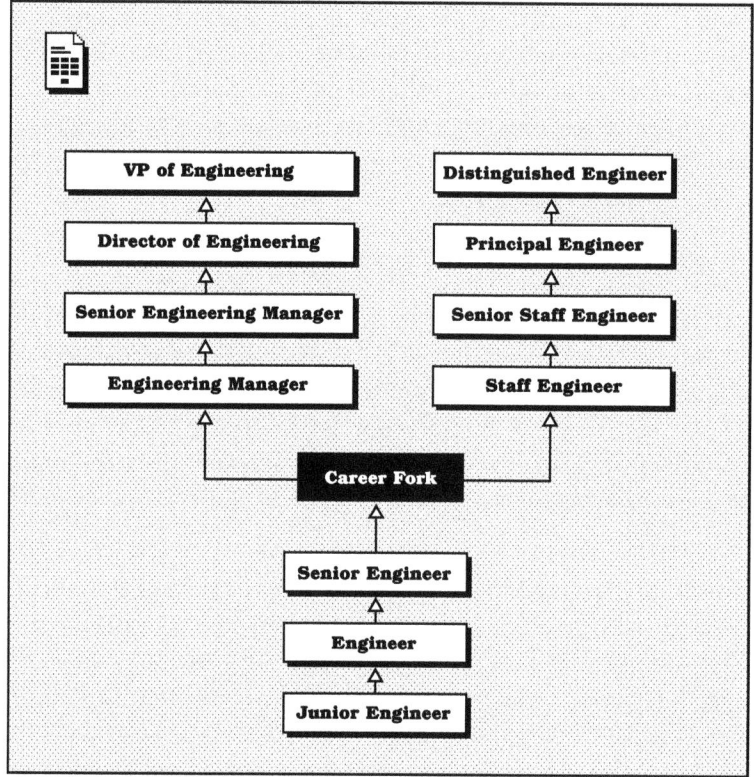

Great leaders can take many forms. Some are hands-on, technical, and deeply involved in the day-to-day work of their team. Others are more hands-off, strategic, and focused on the bigger picture. Some rotate between the two as and when their team needs them to. Some are extroverted and shine in group settings, while others are introverted and are at their most impactful when writing or speaking one-to-one. There are a myriad of shapes to leadership. No one shape is better than another; each has its time and place.

In Chapter 2, Your Place in the Org Chart, on page 23, we saw that there are a number of org chart shapes that deploy configurations of managers and individual contributors in different ways. For example, an engineering manager may have a technical lead reporting to them, and a director may have a singular principal engineer who oversees the technical direction of the area. Depending on what exactly the organization is building, you may choose to assign your senior individual contributors to particular problems or areas of ownership by having them report to different levels of management.

However, this presents a challenge: how do you ensure that your senior individual contributors are able to thrive in their roles? How exactly should they do their job? After all, each area and project may be entirely different. One area may be a long-established piece of infrastructure with performance issues in need of modernization, while the other may be a greenfield project that is bringing an entirely new product to market.

Naturally, the type of senior individual contributor that you would assign to each of these areas would depend on their unique strengths and weaknesses, and also the *archetype* of their role. And, luckily for us, we have a framework for how to think about this.

The Four Archetypes: Pieces of Your Puzzle

A useful way to think about senior individual contributors is to consider the different *archetypes* that they can take on.

Despite, for example, a staff engineer being defined by a description of *what* they do, it's often the case that the *how* will differ from person to person, depending on their strengths, interests, and the particular project they are working on.

In *Staff Engineer [Lar21]*, Will Larson describes four archetypes of senior individual contributors:

- *The Tech Lead.* This archetype typically works closely with a single team and manager to be their lead individual contributor on a project or area of ownership. For example, a Tech Lead could be driving the design and delivery of a new feature that their team is working on.

- *The Architect.* If there is a critically important area of the system, then it may have this archetype associated with it. The Architect is responsible for the ongoing design, implementation, scalability, and quality of that system. For example, a primary database storing critical data that many teams build upon may have an Architect associated with it.

- *The Solver.* This archetype applies themselves to complex issues with the aim of solving them and then moving on to the next big problem. For example, a Solver may be tasked with tackling a particularly thorny performance issue. They may stay associated permanently with one area, or they may move around the organization as needed.

- *The Right-Hand.* This archetype is a partner to a senior manager, which enables them to operate within the manager's scope. The role of the Right-Hand is to increase the bandwidth of the manager when they run large organizations. For example, a Right-Hand may be a distinguished engineer who is a partner to a VP of engineering, helping them to lead the organization.

Each of these archetypes can fit into your organization design in different ways because they work on tasks with varying assignment lengths and focus. You may find that your staff can function as one or more of these archetypes as necessary, and therefore adapt themselves to the needs of the organization.

The following diagram helps to illustrate this. Although it is a simplification and there are always exceptions to the rule, it can be a useful tool to help you think about the interplay between the different archetypes.

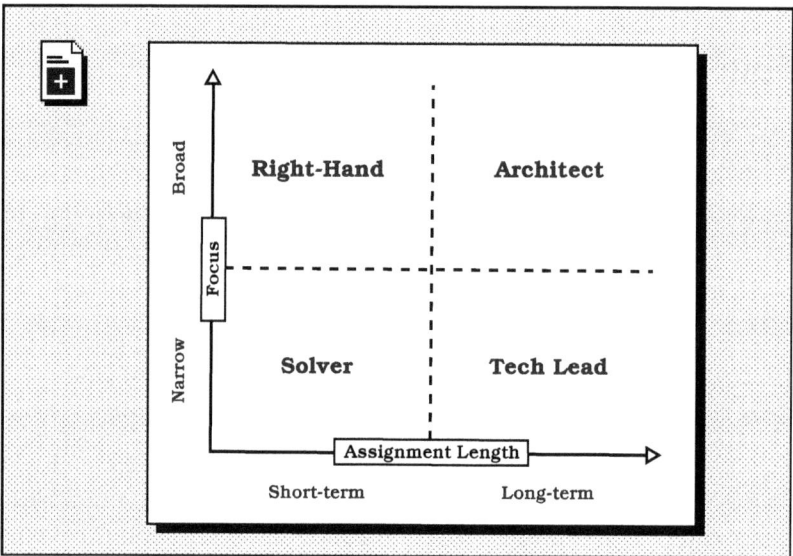

The y-axis of the diagram represents the width of *focus*. A broad focus means that a senior individual contributor will work across many different initiatives, whereas a narrow focus means that they will work on a single one. The x-axis represents the length of *assignment*. A long-term assignment means that a senior individual contributor will work on the same initiative for a long time, typically working with the same team and manager. A short-term assignment means that they will work on many different initiatives across the organization.

Therefore, the archetypes can be mapped onto the diagram as follows:

- *The Tech Lead* is a narrow-focus, long-term assignment. They work closely with a single team and manager on a single initiative.

- *The Solver* is a narrow focus, short-term assignment. They dive into a problem, find a path forward, and then move on to the next one.

- *The Architect* is a broad-focus, long-term assignment. They are responsible for the ongoing design, implementation, and quality of a particular area of the system.

- *The Right-Hand* is a broad-focus, short-term assignment. This is because they extend the bandwidth of a senior manager, and their attention will be drawn to many different initiatives across the organization.

Given that the work is different for each archetype, it follows that the skills and traits required to be successful in each of them will also be different. Importantly, different individuals will suit different archetypes. For example, a senior individual contributor who is a great Tech Lead and Solver may not be a great Right-Hand, and vice versa. The key is to find the right fit(s) for the individual and what your organization needs.

> **Your Turn: Discuss the Archetypes**
>
> Pick one or two of the most senior engineers in your team, department, or organization.
>
> - Based on your observations of them, which archetype do you think they are and why? Do they embody more than one archetype?
> - Book a coffee chat with them and show them the archetypes. What do they think of them? How would they categorize themselves? Which archetype would they like to spend more time in?
> - If they were unfamiliar with the archetypes, has it helped them to think about their current work and how they can grow?

Deploying Senior Individual Contributors

Building on the categorizations of the archetypes by their focus and assignment length, we can now think about how to deploy them in our organizations. In this section, we'll work our way up the management org chart, looking at how to deploy senior individual contributors at each level. We'll see that not every archetype is a good fit for every level: some require partnership with senior managers to work effectively.

Engineering Manager

Let's start at the first level of management: the engineering manager. Given that the scope of an engineering manager is typically a single team with a fixed, narrow focus, it follows that the only archetype that is a good fit for this level is the *Tech Lead*.

The Tech Lead archetype will do as their name suggests: they will be the lead engineer on whatever the team is responsible for, forming a strong partnership with the engineering manager running it. They will typically be the most senior engineer on the team, responsible for the overall technical direction, and also will have responsibilities for mentoring and growing the engineers on the team through pair programming, reviewing code, and so on.

Often, this archetype is the natural evolution of a senior engineer in the team who has already assumed this role and thus receives a backward-facing promotion because they have already demonstrated competency. It is important, however, that the promotion to staff engineer, and thus the realization of the archetype, is not taken lightly; not all senior engineers are able to exhibit the *leadership* traits required at the level above. Senior engineer is, therefore, considered a "tenure" or "terminal" position, and it is not uncommon or bad for engineers to remain at this level indefinitely.

Some engineering managers are able to assume the Tech Lead archetype themselves, although this represents a rare combination of skills in larger companies; it can be more common at start-ups. As such, as a team's area of ownership gets bigger and more critical, and if there is no senior engineer showing the aptitude for demonstrable leadership, it may be a good idea to hire a staff engineer to fill this role instead.

Senior Engineering Manager

The next level of management is the senior engineering manager. With a broader scope than the engineering manager, the senior engineering manager is responsible for multiple teams. This opens up the possibility of deploying multiple archetypes: the *Tech Lead*, the *Solver*, and the *Architect*. Usually, these will be engineers at the staff and senior staff levels.

The application of the Tech Lead archetype was described in the previous section. However, now there is the option to have them report directly to the senior engineering manager for connection to the bigger picture and alignment. The staff engineer gains wider visibility of the organization through their manager, even though their focus is still narrow.

Depending on the area of the system that the senior engineering manager is responsible for, an Architect may be a good permanent fixture. In addition to being responsible for the long-term design, implementation, and quality of that area, the Architect archetype can be responsible for assembling the overall technical roadmap, both in terms of the work to be done and also in the measurement of what success looks like across speed, resiliency, and scale. The Architect can drop in and out of the different teams depending on their needs, offering coaching, mentorship, and guidance.

The Solver archetype can also be a good fit for a senior engineering manager. Some areas continually generate thorny problems, sometimes identified ahead of time by the Architect, but quite often, they are the result of things being on fire. The Solver can be deployed to drop in and become a temporary technical lead on these problems, helping to resolve them and get the team back on track. For example, after a production incident, a Solver may be deployed to help the team get to the root cause and to put in place the necessary improvements to prevent it from happening again. Likewise, a Solver may be deployed to help a team get a project that has drifted back on track, kick a new project off, or even talk to customers to understand their needs and translate them into technical requirements.

Architects and Solvers can complement each other well when there is enough work to do. The key is to ensure that the Solver has the right balance of work, and when there are no fires to fight, that they are partnering with the Architect to help them to move the technical roadmap forward.

Directors and VPs of Engineering

We now move up to the director of engineering, which has a similar archetype deployment to VPs. The Tech Lead, Solver, and Architect archetypes would typically report to the management layer below them, but skip-level meetings can be used to ensure that the director or VP is still connected to the work that is happening.

It is at the director level that the *Right-Hand* archetype becomes a viable option. Usually, this archetype will be a senior staff or principal engineer when reporting to the director and potentially a distinguished engineer when reporting to the VP, depending on the size of the organization.

Right-Hand archetypes are the rarest. This is because, in order to operate effectively, there needs to be a significant amount of breadth within the manager's organization—the kind that hundreds or thousands of engineers generate. The Right-Hand extends the bandwidth of the director and shadows them in communication, meetings, and decision-making. The Right-Hand requires deep alignment with the senior manager and a high degree of trust. It doesn't work if both parties are pulling in different directions. It must be a true partnership.

A Right-Hand removes issues from the senior manager's plate. For example, if there is an architecture review for a critical project with many dependencies with other teams, the Right-Hand can take the lead on it. Similarly, if there are a number of performance issues, the Right-Hand can drop in, work out what needs to be done, and then delegate the work to the appropriate teams.

The leadership that they exhibit is not just technical, but also organizational: they are able to influence, delegate, lead, and get things done. For example, a senior manager may ask their Right-Hand to look into the cost of running their infrastructure in the cloud. They won't do this alone; they will assemble a team from across the organization to help them and then report back to the senior manager with their findings.

The Three Levels of Archetype

If we can map the archetypes into the levels of the management org chart that they report into, then it follows that we can associate them with being strategic, tactical, or operational. The following diagram illustrates this.

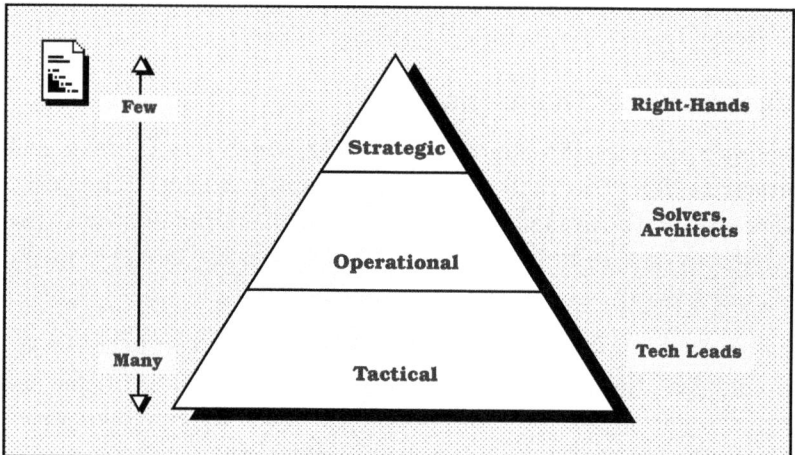

- At the *strategic* level of the engineering department, we may have a small number of Right-Hand archetypes who partner with the most senior executives.

- At the *operational* level, we may have a selection of Architects who own key areas of the system, and a selection of Solvers that can be deployed to help their teams with thorny problems.

- At the *tactical* level, we may have a selection of Tech Leads who are the lead engineers on the individual teams.

When working with staff engineers, both on their career growth and on their eventual archetype preferences, it is important to flag that, like management, there are limited positions in the org chart to deploy them into. Thus, a good strategy is to utilize the Tech Lead archetype, since there can theoretically be one for each team, and then use growth and specialization to evolve them into the other archetypes higher up the org chart as needs become apparent. You cannot set an expectation that all of your staff engineers can eventually become Right-Hands in the same way that you cannot set an expectation that all of your engineering managers can eventually become the CTO. It's just not possible.

The Technical Shadow Organization

Here's what we've covered so far:

- Senior individual contributors have clear career progression paths that run in parallel to management.
- They can operate in various archetypes depending on their strengths and interests.
- They can be utilized in different ways depending on the scope and focus of the area that they are working on.

As such, it follows that the senior individual contributors in an organization are a *collective* with unique technical perspectives on the current and future state of the organization. In a way, this is a *technical shadow organization*: a *virtual* team that is not defined by the reporting relationships org chart but rather by the influence and steer that they have on the work being done. You can see this in the following diagram:

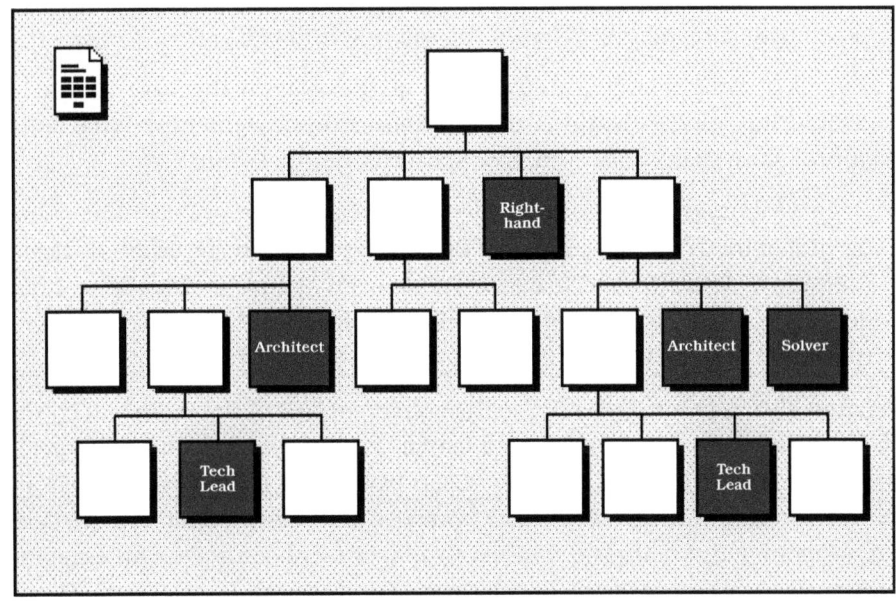

The question is: how can you use this group to its full potential? How can you ensure that they are connected to each other and also to the rest of the organization?

Your Technical Council

One way to engage with your virtual team of senior individual contributors is to create a *technical council*. This is a group of senior individual contributors who discuss and meet regularly to steer the technical direction of the organization.

As a senior leader, you can choose how exactly you want to interface with this group. You can be closely involved by chairing and steering their activities, or you could delegate this to your most senior individual contributor; it's up to you.

The technical council can be used to discuss and make decisions on a number of topics:

- *The technical roadmap*. Based on what the group is experiencing in their day-to-day work, what are the most important technical initiatives that should be prioritized in the future? Are there emerging weaknesses in the system that need to be addressed? Are there new technologies that should be adopted?

- *Technical standards*. Are there any new technical standards that should be adopted across the organization, or do any need updating? For example, what is the current approach to logging, monitoring, and alerting? How is security considered? What is the approach to testing?

- *Technical debt*. Are there any areas of the system that are in need of refactoring, modernization, or performance improvements? What is the approach to doing this, and how should it be prioritized?

- *Deep dives and reviews*. Are there any areas of the system that should be highlighted? For example, is there a new feature or addition that is noteworthy for its technical excellence or even its future risk and technical debt? Are there any areas of interlock or dependencies with external teams that need to be discussed and escalated to you as the leader?

Even just sitting in and listening to the conversations of the technical council can be of immense value to you as a leader. It helps you understand specific issues that otherwise may not have been raised to you directly, and it also gives you input on future technical priorities that can be factored into your own budgeting and planning. Think of the technical council as an extension of your own awareness of the architecture and the code.

We mentioned in Chapter 4, The Games We Play and How to Win Them, on page 91 that the common trait of senior managers and senior individual contributors is *leadership*. The technical council, therefore, is a fantastic arena for your senior individual contributors to practice and improve their leadership skills. If you purposefully step back and assume the role of the group chair and guide the group through coaching rather than directing, you can watch your future leaders emerge.

Building Connections Across the Organization

In addition to looking *down* the org chart at your technical leaders and forming and interacting with a technical council, it is equally important to encourage this group to form connections *across* the organization. Yes, that means outside of your teams. This prevents siloing of knowledge and also indicates that the group actually serves the wider department and company, not just you!

Going back to the archetypes, we can formulate different ways this group can connect with the rest of the organization, as shown in the diagram on page 132. For example:

- Since *Right-Hands* extend the bandwidth of senior leaders, the set of all Right-Hand engineers across the wider organization form a network of technical leaders with a unique insight into the strategic technical direction of the company. They are exposed to the strategic frontier of numerous areas and can ensure there is a high degree of alignment on where the technology needs to go.

- Since *Architects* are responsible for the long-term design, implementation, and quality of a particular area of the system, they form a set of technical leaders who can work on best practices, standards, and patterns that can be shared across the organization. They are uniquely situated to define the primitives of the architecture that will be built upon. They are also best placed to identify upcoming bottlenecks and areas of opportunity.

- Since *Solvers* are deployed to help teams with tough problems, they form a set of technical leaders that can drive up standards by sharing common problems and solutions and also their expertise. They can collectively raise the floor, especially during times of growth or crisis.

- And since *Tech Leads* are the lead engineers on individual teams, they form a set of technical leaders that can collectively advance their craft by discussing, sharing, and communicating what is going on at the front line of the organization.

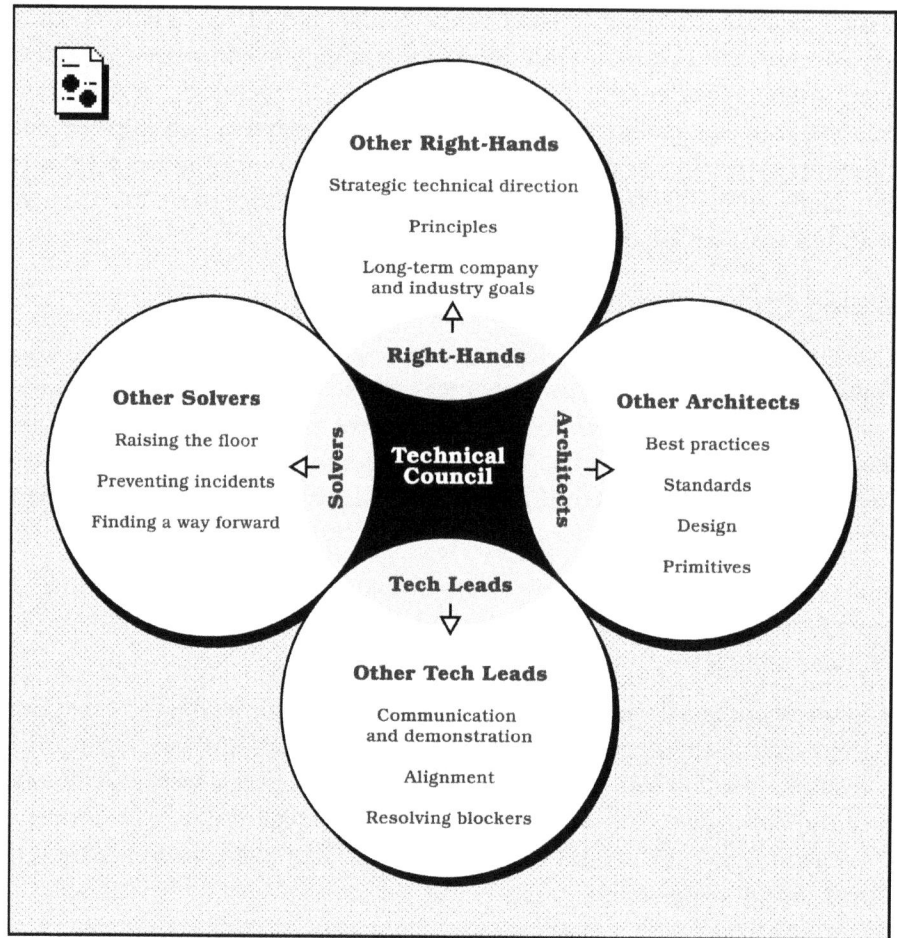

The key is to encourage these connections to happen. If they are not already well-connected, challenge each of your senior individual contributors to pick one or two people across the organization and then reach out and connect with them. This can be as simple as a coffee chat to start with to get to know each other and then a regular catch-up to discuss what is going on in their respective areas.

When it comes to communication from your technical council, we'll enumerate a number of effective ways to do this in Chapter 9, Communication at Scale, on page 191. For now, start by encouraging your senior individual contributors to think of their career path, the archetypes, and how to encourage connections both within and outside of your organization. This team represents your technical leadership; it's time to start treating them as such.

Looking Sideways

We hope that you are leaving this chapter not only convinced that your senior individual contributors deserve your time and attention but that you are also excited about the possibilities that they can bring to your organization.

Here's a recap of what we've covered:

- *We've seen that senior individual contributors have clear career progression paths that run in parallel to management.* These map to strategic, tactical, or operational levels of the organization.

- *We've seen that they can operate in various archetypes depending on their strengths and interests.* We covered the Tech Lead, Solver, Architect, and Right-Hand, and saw how each varies in their focus and assignment length.

- *We mapped the archetypes into the levels of the management org chart that they report into.* This gave us a framework for how to deploy them in our organizations.

- *We saw that the set of all senior individual contributors form a technical shadow organization.* This is a virtual team that is not defined by the org chart, but rather the influence and steer that they have on the technical work being done in your organization. We gave some examples of how to connect this group internally and also externally with other parts of the department.

Reflecting back on what we've covered in the book so far, we've considered the different levels of the org chart that flow upwards and downwards from where you are situated. But what about *sideways*? Your peers are an often overlooked resource that can help you be more effective in your role. In the next chapter, we'll look at how to best utilize your peer group and also how to be a good peer yourself.

CHAPTER 6

The Tragedy of the Common Leader

Bing! Ben joins the video call. "Alright?"

"Alright," you reply. "How's it going?"

"Good, good. Still hacking away at this bug, but making progress. Hoping to get the fix out later today. How about you?"

"So-so," you say. "If I'm being honest, I feel like I've barely spoken to anyone all week. I'm not sure if it's just me, but I feel like I'm not really part of a team anymore."

"Ah, you're missing what our little team used to be like since moving into the big leagues, huh? The glory days in that awful old office with the leaking windows..." says Ben.

"I can't say I don't miss it," you reply.

"That's so weird, though," says Ben. "We've hired some absolutely amazing people into your peer group. Don't you get on with them?"

"Yeah, of course. Well, I've barely interacted with them at all, to be honest. We're all so busy with our own areas that we don't really have time to talk to each other. What's worse is that when we do, it's always some kind of conflict or issue that needs resolving."

"Oh dear. Anything I can help with?" asks Ben.

"Hmm, not really. It's just the continual flip-flop of priorities and nobody ever having enough people to do everything they have to. I think I just need to get used to it. I'm still navigating my new manager, too, so I'm sure that's not helping."

"Does your manager get the group together regularly?" asks Ben.

"Yeah, we meet every week, but the agenda is just full of random topics, and some folks don't even show up because of clashes. Regardless of what we talk about, Jeff seems to take up eighty percent of the airtime, and then we run out of space to talk about anything else. Honestly, how can people be so passionate about QA that they want to jump on a soapbox every single week about it?"

"Sounds like a testing situation," jokes Ben.

"Quite. We need to drive up quality in the group's interactions," you say. "Maybe we could automate Jeff with a chatbot…"

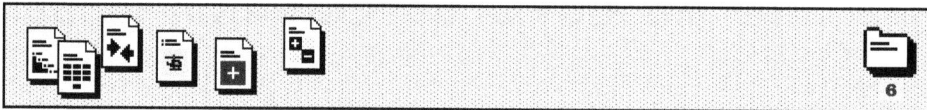

You've probably heard of the phrase "it's lonely at the top." In fact, on a list of one hundred clichéd phrases, it's probably there somewhere, likely near the, erm, top. Although this phrase is typically used to describe the feeling of those sitting in the most senior positions of an organization, it's equally applicable to all of the middle management positions we covered in Chapter 1, VP, Director, What?, on page 3.

Actually, sometimes middle management can feel *lonelier* than the top. After all, company executives have numerous groups in which they work, such as the board of directors, earnings calls, and company town halls. They have a common set of goals and are regularly in the same room together. The C-suite is their *home team*, or *first team*.

Middle managers, on the other hand, can often feel like they lack this comradery. Instead, they exist among other people reporting to the same common manager, caught in the middle of a web of competing people, priorities, and goals. Who is on their side? Who can they confide in? Who is actually on *their* home team?

We spoke about entropy in Chapter 3, Time: Observed, Spent, and Allocated, on page 55—the entropy that your capacity faces when all you do is react and receive without reciprocation from others. Without a home team, you can feel like nobody is on your side. You're trying your best to perform for your manager since you know that performance reviews are lurking around the corner. You're also doing your best to lead those underneath you. You get no psychological comfort either up or down the org chart.

The default state of middle management is entropy, and you need to fight it. During busy periods, you can spend weeks being on the receiving end of escalations and conflict, trying to resolve them with little help from others.

Often the outcome is a feeling of isolation, loneliness, and wishing that you were back in the trenches with a single team to focus on.

In this chapter, we are going to raise our halberds against this entropy by embracing and building the best home team you could ever wish for: your peer group. This is the group of people who are in the same position as you; they have the same issues, the same problems, and the same goals.

You just need to get them to act like a team.

Here's what we're going to cover:

- *We'll look at the tragedy of the commons and see how it applies to your peer group.* An unfortunate default state of middle management is that you and your peer group are competing for the same resource: your manager's praise, attention, and time. However, this competition can lead to a dysfunctional relationship between you and your peers, and we'll look at how to avoid this.

- *Next, we'll see how to build an initial relationship with your peer group based on polarity.* Depending on whether you are generating value or conflict for your peers, you can use this to determine how to approach building a relationship with them. We'll look at some example traits and talking points for each polarity.

- *Then, we'll see that the best way for you to have an ongoing, effective peer group is to act as if your manager doesn't exist.* We'll study the antipattern of a manager as a single point of contact and see how the best way to make things better is to just do it yourself.

It'll take some effort to activate this group, but it might just become the best team that you didn't know you had.

But We Didn't Want This to Become a Dumpster Fire

You've likely seen it before: something with no specific ownership between a group of people falling into disrepair. It could be a shared kitchen in a house that nobody keeps clean, a communal garden that is overgrown, or a shared path that is constantly littered with rubbish.

It seems that despite our best efforts to desire to be altruistic and to do the right thing, we often fail to do so when there is no specific ownership. In fact, this happens in software all the time. Shared codebases that grow in complexity and become a tangled mess, shared infrastructure that nobody wants to touch, and shared processes that nobody wants to own.

There is a name for this phenomenon: the tragedy of the commons.[1] The definition states that should a group of people have access to a shared resource, they will act in their own self-interest and deplete that resource, even if it is not in the group's long-term interest to do so.

Astute readers will notice that the tragedy of the commons is the antithesis of longtermism, which we covered in Chapter 3, Time: Observed, Spent, and Allocated, on page 55. Longtermism is the idea that you should selflessly *invest* in a shared future, even if it means sacrificing the present. The tragedy of the commons, however, is the idea that you should selfishly *take* from the present, even if it means sacrificing the shared future.

Up and Down but Not Sideways

Another tragedy of the commons situation is that of your peer group when you are in middle management. While it is true that your peers are the people who are in the same position as you, also with the same manager, the implied closeness and comradery that this should bring is often lacking.

In fact, it is more than just lacking—it can be nonexistent. This is because the default *outlook* for middle management is to look up and down the org chart, but not sideways. Because you are so focused on your own team and your own manager, you often forget that you have a peer group at all! That is, until you need something from them. At this point, the underinvestment in your peer group becomes apparent: you have limited rapport and trust with them, and an ask to transfer some of your engineering capacity to them is met with hot flushes and heavy and furious typing.

This is the tragedy of the common *leader*. Despite you and your peer group having the same leader in common (access to the same resource), you act in your own self-interest, even if it is not in the group's long-term interest to do so. We can see how this situation can play out in the diagram on page 139.

Assuming a situation where there is a dysfunctional relationship between you and your peer group, the story goes a little something like this:

- *The manager is the common resource you and your peer group have access to.* Since you are acting in a tragedy of the commons, you compete with your peer group for your manager's time, attention, and favor. You want to be the top performer that gets the most resources from the commons.
- *This, in turn, creates a hostile competitive environment.* Like the shared codebase or the shared kitchen, you want everything for yourself. You

---

1. https://en.wikipedia.org/wiki/Tragedy_of_the_commons

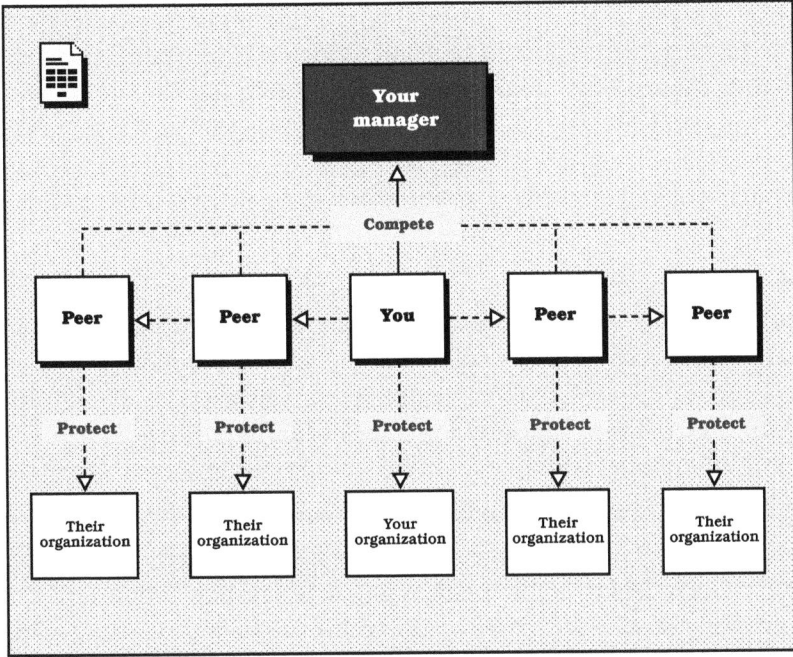

see your peers as competition, and therefore, you communicate and collaborate with them as little as possible. You don't want to give them any advantage over you.

- *You also protect your team at all costs.* You see your team as your own personal resource, and you don't want to give any of it away. They do the same, and slowly but surely, you create a siloed environment that doesn't play well with others.

Is it any wonder that shared codebases degrade when the organizations that look after them are like the ones in the diagram? Is it any wonder that middle management is lonely when your peers are your competition?

We may have just identified why so many organizations are completely dysfunctional. The tragedy of the commons is everywhere. But what can we do about it?

Magnetism and Polarity: Pulling Peers Together

The solution, clearly, is to strengthen the relationships that you have with your peers so that you can create a home team that you all feel a part of and that you can all rely on to help you achieve your collective goals. No surprises there.

If this was a book about being an individual contributor at the beginning of your career, this section would be easy. It would encourage you to do your best in your role and make sure you spend time connecting with your peers in your team individually as well as working together every day. The rest would take care of itself since you all belong to the same team and are working on the same goals, your collective direction is clear, and there is little room for conflict.

However, as we described in the previous section, you exist both in collaboration and in conflict with the other areas of the organization, which in turn means that you also exist in collaboration and in conflict with your peer group. Given the breadth of the area that you, your peers, and your manager cover, you may not find that there is a lot naturally pulling your peer group together. Additionally, you may find that you are all so busy that if you don't have compelling reasons to connect, then you simply won't; your time will be better spent elsewhere.

Your job, therefore, is to create more compelling reasons to connect. The only *true* compelling reason is that both you and your peers are getting something valuable out of the relationship. The good news is that there often always *is* something valuable, but you need to put a bit of work in to find it.

Attraction, Repulsion, and the Middle Ground

Usually, in senior leadership roles the organization that you are running will have various *first and second order effects* on other areas. This could be because you are buildings tools or APIs that are consumed by other teams, or it could be that you are building new product functionality that is requiring other teams to change their systems in order to enable yours.

If you recall, back in Chapter 2, Your Place in the Org Chart, on page 23, we worked through an org chart refactor using the Team Topologies model. Depending on whether a team was a stream-aligned team, a platform team, or an enabling team, it would have different interactions and effects on the teams around them.

A model you can use to think about the effect your organization has on others is that of *polarity*. Magnets have a north pole and a south pole, and depending on which way you hold them, they will either attract or repel each other. The same is true of your organization: you will either attract or repel other teams depending on your polarity, as shown in the diagram on page 141.

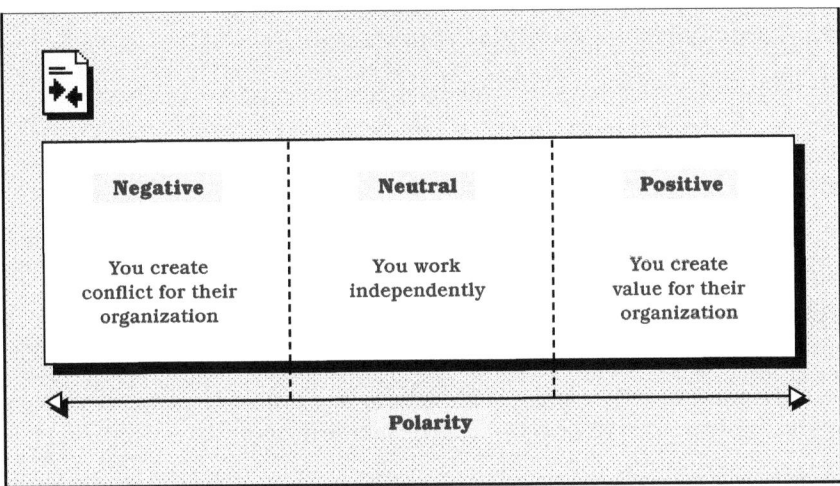

But what do we mean by that? The polarity of your organization is determined by whether you are generating *value* or *conflict* for other teams. If you are generating value, then you are attracting other teams to you. They want to work with you because you are making their lives easier. If you are generating conflict, then you are repelling other teams. They want to avoid you because you are making their lives harder.

As an example of positive polarity, imagine that your team is building a new API that other teams can use to generate product recommendations for users. This API is going to make it much easier for other teams to build new smart features, and so they are going to be *attracted* to you—you're producing things that they want, and you're an enabler for them.

An example of negative polarity is where your ideal product direction is to overhaul the UX of an area of the product that you don't own in a way that conflicts with the ideal product direction of the team that *does* own it. Here, you're going to be *repelling* the other team—you're making their lives harder, and they may want to escalate this conflict so that you change *your* direction.

A middle ground also exists of *neutral* polarity. This is where you are neither generating value nor conflict for another team. This could be two teams that are doing their own thing independently, with zero overlap. They coexist happily with no need to interact.

Depending on whether you are generating value, conflict, or are neutral, you can benefit from different approaches to building relationships with your peers.

> ### Your Turn: Map the Polarity of Your Peers
>
> Take the polarity model and look at your peer group and the areas of the organization that they are responsible for. By peer group, we typically mean the other people who report to your manager, but you may also want to include other people in your organization whom you work with regularly.
>
> - For each area, determine whether you are mutually generating value, conflict, or are neutral. It may be that for some of your peers, you generate both value and conflict.
>
> - For every peer's organization for which you are generating value, think about whether their organization is fully aware of the value that you are generating. For example, are they aware of the APIs or new features that you are building that they can use? If not, how can you make them aware?
>
> - Now, for every peer's organization that exists in conflict, reflect on how that conflict is caused and where it typically shows up. Is it due to a lack of communication, or is it due to fundamental strategic differences? If it's the former, how can you improve communication? If it's the latter, how can you resolve the conflict?
>
> - Finally, for every peer's organization that you are neutral with, consider whether that is intentional or not. Are there ways that you could collaborate or communicate more effectively with them in order to move from neutral to positive polarity?
>
> With these insights in mind, we can now start to think about a framework for improving the relationships that you have with your peers.

Polarity-Led Relationships

Given that we can categorize the polarity of our organization with that of our peers, we can then use this to determine how we should approach building and maintaining relationships with them. The table on page 143 gives some example traits and talking points for each polarity. There are many more that will uniquely evolve from your own situation, but this should give you a good starting point.

Based on these traits and talking points, let's build some hypothetical agendas for your first productive meeting with your peers. To make things straightforward, let's assume that you have three peers: Alice, Bob, and Charlie. In this example, you are running the organization that is responsible for building and maintaining the *design system* used at your company. By design system, we mean the library of reusable components that are used to build the user interfaces of your products in a consistent way.

Polarity	Relationship Traits	Talking Points
Positive	Your team actively collaborates with this team in order for them to get their job done.	Share knowledge with each other from both sides of this collaboration. What's going well? What's not going well? What can be improved? Focus on ways to increase the output of this existing collaboration.
	You are actively building things that this team wants to use that they can't build themselves.	Use your time together to demo new features or APIs that you are building that they could use. Get their feedback and see if they can become early adopters who can offer feedback to improve these systems or features. See the other team as a multiplier of your impact.
	Your team enables this team to do their job, such as by providing tooling, APIs, or infrastructure.	Discuss their experience with the tools that your team provides. See whether they can show you how it's being used and what their pain points are. Offer routes for those pain points to be fixed.
Negative	Your team builds in a direction that strategically collides with this team.	Be open about that fact, and understand what their direction is vs. yours. Build empathy between both sides and see whether you can make the way forward easier. Regardless of strategic clashes, ensure that you are a trusted collaborator, even if you may have fundamental disagreements. Make your stance well understood.
	Your team has difficulty collaborating because of technical, interpersonal, or process-driven reasons.	Use the relationship as a means to understand why this is the case and see whether both parties can change the way that they are collaborating to make the situation better. Challenge yourselves to work together to fix this.
Neutral	Both teams rarely interact because they are working on unrelated things.	Use this as an opportunity to build trust and rapport for the future. Use your interactions as an opportunity to share what both sides are working on, as this context may be useful later on or present opportunities for positive polarity that you didn't know existed.

Firstly, let's apply the exercise from the sidebar to determine the polarity of your relationship with each of your peers:

- *Alice's team is building a brand-new feature from scratch.* You have a *positive* polarity with her team because they are creating net-new functionality and are using the design system in the way it is intended. Some of your engineers have been helping create some of the new components that they need, and they have been contributing back some improvements and bug fixes along the way.

- *Bob's team owns and maintains one of the oldest parts of the product, which has existed since before the design system was built.* You have a *negative* polarity with his team because they are not adopters, and interactions between engineers in both teams around this have created conflict in the past. You are facing increasing pressure from your leadership to get them to adopt the design system and overhaul their area, but you do not control their roadmap, and they are resisting.

- *Charlie's team looks after the data platform that powers insights in the product.* Since it has no front end, you have a *neutral* polarity with his team: you don't interact with them much.

With these polarities in mind, let's build some talking points for your first meeting with each of them. We'll exclude the introductions and pleasantries that are common to each meeting. We'll start with Alice.

- Explore the ways in which her team has been using the design system recently, ideally with a quick demo of the new feature that they are building.

- Get feedback on the current ease of development and whether there are any pain points or improvements that could be made.

- Walk through the current roadmap and see whether the prioritization aligns with her team's needs.

- Share how progress is going with getting other teams to adopt the design system and see whether there are ways in which the success of her team could be used to encourage other teams to adopt it.

- Ask whether any of her team would be interested in meeting one-to-one with you or some of your engineers to share their experiences and feedback and build connections.

Next, let's look at Bob.

- Be transparent about the conflicting strategic direction that your teams are taking: his area is long overdue for an overhaul of the UI, but there is resistance. Where does this come from? What are the current blockers to making this happen?

- Explain how the strategic direction from leadership is impacting your own team since so much of it is outside of your control.

- Ask Bob to share his current roadmap priorities with you, detailing his stakeholders, strategic direction, and which parts of his team are working on what. This is key to understanding the influences that steer his team's direction.
- Share the roadmap for the design system and see whether there are ways in which it could be changed to make it easier for his team to adopt it.
- If needed, demo the process for switching out components in the design system and how it can be done incrementally, including the additional value that it brings other than just visual consistency.
- Ask whether there are any ways in which your team could help his team to adopt the design system, such as by providing training or support with implementation.

Finally, let's look at Charlie.

- Spend some time doing a deep dive into your design system: What is it? Why does it exist? How does it work? What are the benefits of using it?
- Ask for a similar outline and demonstration of the data platform that his team looks after.
- Share how your team is organized, including who works on what. Get the same knowledge from him, too.
- Consider whether there are any ways in which your team could collaborate more. For example, has there ever been a desire to build a simple UI for the data platform to allow people to do ad hoc queries? Could the design system be used to build this? Also, what sorts of usage metrics could be recorded in the data platform to give you a better idea of how the design system is being used compared to older parts of the system? Are there any ways of embedding telemetry into the design system to make feature tracking available out of the box?

Although fictional, these examples should give you some inspiration on how to make your first meetings with your peers more focused and productive. Typically, the way to break through to busy people like yourself is to have a clear focus on how you can make *their* lives easier by connecting regularly, sharing knowledge, and encouraging collaboration. Even when it looks like there is no common ground, there often is; you just need to find it.

You can build on these first meetings by making them regular and by making sure that you follow up on any action points that you have. You can also use them as a means of sharing knowledge and building trust with your peers;

the more that you share, the more that they will share, and the more that you will all benefit from each other's experiences.

Actually, It's All on You: Do It Yourself

The first section of this chapter sketched out what happens in the tragedy of the commons. When you and your peer group are *competing* for the same resource, which is your manager's time, the same thing starts to go wrong as when ten housemates share a kitchen: nobody takes responsibility for the situation, and it falls into disrepair. The following section then showed that the only way you can fight this entropy is to be proactive in establishing the connection you want with your peer group and continually working on it to show you are a trusted partner and collaborator.

What this highlights is it's in your best interest to selflessly put in the work for the group—you shouldn't expect your manager to do this for you. In fact, the more senior you become, the more you should expect to be self-sufficient in this regard. When your manager is a busy executive, making sure their reports are collaborating together is going to be something already *expected* rather than something they are going to be actively working on.

The dynamics of a good peer group should be like musical theater: there is a diverse set of characters, each with their own strengths and weaknesses, but they all come together to create something that is greater than the sum of its parts. The performance is done for the audience, not for the director. And, in fact, as a musical tours the country or takes up residency in a theater, the director isn't even needed; the group of actors and actresses are a self-sufficient and well-oiled machine.

The performance is judged as a whole rather than on specific parts or performers. Sure, from time to time, there may be a standout individual performance, but people are there to watch and feel what is created by the group. Thus, the individuals who are taking part are not there to sabotage each other because it ruins the performance for everyone. This is exactly the mindset of a good peer group: you do not compete for your manager's favor as a *goal*; instead, it is a *side effect* of the contribution that you make to the collective.

Peer groups that are dysfunctional are similar to reality TV shows. Each individual is there to compete for a single prize to the detriment of everyone else. When one individual gets to sign for Simon Cowell's record label, everyone else loses and is likely never heard of again. When you're working together to build software and an organization that will likely outlast your own tenure at the company, this is a poor mindset to have.

There is clearly a paradox here: the performance of individuals is judged independently of the performance of the group, but not everyone can have the highest performance rating. We will explore this dichotomy between individual performance and group performance in more detail in Chapter 10, Performance Management: Raising the Bar, on page 223.

When thinking of how to perform within your own peer group, it all comes back to *longtermism* and *infinite games*, which we covered in Chapter 3, Time: Observed, Spent, and Allocated, on page 55 and Chapter 4, The Games We Play and How to Win Them, on page 91. It is a positive-sum rather than a zero-sum game. You are investing in the collective future by putting aside your individual agenda and working for the common good. This is the only way that you can fight the tragedy of the commons.

Your Manager Is Not Your Single Point of Contact

Another common peer group dysfunction is when the shape of the org chart dictates the flow of *communication*, meaning that a set of peers only talk with each other through their manager. This is a common pattern in organizations that are structured around a functional hierarchy, where the manager is the single point of contact for the group.

However, this is a poor pattern for a number of reasons:

- *The manager becomes a bottleneck.* Just by looking at an org chart, if your manager has to be the single point of contact for every one of their direct reports, then you can imagine what their inbox looks like and the effect it has on response time. For regular day-to-day, not-particularly-important communication, this means it can take a long time to get a response.

- *It encourages games of "telephone."* If you're not autonomously communicating with your peers, then you can't guarantee that exactly what you want to communicate will be relayed to the right people in the right way. This can lead to misunderstandings and miscommunication.

- *It encourages a lack of transparency.* An ideal organization works in the open, and the same should be true of your peer group. Every single private conversation that you have with your manager is a missed opportunity to share knowledge and build trust with your peers. Instead, communicating in the open means that everyone can benefit from the conversation, and it can bring new ideas and perspectives to the table.

- *It encourages politics and snide behavior.* This is often most apparent during times of conflict, where a peer will try to get their manager to side with them over another peer. Examples of this include prioritization tie-breakers or when different parts of the manager's organization are competing for more engineers. Private conversations tend to just avoid the conflict rather than resolve it.

The solution to this is the same theme that we're repeating again and again in this chapter. If it isn't already happening, start making cultural changes in your peer group to encourage all but the most sensitive of conversations to happen in the open rather than in private between your peers and your manager.

Here are some ways in which you can lay down the foundations for this to happen:

- *Set up a chat channel for your peer group.* Make it private so that you can have sensitive conversations, but encourage everyone to use it as a means of communication. Have your manager be a member of the channel as well so they can get involved in any conversations that they need to and, at the very least, see what is going on.

- *Hold a regular meeting with your peer group and have your manager attend optionally.* Typically, people wait for their manager to set up a regular staff meeting, but you can do this yourself. Decide on the regularity and invest in making it a productive meeting by calling for agenda items ahead of time. If your manager wants to attend, then they can, but it's not a requirement. In fact, having them attend some, but not all, meetings, ideally on a rotating schedule, is a great way of encouraging the peer group to be self-sufficient.

- *Change the balance of communication in the peer group from one-to-one to one-to-many.* If you find yourself talking to your peers about anything privately that you think would be useful for the group to know, then make sure that you share it via either chat or a meeting. This could be anything from how you resolved a blocker with deployment tooling to how you're managing prioritization conflicts with another team. The more you share, the more others will share, and the more you will all benefit from each other's experiences.

- *Proactively bring discussion topics to the group.* Your peer group doesn't have to just talk about functional things; you want to encourage interactions that build trust and rapport. Share interesting articles or papers that you've read that could provoke discussion, or use them as a sounding board as you're working through a particularly tricky problem. Day by day, you can create a positive culture of sharing and collaboration.

The Best Way to Build Trust: Deliver Something Awesome

The fastest path to building a strong, trusting relationship with your peers is to deliver something awesome for the group. In Chapter 3, Time: Observed, Spent, and Allocated, on page 55, we talked about how, ideally, you should find ten percent of your capacity for working on things that make your organization better. One way of making your organization better is to make your wider department better, which means that you should be looking for opportunities to do so.

Some of the most frustrating leadership peer groups contain individuals who are quick to spot problems and quick to escalate them but rarely step up to the plate to actually fix them. The tragedy of the commons strikes again. However, if you're planning your capacity well, you can execute some of these fixes yourself, sometimes with little outside support or additional resources.

Delivering something for your peer group, and hence your wider department feels *brilliant*. Not only is it good for everyone else, but it also replenishes your capacity by giving you controllable, tangible projects that you can work on yourself. Deep work on something that you own will make you feel happy and productive.

As such, see your peer group as a source of inspiration for things that you can work on for them. Here are some examples:

- *Codifying best practices.* Your peer group is in a great position to see what works well and what doesn't across the department. Work with your peers to gather the best practices that you've seen, from coding standards to deployment processes to how to run projects and meetings. The eventual deliverable here could be a handbook for your department that you can all contribute to and maintain. What's more, it gives you plenty of opportunities to communicate widely with your peer group and to raise your visibility.

- *Automating common tasks and issues.* Similarly, your peer group is in a great position to see what the common issues are that are affecting everyone. You can work together with them to understand how to build tooling to make them better. You may be able to do this yourselves, or if the issues are bigger, you could work together to get them prioritized and resourced. For example, if there are issues with code review, can you improve the mapping of code ownership to ensure that the right people are reviewing the right code when pull requests are raised? Is it possible to surround particularly dangerous parts of the codebase with virtual tripwires that alert the right people when they are being changed?

- *Identifying directly responsible individuals (DRIs) for your technology real estate.* A DRI is a person with whom the buck stops for a particular area—the key person who should be consulted about upcoming major changes. A simple crowdsourced project is to create a living list of DRIs for your department and make sure that it is kept up to date. Then, everyone will know who to talk to when they need to make a breaking change to a key area. You can combine this initiative with the first two. You could automate the process of identifying DRIs by embedding the information in your codebase, and you could codify the process of how to become and act as a DRI in the handbook.

- *Unifying reporting on the health of your code and production environment.* Often, individual teams will have their own dashboards and reports that they use to monitor the health of their services. However, is it possible that you could create a unified approach and dashboard that shows the overall health of the whole product? You could define the information that you want to see with your peers and see whether standardization could lead to better tooling and reuse. Again, with the previous points, you can codify the process of how to add new metrics to the dashboard, automate reporting, and identify DRIs for the areas that are being reported on.

- *Running regular developer experience surveys.* If you work in a large department, it can be challenging to spend time with each engineer to understand how they are feeling about their work. However, defining a survey that helps you track key indicators such as happiness, autonomy, the ability to get things done, the presence of blockers and broken processes, and so on can be a great way of getting a pulse on the department. Once you have created the survey, you can run it at regular intervals (for example, once per quarter) and, with your peer group, report on the results and trends over time to the rest of the department. The results of this pulse survey can generate new initiatives for you to work on together.

This is a short selection of ideas, but the key point is that you do not need your manager to tell you that you should do them; you can work autonomously with your peer group to identify and execute on them. The more that you do, the more that you will be seen as a trusted collaborator and a leader in your peer group.

It's the only way that you fight the tragedy of the common leader; ironically, you all operate as if you didn't need them to be there in the first place. Strange, isn't it?

And Now, Let's Work on Your Manager

If you reframe your relationship with your peer group and then continually put in the work to make it better, it can become one of the best home teams that you've ever had. This chapter has outlined how to frame this relationship and also introduced methods and tools to get the best out of it.

Here's what we've covered:

- *We started by looking at the tragedy of the commons and how it applies to your peer group.* Nothing will be successful if you are competing in a zero-sum game with your peers. You need to be part of a positive-sum game that benefits everyone in the long term.

- *Next, we saw how to build an initial relationship with your peer group based on polarity.* We saw how, depending on what you work on, you may have positive, negative, or neutral polarity with your peers. We then saw how to use this polarity to determine how to approach building a relationship with them.

- *Finally, we saw that the best approach to making your peer group better is to just do it yourself.* Imagine that your manager didn't exist and that it was up to *you* to direct the group. What would you do? What does amazing look like? Just do that. It's that simple. We also saw a number of examples of projects that you could deliver for your peer group either by yourself or with their collaboration.

Now that you've got your peers in the bag, it's time to put the work into another relationship that can make or break your happiness: the one you have with your manager. Like your peer group, you get out what you put in. Also, you'll need to deal with a particular individual who can make that relationship more challenging than it needs to be: *yourself*.

CHAPTER 7

Of Clownfish and Anemones

Bing!

You join the video call, ready to apologize for being late. However, as you're about to speak, you realize that you're the only one there. You turn off your camera and mute your microphone while you wait for your manager to join.

After a few minutes of sitting in silence, you open up your chat client to see if you've missed a message. Nope, nothing there. You open up your email to check the same thing. Nothing there either. You figure they're probably running a bit behind.

You jot down a few additional notes into the agenda that you'd like to speak to them about. First up: one of your direct reports is a flight risk, as you know they are interviewing at another company. You want to get your manager's input on how to handle this and what to do if they get an offer. Next, there's an upcoming escalation about a technical decision that you want to run by them so it doesn't catch them off guard. Oh, and yeah, there's also the speed of builds in the monolith, which has been causing your engineers a ton of grief recently. There's lots to cover, so you're glad you've managed to get some rare time with them.

You fiddle around with the video call settings, which have been updated recently. There are some new backgrounds, which you click through to kill some time before they arrive. They're ten minutes late now. You look at chat and email again. Nothing. You answer a few outstanding messages in your team channel while you wait. Hmm.

Fifteen minutes late now. That's 50 percent of the meeting gone. You open up your chat client and send them a message to see whether they're coming. They're online, but you don't get any reply.

You go back to your messages and start to read them, and you hear the familiar *bloop* notification sound. You have a direct message from your manager's executive assistant.

"Hi, I'm sorry to say that Lisa is unable to make the meeting today. She's been called into an urgent meeting with the CEO. She's asked me to reschedule the meeting for next week. I'm sorry for the inconvenience."

You sigh and reply to the message. "No problem, thanks for letting me know." That's the third week in a row that's happened. Another message comes in from your manager's executive assistant. "I've rescheduled the meeting for next week at the same time. Lisa's also asked if you can send her an update on the resiliency work that your team has been doing. She's keen to understand how it's going, and the CEO just asked her about it."

You reply, "What resiliency work?" You've not heard anything about this, and you're not sure what she's referring to.

"I'll find out and get back to you," she replies.

You disconnect from the call, frustrated, for the third week in a row. You're not sure if Lisa even knows what your team is working on anymore. Resiliency project? What resiliency project? You stare out of the window, wondering how you can make this relationship work.

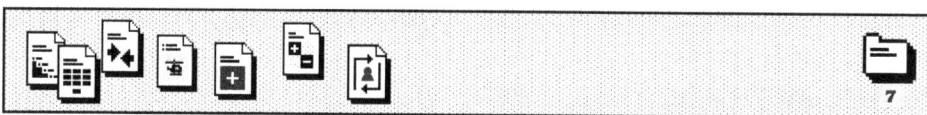

Ah, we've reached the chapter about how to deal with your manager, who is likely a senior manager, in a book that is all about being a senior manager *yourself*. This is getting a little bit meta, isn't it? The recursion is strong with this one.

Jokes aside, this chapter is one of the most important ones in the book. Having a productive, symbiotic relationship with your manager is critical to both your own success and the success of your team. It's also one of the most difficult relationships to get right, especially since the further you go up the org chart, the more that you are expected to be self-directing and self-sufficient by default, and you may get little to no guidance on how to do your job. That's why you're in your role; after all, *you're* the expert, not your manager.

The previous chapters in the book have built out a strong foundation for you to be able to manage upward effectively. This is because you now know that all of the challenges that you have learned about are not unique to you. Your manager is likely experiencing them, too, often at a larger scale where the stakes are higher. If they sit on the strategic rung of the company, then you now know all about the scope of their role and what you need to take *off* of their plate in order for you both to be successful.

You understand the infinite games they are playing and how you can help them win. You can do so by taking care of the operations containing the finite games that contribute to the long-term success of the company. You know all about how to build relationships with your peers so that the entire organization under your manager functions as a cohesive unit, and you also know what a healthy and productive partnership between a manager and their direct reports looks like. You know how to start building a relationship that starts with contracting and then continues to improve with regular one-to-ones and coaching.

So, it's all in the bag right? Will your manager be doing all of these things for you in the same proactive and thorough way that you are for your own direct reports? Well…let's see.

Here's what we're going to cover in this chapter:

- *We'll begin by saying the thing you don't want to hear: your manager will always disappoint you.* However, we'll explore why that is, how it's actually your problem, and how you can have a productive relationship with them regardless.

- *We will explore using tools, not prescriptions.* Broadly applicable to all of the chapters in this book, we'll dig into why there is no one-size-fits-all approach to managing upward and how thinking there is will lead to failure.

- *Then, we'll define the kind of relationship that you want with them and help you articulate it.* This will help you understand what you need from them, and what they need from you.

- *Next, we'll frame your relationship with your manager as symbiotic.* Symbiotic relationships, often observed in nature, are ones where both parties mutually benefit, and it is by far the most productive way to think about your relationship with your manager.

- *Finally, we'll explore what to do when things go wrong.* We'll debug common scenarios such as escalations, the Eye of Sauron, and unpleasant surprises and how to handle them.

There's a lot to cover, but don't worry; we've got your back!

Teenage Rebellion: Raging Against the Machine

Let's start with the thing that you don't want to hear: your manager will always disappoint you. This isn't necessarily because they are bad at their job or because they have a specific grudge against you. In fact, generally speaking, they may consistently do an excellent job of managing you and your peers from the perspective of the outputs that the organization produces.

However, as you become an increasingly senior leader, there are a number of traits you'll develop and be expected to master that will lead to friction:

- *You will be expected to be self-sufficient.* This means, in the long term, you will be the one responsible for your own development, and you will be expected to be able to self-coach and self-direct. Exactly what you spend your time on will be up to you, and you will be expected to prioritize your own work as well as that of your team.

- *You will be the expert in your domain.* This is especially true if you run a large organization or a team of domain experts such as machine learning or security. You will be expected to be the expert in your field and know more than your manager does about it. This means that you will be expected to make decisions and trade-offs without their input.

- *You will develop your own leadership style.* This means harnessing your strengths and developing your weaknesses in order to be the best leader you can be, which is a unique function of your skills and personality. Perhaps you are a great coach, a great communicator, or an avid, concise writer. Every senior manager has their own style, and it will likely be different from that of your manager.

- *The lens through which you view the organization will be unique.* Your global maxima may be one of your manager's local maxima. This is especially true around strategic decisions and resource allocation. This can put you on the path to conflict in the same way that you may have experienced conflict with your peers.

- *If you are a high-growth individual, your next career move might be the seat they are sitting in.* That means you can have an extremely high standard for what you expect from your manager, and you may be disappointed if they don't meet it.

There may be another time in your life when you experienced growing self-sufficiency, development of your own character and style, and a differing long-term view of the world: your teenage years. These are the times in your life when, despite having been created, born, and raised by your parents over the course of *at least* a decade, you can rebel and develop a fractious relationship with them. You may have, in fact, called them rubbish and expressed your displeasure at the fact you are related to them. Ah, the folly of youth.

However, the same thing can happen with your manager. Despite the fact that they may have given you the opportunity to do the job you are doing, and despite the fact that they may have coached you and helped you develop your career, you will likely always hit a ceiling where your own developing independence and self-sufficiency will lead to friction. This is especially true if you are a high-growth or competitive individual.

The Reporting to Peter Principle

The Peter Principle,[1] coined by Laurence J. Peter in 1969, states that "in a hierarchy, every employee tends to rise to their level of incompetence." The idea is that if you are good at your job, you will be promoted, and you will continue to be promoted until you can no longer get promoted. This is *Peter's plateau*; the level at which you are no longer competent. This is a somewhat overly simplistic view of the world, but a gradual regression of talent to the mean is a common phenomenon in organizations.

With that in mind, I'd like to propose a new principle: the Reporting to Peter Principle. It's a useful way to think about the relationship between you and your manager. The Reporting to Peter Principle is as follows: in every organization, you will rise to a point where you will experience extreme internal conflict with the way that your manager does their job. This will manifest as disappointment, frustration, and a feeling that you should be doing their role instead of them. More often than not, this is an invention of your own mind rather than them actually doing a bad job.

This represents a key inflection point in your own development as a senior leader, which builds upon other principles that we have explored earlier in this book: notably, longtermism in Chapter 3, Time: Observed, Spent, and Allocated, on page 55 and the tragedy of the commons in Chapter 6, The Tragedy of the Common Leader, on page 135. At the point that the Reporting to Peter Principle becomes true, you have two choices:

1. *You can continue to be frustrated and disappointed with your manager, and you can let this develop into resentment.* This will lead to a breakdown in your relationship with them and will likely lead to either you leaving

---

1. https://en.wikipedia.org/wiki/Peter_principle

the organization or forcing a change in your manager through a risky, high-stakes escalation. This is short-term, selfish thinking that turns a functioning organization into a dysfunctional one to the detriment of everyone. For reference, read any news article about politicians fighting each other instead of making progress for their constituents.

2. *You can embrace your differences and consider them a strength insofar that you can both learn from each other and develop a symbiotic relationship.* This is noble, selfless thinking that improves your performance, their performance, and the performance of the organization as a whole. This is longtermism and altruism in action.

The key is noticing when the Reporting to Peter Principle becomes true and then taking action to ensure that you take the second path. This will serve you and your organization in the long term and will help you develop a symbiotic relationship with your manager. We dig deeper into symbiosis in Symbiosis: Defined, Observed, and Applied, on page 160.

> **Your Turn: The Difference Between You and Your Manager**
>
> Take a moment to think about the traits that you and your manager have. These could range from the way that you communicate to the way that you make decisions to what you both value.
>
> - What are some of the shared traits that you have? For example, are you both good at written communication, or do you both share a primary focus on system performance and reliability?
>
> - Conversely, what are some of the biggest differences between you? For example, is one of you extroverted and the other introverted? Does one of you value autonomy and the other value collaboration, such as in your approach to how teams are structured?
>
> - Have any of the differences between you and your manager caused friction in the past? Was this because of a real conflict, or was it *internal* conflict that you felt toward your manager?
>
> - Do you fundamentally think that you can do a better job than your manager? Why is that? Could it be you are experiencing the Reporting to Peter Principle?

Prescriptions Don't Work: Tools Do

In addition to fighting the Reporting to Peter Principle, there is another thing that you need to be aware of when it comes to managing upward: there is no one-size-fits-all approach to doing it. This is because every manager is different, and everyone who has ever given advice is different to *you*.

It's worth zooming out a little and touching upon a maxim that holds true for the whole book and, in fact, your whole career too. It's the idea that there are no silver bullets, no quick fixes, and no one-size-fits-all approaches to *anything*. As you become more senior, the more nuanced and complex the problems you will face will become and the more you will need to develop your own style and approach to solving them. This is why the book is full of *tools and techniques, and not prescriptions [Gup17]*.

Prescriptions, that is, prescriptive advice, have become prevalent in the world. They feed clickbait titles and are easy to consume. As a reader, you feel like you are only one blog post away from being able to solve all of your problems, whether they be personal or professional. You can even see it creeping into newspaper headlines because it draws in readers. Three easy ways to live longer? Yes! I'm reading that.

However, prescriptions are dangerous because the reality is that nobody has faced the exact same situation as you, and nobody else *is* you. They strip away nuance, experience, and, bluntly, intelligence. When it comes to being a fantastic senior leader, parent, caregiver, or anything else, prescriptions may get you a little of the way there, but they will soon fall short when the rubber hits the road.

As a senior leader, you develop your own unique style and approach to solving problems by treating what you learn as *tools* rather than prescriptions. Tools are things that you can use to solve problems in your own way, in the same way that a carpenter uses a hammer for a multitude of different tasks.

Similarly, you should be wary of how you treat stories of successful leaders. For example, if you read Steve Jobs' autobiography and then tomorrow decided to copy exactly what Steve Jobs did, you wouldn't be as successful as Steve Jobs. He was a unique product of a situation, time, and application. The same is true when trying to copy the mechanical technique of any sportsperson. There's much more to becoming Michael Jordan than the exact way that he jumps and shoots.

When it comes to building a productive relationship with your manager, the same is true. There are no prescriptions. Instead, the tool that you need to use is the ability to observe and understand the strengths and weaknesses of both yourself and your manager, using that understanding to build a relationship that works for both of you. By understanding additive and subtractive actions, you can build a relationship that is symbiotic, and that is the key to managing upward.

Symbiosis: Defined, Observed, and Applied

When you are an individual contributor working on a front-line team, you are united by a common goal, which is to deliver the outputs that your team is responsible for. You and your peers are likely collaborating closely, writing code and designing features together, and shipping dependent and interrelated work. The relationship with your manager is also clear. They are accountable for the outputs of your team, and you are responsible for delivering them.

As we explored in Chapter 6, The Tragedy of the Common Leader, on page 135, as you become more senior, the mutually beneficial interactions between yourself and your peer group become less obvious and require work; hence why we went through an exercise around polarity mapping. At this level, the relationship with your manager also requires work. This is because you may find without that work, at best, you'll have a transactional and low-touch relationship with them, and at worst, you'll have a dysfunctional one.

The key to building a productive relationship with your manager is to understand that it should be a *symbiotic* one. Symbiosis is a biological term that describes a relationship between two organisms that is mutually beneficial.

Clownfish have a symbiotic relationship with anemones, hence the cryptic title of this chapter. The clownfish is immune to the anemone's sting, and it uses this to its advantage by hiding in the anemone's tentacles when it is threatened by predators. In return, the clownfish cleans the anemone, brings it food, and even protects it from parasites. These two organisms are nothing like each other, but they depend on each other for survival.

The reason that symbiosis is a good model to think about your relationship with your manager is because, by definition:

- *Symbiosis benefits you both.* You and your manager doing your job well should work both ways. Your success ensures that a part of their organization is functioning well, and their success ensures that you have the resources and support that you need to continue.

- *It is a critical relationship for mutual survival.* If the org chart were a biological ecosystem, the relationship should lead to the growth and survival of both of you: a win-win for longtermism. If you succeed, your team can continue to grow in impact, and, in turn, your manager also succeeds. A virtuous cycle.

- *Even the most disparate organisms can have a critical symbiotic relationship.* Most importantly, symbiosis can happen between two very different organisms. For example, a bee and a flower are *nothing* like each other, but the bee needs the flower for food, and the flower needs the bee for pollination. The same is true for pistol shrimps and gobies, coral and algae, and even humans and the bacteria in our colon.[2] You don't need to have the same style, character, or approach to work as your manager in order to have a symbiotic relationship with them. The most unlikely pairings can be the most productive.

The key, therefore, is to understand the actions you and your manager perform that are additive and subtractive to your relationship and then use that to build a relationship that is symbiotic. However, you'll have to decide whether you or your manager is the clownfish. I'll leave that to you to work out.

Skip to the End: Defining the Relationship

Exploring additive and subtractive actions is a useful additional step to the contracting exercise we covered in Chapter 4, The Games We Play and How to Win Them, on page 91. It allows you to dive deeper into what it means to work together closely and also to understand what you both need, what can be a source of friction, and, most importantly, what concrete actions you can both take to ensure symbiosis. This is because having a good working relationship with your manager at a senior level isn't just about getting on well and having a good rapport; it's about being able to have a mutually beneficial impact as part of a virtuous cycle.

- *Additive actions* are ones that you can both take that will explicitly benefit your relationship—things you can do that help your manager and things that your manager can do that help you. Naturally, it is in your mutual interest to define and perform these actions. A small example could be holding regular one-to-ones, or a larger example could be building dashboards that allow your manager to see your organization's progress against defined metrics without having to ask you for them.

- *Subtractive actions* are ones that can be a source of friction in your relationship. These are things that you can do that will make your manager's life harder and vice versa. The key is to identify these actions, have a strategy for calling them out when they happen, and then *transform* them into additive ones. A small example could be not inviting you to meetings

---

2. https://www.nhm.ac.uk/discover/mutualism-examples-of-species-that-work-together.html

that have a direct impact on your team, or a larger example could be not agreeing on a clear set of metrics for which you are both accountable.

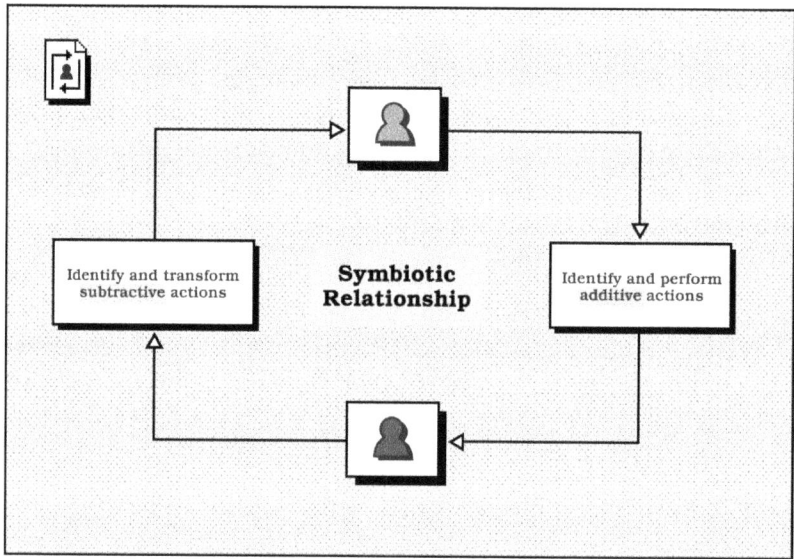

You can categorize these additive and subtractive actions into different aspects of your relationship, such as communication, decision-making, process and structure, and so on. You can define the categories yourselves. This is best explained in practice, so let's look at a worked example of a senior manager who reports to the CTO of a large organization as shown in the table on page 163.

Try it out. Take a moment to think about your relationship with your manager, and then write down some additive and subtractive actions that you can both take to improve it. You don't even need to do this collaboratively—you can do it yourself and then talk to them about the solutions that you've come up with as part of contracting.

How Do You Actually Want to Be Managed?

So far, we've talked about managing upward by understanding the strengths and weaknesses of both yourself and your manager and then laying the foundation for a relationship that's symbiotic. However, there's a fundamental question you need to ask yourself: *how do you actually want to be managed?* And, more importantly, do you even know the answer to that question?

What do we mean by this? Well, we identified at the beginning of the chapter that, in some ways, your manager will always disappoint you. This is because you will always have a different style, approach, and view of the world to them. But have you considered what an ideal relationship with them would

Aspect	Action	Situation	Solution
Communication	Keeping the CEO up to date on progress	Additive	You will build a dashboard that displays your organization's KPIs in real time. Your manager can use this whenever they need to report upward without needing your involvement. You can also use this to align all of your teams.
Communication	Meeting one-to-one	Subtractive	Your manager's schedule often changes at the last minute due to external and board interactions. This leads to your one-to-ones being frequently cancelled. You will transform this situation by writing an update once a week that allows you to keep up to date asynchronously at the very least.
Decision-making	Understanding project priorities	Subtractive	Your CEO can often have strong opinions about changing priorities that can seemingly come out of nowhere. They seriously affect the morale of the team. You will transform this situation by having the CEO come to you and your manager directly, then jointly agree on the next steps from there.
Process	Ensuring frequent progress within your teams	Additive	Your team already demonstrates a healthy weekly cadence in their work: setting goals on Monday and then reporting on Friday. You will both work to highlight the team's work here as best practice across the wider department.
Style	Ways of exchanging information	Subtractive	Your manager prefers to talk in person rather than writing, and you are the opposite. You will transform this situation by leading with written updates to them, and your manager can have clarifying calls with you if needed. You'll work together on the format so you both get what you need.
Peer group	Getting connected to the wider group	Additive	You are demonstrably good at running effective meetings, so your manager is going to let you be the chair of their weekly staff meeting so you can steer the discussion topics and assign follow-up actions throughout the week.
Access to information	Understanding what your manager gets up to	Subtractive	By default, your manager's world is a closed box that you don't see into, so you don't know what they spend their time doing. You both agree to transform the situation by having them bring one to two interesting things they have seen or are working on to the weekly staff meeting for everyone's visibility and discussion.

look like? What would be happening each day, week, and month? Would you be talking to them frequently and appreciating their close steer? Or would you be operating autonomously, with them only stepping in when you need them to?

Earlier, in Chapter 4, The Games We Play and How to Win Them, on page 91, we covered delegation, specifically, how doing so effectively is a trade-off between delegation and control. Oftentimes, feeling like you are not receiving enough support from your manager is a symptom of an impedance mismatch in the placement of that trade-off. For example, if you're a high-growth individual, you may want to be given more autonomy than your manager is comfortable with giving you. Conversely, and more commonly at senior levels, you may want more frequent check-ins and steer than your manager is providing.

The key is to understand where you want to be on the delegation-control spectrum, shown in the following diagram, and align on that with your manager. It may change over time, and it may be different for different aspects of your role, but it's important to understand where you want to be, and then use that to get the input and feedback that you need.

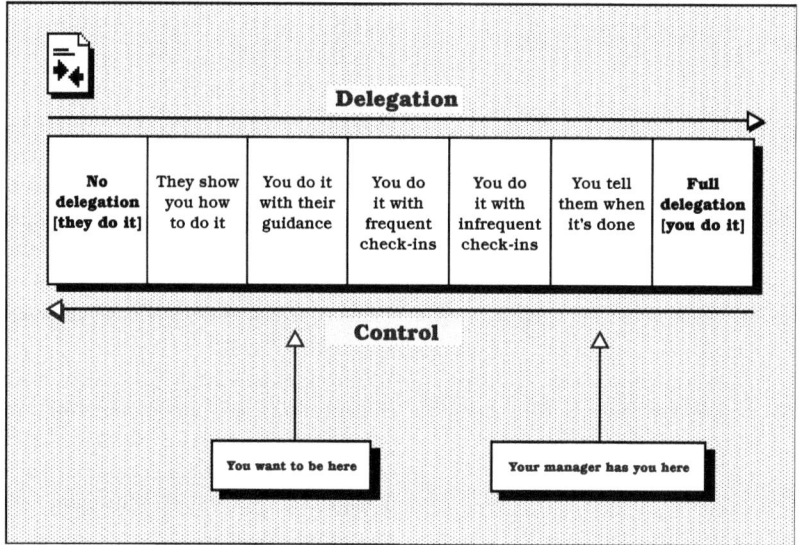

As per the diagram, if your manager has you placed somewhere on the spectrum that you don't want to be, then it generates an impedance mismatch that can generate friction:

- *If they are delegating too much to you*, then you can feel like you are not getting enough support from them. Despite this being a vote of confidence in your ability, it can leave you feeling like they are not investing enough time in you or giving you any validation.

- *If they are delegating too little*, then you can feel like you are not being given enough autonomy and are being micromanaged. Despite this potentially being because they want to give you the support that you need, it can leave you feeling like they are not trusting you to do your job.

There are landmines either way when there is an impedance mismatch. The key is to understand where you want to be and then use that to set expectations with your manager. It may be the case that you want them to be extremely close to you on one particular aspect of your role or critical project and then the opposite on another. However, if you don't take control and communicate this to them, how will it ever get any better? Take control and be clear about what you need from them. They will be thankful for it; trust me.

When the Stuff Hits the Fan

So far, we've covered how to figure out a productive relationship with your manager: one that builds on your strengths and weaknesses and is symbiotic. However, this is only one side of the coin. You also need to be able to handle the inevitable situations where things go wrong.

It is important to define the word "wrong" since it does not necessarily mean that you have done something wrong yourself. Instead, we broaden the definition of "wrong":

- *Escalations.* These are situations where you need to escalate a problem to your manager because you are unable to make the decision yourself. This could be because you don't have the authority or because you don't have the information.
- *The Eye of Sauron.* These are situations where an external event or internal scrutiny throws everything up in the air amongst intense pressure. This could be a major incident or a sudden change in direction from the CEO.
- *Unpleasant surprises.* This is where you or your manager are caught off guard by something that you didn't expect. For example, there could be a critical security vulnerability in your product, or maybe you are being billed a large amount of money for a cloud service that you didn't know you were using so much.

We'll explore each of these in turn and see how you can handle them in a way that is proactive and productive.

Escalations

Escalation has long been a dirty word in the world of management. It is often seen as a sign of weakness or indecision and a sign that you are unable to do your job. However, this is not the case. Escalations are a healthy part of any organization, and they are a sign that you are able to recognize when you need help and that you are able to ask for it.

Escalations, when managed well, can be highly productive. They can build trust between you, your manager, and others that are involved and can lead to better outcomes for the organization as a whole.

Generally speaking, an escalation is required when you are unable to make a globally optimal decision at your level of the organization. This could be because you don't have the authority to make the decision or because you don't have the information to make it. In either case, you need to escalate the problem to somebody who *does* have the authority or information to make the decision.

Examples of escalations can include:

- *A disagreement between two teams that you are unable to resolve.* For example, perhaps there's a disagreement between your team and another team about the best way to integrate your systems. Both parties refuse to budge, and you are unable to make the decision yourself.

- *A disagreement about staffing across groups.* For example, another part of the organization is requesting three of your engineers to work on a dependent project, but you are unable to spare them because you are already understaffed.

- *A disagreement between priorities.* For example, you want to deprioritize a project because of a critical security vulnerability, but your peer wants to continue with it because it is the foundation of a new product that they are launching.

The commonality between all of these examples is that you are unable to make the decision yourself, and you require others who have more context, authority, and a global view of the organization to help make it for you. This is a good thing.

When you are faced with a situation that looks like it needs an escalation, you should follow the recipe provided here:

- *Identify the problem.* What is the problem that you are facing? What decision needs to be made? What is the impact of not making the decision?

- *Have all parties involved in the escalation agree to it being escalated.* This is important. You need to ensure that all parties involved in the escalation agree that it is the right thing to do. This is because you need to ensure that they are brought into the process and that they are not going to be surprised by it.

- *Work together with the other parties to define the problem, the choices, and the ramifications of each choice.* This is a collaborative process. For example, if the escalation is around staffing, you need to explain the different options of where to allocate staff and what the impact of each option is. Your manager and others who are receiving the escalation need to understand the full picture from the information that you provide.

- *Make a recommendation.* Both parties will have their own recommendation, so make this clear about what you prefer and why.

- *Escalate!* Let your manager know it's coming, and then put it in writing. A useful method is to start a private chat channel for the escalation and get everyone involved to join it. Then, write up the problem, the choices, the ramifications, and your recommendation, asking for feedback. Ensure the conversation happens in the open, where everyone can see it.

- *Don't take it personally.* If your recommendation is not selected, don't take it to heart. You presented the facts, and the organization chose another way. It has nothing to do with you; it has everything to do with the long-term view of the company.

As you get more experienced with escalations, you'll come to understand that they are a powerful tool to have in your arsenal. By working through disagreements and problems in a collaborative way, you can build trust with your peers and your manager, and you can ensure that the organization is making the best decisions possible.

An Example Escalation

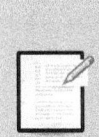

Hey, we'd like to escalate a problem to you. We have a critical security vulnerability in the open source libraries that handle our auth system, which we need to fix. However, we are also helping Alice's team with a new product that is due to launch in two weeks. We have two options:

- We can deprioritize the new product and fix the security vulnerability. This'll mean the new product will be delayed by two weeks. However, this has knock-on effects to our marketing team, who have already started to advertise the new product.

> **An Example Escalation**
>
> - We can continue to work on the new product and fix the security vulnerability after it launches. This will mean that the new product will launch on time, but we will be vulnerable to attack for two weeks. The vulnerability is not public, but it has been published widely online. In fact, it was on Hacker News this morning.
>
> Our recommendation is that we deprioritize the new product and fix the security vulnerability. We think that the risk of being attacked is too high and that the delay to the new product is worth it. However, this is causing obvious conflict with Alice's team, who is already under pressure to launch the new product.
>
> Please help us make the right decision here.

As a senior leader, your staff will also escalate to you. When helping them through this, ensure that you coach them to follow this same recipe. Pay close attention to the following bugs that can occur, which can also occur in your own escalations upward:

- *Your staff don't enumerate the options.* This is a common one. Your staff may come to you with a problem, but they don't have a clear set of options for you to choose from. This is an essential part of the escalation since it forces them to think through the situation clearly. Also, bluntly, if they don't, they are expecting you to do their work for them.

- *Your staff don't make a recommendation.* Building on this, you should not be doing their work for them. Ensure that a recommendation comes with any escalation, and push back on them until they can provide one.

- *They initially opt for solutions outside of their span of control.* When escalating, it should be because one either has exhausted all options or needs help choosing. If a recommendation, for example, is to do less on project A and more on project B, and both A and B are within their organization, then that's fine. However, if the initial recommendation is that they think you should transfer staff from outside because they feel their project is more important than others in your organization, then that's not okay; only you can offer that solution because you have more context.

Escalating well is a skill that you and your staff will develop over time. It is a key part of being a senior leader, and when done well, it is effective and the bedrock of strengthening trust between you, your staff, and your manager.

The Eye of Sauron

In the *first book in this series* [Sta20], we covered situations called the Eye of Sauron, where an external event or intense internal scrutiny means that your engineering team is being watched extremely closely. As you go further up the org chart, these situations can still occur, but they can be much more intense, the communication can be more unfiltered and candid, and you alone cannot solve the problem yourself by working on it; you have to delegate and coach others to do so.

The Eye of Sauron can be caused by a number of things, such as:

- *A major incident.* This is where a critical part of your product or infrastructure is down, and it is causing a major impact on your customers. This is a high-stakes situation, and suddenly, you are in the spotlight from your peers, your manager, and your CEO.

- *A sudden increase in interest, scrutiny, or change of direction from an executive, like the CEO.* Although yesterday it was business as usual, today the CEO has decided that the direction of your team and their priorities are all wrong, and they seem to know better. This can manifest in them thinking you should be working harder, faster, or on something else entirely.

When you are in the spotlight, you can begin to question yourself and your judgment, and you are under intense pressure to resolve the instability as quickly as possible. This instability can manifest as actual issues with your product or infrastructure, or it can manifest in what yesterday felt like a clear direction and set of priorities suddenly being questioned.

When these situations happen, your job as a manager is to remain calm, execute diligently, listen to all inputs, make decisions and escalate where needed, and communicate clearly and frequently. As before, never take it personally: you are not the problem; the situation is. However, you can be the solution.

Here's a recipe for handling the Eye of Sauron:

- *Remain calm.* This is the most important thing. You need to be the calmest person in the room, and you need to be able to think clearly and rationally. If you are not calm, then you will not be able to do your job effectively.

- *Listen to all inputs.* You will be receiving a lot of information from a lot of different sources. You need to be able to listen to all of them and then make decisions based on the information that you have. If you disagree with an input, then you should be able to push back on it and explain why. However, always work with *strong opinions, loosely held.* You need to have strong opinions to create action, but you need to be able to change your mind when presented with new information.

- *Come up with a communication plan.* Depending on the type of situation, you may decide putting out updates to stakeholders (which can be the whole department or company) is something that needs to happen hourly, daily, or weekly. This is important because it shows you're in control of the situation, are able to set clear expectations, and don't need to be chased for information. A production incident may require hourly updates, whereas a change in direction from the CEO may require weekly updates to show the progress your team is making.

- *Coach others to see these situations as a learning opportunity.* The Eye of Sauron is a great opportunity to have high-growth individuals on your team step up and prove themselves on a wider stage. Don't feel like you have to do everything yourself. Delegate and coach others to do so. Not only will this help them grow, but it will also mean that you can focus more clearly on specific tasks such as communication.

- *Retrospect after the situation is over.* Once the whirlwind has passed and you are back on track, regroup with your team and your manager to understand what went well, what didn't, and what you can do better next time. Could the whirlwind have been prevented altogether? How can you work to prevent it in the future? What can you do to ensure that you are better prepared next time? Publish a postmortem if you think that it could help others deal with similar situations.

Like escalations, incidents of the Eye of Sauron do not need to be entirely negative. They are a great opportunity to gain exposure to the wider organization and show that you are able to handle high-stakes situations. They are also a great opportunity to coach others to do the same. As hard as it may be, embrace them. They might just be the place where you can shine.

Unpleasant Surprises

Unpleasant surprises are situations where you or your manager are caught off guard by something that you didn't expect. A classic example is when the finance team informs you that you have completely blown your budget because of a spurious cloud spend that you didn't know about.

Unpleasant surprises are a fact of life, and given the complexity of the domain that you work in, they are inevitable. The way that you deal with unpleasant surprises is that you understand what is outside of your control (the surprise itself) and what is within your control (that is, how you react to it). Like the Eye of Sauron, extracting blame, taking it personally, or getting angry or upset will not help you solve the problem. Instead, you need to be able to react to it in a calm and rational way.

Here's a recipe for handling unpleasant surprises:

- *Assess and confirm the situation.* What exactly is the situation? What is the impact? What is the root cause? Importantly, is the unpleasant surprise true? Verify the facts. For example, is the cloud spend actually real, or has there been some kind of clerical error on your end or the provider's end? Get the facts, and be clear with your manager about what they are.
- *Come up with a clear plan.* Work with your team and your manager to come up with a plan to mitigate the situation. If you can make the situation go away by reprioritizing work, then do so. If the situation cannot be changed, then focus on how you can mitigate the impact and prevent it from happening in the future. If that cloud spend is because of a service that has been sending far too many logs, then work with your team to immediately reduce the amount of logs that are being sent.
- *Execute on the plan.* Once you have a plan, execute on it. Depending on the seriousness of the situation, follow similar communication protocols to the Eye of Sauron: communicate frequently and clearly, and ensure that you are not being chased for information.
- *Retrospect after the situation is over.* Once the unpleasant surprise has passed and you are back on track, regroup with your team and your manager to understand how it will never happen again. Publish a postmortem and move on.

Three Is a Magic Number

Here we are at the end of the chapter. Building a productive relationship with your manager is *critical* to your happiness and success in a senior manager role, but as we've seen, it's not always straightforward.

Here's what we've covered:

- *We started off by exploring why your manager will likely always disappoint you.* You will have different styles, approaches, communication preferences, and views of the world, and this will always lead to friction. We saw that in order to combat this, you need to realize that you will always be promoted to a level where you experience this and that the solution is in how *you* deal with it, not how they do.

- *Next, we touched upon how there is no one-size-fits-all approach to managing upward.* This is because every manager is different, and every relationship is different. Re-using advice from others will only get you so far. Instead, we saw that you need to treat advice as tools, not prescriptions, and experiment with them to find what works for you.

- *Then, we explored how to define the relationship you want with your manager.* Building a symbiotic relationship with them is critical to your success, and we saw how to do that by understanding additive and subtractive actions and how you can do more of the former and then transform the latter.

- *We closed out by explaining how to handle situations where things go wrong.* We saw that escalations, the Eye of Sauron, and unpleasant surprises are inevitable, and we saw how to handle them in a way that is proactive and productive.

It may take time to get to a place where you and your manager are working together in a symbiotic way, but it is one of the most important things that you can do to ensure that you are happy and successful in your role. And, always remember to just talk to them about it if you are unsure. They are just another human being too.

In the next chapter, we're going to look at different parts of the org chart to understand how to form and utilize trifectas and multifectas and how to build allies, all of which will add to your ability to have an impact at scale.

CHAPTER 8

Trifectas, Multifectas, and Allies

It's a drizzly morning. You open your laptop to perform your usual ritual of reading your messages and emails with your coffee in hand. You click through them one by one, archiving them as you go.

Ah, so the latest update to analytics dashboards just shipped. That's cool. Users can now drag and drop them in the configuration they want rather than having to use preset layouts. You make a mental note to check it out in the product later. You archive the email.

Next, you read a discussion around hiring plans for product managers for next year. You're not sure why you're on this thread since you're in engineering, but you read it anyway. It seems like product management headcount is growing significantly next year in all parts of the department. You make a note to chat with Zach, who is the lead product manager for your area, to see which teams he thinks need more support. You archive the email.

Oh, and speak of the devil—the next email is from Zach himself. It's addressed to you, your UX counterpart Brian, and the executive team. The subject of the email is "Next year's roadmap." This is unexpected. You open it up and read it.

```
Hi all,

Please find attached our roadmap for next year.
It is broken down into quarters, and each quarter
has a theme. You can find the engineering estimates
attached to each item, and what each team is going
to be working on.

Let me know if you have any questions.

Best,
Zach
```

You open the attachment and feel your pulse quicken. There's enough work in here for a thousand engineers, let alone a hundred. You rub your eyes vigorously, then send Brian a message on chat.

```
[09:04] <you> hey Brian, did you see Zach's email?
[09:04] <brian> what email?
[09:05] <you> look at your inbox
[09:05] <brian> OK, hang on
[09:05] <brian> what the hell?
[09:05] <you> I think we have a problem
```

It's going to be a long day.

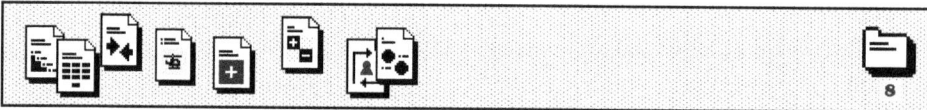

We've spent a number of chapters navigating our way around the org chart, following the lines of reporting. Everything we've covered so far has been achieved by traversing the tree of reports, peers, and managers.

However, this misses a key part of the picture: the vital cross-disciplinary relationships that get stuff done. Software companies are not just made up of engineers; it takes a whole host of different crafts to design, build, market, sell, and support a product.

Since this is the case, we are going to spend this chapter looking at ways in which you can think about these cross-disciplinary relationships, exploring how to unify them behind common group structures, which will allow you to achieve your goals together, collaboratively.

After all, the need to work closely with Product, UX, Marketing, Sales, Support, and other teams does not disappear when you become a senior manager—it becomes even *more* important. These relationships are not just a nice-to-have; they are a core part of the way innovative companies function.

Here's what we're going to be covering:

- *We'll start by looking at the concept of trifectas*, which is a group of three people from different disciplines who work together to achieve a goal—typically engineering, product, and UX. We'll look at how these trifectas are defined, how best they should work together and how, ideally, they should go all the way up the org chart to senior levels. We'll look at how trifectas can help resolve escalations and blockers, how they can negotiate and make decisions, and how they can drive up the quality of execution of their individual crafts in their teams.

- *Then, we'll look at multifectas*, which is where you add additional disciplines into the mix, such as product marketing, support, or sales. A multifecta is an extension of a trifecta that can differ in size and composition depending on the problem at hand. We'll look at different kinds of multifectas for different parts of the engineering department and how they can work together to achieve a common goal.

- *Finally, we'll look at allies*, who are people who aren't in your discipline but who you can rely on symbiotically for help and support. We'll cover the concept of the periphery and how you should be looking to build connections and relationships with people who are at the edges of the company since they offer crucial insights and perspectives you may not have considered.

Are you ready? Let's get going.

Omne Trium Perfectum

There's something special about the number three. It crops up everywhere. In stories we tell children, three is the number of wishes you get from a genie, the number of little pigs, musketeers, blind mice, the number of times you have to say "Beetlejuice" before he appears, and the number of bears that Goldilocks encounters.

In Christianity, three holds significance within the Holy Trinity, and in Hinduism, three is the number of forms of God in the Trimurti. Outside of religion, we sometimes consider our own well-being in terms of mind, body, and spirit. The number three is everywhere.

Three is also a key tenet of speechwriting. Next time you listen to a public figure, such as a politician giving a speech, listen to how they structure their points. They will often use the rule of three: sentences and ideas are grouped into triplets in order to make them more memorable. Sometimes, an election campaign is about "education, education, education," or perhaps it's about "hope, change, and progress."

And you've guessed it: the number three is also important in the world of software. It's likely that when trying to plan priorities for your team, you've had to make a decision between three options: scope, resources, and time. You can have two of the three, but not all of them.

This is often called the "iron triangle" or the "triple constraint":

- The *scope* is the amount of work that needs to be done.
- The *resources* are the people who are available to do the work.
- The *time* is the amount of time you have to do it. See the diagram on page 176.

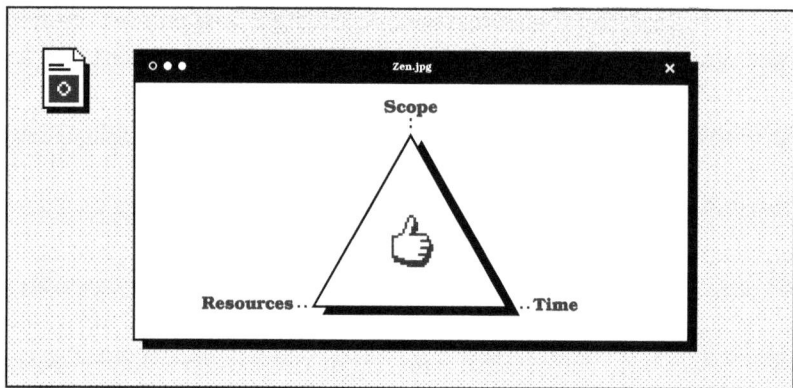

If you have a fixed scope and a fixed amount of time, then you can only change the resources. Conversely, if you have a fixed scope and a fixed amount of resources, then you can only change the time it takes to do it. Lastly, if you have a fixed amount of resources and a fixed amount of time, then you can only change the scope. There's always a trade-off; you can't have all three.

There is something immensely clarifying about this dilemma with three variables: it *forces* you to make a decision about what you're going to do and the trade-offs that you are going to make in order to achieve it. Having three variables injects just the right amount of *tension* into the decision-making process to force progress while not making it so complicated and highly multivariate that you get lost in the weeds.

Trifectas: Your Own Perfect Triplet

One of the most powerful groups that you can be part of as a senior leader is a trifecta. A trifecta is a group of three people from different disciplines who work together to achieve a goal. Typically, this is a group consisting of engineering, product, and UX.

- *Engineering* is responsible for building the product, that is, writing the lines of code that make it work.
- *Product* is responsible for defining what the product should do, that is, what features it should have and how it allows a user to achieve their goals.
- *UX* is responsible for designing how the product should work, that is, how the user interacts with it and how it looks.

With these three disciplines working together, you have a powerful combination of skills and perspectives that can create a product that is scalable, useful, and beautiful.

We often think of trifectas as being an artifact of a single front-line team rather than anything to do with senior management. For example, a team may have a product manager, a UX designer, and a number of engineers who report to a single engineering manager. The three disciplines work together to define, design, and build the product, and in doing so, they experience positive tension that helps them to make better decisions.

For example, some of these trade-offs can be:

- *Scope vs. effort.* Engineering might emphasize building robust, extensible solutions, while Product might prioritize faster delivery to validate a hypothesis of product-market fit first. The right balance will be up for debate.
- *User needs vs. technical constraints.* Product or UX may advocate for a feature that is simple to use but highly challenging to implement, while engineering may advocate for a simpler solution that is easier to build and maintain with a less-optimal user experience.
- *User education vs. product simplicity.* Product may advocate for a feature that is complex and customizable but powerful, while UX may advocate for a simpler solution that is easier to understand and use by the majority of users.

These trade-offs and debates are not bad—they are, in fact, extremely healthy. They force the team to make better decisions, and in doing so, they create a better product.

You may find that different parts of the department may have different trifecta members. For example, a platform team may have a trifecta consisting of engineering, product, and developer relations instead. Essentially, it's the core leadership of an area.

In terms of their responsibilities, a team's trifecta will:

- *Ensure strategic alignment.* The trifecta will work together to ensure that the team's work is aligned with the wider organization's strategy. They will also ensure that the team's work is aligned with the work of other teams, identifying and resolving gaps or overlaps.
- *Define the team's roadmap.* The trifecta will facilitate the idea-generation process and then work together to define the team's roadmap. This includes getting the right balance between new features, technical debt, UX improvements, and other work.
- *Make decisions.* The quality of the work outlined in the two previous bullet points is dependent on the quality of the decisions that the trifecta makes.

Daily, weekly, monthly, and quarterly, the trifecta will make decisions about what needs prioritizing, what needs to be cut, and what needs to be changed.

- *Drive up the execution of their individual crafts.* Achieving excellence in engineering, product, and UX does not happen by accident. It requires a concerted effort to ensure the team is constantly improving in each of these areas in balance with delivering the roadmap, and each member of the trifecta will represent their craft. For example, the engineering lead will have an eye for scalability, resilience, and performance, while the UX lead will have an eye for usability, accessibility, and aesthetics.

- *Resolve escalations and blockers.* The trifecta will be the first port of call for any escalations or blockers that the team encounters. They will work together to resolve these issues, and if they can't, they will escalate to the next level of management.

- *Communicate with stakeholders.* The trifecta is responsible for communicating with stakeholders, including other teams, senior management, external partners and users, and other parts of the organization. They will work together to ensure that the right information is communicated to the right people at the right time.

> **Your Turn: Do You Have Effective Trifectas?**
>
> Before we start looking at trifectas from a senior leadership perspective, let's take a moment to think about the teams that you are currently responsible for:
>
> - Do you have a trifecta for each team, that is, a clearly assigned Engineering, Product, and UX lead? If not, why, and how are you compensating for this? Are UX or Product staff split across multiple teams? If so, how are they managing their time? Is this ideal?
>
> - Do your trifectas actually know that they are part of one? Specifically, do they act like a leadership team that has jointly shared accountability for the direction of the team's work? If this is not the case, you should talk to them about formalizing their relationship. The simple act of naming them as a trifecta will help them to understand their role and responsibilities.

However, there is something important you need to consider as a senior leader: even if you have clearly defined trifectas for each of your teams, a critical bug that creeps into organizations is that healthy, collaborative trifectas are *only* found within the front-line teams and nowhere else. This is a problem, but you can fix it.

Trifectas Should Go All the Way Up

In many organizations, as you progress up the org chart, trifectas, along with their benefits, disappear.

This happens because organizations usually form their reporting lines around each discipline: engineering managers report to directors of engineering, VPs of engineering, and beyond, and the same is true for VPs of product and UX. Now, it's worth stating that there is nothing wrong with this at all. In fact, it's a great way of ensuring that each discipline has a clear career path and that each discipline has a clear voice at the senior levels of the organization.

However, it does mean that the trifecta structure and the positive tension that it brings can be lost, and senior leaders become isolated from all of the benefits of cross-functional collaboration. At best, this is a missed opportunity. At worst, it can lead to a dysfunctional organization that doesn't have home teams for its senior leaders.

Looking at the following diagram, we can see what happens when trifectas are only found within the front-line teams. Where they exist, we get the cross-functional collaboration we want, but as we move up the org chart, we lose it.

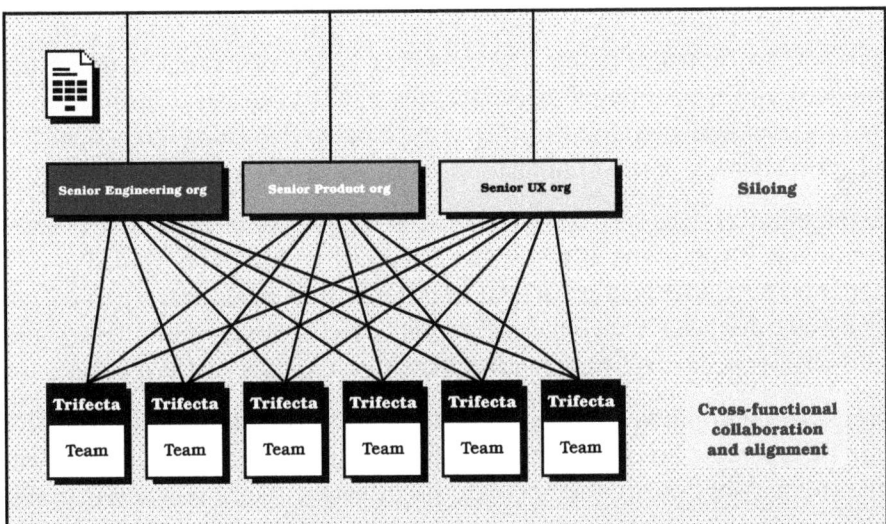

The result is that the senior leaders are isolated from each other as part of warring factions, leading to dysfunctional behavior:

- *Lack of visibility.* Senior leaders only view the world through the lens of their own discipline. They are not exposed to the perspectives of other disciplines, and as a result, they struggle to make decisions in the same unified way that the front-line trifectas do.

- *Lack of alignment.* The lack of visibility leads to a lack of alignment between the different disciplines because they are not jointly accountable as part of a trifecta. For example, senior engineering leaders may only hear that not enough technical debt is being paid down, leading to a myopic, unbalanced view of the work that is being done. This leads to increased tension and conflict between the disciplines as a whole.

- *Lack of accountability.* While each trifecta-led team is wholly accountable for the work that they do and for managing the trade-offs between the disciplines, the senior leaders are not; they are only accountable for their *own* discipline. This makes it far harder to make decisions that span the org chart. It can feel like an adversarial situation where each discipline is trying to get the best deal for themselves. This is not the behavior of senior role models—they should unite rather than divide.

- *Lack of escalation paths.* When a trifecta-led team encounters an escalation or blocker that they cannot resolve themselves, they need a route to escalate it to the next level of management. However, if the next level of management is not part of a trifecta, then the escalation path is unclear.

As such, it is in your best interest to ensure trifectas are present among the senior leadership team and middle management in the *same way* they are present in the front-line teams. Not only does this work against dysfunctional behaviors, but it also helps to ensure the senior leadership team is unified behind a common goal and they are able to make decisions aligned with the long-term strategy of the organization, not just their own discipline.

The diagram on page 181 shows what this might look like. In it, we can see the trifectas are present at all levels of the org chart. Every front-line team ladders up to a more senior trifecta, and these, in turn, ladder up to trifectas at the executive level. This means the trifecta structure is present everywhere and the benefits of cross-functional collaboration are present everywhere, too.

It is worth mentioning that this trifecta organizational structure is *not* the same as reporting lines. Therefore, it doesn't matter if the reporting lines of senior managers line up directly with the trifecta ownership structure. What matters is that the trifectas are *defined, present, and accountable* for the areas that they oversee.

For example, if a large technology company develops multiple products, each with tens of front-line teams, then you would expect to see a trifecta for each of those products that those teams work on, with all of the front-line teams laddering up to those senior trifectas. Above them would be the most senior trifecta, which would be responsible for the entire product portfolio.

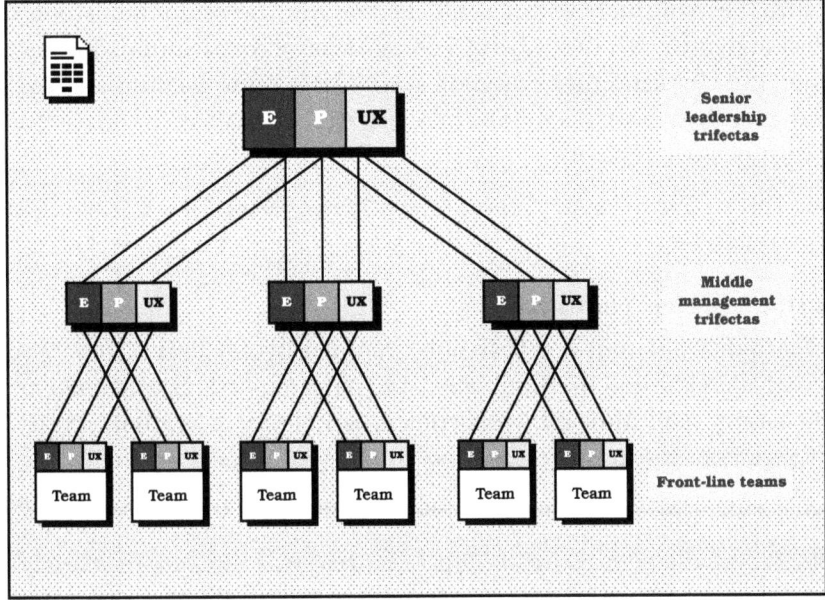

There are many benefits to having trifectas all the way up the org chart:

- *Accountability is clear.* Each trifecta is accountable for the work that it oversees, and each piece of accountable work has a clear cross-disciplinary group of owners. They vouch for the product and the company first, *not* their own discipline.

- *Positive tension is present at all levels.* Each trifecta is responsible for managing the trade-offs between the disciplines, and this positive tension is present at all levels of the org chart. This means that the decisions that are made are more likely to be balanced and well-considered in the same way that they are in the front-line teams.

- *Escalations are resolved quickly.* If a front-line team encounters an escalation or blocker that they cannot resolve themselves, they can escalate it to the trifecta that they ladder up to. If that trifecta cannot resolve it, they can escalate it further, and so on, until it reaches a trifecta that has the accountability and authority to resolve it.

- *The trifecta structure maps neatly to the roadmap and project approvals.* The trifecta structure is a natural fit for this process. Every trifecta will own its own piece of the roadmap, and senior trifectas own the roadmap for broad areas. Overlaying the escalation process on top of this means that the trifecta structure is also a natural fit for project approvals, resourcing debates, and other prioritization discussions.

Ensuring that you have trifectas all the way up the org chart is one of the simplest and most effective ways of raising accountability, improving decision-making, and ensuring that everyone is unified around a common goal while vouching for their own disciplines in a way that is healthy, constructive, and filled with positive tension.

Getting this in place doesn't even require a reorganization—it just requires a change in mindset.

Setting the Stage for Your Trifecta

Trifectas that work well together don't happen by accident. They require a concerted effort to build trust, rapport, and, most importantly, *actually* working together every day. After all, your trifecta is not just a symbolic entity; it is one of your core working groups, and you should treat it as such.

Here are some tips for setting the stage for a healthy trifecta relationship:

- *Start a private chat channel.* This is a great way of asynchronously communicating with each other and building rapport. Be proactive in starting conversations, such as highlighting updates of note, asking questions about current projects and priorities, and sharing what you're working on.

- *Consider a regular meeting.* Weekly interactions in this channel, plus each of your individual observations and experiences, should generate enough content to meet for thirty minutes every week. Again, be proactive and take control of the agenda: What blockers are the group facing? How are each of the front-line teams progressing, and what are the challenges that they are dealing with? What is going on in adjacent teams that you should all be aware of? What are the priorities for the coming week?

- *Consider office hours or regular syncs with front-line trifectas.* In order to ensure that each team has a touchpoint, you can schedule thirty-minute office hours or syncs with each of them on a regular schedule. Weekly or fortnightly is a good cadence. This is a great way of ensuring that you are aligned with the work that they are doing and that you are able to provide them with the support that they need. In order for these to work well, ask each team to come prepared with an agenda. One template to use is to ask them to come prepared with three things: what is going well, what is not going well, and what they need help with. This will help to ensure that the meetings are focused and productive and that they make the most of your collective time.

- *Develop a process for project approvals.* We want front-line teams to be autonomous, but we also want to make sure that they are working on the most important things. One way of doing this is to establish a process for project approvals. For each new block of significant work, the front-line trifecta should present a short, concise proposal to the senior trifecta. This proposal should include the problem that they are trying to solve, the entry and exit criteria, the resources that they need, and the expected, measurable outcomes. The senior trifecta should then review the proposal and either approve it or ask for changes. This process should be lightweight and not onerous. It should be a way of ensuring that the work is aligned with the strategy and that the right resources are being allocated to the right work. It injects positive tension from the top down.

- *Develop a process for reporting on progress.* In order to ensure that the senior trifecta that you are part of is able to keep track of the work that is being done, the front-line trifectas should report on progress on a regular cadence. For example, this could be a weekly or monthly written report highlighting progress against goals, what was shipped, what challenges were encountered, what's next, and what help is needed. Not only does this help the senior trifecta to keep track of the work, but it also helps the front-line trifecta to reflect on their own progress and identify areas for improvement.

Your Turn: Establish Your Senior Trifecta

Now that you've read about trifectas, it's time to think about your own.

- Do you have a trifecta that you are part of? If not, why, and how are you compensating for this? Are you working with your peers in other disciplines in a way that is healthy and constructive? If not, why?

- If you are not part of a senior trifecta, how can you make that happen? Who should be in it? If it's not clear, how can you work with your peers and your manager to make that clear?

- If you are part of a senior trifecta, how can you make it more effective? Are you meeting regularly? Are you communicating regularly? Are you aligned on the work that you are doing? Are you aligned on the strategy? If not, how can you improve this?

- Have you observed, or are you part of, trifectas that don't map well to the org chart? For example, is one member several organizational levels above or below the others? Is this an antipattern, and does it affect the decision-making ability of those involved?

Extending to Multifectas

Getting a new feature to market needs more than just a trifecta. This is especially true at the senior levels of larger organizations, where running a portfolio of products requires a *multifecta* of disciplines to work together.

When we use the term multifecta, we are referring to a trifecta plus other disciplines in an extended group. Sometimes, you might see this being called a stakeholder group.

So, in addition to engineering, product, and UX, this could include:

- *Product marketing.* Product marketing is responsible for the product's go-to-market strategy. This includes the messaging, positioning, pricing, and launch strategy.
- *Developer relations.* This is a hybrid marketing-engineering role that is responsible for building relationships with the developer community. This includes developer advocacy, developer education, and developer events.
- *Customer success.* These folks are responsible for ensuring that new and existing customers are able to get value out of using the product so that they continue to be customers for a long time. This includes onboarding, training, and management of strategic accounts.
- *Sales.* Unsurprisingly, they are responsible for selling the product to new customers and upselling additional features and functionality to existing ones. This includes prospecting, pitching, and closing deals.
- *Support.* This staff is responsible for supporting customers who are using the product and is positioned on the front line. In addition to providing technical support, they also answer common questions and resolve common issues. Being close to the customer, they are a great source of feedback.
- *Legal and compliance.* This group is responsible for ensuring that the product is compliant with the law and that the company is not exposed to unnecessary risk. This includes privacy, security, and data protection.
- *Security.* This group is responsible for ensuring that the product is secure and that the company is not exposed to unnecessary risk. This includes threat modeling, penetration testing, and incident response.

As such, the area that you run may benefit from a formally defined *multifecta*. What the shape of that multifecta looks like will depend on your organization and the work that you do. For example, if you run a feature-driven product area, then you may want to have a multifecta that includes product marketing staff who work closely alongside the trifecta to ensure that each new addition to the product is well-positioned and well-understood by the market and that releases are communicated effectively.

Conversely, if you run a platform team that provides APIs to the community to build with, then you may want to have a multifecta that includes developer relations staff who ensure that the APIs are well-documented, that there are examples and tutorials for developers to use, and that the developer community is engaged and excited about the platform. These activities can include running an online community that allows developers to get high-touch contact with the team and each other and running events such as meetups and conferences.

In practice, multifectas are not as tightly knit as trifectas. Whereas a trifecta may work together every day with a shared focus, staff in multifectas may be supporting multiple teams. For example, a product marketing function may span multiple product areas since those areas combined provide enough work for a full-time product marketer but not enough for each area to have its own.

However, what is most important is that you arrange your multifectas for sustained context: that is, you work with the same people over a long period of time. Not only does this give you the highest chance of forming relationships that have high trust and rapport, but it also means that you can build up a shared, deep understanding of the work that the organization is doing. This is especially important for developer relations. Engineers will call you out really quickly if it's clear that you don't understand the technology that you are advocating for.

With this in mind, all that we've covered in the previous section about trifectas is equally applicable to multifectas, including that they should go all the way up the org chart. Formally defining the multifectas, ensuring that those in them communicate and meet regularly, and ensuring that they are aligned on the work that they are doing is essential.

You may find in practice, however, that you do not get as much time with your multifecta as you do with your trifecta. As such, you should be mindful of this and ensure that what you need from them, and when, is made clear. For example, the most important thing that you need to give product marketing is a clear roadmap with dates so they can work ahead of time on the go-to-market strategy.

Speak to your multifecta and ask them what they need from you and when and how they would like to engage. Often, they are working on multiple projects at once, and they will need to plan their time effectively.

Snow Melts at the Periphery

Writing as the CEO of Intel, in *High Output Management [Gro95]*, Andy Grove said, "the snow melts at the periphery first." What he meant by this is that the initial signs of trouble in an organization are not at the center where engineering or management are situated but at the edges. This is because the people at the edges are the ones who are most exposed to the outside world.

The definition of the outside world could mean many things. It could mean the market, the competition, the customers, the users, the partners, the ecosystem, or the community. It's where bad reviews of your product are posted, where your customers are asking for help, and where social media threads are posted complaining about unacceptable bugs.

As you become more senior in an organization, it is easy to become isolated from the outside world. You exist with senior managers and individual contributors above, below, and by your side, and with time, you can put more energy into fixing internal problems than you do into understanding the fundamentals. This is a dangerous place to be.

As such, it is important that you make a concerted effort to be connected to the outside world. This is where your *allies* come in. An ally is someone who is not in your discipline and also not necessarily anywhere near you in the org chart but who you can rely on for opinions, insights, and perspectives that you may not have considered. They do not necessarily have to be as senior as you, either. They could be a member of the support team, a junior engineer working closely with customers, or sales staff who closely advocate for the parts of the product that you look after.

You can see a visual representation of this in the diagram on page 187. The periphery is where the outside world is, and the allies in different disciplines are the groups that are closest to it. By forming strong bonds with these groups, you increase your exposure to the outside world, and you can make better decisions as a result.

One of the reasons that start-up companies move so quickly is that they are small enough that *everyone* is building, selling, and talking to users. This superpower allows them to move quickly, make decisions, change their minds just as quickly, and see the true effect of the rubber hitting the road. Building connections with allies is one of the ways that you can retain this superpower no matter how large your organization gets.

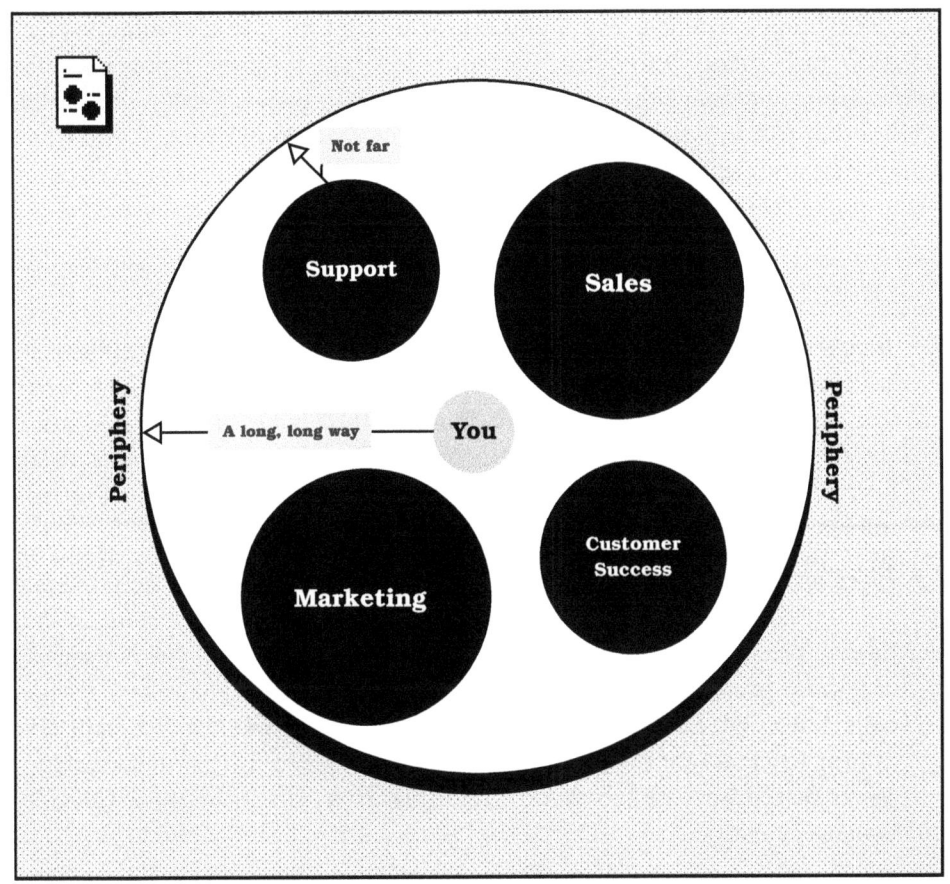

Well-Mannered Snooping

One of the best ways to begin to build connections, especially if you are new to an organization, is to do some well-mannered snooping.

A wealth of open information exists in many different places: your company's chat system, internal wikis, email lists, and more.

Identify the different parts of the organization that are close to the periphery and read what they are talking about. Join their public email lists and chat channels, and dig into the projects that they are doing. You will learn a lot about what is going on, and you will identify key people involved in the work whom you can reach out to.

In identifying your allies, you should do your best to form a symbiotic relationship with them. Otherwise, they may feel like they are being used for information and that you are not giving anything back. Without knowing, your senior role and job title may make them feel uncomfortable if you don't build trust and rapport first. Imagine what a new and inexperienced support agent might feel when the VP starts messaging them regularly: *stressful!*

As such, when building connections with folks at the periphery, you should consider reciprocating in the following ways:

- *Give them useful, actionable information.* You will know many things that they don't because of your position in the org chart. This could range from specifics of the upcoming roadmap, to the people in the organization they can connect to for help with specific questions, to better details about how to support and debug the product. Be proactive in sharing this information with them and offering up connections to others.

- *Be available to talk to customers.* Having a senior engineering presence on a customer call can be a huge boost for support or sales staff. It can help to build trust, resolve issues quickly, and show that your company cares. Be proactive in offering to join calls and be available for ad hoc calls if needed. Sometimes, just picking up the phone (or webcam) and talking to a customer can prevent weeks of back and forth and escalation. Never be too busy or too afraid to do this. It is one of the most valuable uses of your time.

- *Be a point of contact for unblocking issues.* Sometimes, engineering organizations can be structured in a way that makes it nearly impossible for small bugs, feature requests, or other issues to be raised and worked on. You can be a point of contact for these issues and devise ways for them to *not* get lost in the ether. For example, you could set aside periods of time during the year where you work to prioritize, triage, and burn down stacks of these issues and then communicate the results back to those who initially raised them. One of the most encouraging things for a member of the customer-facing organization to know is that their issue has been heard, resolved, and shipped to production. They can then deliver the good news.

- *Offer coaching and mentorship.* For less experienced staff, your experience and perspective can be invaluable. You can offer to mentor them or coach them on a particular topic. Many staff may be interested in a potential route into engineering, and you could open the door for shadowing opportunities or even secondments. Organizations have had a lot of success over the years in finding in-roads for support staff who want to become engineers and are currently working on their skills in their spare time. Often, it just takes one good connection to make it a reality.

- *Offer to be a sounding board.* Your perspective from higher up in the organization can be invaluable. You can meet occasionally to hear how things are going for them and offer advice. In doing so, you will learn a lot about what is going on at the periphery, which you can then use to inform your own decisions.

The senior levels of the org chart are not somewhere that you want to hide. Isolation, over a long period of time, will mean that you will become thoroughly out of touch with the outside world—the *real* place where the product is being sold, used, and supported. As such, you should be proactive in building connections with those at the periphery.

Some senior leaders will do *anything* to not have to talk to customers or customer-facing staff. Don't be one of them. In fact, they can be one of the strongest tools in your arsenal. There is so much to learn from them.

> **Your Turn: Identify Your Allies**
>
> Pause for a moment and think about the periphery of your company.
>
> - How would you define the periphery? Who are your existing and potential customers, and who is the closest to them? Which departments do they work in? Who runs those departments? Who is working on the front line within them?
> - Write down a list of ten people who could become close allies. What do you know about them? What do you think they could teach you? What could you offer in return? What could you do to begin to build a relationship with them?
> - Reach out to each of the people on your list and introduce yourself if you don't know them already. State your intention of wanting to understand more about their work and get closer to the periphery, and see whether they'd be open to having a conversation with you.

And Now for Something Completely Different

That now finishes our tour of the multifecta of disciplines that you are going to collaborate with. Hopefully, you are leaving this chapter excited by the possibilities of working with many more people than just your reports, peers, and manager. You can still be incredibly close to the real world despite your seniority.

Here's what we covered:

- *We looked at trifectas*, which are generally the engineering, product, and UX leaders jointly accountable for the work their team does. In addition to defining them, we covered collaboration and how they should go *all the way* up the org chart to ensure the benefits of cross-functional collaboration are present at all levels.

- *Then we expanded our definition to multifectas*, which is where additional disciplines such as product marketing, developer relations, customer success, sales, and support are added into the equation. We looked at how different multifectas can be formed for different parts of the engineering department and how they can work together to achieve a common goal.

- *Then we looked at allies*, who are people who are not in your discipline but with whom you can form a symbiotic relationship. We saw how the periphery of the organization is where the snow melts first, and therefore, it is important to build connections at the edges of the organization in order to stay informed and to ensure you are not isolated.

With that behind us, we're going to step away from the org chart and look at how you can communicate effectively as a senior manager. This is a crucial skill that you will need to master in order to be successful, and often, it is one that is overlooked in its importance. Get the kettle on for a cup of tea, and we'll see you in the next chapter.

CHAPTER 9

Communication at Scale

Bing! Ben joins the video call.

"Hey," you say, "I saw your message that you needed to talk to me. Is everything okay?"

"I'm having an absolute nightmare," Ben replies. "The platform team is refusing to merge my pull request. It's not just code changes either; they think the entire architecture is wrong."

"Okay, let's take a look," you say, and Ben shares his screen so you can see the comments. Multiple people from the team, including their director, have said that the changes can't be merged. In fact, they want the whole thing rewritten. Getting the code to this point has taken the best part of a month, and Ben is clearly frustrated.

"Okay, let's take a step back," you say. "Who did we talk to before we started this work?"

"It was someone on the platform team that was in our channel," Ben replies. "I can't remember who it was, but they said it was fine."

"And what did they say was fine?"

"We had a call and walked through the design."

"And where is the design? If we can find that, we can show the team that we did talk to someone and that they said it was okay."

"I just did a quick sketch on a shared whiteboard," says Ben. "I didn't think it was important enough to write down."

"Okay, and what about the chat logs from when we spoke to them?"

"We have a two-week retention policy on chat logs," says Ben. "They've gone."

"So we have no record of the conversation and no record of the design. That's less than ideal, isn't it?" you say.

Ben puts his head in his hands. "What a mess. Looks like we're going back to the drawing board on this one. Can you help me talk to marketing about the delay and to the rest of the team?"

"Sure," you say. "If you start a design document now, I'll get everyone on the same page. We'll get this sorted."

"Argh," says Ben. "I honestly thought that for *once* we'd have everything done on time and with no stress…"

"And how long have you worked in software now?" you ask, laughing.

No matter how talented or how brilliant you are, working in a large organization is to exist within a swirl of complexity. There are so many people, so many moving parts, and so many things that can get forgotten about, communicated poorly, or just lost somewhere between the proverbial sofa cushions.

Therefore, the larger the organization, the more important it is to be able to communicate *clearly* and *concisely*. Lack of alignment, understanding, and clarity inevitably leads to confusion, frustration, and wasted time.

One could posit that the utopian ideal for an engineer is being able to work on big, interesting, and challenging problems, spending as much time as possible doing so. No meetings, no distractions; just pure, unbridled creativity.

However, as you know, this is not what work is like. The reality is that most engineers spend a significant amount of their time communicating with others—ensuring that everyone is on the same page, that the right people are involved in the right conversations, and that the correct decisions are made. Nobody wants to rewrite their pull request at the last minute because of a misunderstanding.

Therefore, as a senior leader, one of the key aspects of your role is to use your communication skills to ensure the organization is aligned, your engineers are able to find their focus and be productive, and the organization is continually *learning*.

But what do we mean by learning? Think of a company as an organism that is evolving over time. Each day, week, and month, it faces new challenges that it must overcome in order to survive. These challenges come in many forms, from working out how to build new features to make the product better to figuring out how to hire the right people to do more of the former to dealing with threats from competitors. Each of these challenges is an opportunity for the company to learn and evolve. And if a company has mastered communication, then it can ensure that the lessons learned from each completed challenge are a scaffold on which to build the solution to the next challenge.

However, if a company has not mastered communication, then it is destined to repeat the same mistakes over and over again. There will be duplicate effort, wasted time, confusing and conflicting priorities, and a general sense of "what on earth is going on?" Learning is not possible without artifacts to learn from, and good communication is the process of creating those artifacts to keep moving forward.

This chapter is all about communication at scale, and it will level up your own communication skills and those of your team. Here's what we're going to cover:

- *We'll begin by seeing how progress is fueled by communication.* Society and humanity as a whole have come a long way, fast, since we mastered communication. We'll see how the most effective leaders are those who are able to communicate clearly and concisely and how the most effective organizations are those who are able to learn from their mistakes and progress.

- *Then, we'll lay some groundwork with patterns of communication.* These abstract patterns will be applicable to many situations and will speed up the flow of information. We'll touch upon the spectrum of synchronousness, Parkinson's Law, the importance of writing, optimizing for decision speed, recommendations, and keeping a second brain.

- *Finally, we'll construct a communications architecture that will produce artifacts that will enable your organization to learn and progress.* By revisiting the three levels of warfare, we'll see how information should be generated at the tactical level and then aggregate upward through the operational and strategic levels. All the artifacts this architecture produces will be your organization's commit log of history and will be the scaffold that supports tomorrow.

Grab your pen and paper, and let's get started.

Standing on the Shoulders of Scribbles

In Tim Urban's book, *What's Our Problem?* [Urb23], the history of civilization as we understand it is visualized as a 1000-page book. Each page of the book represents 250 years of human history. As such, the first 949 pages of the book are blank, as they represent the period of time when humans were hunter-gatherers. The remaining 51 pages represent ancient history as we know it, beginning with the Agricultural Revolution.

In fact, the last page of the book would cover the early 1770s to the early 2020s: a period of time that began with humans still discovering parts of their own planet for the first time and ending with smartphones, the Internet, and the Higgs boson. Whew! That's a lot of progress in a short amount of time.

Looking at the last page, Urban posits that the collective knowledge of society is advancing so quickly now that if you took a human from the previous 250-year page of history and magically transported them to the present day, they would be completely unable to function. They may even go mad from the shock of the change. This will only get worse for the future pages that we have yet to write. Given that so much has changed in the last 250 years, what will the next few pages of human history bring?

What is driving this increasingly rapid change? The answer is *technology*. The creation of new technologies and the application and adaptation of existing technologies to new problems is making innovation and discovery happen faster and faster. And what do we mean by "technology"? Fundamentally, it's the creation of new tools that allow us to do things we couldn't do before.

New technologies at the time of writing cover robotics, software, hardware, and AI, but in the past have included the wheel, the printing press, the steam engine, and most importantly, *writing and language*. Each new technology becomes a scaffold that allows us to stand on the shoulders of the previous technology, and in one sense, we are all standing on the shoulders of the first human who picked up a stick and drew a picture in the sand. Thanks, whoever you were.

The reason that writing and language are so important is that they allow us to communicate with each other. They allow us to share ideas, to learn, and to build further technologies on top of those that already exist. I am writing this book on my computer, which I did not build, and I am syncing my progress to a server that I have never seen (but can ping), using version control tooling that I did not write, over the Internet, which I did not create. I am standing on the shoulders of millions of people who have come before me.

This is possible because those millions of creative and inventive people have been able to create, share, and implement their plans together. This spans from the conceptual design of packets and circuits to construction workers digging up the ground to install cables. When humans communicate well, we can progress as a *collective* rather than as individuals. I can learn from you, and you can learn from me. We all prune our parts of the grand decision tree of knowledge, and we progress as a species.

The same is also true of organizations. In a way, each organization is like a mini civilization. They have their own beginnings, aims, culture, and place within the solar system of other organizations. And, just like civilizations, organizations can only progress if they are able to communicate well, innovate, discover, and learn from their mistakes.

As a senior leader, you have an important role to play in ensuring that your organization is able to progress and learn. You are the one who is able to see the bigger picture, and the needle that threads together the division of labor into a cohesive whole is *communication*. This is why communication is one of the most important skills to invest in.

When we talk about communication, we are talking about specific skills that you, your peers, and your team can learn and practice. Communication occurs in many forms, from one-to-one conversations to group meetings, decision logs, and how you write documents for yourself and others. As such, we're going to hold a lens up to communication from a variety of angles and explore how you can use it to help *your* organization progress and learn faster and more effectively.

Patterns of Communication

When we design software, we often talk about *design patterns*. A *design pattern* [GHJV95] is an abstract description of a solution to a problem that we can apply to many different situations. For example, the singleton pattern is a way of ensuring that only one instance of a class is ever created. We can then pick this pattern up off the shelf and apply it to whichever codebase, context, and language we are working in.

By widening our lens, we can see that there are common patterns in system design. For example, when designing a new system, we might think about some of the following patterns to reason about how the system will work, which, in turn, will determine how we build it:

- *Synchronous vs. asynchronous*: Does the system need to be real-time with regard to the speed at which it reads or writes data, or can it be eventually consistent? If asynchronous is acceptable, then our system may be simpler to build and operate.

- *Stateless vs. stateful*: Does the system need to remember state, or can it be stateless? Stateful systems may be more powerful, but stateless systems are often easier to maintain and scale.

- *One-to-one, one-to-many, many-to-many*: How many entities are involved in the system, and how do they communicate with each other? This is often referred to as the *fan-out* and *fan-in* of the system in data pipelines and can also determine how tables are joined in a database.

As we gain more experience writing software, we learn to recognize the situations and outcomes that these patterns are useful for, and we can apply them to our work. We can also learn to recognize when a pattern is not appropriate so we can avoid it. Some of the best engineers are able to draw upon their experience and knowledge of these patterns to turn challenging, new, and complex problems into elegant, simple, and maintainable solutions. As an engineering leader, you'll know that solid software design makes your whole organization more productive.

However, despite the fact that we recognize the importance of design patterns in software and hold ourselves and our engineers to a high standard of rigor, we often don't apply the same level of rigor to our communication. Many leaders communicate poorly, from the way that they express themselves to the patterns that they use to communicate information to their teams.

We previously mentioned that the progression of human civilization has been driven by the creation of new technologies and that documentation of these technologies and efficient communication of their ideas is what has allowed us to ever more rapidly build on the work of our ancestors. As a senior leader, you need to get serious about the way in which you communicate, and you need to learn to recognize the patterns of communication that you can apply every day. These patterns will ensure that your organization is able to progress, learn, and evolve.

The Spectrum of Synchronousness

Effective communication that allows your organization to learn, progress, and succeed, especially when globally distributed, requires a variety of different modes of communication. Specifically, as a senior leader, much more of your communication will need to cross time zones and geographies and be in a format that busy people can consume. As such, you need to shift your primary communication style from being synchronous to asynchronous.

When leading a single front-line team, much of your day-to-day leadership can be done synchronously, especially if your team is physically co-located in an office. From doing your daily stand-up to having one-to-one and team meetings to having ad hoc pairing sessions, you can communicate with your team in real time.

However, as you progress in seniority and org size, the ability to efficiently communicate synchronously becomes more difficult. This is not only true of your own organization but also of your peer group and those who are more senior than you. Even if you are all in the same office or time zone, good luck getting everyone in the same room at the same time.

You need to lean strongly into asynchronous communication. This means developing a mindset where you always think about how best you can communicate information to your team, your peers, and those senior to you in a way that allows the creation and consumption of that information to be decoupled. This means that both you and they can interact with that information in a way that is most efficient for everyone's collective pressing schedules.

A model that you can use to think about how to do this is the *spectrum of synchronousness [Sta22]*. We can use this model to categorize different modes of communication and reason about how we can best use them. We illustrate this model in the following diagram:

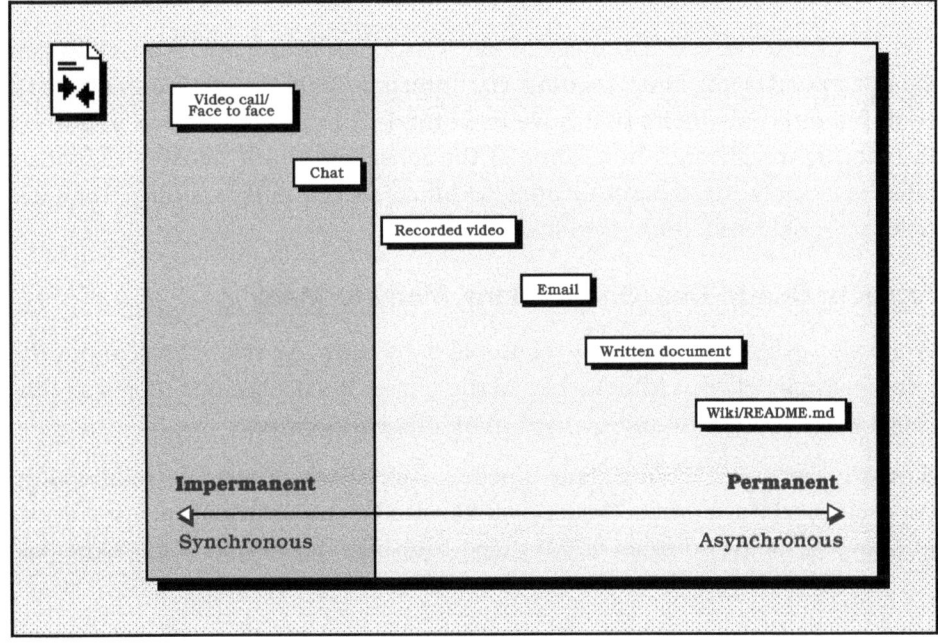

Reading the diagram from left to right, we can see common formats of day-to-day communication plotted. On the left-hand side, we have the most synchronous modes of communication, and on the right-hand side, we have the most asynchronous.

A common pitfall for leaders is that they tend to default to the left-hand side of the spectrum; in fact, many classic leadership books put a strong emphasis on the performant aspect of in-person synchronous communication. However, the reality is that the most effective leaders are those who are able to use the full spectrum and are also strongly biased toward the right-hand side. This is even more true in large technology organizations that are globally distributed.

One of the most important aspects of the middle-to-right-hand side of the spectrum is also indicated on the diagram: it is where communication is *permanent*. When you communicate asynchronously, you are creating a permanent record, whether it be an email, a document, or an entry into a wiki. This is important, as it allows you to create a scaffold of information that your organization can read, search, discover, and learn from.

Traditional, stereotypical leadership is ephemeral: it is a performance that is only witnessed by those who are present. Conversely, asynchronous-first leadership is slower, more considered, and more archival and allows you to reach more people more efficiently. It is also more inclusive, as it allows people to consume information in a way that is most accessible to them.

If you want to see real examples of asynchronous-first leadership, then you should spend some time reading the Internal Tech Emails newsletter.[1] It contains internal emails that have been made into public records and are a fascinating insight into how some of the most important matters that have affected society are communicated within organizations. Usually, they are written, considered, and asynchronous.

Artifacts: One-to-One, One-to-Many, Many-to-Many

When we design the schema of relational databases, we often think about the relationships between tables—hence the name. We design our tables so that they can be written to and queried in an efficient manner.

Similarly, when designing data pipelines, we think about the relationship between the data sources, the data sinks, and the transformations that occur in between. Some sources of data feed multiple sinks, and some sinks are

---

1. https://www.techemails.com

> **Your Turn: Shift Right**
>
> With the spectrum of synchronousness in mind, bring the following mindset to your next few days of work.
>
> - How can you approach each part of your coming day with an asynchronous-first mindset? What are you doing that could be done asynchronously?
> - What communication are you doing right now that is entirely ephemeral? How can you make it permanent?
> - Can you introduce brand-new practices to your team that are asynchronous-first? For example, can you introduce a weekly update that summarizes the week's highlights, lowlights, and what's coming up next week?
> - Are there any leaders in your organization who already practice asynchronous-first communication, which is predominantly on the right-hand side of the spectrum? How can you learn from them?

fed by multiple sources. Data fans in and fans out, and therefore, we need to think about how we can design our pipelines to be efficient and scalable.

Ensuring that we have the right relationships between where our data rests and where it is transmitted and consumed is important because it means that we can build efficient systems that are easy to maintain and scale. If the design of a database or a data pipeline is poor, then we will end up with, at best, a system that is duplicitous and inefficient and, at worst, a system that is impossible to look after.

We apply serious scrutiny to the design of these systems, ensuring that, ideally, data is never duplicated unless absolutely necessary and that the relationships and joins between different parts of the system are logical and easy to maintain throughout its lifetime.

As a senior leader, you need to apply the same level of scrutiny to the design of your communication. After all, the communication that you create and consume is the data that your organization uses to learn and progress. Artifacts such as documents, emails, and meeting notes are the scaffolds that your organization uses to build on top of, and if you communicate with little thought to the design of these artifacts, then, like a poorly designed database, your organization will be inefficient, duplicative, and difficult to maintain and scale.

If you are in an operational or strategic role, you will spend a lot of time reviewing, discussing, and generating ideas. Often, the best ideas will come when you least expect them: while you're in the shower, out for a walk at lunch, or in an offhand comment or interaction with a colleague. These ideas are the seeds of progress, and it is your job to ensure that they are captured, nurtured, and grown into something that can be used by your organization.

Looking back at the spectrum of synchronousness, we can see that the left-hand side of the spectrum is where most of these ideas will be generated, including in real time inside your own head. However, the right-hand side of the spectrum is where these ideas will be consumed. As such, you need to ensure that you are able to efficiently move ideas from the left-hand side of the spectrum to the right-hand side. Consider this diagram:

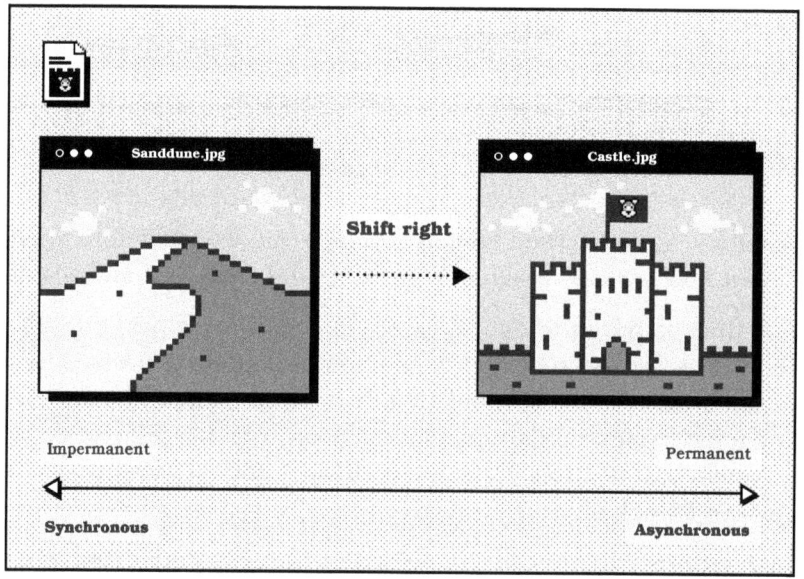

Any communication on the left-hand side of the spectrum will be impermanent; like sand, it will just blow away in the wind. Moving the communication of your organization to the right-hand side of the spectrum is like turning sand into stone: it becomes permanent, and it can be built into something strong, long-lasting, and even beautiful. Every artifact you create is a gift to the future.

We will look in more detail at how to do this in Leadership Is Writing, on page 204 and what types of artifacts you can create in The Grand Commit Log of History, on page 209, but for now, know this: no matter how good your ideas are, if you are unable to document and share them with others, then entropy will erase them, even from your own head. You need to start carving out time every day to think and write about the future of your organization, even if most of what you write is never read by anyone else. If you have a good idea about how your storage should be sharded at some point in the coming years, get it down on paper. You'll thank yourself later when you need to make that decision.

Likewise, every time you partake in a conversation, think about how you can shift it to the right-hand side of the spectrum. If you are in a meeting, can you take notes and share them with the attendees? If you are having a one-to-one, can you take charge of keeping the agenda? If you happen to have an interesting idea in a direct message, can you write it up and share it with everyone on the team? All of these actions *shift right* along the spectrum of synchronousness, and they are the building blocks of your organization's future.

Doing this is an application of the engineering mindset that you have honed over the years. If you take the time to write any pertinent information in a way that can be immediately shared with others if needed, you are creating a one-to-many relationship between that information and those who may consume it. Capture everything that you can, and have the default sharing permissions as wide as possible.

Optimizing for Decision Speed

Having an organization that habitually creates artifacts as a way of making ideas sharable, discoverable, and permanent is a great start. However, the creation of these artifacts is not the end goal: the end goal is to *make decisions*.

A decision is anything that progresses the thinking of your organization. It could be a decision to build a new feature, hire a new person, or invest in scaling a piece of your storage infrastructure. A decision may be to *not* do those things based on the information that you have. Artifacts such as design documents, interviewer feedback after an interview, and post-mortems are all examples of artifacts that are created to help make those decisions.

As a leader, you should be optimizing for *decision speed*. The faster that you can make decisions, the faster that your organization can learn and progress. However, this does not mean that you should be making all decisions quickly as a primary goal. Instead, you should be making decisions as quickly as possible *without* sacrificing the quality of the decision.

Without an important distinction, you will find yourself in a dichotomy: your teams and the organization as a whole will want to move quickly, but you will also feel the weight of responsibility to make the right decisions, thus slowing things down. The distinction that you need to use to navigate this dichotomy is the difference between *one-way doors* and *two-way doors*.

- *One-way doors* are decisions that are difficult or impossible to reverse. For example, if you decide to make a breaking change to your API that will, in turn, break all current third-party integrations, then you need to be extremely sure that it is the right thing to do. The same is true of firing decisions—it's unlikely that a member of staff is going to want to come back if you've made a mistake letting them go.

- *Two-way doors* are decisions that are easy to reverse. For example, if there is indecision on exactly how a particular chart component should look in the UI, you can always pick one choice for now, roll it out, and then change it later based on customer feedback. The world won't end if you make the wrong decision here.

In order to optimize for decision speed and correctness, you need to train your organization to adhere to the following protocol when making decisions:

- *Identify whether it is a one-way door or a two-way door.* This is a topic that you can bring to your one-to-ones with your direct reports, or you could give a short talk about it. Fed with enough examples, your team will easily be able to recognize the difference between the two.

- *If the decision is a two-way door, then it should be decided as close to the front line as possible.* This means that if one of your engineering teams is faced with a two-way door, you should empower them to autonomously choose a path forward themselves. If it's wrong, then they can change it later; either way, they move forward quickly.

- *If the decision is a one-way door, then it should be escalated to the appropriate level.* This means that if one of your engineering teams is faced with a one-way door, then they should follow the escalation protocol that we covered in Escalations, on page 166. This means that any one-way doors could go all of the way up to the CEO if needed, and that is *exactly* the right behavior. You want to ensure that the most important decisions have buy-in from the top.

For example, building on our one-way door of a breaking API change, the team should escalate this upward. One could imagine it going to the director level, where the appropriate multifecta would be involved in the decision since it would include product, engineering, product marketing, and customer success.

By having your organization follow this protocol, 90 percent of decisions will be made quickly and safely, and the remaining 10 percent that deserve higher levels of scrutiny will slow down and be carefully considered. This empowers teams to move fast and to know that leadership has their back when they need it.

Parkinson's Law: It's Real, So Use It

Parkinson's Law states that "work expands so as to fill the time available for its completion."[2] Although it is counterintuitive, you will find through practice and experience that there is a *lot* of truth to this. Projects that don't have deadlines imposed on them, even if they are self-imposed, will take a *lot* longer than they need to and may suffer from feature creep and scope bloat.

By setting challenging deadlines, you will actually get better results. It's all about manipulating the Iron Triangle of scope, resources, and time (see Omne Trium Perfectum, on page 175). You can't change one part of the triangle without affecting the others. For example, if you want to do *more* work, then you're either going to need more people or more time. It's the embodiment of the "pick two" rule: you can have it good, fast, or cheap, but you can't have all three.

Back to Parkinson's Law: without tight time constraints, the scope of a team's project will expand to fill the time available. This is just human nature. Just look at how long my clean washing sits in the basket before I actually put it away or how long those little DIY jobs around the house take to get done. With no deadline, there's no urgency, and so things just don't happen.

So, deadlines work. Now, the usual hip-shoot counter to deadlines is that "fake" deadlines lead to *poor* work being done, and look—there is *sometimes* truth to that. However, that situation occurring usually represents *poor application*, rather than issues with the methodology. Putting challenging timeboxes on projects in a *healthy* environment can lead to serious innovation and creativity. Doing the same with impossible timeboxes in a toxic environment will lead to all of the bad things that you expect.

Deadlines *really* help human beings get things done. The only way that I've written books is because I set myself a challenging, but not impossible, schedule with the publisher. This contract of *external accountability* keeps the fire going through the long slog, and it forces me to make clear-cut decisions about what to include, what to leave out, and how to manage my spare time so I make progress. The *exact* same thing is true with communication and software projects.

When you are asking people to do something, lead with a recommendation of when it should be done. Be explicit about this but open to negotiation. It's such a simple technique, but when you compound its usage over a year at a big company, you will be amazed at the difference it makes.

---

2. https://en.wikipedia.org/wiki/Parkinson%27s_law

Deadlines force a clear tempo and cadence, and fundamentally, they make things happen. A canonical example of this is sending around a survey that can be filled in *whenever* vs. one that needs to be filled in *by tomorrow*. Just by asking, you will get a much higher response rate far faster. Learn from this and apply it to your own communication.

This tempo and cadence are crucial for effective leadership. Even though you may not think people want it, and even if people *themselves* think they don't want it, knowing things need to be done by deadlines that are *just on the cusp* of the comfort zone forces real, tangible progress. If you think a prototype might take a month, why not challenge the team to see what they can deliver by the end of the week? You will be surprised, and so will they.

To get started, be aware that humans *always* underestimate what they can get done in one week. See how many teams, projects, and tasks you can inject a weekly reporting cadence into: have teams plan, execute, and report on what they've done weekly, writing up their progress in an update that is shared widely in a place that anyone can see. This discipline is energy-giving, and soon, you will find that it completely reshapes how people think about their work. Your staff will actively look forward to getting things done so they can write up and share their progress each Friday afternoon.

When wielded with grace, good intentions, and knowledge of what gets humans moving and feeling good, deadlines are a powerful tool. Parkinson's Law is *real*, and the larger your organization is, the harder you'll need to fight it. If you succeed in this fight, you can grow and still ship quickly with an org size of tens of thousands. If you don't, then one day, you'll look around and wonder why your startup turned into the software equivalent of your local DMV office.

Leadership Is Writing

Given that we have established that good communication is what allows your organization to learn and progress and that the most effective leaders are those who shift right along the spectrum of synchronousness, it follows that much of leadership is *writing*. As you progress in seniority, you will spend more and more of your time reading and writing when it comes to the most important aspects of your role.

The Paper Triangle

Writing is the most efficient way to communicate complex ideas to other people. Reading is faster than listening. Additionally, the kinds of complex ideas that you will be generating and considering are best expressed in written form for others to consume; there's simply too much to understand otherwise. Combine this with collaboration tools that allow for asynchronous commenting and discussion, and you're left with no other viable alternative for communicating complex ideas. Embrace it.

In fact, writing is actually the process of thinking.[3] When you write, you are forced to organize and structure your thoughts in a way that is logical and coherent. Often, it may take writing your ideas down to formulate them in the first place. As such, you should find as many opportunities as possible to write down your thoughts since it is one of the most efficient ways to think.

What is important to highlight is that the text that you generate while thinking is *not* the finished text that you would want to share with others. If you've ever read a proposal or design document that is muddled or incoherent, then it's likely that the author has done the writing to help themselves think but has not gone back and put on their reader's hat and edited it so that it is clear and concise for others to interface with.

Remember the following algorithm when you need to explore ideas and think through problems:

- *Write to think.* When you need to think through a problem, write it down. Don't worry about how it reads; just get your thoughts down on paper.

- *Interrogate your thoughts.* Once you have written down your thoughts, interrogate them. Ask yourself questions about what you've written, and try to find the holes in your thinking. Pretend it was written by someone else. Make it better.

- *Edit to read.* Once you've gathered your complete thoughts, go back and edit them so that they are clear and concise for others to read. *This* is the text that you will share with others.

Similar to the Iron Triangle of scope, resources, and time, we can think of this as the Paper Triangle of thinking, interrogating, and editing, except this time, you *have to do all three* to communicate effectively from your brain to others. The diagram on page 206 illustrates this.

If you iteratively follow this approach, not only will you surprise yourself at the clarity of thinking you can achieve, but you'll also be able to create artifacts that progress the thinking of your organization once you've shared them. If you produce an artifact that's poor, then it's likely you've missed one of these three steps. Keep the Paper Triangle in mind whenever you are communicating.

---

3. https://www.youtube.com/watch?v=vtIzMaLkCaM

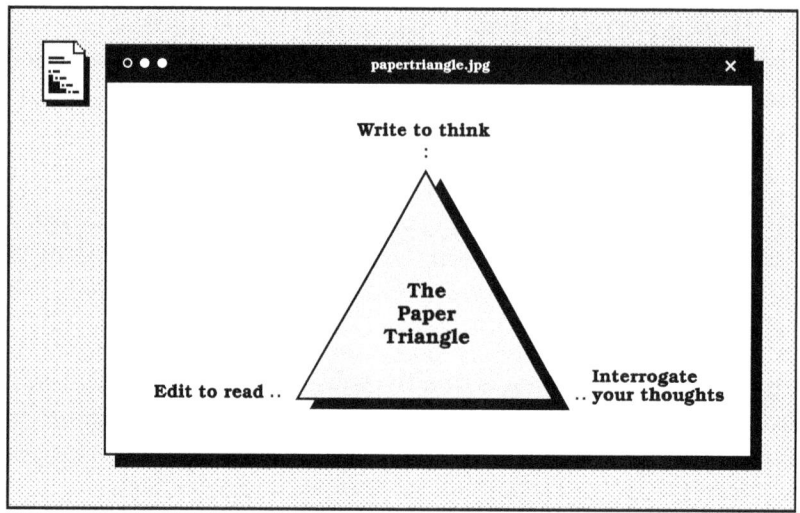

What Is Your Recommendation?

Since we're optimizing our communication to improve decision speed, we need to ensure that whatever communication we create strongly suggests where we should be going next. Oft-repeated advice is to have a "strong opinion, loosely held," which means that you should, by default, be communicating in a way that has a clear direction of travel ("We are doing this" vs. "Should we do this?"), but doing so while ensuring that you are open to changing your mind if presented with new information.

The common bug with this advice is it's often interpreted as "have a strong opinion *first*, and *then* be open to changing your mind." In the hands of the wrong people, especially those who hold senior positions, this can lead to a culture of decisions being railroaded because others are afraid to speak up.

Instead, discard the "strong opinion, loosely held" phrase and replace it with a fresher and gentler one: *what is your recommendation?* This is a phrase that you should be using in your writing and in your conversations. Ask it from yourself and others whenever they are communicating a complex idea with multiple potential outcomes.

For example, if you are reviewing a design document, then the author should ideally lead the document with a recommendation of which path to take before iterating through them all. It helps frame the complexities and cuts right to the chase. If you are in a meeting and someone is presenting a problem or seems to want you to make a decision on their behalf, then ask them what their recommendation is. It's an incredibly powerful question.

Make it a part of your team's culture to always state a recommendation when communicating ideas. Anyone can make recommendations whether or not they have the authority to make the decision. It helps with escalations, reduces the time taken to understand written artifacts that you are consuming, and, most importantly, sets the tone that *every* communication should be a recommendation that progresses the state of the organization forward.

Building Your Second Brain

Some of the most important communication that you will do is with yourself. As we've already discussed, writing is the process of thinking, and you should be writing down your thoughts as often as possible. However, aside from the artifacts that you create for others, you should also be creating artifacts for yourself.

At the senior levels of an organization, you will be dealing with a great deal of information: conversations, meetings, emails, documents, and more. Context-switching is an inevitable part of the job, so you need to ensure that you are able to capture and recall information as efficiently as possible.

The Internet is chock-full of ways for you to capture and process notes, and the most important thing is to find a system that you like using. More recently, at the time of writing, the concept of a *second brain* has become popular, and it is something that I have also had success with.

The idea of a second brain is that you have an interconnected system that allows you to capture, process, and recall information in a way that suits you. Popular second brain systems include Roam Research,[4] Notion,[5] Obsidian,[6] and Logseq.[7] You should spend some time exploring these systems and finding one that works for you.

The key to a second brain is that it is *interconnected*. Notes are created in plain text, often using a superset of Markdown, and they are linked together by simply surrounding particular words with double square brackets. When using the application, you don't need to actually create a new page for a note; you can just link to it, and the application will create it for you to write later. This means that you can create a note for anything and link it to anything else. It's a very powerful way of organizing your thoughts into a knowledge graph.

---

4. https://roamresearch.com
5. https://notion.so
6. https://obsidian.md
7. https://logseq.com

I have had the most experience with Logseq and Obsidian, which use plain text files that can be tracked in version control. This allows for easy syncing across different devices. In a similar way to the org-mode in Emacs, you can also use these applications to create a daily journal. The default home page of Logseq is an entry per day, which doubles as a to-do list.

Getting into the habit of more serious note-taking is a skill you should invest in. It can feel like a chore at first, but it'll pay dividends in the future. See whether you can keep your second-brain system open on the side of your screen all day while you work, and try to capture your thoughts when reading emails and documents and having conversations with others in meetings. You'll be surprised at how much you can capture, how much easier it'll be to understand that information as a side-effect of writing it down, and also how much you'll be able to recall in the coming weeks and months when you need it.

A second-brain system is like your own personal Paper Triangle. You are the writer and also the audience. The other neat side-effect, apart from better organization and recall, is that if your notes are good, then with only a little extra editing, you can share them with others. The second brain is the primordial soup from which further artifacts are born.

Here's a simple recipe for getting started with a second brain. We'll use the syntax of Logseq, but you can use any system that you like:

- *Create a new note each day.* This is your daily journal. Write down anything that you're thinking about, from your ideas to meeting notes. You can also use it as a to-do list.

- *Proactively create links for concepts that seem important to your context.* For example, if you are writing some notes about the API, then surround that word in square brackets, which will create a new note for it and link it in the knowledge graph. Essentially, anything that is an important noun in your knowledge domain should be a note.

- *Proactively use it as a reference.* If you think that something should exist as a note, and you look for it and it doesn't exist, create it, even if it's just a stub. That way, you can link to it and come back to it later, and your knowledge graph is growing closer to how you intuitively think about connections in your actual brain.

- *View your knowledge graph regularly.* Daily or weekly, use the graph view to look at which concepts are becoming highly connected. For example, if you did a lot of thinking on the API this week, it might be worth developing that page further with more links and more content.

It may take a number of weeks or months for your second brain to feel like home, but it is well worth the investment. You will be surprised at how much you can recall from it and how much easier it is to understand complex ideas.

> **Your Turn: Create Your Second Brain**
>
> Spend some time exploring the different second-brain systems that are available. Try to find one that works for you, and then start using it.
>
> - What kind of system works best for you? Is it a page of notes per day, or do you think in terms of projects and tasks? Do you prefer to write in a linear fashion, or do you prefer to link notes together?
> - Pick an approach and use it for a week. Be mindful to capture your thoughts as you go about your day, even if it feels unnatural at first.
> - At the end of the week, review your notes. If you are using one of the systems mentioned, you can view a graph of your notes and see how they are linked together. What can you derive from this? What can you learn about what you've been working on and thinking about?

The Grand Commit Log of History

We have established that the most effective leaders are those who are able to communicate clearly and concisely and who are able to do so in a way that allows their organization to learn and progress. We have also established that the most effective way to do this is to shift right along the spectrum of synchronousness and that writing is the most efficient way to communicate complex ideas to others.

As such, an efficient and effective organization, such as the one that we are sure you will run, will be one that has systems in place that can predictably take ideas as input and produce great software as output. These systems will be made up of people, processes, and technology, and they will be designed to ensure that the right people are involved in the right conversations and that the right decisions are made. This is something that does not happen by accident—it is a *communication architecture* that you will need to design and implement.

In a sense, over time, any organization's current state can be reasoned about as a function of the ideas, decisions, and actions that have been made in the past. If those ideas, decisions, and actions were also captured in a way that's permanent and discoverable, then we can think of them as a *commit log of history*, in the same way you have a commit log for your codebases. The communication architecture of your organization is what continually appends to it.

In this section, we'll look at an example of communication architecture and examples of the artifacts and related processes that you and your teams can create. We'll avoid being prescriptive about exactly *how* those artifacts should be structured, opting instead to focus on the *why* and the *what*. There will be plenty of links to further reading for each specific example, and you should spend some time exploring the different approaches and finding what works for you. You can then make templates available for your teams to use.

We'll use the framework of the The Three Levels of Warfare, on page 9 to categorize the different artifacts and processes. This will also help you think about who is accountable for creating and maintaining them at each level of the organization.

We'll begin at the tactical level and work our way up to the strategic. This is important because a well-designed communication architecture *propagates information upward from the front line* of the organization.

The Tactical Level

Let's start piecing together the communication artifacts and processes frontline teams should produce. We'll group these by the type of artifact that they are. In order to aid visualization, we've also illustrated them in a diagram as shown on page 211.

In order for everything else to work efficiently, you will have to decide which tools or frameworks your teams are going to use. For example, consistently using the same software to track all projects and tasks is important, as it will allow subsequent levels to aggregate and report on them. This doesn't mean paying for an expensive software subscription; it might just mean using the same templates for everything. We'll cover this in more detail in the next section.

Codebase

The codebase is the most important communication artifact that your teams will produce. It is the source of truth for the current state of the software that your organization produces. When using tools built on top of version control, such as GitHub, you also get a lot of other important communication artifacts for free, such as pull requests, issues, project management, and more. Exactly which systems you use is up to you, but you should ensure that you have a consistent approach across the organization.

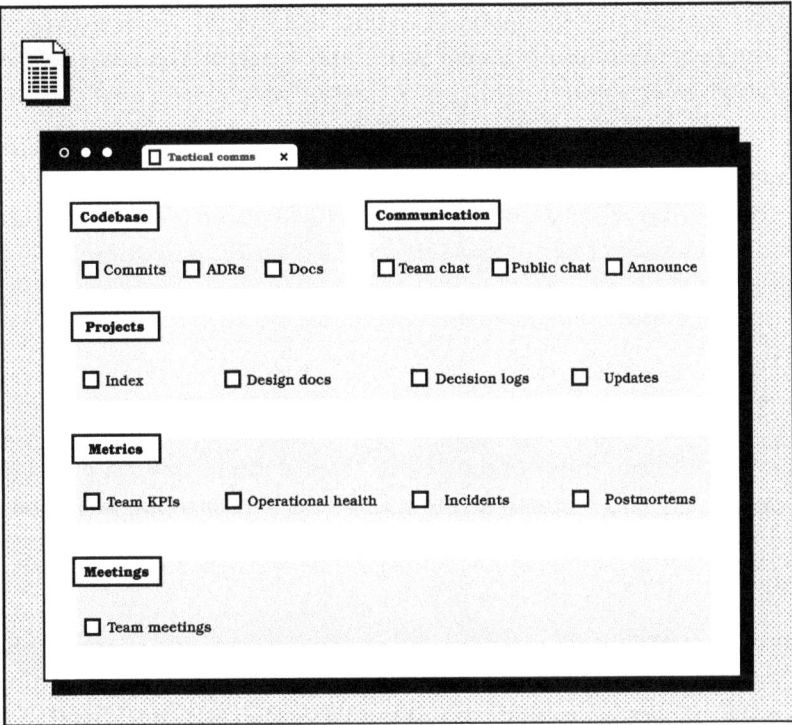

Many important communication artifacts are baked into the codebase. Notably:

- *Good commit messages.* These should be clear and concise and should be written in a way that is understandable by anyone in the organization. They should also be written in the present tense as if the commit is happening right now. This is because the commit message is the *why* of the commit, and the code is the *how*. There are detailed guides on how to write good commit messages, such as the one on the GitHub blog.[8]

- *Architecture Decision Records (ADRs).* Whenever a significant architectural decision is made, it should be captured in an ADR. This is a document that describes the decision, the context in which it was made, and the consequences of the decision. ADRs are typically kept within a dedicated folder within the codebase that they describe. This article provides a baseline template.[9]

- *Documentation.* Any documentation that is relevant to the codebase should also be kept within the codebase itself. This includes READMEs, links to

---

8. https://github.blog/2022-06-30-write-better-commits-build-better-projects/
9. https://cognitect.com/blog/2011/11/15/documenting-architecture-decisions

design documents, and more. The codebase should be the source of truth for the current state of the software, and it should be self-documenting as much as possible.

Always optimize for keeping as much information as possible *within* the codebase where you can. The code is always the source of truth, so hang as much information off of it as possible. This will make it easier for others to discover. You want your leaders to be comfortable dipping into the codebase and related tooling, not afraid of it.

Projects

At any given moment, a team will be working on one or more projects. How your organization defines a project is up to you, but typically, it should be a finite game with clear entry and exit criteria (see Finite Games, on page 110). For example, a project could be to build a new feature or to migrate a database. It should be something that can be tracked and reported on.

Each team should have the following:

- *A project container.* This is where all of the information about the project is kept. This could be a GitHub project, a JIRA project, or something else. What is important is that you should standardize the way that teams track their projects to allow for aggregated roll-ups later.

- *Statuses for their projects.* Each project should have a status that's updated regularly, reflecting the current state of affairs. This could be as simple as a traffic light system of red, yellow, or green, or it could be a finite list of phrases such as "at risk" or "on track." What is important is that the status is up to date, visible to others, and standardized across the organization.

- *Design documents.* Where needed, each project should have a design document that confirms the technical approach and has consensus recorded with others if required. It should be linked from the project container, and it should be kept up to date as the project progresses. Like commit messages, design documents should be written in a way that is understandable to anyone in the organization. For advice on how best to structure and write design documents, see this article from Google.[10] You should keep a template for design documents available for everyone to reuse.

- *Regular updates.* Every team should have a way of providing regular updates on their projects at a defined cadence. It is your choice as a

---

10. https://www.industrialempathy.com/posts/design-docs-at-google/

leader to define that cadence, but short weekly written updates of highlights, lowlights, and what's coming up next week are a good place to start. Updates can be coupled with updating the status of the project container.

Communication

Teams interface internally with themselves and also externally. Typically, each team should have the following:

- *A private team chat.* This is used for day-to-day communication.

- *A public team chat.* This is the interface that the team uses to communicate with the rest of the organization. Typically, this is an inbound channel where people from other engineering teams or departments come to ask questions or request help. There are various automation tools that can be used to help with request triage, such as Slack's Workflow Builder.[11]

- *An announcement mechanism.* This may be part of wider mailing lists or a dedicated channel. However, there should be a clear way for the team to make announcements to the rest of the organization. This could be used for broadcasting shipping announcements, notifying others of upcoming changes or outages, or sharing other important information.

For any public communication channels, you should ensure that discoverability is paramount. For example, you should have a clear naming convention for channels and ensure teams link it from within their documentation, or you could have them discoverable in a directory.

Metrics

Organization-wide metrics begin with what is being tracked within the frontline teams. As such, each team should have the following:

- *Key Performance Indicators (KPIs).* These are the metrics that the team is tracking to measure their performance. They should be clearly defined, tracked over time, and visible to the rest of the organization. Typically, KPIs are strongly linked to the output that the team is producing, such as the number of daily active users, dollars attributed to the team's work, or average session duration. We'll dive much deeper into this in Chapter 11, Strategy 101, on page 253. Fundamentally, if there are issues here, then the team is not achieving its mission.

---

11. https://slack.com/intl/en-gb/features/workflow-automation

- *Operational health metrics.* These are the metrics that the team is tracking to measure the health of their systems. Examples of these metrics include error rates, latency, uptime, and more. We'll also dive deeper into this in a later chapter. If there are issues here, then the team is not succeeding at producing scalable, efficient, and reliable systems.

- *Logs of incidents and post-mortems.* When things go wrong, the team should be capturing the incident and the post-mortem in a standardized way. You can find an index of templates as a good starting point.[12] You should choose a template for your organization and ensure that it is used consistently.

Meetings

Lastly, each team will have a variety of meetings that they attend. However, meetings are expensive, so you should ensure they are used sparingly and they are as efficient as possible. As such, it is not recommended to force each of your frontline teams to have particular meetings but instead to allow them to decide which meetings to create and attend for themselves.

In terms of a contract with the rest of the organization, if all of the tactical communication architecture is in place and functioning correctly (the team is providing regular updates on their projects, is shipping regularly, and is running stable systems), then they are free to have as little or as many meetings as they please.

Meetings themselves *do not* roll up to the next level of the organization, but the *artifacts*, from designs to code to documents that they produce, *do*.

The Operational Level

Next, we'll look at the operational level. We'll begin to see how the artifacts and processes that we've covered at the tactical level roll-up. Ownership of these artifacts and processes will typically be at the director level in a larger organization. As before, we have illustrated them in a diagram as shown on page 215, and we'll group them by the type of artifact that they are.

We have excluded the codebase grouping from the tactical level. Depending on whether you have a monorepo or a polyrepo, you may have one or many codebases. The larger the monolith, the more steer that will need to come from higher levels of the organization; what kind of steer has already been covered in the previous section.

---

12. https://github.com/dastergon/postmortem-templates

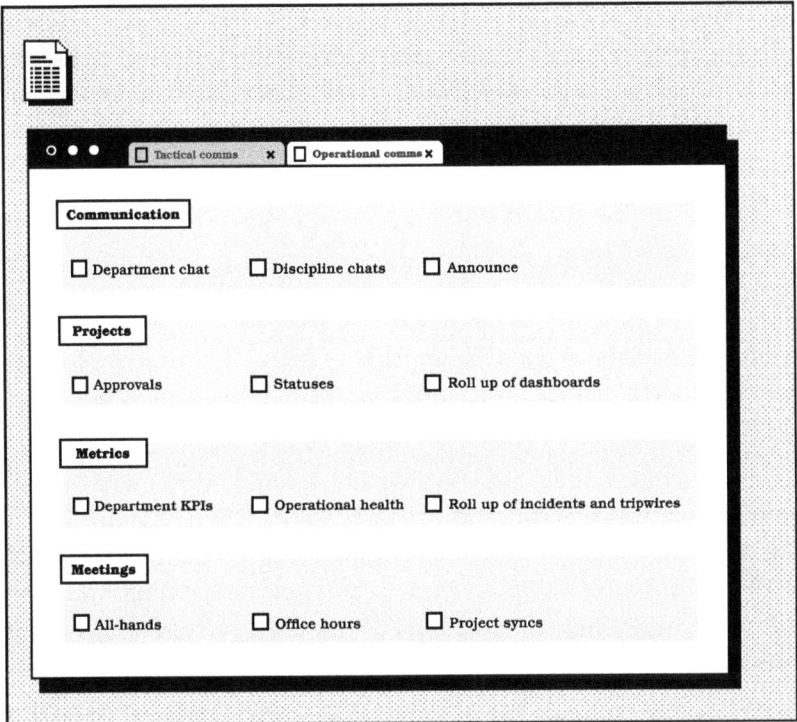

Communication

Typically, the operational level in an organization is grouped around some specific part of the system, such as a product, group of products, or functional unit. As such, each operational grouping should have the following:

- *Public department chat.* This is the interface that the operational grouping uses to communicate with the rest of the organization. Similar to public channels for frontline teams, this is where people from other engineering teams or departments come to ask questions or request help.

- *An optional private department chat.* However, given that frontline teams have their own private chats, these aren't always used or needed.

- *An internal announcement mechanism.* This is so the operational leadership can broadcast important messages, such as information on upcoming changes, outages, or other information that needs to be shared.

- *An external announcement mechanism.* Again, similar to frontline teams, this is for announcements that are relevant to the rest of the organization, but this may roll up into the announcement mechanism of the next level of the organization.

- *Discipline-specific private chats.* Often, it is useful and also builds trust and rapport for leaders of disciplines, or even whole disciplines, to have their own private chat. For example, engineering managers or product managers may have one where they can talk with their peers in confidence and share information.

As before, ensure that public channels are discoverable and that there is a clear naming convention.

Projects

This is where we begin to reap the benefits of using the same project tracking and reporting mechanisms across the organization. Each operational grouping should have the following:

- *Roll-up dashboards.* By aggregating the project containers of the front-line teams, you can create roll-up dashboards that show the status of all projects within the operational grouping. This is useful for reporting and for identifying where help is needed. You can review this information as leaders on a regular cadence and use it both to report upward and to focus your attention on where it is needed.

- *Clearly visible statuses.* At a glance, the status of each project should be clear. This is why it is important to standardize the statuses that are used across the organization. By sorting and filtering, operational leaders should be able to quickly identify what is on track, what is at risk, and why.

- *Approval information.* If you have designed a process for approving projects before they begin or before they transition from phase to phase, this information should be clearly visible. Again, this is so that operational leaders can identify where they need to focus their attention so the organization can keep moving.

For operational leadership, roll-up dashboards are one of the most important artifacts derived from the front-line teams. They are the source of truth for the current state of the world, and they also represent the interface between the tactical and the strategic levels of the organization. Always invest in making these as effective and useful as possible, even if it means dedicating some resources to building custom tooling.

Metrics

Similar to project roll-ups, operational leadership should be able to roll up the metrics of the frontline teams. This is also facilitated by using the same metrics-tracking mechanisms across the organization. Each operational grouping should have the following:

- *Department KPIs.* We will touch upon strategy in a later chapter, but good department KPIs are typically a roll-up of a subset of the KPIs from the frontline teams. Operational leadership should be able to see at a glance how the department is performing, and similar to project statuses, they should be able to sort and filter to identify where they need to focus their attention.

- *Operational health.* For the suite of software, services, and systems that the operational grouping is responsible for, there should be a roll-up of the operational health metrics. If the operational layer's systems were a company in their own right, what would the board of directors be looking at? This is what operational leadership should be invested in tracking. Like before, much of this can be derived from aggregating the metrics of the frontline teams.

- *Roll-up of incidents and post-mortems.* As before, the operational leadership should be able to see a roll-up of the incidents and post-mortems of the frontline teams. This gives them a view into which parts of the system are most fragile and can be used to identify where there is under or overinvestment in reliability moving forward.

The metrics roll-ups combined with the project roll-ups form great discussion points for operational leadership each week.

Meetings

At the operational level, there are some wider meetings that are useful since they uniquely facilitate unblocking or help inform the rest of the organization. For example, each operational grouping could have the following:

- *A regular all-hands.* This is usually a synchronous meeting where the operational leadership can get everyone together and celebrate achievements, review progress, and share information. It's also a great opportunity to invite guest speakers from other parts of the organization to share information. All-hands are expensive to run, so you should ensure that they are used sparingly—maybe once per month or quarter.

- *Office hours.* Having operational leadership available for office hours via bookable calendar slots is a great way to unblock teams on the ground. For example, teams may want to get ad hoc feedback or advice on a project, or they may want to discuss whether to escalate a decision. A few hours a week of office hours goes a long way to keep everything moving.

- *Project syncs.* As projects move through different transitions (from proposals to prototypes to build), it may be necessary or desirable to have the team go through a project sync with operational leadership. This is a great way to ensure that the project is on track and to identify any blockers or issues that need to be resolved so that there are no surprises later. These should be opt-in for the teams, as not all projects will need them.

The Strategic Level

Lastly, we will look at the strategic level. We will take the same approach as before, grouping the artifacts and processes. For subsequent roll-ups of the operational level, we will avoid duplicating explanations that have already been covered, opting for brevity instead.

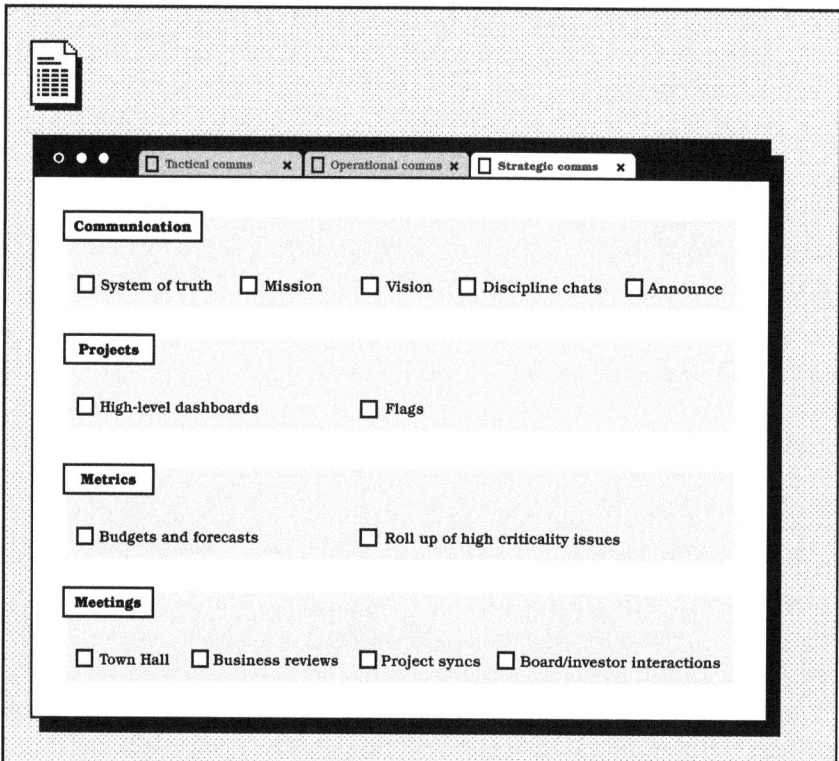

Communication

One unique aspect of the strategic level is that they typically own the tools and mechanisms as well as being users of them. As such, the strategic level should have the following:

- *Ownership of the system of truth.* Whatever systems are in place for storing and sharing information, the strategic level owns them. What this means is that clear decisions should be made about what tools are used and how. This means, for example, deciding to use GitHub for code, Slack for chat, and an internal wiki for documentation. It also means deciding how those tools are used, such as how to structure repositories, how to name channels, and how to structure documentation. The strategic level should also be responsible for ensuring that the tools are fit for purpose and that they are maintained and improved over time. They should also decide through delegation on the permissions and access levels for each tool.

- *The vision.* The vision is the future state of the organization; it's where it's going. The strategic level should own or contribute to the vision, and they should ensure it's clearly communicated to the rest of the organization. Linked to the previous bullet point on ownership of the system of truth, the mission should be clearly documented and discoverable. Consideration should be given to how the mission can be front and center in everything that the organization does.

- *The mission.* The mission is the iterative process of discovering the path to make the vision a reality. Whereas the vision stays relatively constant, the mission is constantly changing as the organization learns and progresses. As such, leadership should decide how to embed the mission into all other relevant artifacts and processes. One approach is to review and update the mission on a regular cadence, such as yearly, and cascade this outward. Previous versions can be versioned and archived.

- *Discipline leadership chats.* Similar to the operational level, it is useful for leaders of disciplines to have their own private chats for distributing information and building trust and rapport.

- *Announcement mechanisms.* Likewise, company-wide announcement mechanisms should be defined here.

Projects

The strategic level will have a broad view of everything that is going on in the organization. As such, they should have the following:

- *High-level dashboards* that roll up the projects of the operational groupings. The granularity of these dashboards will depend on the size of the organization, but they should be able to see at a glance the status of all projects, and they should be able to sort and filter.

- *Flags* for projects that are at risk or need attention. Executives have limited time, so they should be able to quickly identify where they need to focus their attention.

The strategic level should decide on the cadence of reviewing the high-level dashboards and flags. Doing so effectively typically will require support from dedicated staff to aggregate, summarize, and action follow-ups, such as facilitating deep dives, escalations, or requesting more information.

Metrics

Further roll-ups from the operational level build the picture here, plus a stricter focus on financials. The strategic level should have the following:

- *Company or department-wide KPIs.* These are the metrics the strategic level is tracking to measure the performance of the organization. They should be clearly defined, tracked over time, and, ideally, visible to the rest of the organization.

- *Budgets and forecasts.* Here, rolling forecasts of variables such as headcount, revenue, and costs should be tracked. Modeling these variables over time allows for better present-day decisions to be made. Typically, these artifacts are private to the strategic level, but they may be summarized and shared where relevant (progress against cloud spend, headcount, and so on).

- *Roll-ups of high-criticality issues.* These are taken from the operational level, mixed with any other escalations from other parts of the business (VIP customers, customer success, support, and so on). The strategic level often will need to be involved in resolving these issues by speaking to customers directly, so they should be able to quickly identify the most pressing issues.

Meetings

You can't escape meetings at this level. The strategic level should have the following:

- *Town halls.* These are regular company all-hands meetings that you've likely experienced before. Used sparingly and seriously, they are a great way to communicate the vision and mission, celebrate achievements, and share information. Ownership of the schedule and content of town halls should be decided here. At larger organizations, doing town halls well can be a full-time job curating content and internal and external speakers.

- *Regular business reviews.* For each operational grouping, there should be a regular business review where the strategic level can review the state of the business. A typical cadence is quarterly. We'll look more closely at templates for running these sessions in Chapter 11, Strategy 101, on page 253.

- *Project syncs.* Some projects may require approval or guidance all the way from the top, so the strategic level should be available for project syncs where needed.

- *Board or investor interactions.* The strategic level forms the interface between the organization, the board, and investors. As such, they should be available for regular interactions, such as board meetings, investor updates, and more.

We've now reached the top of the communication architecture. Yes, it's involved, but it's also necessary to bring order to what can become increasingly chaotic as the organization grows. The key is to ensure that the artifacts and processes that you put in place are the minimum viable set that generates the commit log of history that you need to progress the organization forward. What you choose to put in place will depend on the size of your organization, but the principles remain the same: it all starts with the front-line teams and succeeds through aggregation upward. Implemented well, your organization will progress faster and leave an audit trail of how it is doing so.

> **Your Turn: Design Your Commit Log**
>
> Spend some time thinking about the artifacts and processes that your organization currently generates from its communication architecture.
>
> - Is ownership of each of these artifacts and processes clear? If not, who should own them based on the framework that we've covered?
> - What is missing? What artifacts and processes do you need to put in place to ensure that your organization is progressing efficiently and effectively?
> - If you had to rip everything out and design the communication architecture from scratch, what would it look like? What would you keep, and what would you change?

And Now for Our Favorite Parts of the Job

We've covered a *lot* in this chapter. It turns out that communication is important and complex and requires you to design the right architectures to enable it. However, it is also one of the most rewarding parts of the job. As a leader, you are in a unique position to help others learn and progress and to help your organization achieve its mission. Here's what we've covered:

- *We started by seeing that communication enables progress everywhere.* We saw how rapidly humanity and society have progressed over the last few hundred years and how communication has been the catalyst for that. We also saw how the same principles apply to organizations and how the most effective leaders are those who are able to communicate clearly and concisely.

- *Then, we laid some groundwork with patterns of communication.* We covered the spectrum of synchronousness and how the most effective leaders are those who shift to the right along it, enabling them to have their messages heard far and wide. We saw how leadership is writing, how to optimize for decision speed, how to take advantage of Parkinson's Law, how to use recommendations to drive progress, and how keeping a second brain can help you organize your thoughts and practice your craft.

- *We finished by looking at designing a communication architecture.* This is a series of processes and frameworks that go from the tactical to the strategic, enable efficient communication, and generate artifacts that can be used to progress the organization forward. We saw how the commit log of history that comes out of this is the scaffold that new ideas are built upon. We finished by having you consider what your organization currently produces and what you would change if you had to start from scratch.

For the final chapter in this part of the book, we're going to be doing a deep dive into performance management. Although it is one of the areas that can be fraught with difficulty, it is also incredibly rewarding and can send your staff and yourself to new heights. See you there.

CHAPTER 10

Performance Management: Raising the Bar

It's another cold morning. Why doesn't the heating seem to work in this room? Never mind. Coffee in hand, you open up your email to see what's in there. To your surprise, there's an email from the CEO. You open it up and read it.

> Hey,
>
> I talked to Lisa yesterday, and I think that our process for doing performance management in engineering, and maybe even the whole company, could use a revamp.
>
> She was telling me you had a lot of ideas about this, so I think we should start working together with HR to figure out how we can overhaul it in time for the next performance cycle, which begins next month.
>
> I've put some time in your calendar later today with Lisa and the head of HR. If you can prepare a one-pager on your ideas ahead of time, that would be great.
>
> Corie

Okay, so this wasn't exactly how you were expecting to spend your time today. What was Lisa saying with regard to your ideas? What even *were* your ideas? You think back to the last few weeks, and you can't remember saying anything specific about performance management. You must have said something, though, right? Never mind. You can see the meeting in your calendar. It's in two hours, so you'd better get started.

You open up a new document and write the title, "Performance Management: Raising the Bar." You stare at the blank page. You make a new bullet point. It's blank. You stare at it again. You type, "The most important part of performance management is ensuring that it is fair, transparent, and consistent." You stare at it again. You delete it. You retype it. Isn't this just obvious? Hmm.

You take a sip of your coffee and stretch. It's going to be a long two hours.

When becoming a manager for the first time, one of the most daunting new responsibilities is performance management. You can no longer get frustrated if somebody on your team isn't pulling their weight—now it's your problem to fix!

Typically, first-time managers are well supported in navigating this new responsibility. For example, companies often provide training and guidance on how to do it within the system that they have in place. Generally speaking, staff will receive performance reviews one or more times a year and will often be given a rating that feeds into their career progression and compensation increases. In this system, if someone is identified as not performing, guidelines will be followed for how to put them on a performance improvement plan (PIP), which results in them either improving or being exited. None of this process is particularly innovative or new. It's likely that you've experienced various flavors of it at every company you've worked at.

However, as a senior leader, there are a number of *new* challenges that you will face when it comes to performance management. These new challenges are what we are going to cover in this chapter. Some of these are because you are managing increasingly senior staff along with a large organization, and others are because you are now responsible for ensuring that the performance management system is working as intended.

Here's what we are going to cover in this chapter:

- *We'll take a whistle-stop tour of performance management*, recap some of the broad themes, and focus on how larger technology organizations do it.

- *Then, we'll zero in on the performance management of senior staff* and investigate how to build a complete picture of their impact. We'll expand on this to look more broadly at how you could design a performance framework for your whole team, department, or company.

- *Next, we'll look at the calibration process*, which is how large organizations attempt to ensure that performance management is fair and consistent across the entire org chart.

- *Finally, we'll look at some common performance management issues and how to debug them*, including how to deal with brilliant jerks, job title inflation, and how to avoid being held hostage by what someone wants.

This might be one of the most important chapters in the whole book because *you* are responsible for how your organization performs, regardless of how many tens, hundreds, or thousands of people are in it. It's a big responsibility.

The Rising Tide: Why We're Doing This

To understand more deeply why performance management is so important, let's revisit some of the broader themes that we've covered earlier in the book. In Chapter 3, Time: Observed, Spent, and Allocated, on page 55, we looked at the concept of *longtermism*, which is a lens that we should hold up to everything that we do, allowing us to ask ourselves whether we are acting altruistically toward the future, even if it means sacrificing some short-term gains.

Additionally, in Chapter 9, Communication at Scale, on page 191, we considered that the speed of progression of society is an ever-accelerating function based on the ability to continually build upon the work of those who came before us. We saw that organizations that are able to continually *learn* become better, smarter, and more effective in the long run and that this is a key competitive advantage that senior leadership should focus on.

The philosophy behind performance management is extremely similar: we expect everyone in the organization to continually improve, and we want to ensure that we have a system in place that allows us to keep raising the bar higher and higher over time. Similar to how in the previous chapter we noted that a human transported from 250 years ago to today would not be able to comprehend the world around them, the same is true of our company: we want the collective capability of our organization to advance rapidly under our leadership. General Electric was founded in 1892 and is still a Fortune 500 company today. Employees from 1892 would not be able to comprehend what current-day employees do, which is a function of this ever-increasing bar of capability and performance.

As a senior leader, you are responsible for the *positioning* of the performance bar and for ensuring that it is continually raised over time in such a way that you are able to attract and retain the best talent. The bar last year is lower than the bar this year because this year's bar is a function of the bar of last year, plus the collective learning and improvement since that time.

This is a key insight because without continually raising the bar, your organization will stagnate. Performance management isn't primarily about checking that everyone is doing okay, nor is it primarily about ensuring that everyone is fairly compensated (although these are second-order effects). It's about ensuring that your organization is getting better every week, month, and year.

A good performance management system typically encompasses the following elements:

- *A clear definition of what good performance looks like*, which is usually a set of competencies expected of everyone in the organization. It's likely you're familiar with these concepts already. We covered this earlier in the book in Chapter 1, VP, Director, What?, on page 3, and there is also a deep dive on defining a career ladder in *the previous book [Sta20]*.

- *A regular performance review process*, which is typically done once or twice a year. This is comprised of numerous parts, which we'll look at in the next section, but commonly includes a self-assessment, a manager assessment, and a peer feedback process that results in a rating.

- *A calibration process*, which is a way of ensuring that the performance management system is fair and consistent across the entire organization. We'll cover that later in this chapter.

- *A PIP process*, which is a way of ensuring people who aren't performing well are given the opportunity to improve or are exited from the company.

- *A compensation process*, which rolls up the performance management process outcome into opportunities for pay increases. This is generally done once or twice a year and is often done in conjunction with the performance review process. The idea is that your best performers have the greatest opportunity for the largest compensation increases, and your worst performers have the least. This provides incentives for people to perform well and also provides a way of ensuring that your best performers are retained.

This is a lot of work, and ownership of the whole process may sit within your HR function. However, as a senior leader, you are responsible for ensuring that this process is working well, that you are leveraging it to its full potential, and that you are working with the owners of the process to iteratively improve it. With time, the effects of good performance management will compound, as you can see in the graph on page 227.

What does this mean? It means that:

- An effective performance management system, applied consistently, *positively compounds whole company performance over time*. Similar to how humanity's capabilities are accelerating through ever-improving technology and communication, so too will the capabilities of your organization.

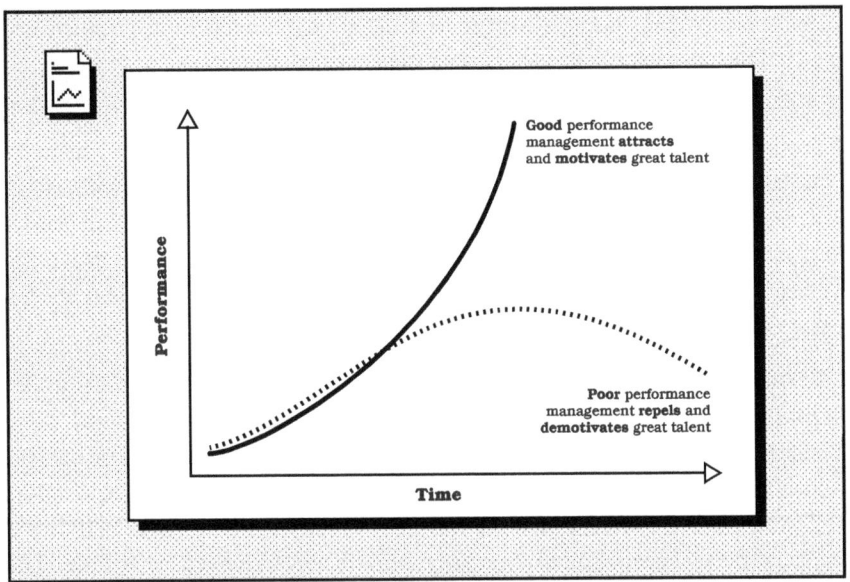

You will attract and retain the best talent, which will result in you outperforming your competitors, which allows you to attract and retain the best talent, and so on, in a *virtuous* cycle.

• A poor or non-existent performance management system, applied badly, *negatively compounds whole company performance over time.* This is because your best performers will leave, and your worst performers will stay and stagnate. You will not be able to attract the best talent because they would rather work at companies that are filled with other people who are performing well. This is a *vicious* cycle.

To apply a video game analogy, your performance management system is the company's *power curve*. The term power curve is used to describe the rate at which the various elements of a game improve over time, such as the power of the player, the power of the enemies, and the power of the items and equipment.

For massively multiplayer online games like World of Warcraft, which has been around for decades, the power curve is continually increasing, and the game is getting harder and harder at the highest level of content. Players who have been playing for a long time have invested in their characters and have obtained the best equipment, and are therefore able to take on the biggest challenges. Players who tried the game for a few months in 2005 and then stopped playing will find that if they log in today, the high end of the game is now unrecognizable: they simply do not have the skills or equipment to compete. The power curve has moved on without them.

So, performance management isn't just about getting some administrative stuff done a few times a year; it's actually critical to the long-term health of your organization. You set the power curve in a way that ensures everyone is continually improving and that new players want to come and join your game. For players who aren't up to the challenge, you invest in more opportunities for them to improve, and if they don't, it's probably best if they go and play something else.

This chapter does not intend to be an in-depth description of every aspect of performance management, along with templates and guides. Instead, we want to use this chapter to highlight the key considerations and new processes and experiences around performance management at the senior leadership level. If you *are* interested in the former, however, there are over one hundred pages dedicated to performance management culture in Scaling People. [Hug23]

> **Your Turn: Audit Your Current Performance Framework**
>
> Before we go further, take a step back and think about the performance management process that you have at your company.
>
> - Looking at the previous list of performance framework elements such as reviews, calibration, PIPs, and links to compensation, what do you have in place today? What is missing?
>
> - How effective is your company at rewarding and retaining your best performers? How effective is your company at exiting your worst performers? If either is lacking, why do you think that is?
>
> - How effective is your company at ensuring that your performance management system is fair and consistent across the entire organization? Do some managers have a reputation for being too harsh or too lenient? Is anything done about this? Are there checks and balances?
>
> - What are some of the common gripes that occur around performance review time? For example, is it too much work in too short a time? Do managers need to produce lots of evidence and documentation? What are some of the ways that the process could be streamlined?

Performance Management of Senior Staff

As a senior leader, it's likely that you've spent a lot of time in less senior roles applying performance management practices to staff who are on the front line. Once you've done this a few times, it becomes just another part of managing people.

However, the new challenge that you face as you work your way up the org chart is how to effectively performance manage your managers and your most senior individual contributors. These are people who are further from the peripheral work of the organization, and therefore, it can be harder to get a clear, unified sense of how they are performing. For similar reasons, it can be harder to give them tangible, actionable feedback that will help them improve in line with the power curve.

Back in It's All Just Leadership After All, on page 103, we saw how progression into the most senior positions in engineering, both in management and in individual contribution, have more in common than we might think. Rather than being totally separate career paths, they are actually two sides of the same coin: they are *leadership* positions that produce *similar outputs through different implementations*.

Given that this is the case, your performance management focus around your senior staff needs to center around *measuring the output of their leadership*. This is a subtle but important distinction: you are not solely measuring their individual contribution, but rather, you are measuring their observed aggregate impact.

In *High Output Management [Gro95]*, Andy Grove describes the output of a manager as being the output of their organization plus the output of the neighboring organizations under their influence. This is also true of senior individual contributors, whose organization is defined as the set of people who they are influencing through their applied craft: that is, the services, teams, codebases, and processes that they are responsible for.

But how exactly do we measure the output? Well, assuming that we have a well-structured performance framework, we can piece together a picture of the output of a manager or senior individual contributor by looking at the following:

- *Self-assessment*, which is a way for the person to reflect on their own performance and to identify areas for improvement. In Brag Docs: The Greatest Gift You'll Ever Receive, on page 102, we showed how your staff keeping their own records throughout the year can be an efficient way of producing self-assessments.

- *360 feedback*, which is a way for the person to receive feedback from their peers and those above and below them in the org chart.

- *Metrics or Key Performance Indicators (KPIs)* that show the tangible output of their work. If the performance or resiliency of the system is improving, or if they have shipped key features that positively affect the organization's KPIs, then this is undeniable evidence of their impact.

- *Your own observations*, which is a way for you to provide feedback based on your own experience of working with them. This is the most subjective of the four, and therefore, it's important that you have a way of backing up your observations with evidence by using the content from the other three bullet points.

These four aspects form a holistic picture of a senior staff member's performance, and we've visualized them in the following diagram:

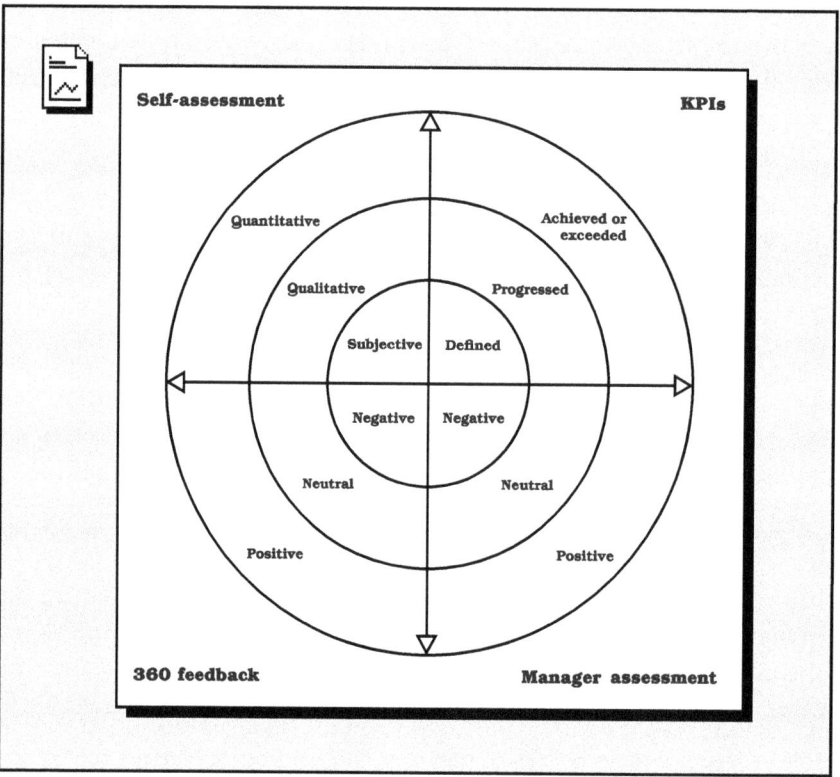

Each quarter of the circle represents each of the dimensions of their performance. The further you move from the center, the better the performance is in that dimension. We can measure against these in order to get a holistic picture of how someone is performing, highlighting areas for improvement and also areas of strength.

Let's take a look at each of these in turn.

Self-Assessment

Self-assessment is a way for the person to reflect on their own performance, highlighting what they believe they have done well and what they believe they could improve on. The three increasingly desirable levels of self-assessment, starting at the bottom, are:

- *Subjective.* This is where a person is analyzing their own performance based on their own opinion and feeling. Since this is inward-looking, it's not representative of how you want your senior staff to be thinking. Ideally, they should be aligned with broad organizational impact. However, it's a good starting point, and you can use this as a way of coaching them to think about their impact in a more objective way.

- *Qualitative.* This is where a person is analyzing their own performance based on qualitative evidence. For example, they might say they've been a good manager because they've been able to retain their staff or have them perform well, or they might say they've been a good individual contributor because they've been able to ship a key feature or keep the system running smoothly. This highlights an increased level of self-awareness about their impact on the organization but is lacking in quantitative evidence. Coaching someone from here to the next level is about helping them to think about measurement.

- *Quantitative.* This is the ideal level of self-assessment, where a person is able to provide quantitative evidence of their impact on the organization. For example, an individual contributor might be able to show that they have improved the throughput of the system by 20 percent, or a manager might be able to show that the features their team worked on have increased annual revenue by 9 percent and monthly user retention by 22 percent. When your staff self-assess quantitatively, you know that they are thinking about their impact in the right way for their level.

Quantitative Self-Assessment Through Brag Docs

Throwing together a cohesive quantitative self-assessment at the end of a performance period can be a lot of work, and it's easy to miss things or simply not have time to do it.

A solution is to use a tool that we already covered earlier in the book: brag docs. Have your staff keep daily or weekly digests of what they have been working on and what effect it has had, with clear evidence. That way, rolling this up a few times a year becomes a breeze.

Think about how your company does self-assessment today and see how it lines up with the shift toward qualitative measurement. If the process itself lacks guidance on how to make self-assessment data-driven, then you should consider adding this in and providing training and examples.

KPIs

Next up, we have KPIs, which shouldn't need specific self-assessment or management assessment; they should speak for themselves. There are three increasingly desirable levels of KPIs, starting at the bottom:

- *Defined.* A baseline assumption is senior staff should have, at the very least, *some* KPIs that are defined for their role. For example, a manager may be accountable for their team's KPIs, such as a product's revenue, daily active users, or system uptime. A senior individual contributor will likely contribute into the same technical KPIs for their team and may also have additional metrics that they are tracking, such as the number of outages or various additional performance metrics, such as page load time or latency. If someone doesn't have any KPIs defined, then this is the first thing that you should work on with them.

- *Progressed.* The next level is where someone is able to show that they have made progress on their KPIs for the period but may not have achieved them. The fact that the KPIs exist is key since they are able to see which areas are getting better (or worse!), and you can work on them together to create a plan to improve them.

- *Achieved or exceeded.* The ideal level is where someone is able to show that they have achieved or exceeded their KPIs for the period. This is a great sign that they are defining KPIs well in the first place (not over or under-committing) and that they are able to execute on them.

KPIs have a close link with self-assessment: the better that your senior member of staff is at defining and achieving their KPIs, the easier it is for them to achieve a quantitative self-assessment.

360 Feedback

Getting 360 feedback is critical for senior staff because it's a way of getting a sense of how they are perceived by those who they should be having a positive influence on. There are typically three levels of 360 feedback, starting at the bottom:

- *Negative.* Receiving negative feedback in aggregate can typically cover interpersonal problems (for example, being a jerk regardless of how good they are), not being seen as performing well (for example, not delivering on expected commitments), or not being seen as having a positive influence on those around them (for example, not being a good manager or leader). If someone is receiving negative feedback across the board, this is a very bad sign, and you need to work with them and those who are giving the feedback to understand why this is the case and plan a way forward, which may be a PIP depending on the severity of the feedback.

- *Neutral.* Receiving neutral feedback in aggregate typically means someone isn't having a *visible* impact on those around them. For example, peers may give feedback they aren't sure what the person is working on. That's bad, and assuming you know they are doing good work, you need to coach them on how to be more visible through communicating their outputs and also collaborating more, such as through pair programming, code reviews, design reviews, and so on. At the senior level, sustained neutral feedback isn't good enough; good solo work by seniors should be clearly visible to others.

- *Positive.* This is the default level that you want your staff to be at. It shows that they are aligned with having a strong impact and that others notice this through observing them and interacting with them.

Qualitative and Quantitative 360 Feedback

When your organization designs 360 feedback, it should ensure it combines both quantitative and qualitative feedback. Quantitative feedback is typically in the form of ratings on a scale, and qualitative feedback is typically in the form of written comments. Both are extremely valuable.

Quantitative feedback can be captured via a selection of statements the feedback giver can rate, such as "I would fight hard to keep this person on my team" or "This person levels up everyone around them." A scale of 1 to 5 can cover disagreement through to agreement. Qualitative feedback can be captured via a free text field, where open-ended questions such as "What is this person doing well?" and "What could this person improve on?" can be asked.

Pro tip: if you aim for high overlap between the questions in 360 feedback and manager assessment, then you can calculate outliers. For example, if someone is rated highly by their manager but low by their peers, then this is a flag that needs investigating. It also feeds into calibration, which we'll cover later.

Your Assessment

Finally, there is your own assessment. Your company may have its own performance categories, such as "outstanding," "good," or "needs improvement," but to keep things simple, we'll just use three, which you can adapt as you see fit.

It is a good idea to take a multiphase approach to writing your assessments. First, write the assessment without looking at any of the other evidence: do it based on your own judgment alone. Then, once you have access to their self-assessment, read it and see whether it changes your opinion (for example, you may have missed something, or perhaps it highlights some areas of improvement you hadn't thought of). Finally, read all of the peer feedback and make another pass. This is a good way to ensure that you are not being biased by the other evidence but you are still able to take it into account.

- *Negative.* This is where you believe that someone is not performing well, and the next step should be a PIP. Negative assessments should be representative of being far below the performance bar that you have set for your organization.

- *Neutral.* This is where you believe that someone is performing okay, but there is clear room for improvement. Neutral assessments should be representative of staff who have had an irregularly off-kilter period and are an indicator that they need to step things up for the next cycle. Think of a "two strikes" policy here. Neutral assessments represent being slightly below the performance bar that you have set—they are not improving at the same rate as the rest of the organization.

- *Positive.* This person is hitting or exceeding the bar. Your organization may or may not have a category differentiating between those who are good vs. great. Good would mean that they are hitting the highest levels in *most* of the categories in the diagram, and great would mean they are hitting *all* of them.

Always write your assessments in a way that is *actionable*. Based on the other three quadrants, you should have plenty of evidence to back up your assessment, and you should be able to provide specific examples of where they have done well and where they could improve.

Performance Improvement Plans

 If some of your staff are getting a negative rating or consecutive neutral ratings over a longer period of time, a recommended course of action is a PIP.

> **Performance Improvement Plans**
>
> PIPs are a way of agreeing on a clear set of actionable and measurable goals to achieve over a period of time, and if they are able to achieve them, then they will be able to get back to a positive rating. If they are not able to achieve them, then it's likely that they are not a good fit for the organization, and you should work with them to find a new role or exit them from the company.
>
> PIPs are a win-win: if someone is willing to work hard to improve, then they will, and as a result, you'll have a better-performing staff member. If they're not willing to work hard to improve, then you'll have a clear path to exit them from the company, ensuring your performance bar is continually raised, as per the power curve.
>
> PIPs are not just for those in frontline teams: leaders do not get a pass. Setting the bar high for your leaders is critical since it sets the tone for the rest of the organization. If you are not willing to hold your leaders to the same standards as everyone else, then you are sending a message that you are not serious about performance management.

For staff who are performing well but have areas for improvement, you can use the previous diagram as a way of discovering and suggesting where to focus your coaching over the next period. There is an example in the diagram on page 236.

Here, we have a member of senior staff who, according to their KPIs and your own observations, is performing well but, according to their self-assessment and 360 feedback, has areas for improvement. Their self-assessment lacks quantitative evidence of their impact despite the KPIs of their area being good. Their 360 feedback is also neutral, and when digging deeper and reading written comments, you find that their peers don't have much visibility on what they are doing; typically, they work alone with little collaboration.

Based on this, you can work with the senior staff member to increase their visibility and also better understand how their work is impacting the organization (because it is!). In your plan for the next period, you encourage them to:

- *Start a brag doc.* This is a way for them to keep a record of their work throughout the period, including links to projects, KPIs, and other evidence of their impact. This will help them to write a quantitative self-assessment next time, but most importantly, it will shift their mindset to this way of thinking about their work. You will review it weekly in your one-to-ones.

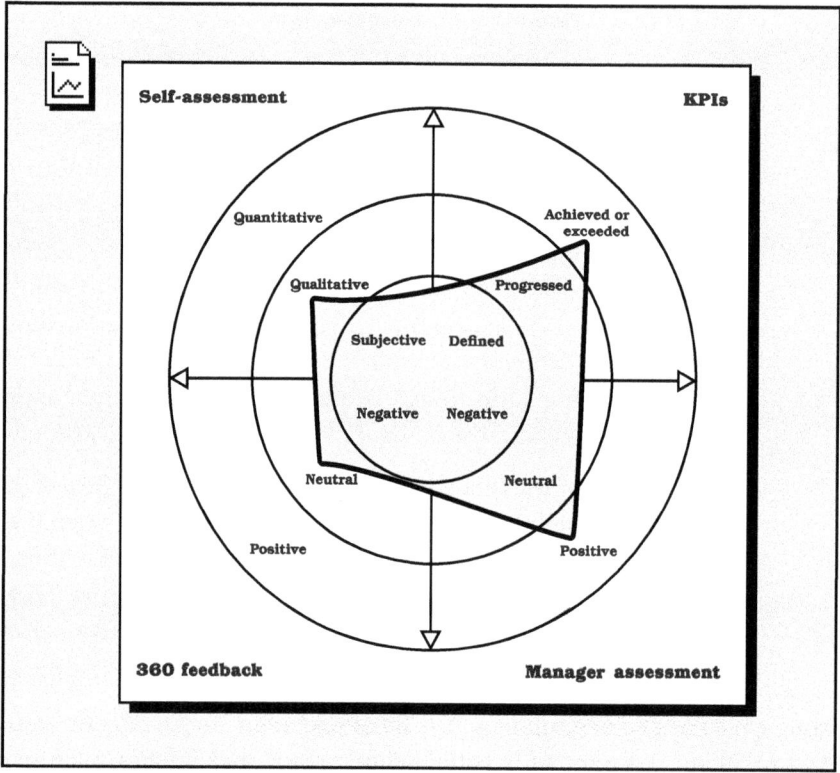

- *Start mentoring a high-growth individual in your org.* This will increase their visibility of themselves and their area and help them improve their collaboration and mentorship skills.

- *Write a monthly detailed update for their area,* and share it widely. They'll focus on the changelog of their area and highlight any impact on their KPIs.

Expanding the Model to the Whole Organization

If you find yourself in a position where you need to help design the performance management system for your whole organization, then the model we covered for senior staff has a high degree of re-use. The main difference for those not in leadership roles (non-managers and individual contributors below the staff engineer level) is you'll need to replace the KPI assessment with a more traditional assessment of their competencies (see Competencies, on page 16) compared to those defined in your career tracks. This is because they're not typically singularly accountable for KPIs, but they contribute to them through their craft, so their focus should be getting better at it.

As such, the model for non-leadership staff in the top-right quadrant looks like this:

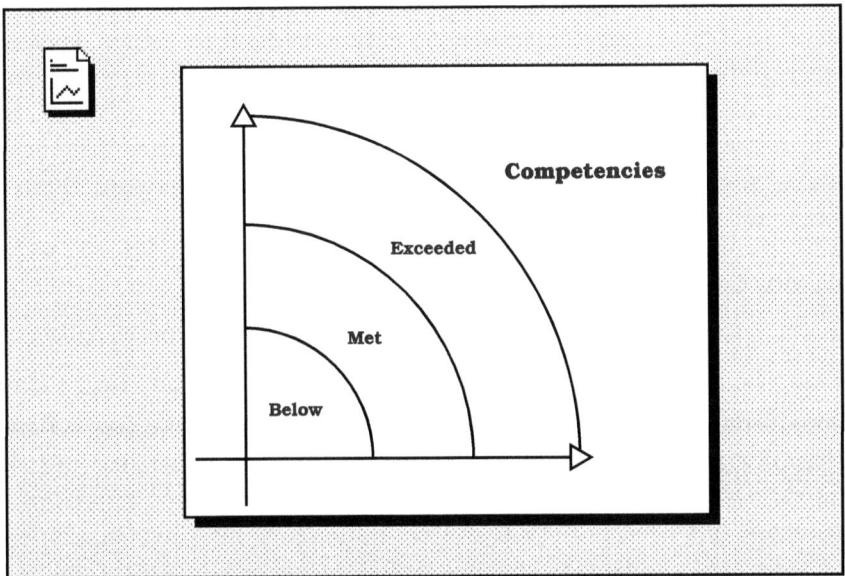

Note that meeting the bar for competencies is a baseline expectation. Those exceeding the bar are those who are performing well and are thus stretching into the next level of their career track, increasing the capabilities of the whole organization in line with the power curve.

Calibrations: Converging on Fairness

Even with a perfect performance framework in place, all of the actors in the system are human, and therefore, there is a high degree of subjectivity involved. Some managers may be more lenient than others, and some engineers may have different ideas of what good looks like.

This is why large organizations run *calibration* processes. If you are new to senior leadership, you may not have been involved in calibration before, so let's take a look at what it is and why it's important.

What Is Calibration?

Calibration is a process that is run to ensure that performance management is *fair and consistent across the entire organization*. It is typically run by HR and involves a group of senior leaders coming together to review the aggregate performance data of all of the staff in the organization to ensure it is as free from bias as possible.

Now, you may already be asking yourself: "How do you *guarantee* that calibration is fair and consistent?" The answer is, truthfully, that you can't. Again, humans are involved. However, calibration gives opportunities to prune outliers and to ensure that the performance management system is working as intended. When viewed at a macro level, it should be clear when certain managers are being too harsh or too lenient or when certain cohorts are being over or under-rated, and it also gives you a chance to spot inconsistencies in the data, such as staff who have large discrepancies between their peer feedback and their manager assessment.

How Does Calibration Work?

Generally speaking, calibration can be broken down into three phases:

- *Preparation.* This is where the performance review process runs as normal, generating all the supporting evidence for each person. Those running the calibration process will also gather any other evidence they have, such as ratings from previous performance reviews and the amount of time someone has been in their role. Initial questions and investigations may be generated at this point that can be followed up on during the calibration process.

- *Calibration.* This is typically a series of meetings where a group of senior leaders come together to review the aggregate performance of staff in the organization. They'll look at performance ratings given by managers, aggregate scores from peer feedback, the scope of their roles, and so on. Usually, people are grouped into cohorts, with the most typical cohort being those of the same level (for example, all senior engineers). Data will be gathered in such a way that allows the group to see ratings distributions per manager, per team, and so on so outliers can be identified. Larger organizations may have dedicated tools for analysis so correlations can be found between different factors. Senior leaders may be expected to answer questions about the data.

- *Actions.* After the calibration process, numerous actions may be generated. For example, there may be follow-ups with managers who have outlier data that need to be explained or adjusted. Additionally, the calibration process may highlight inconsistencies in pay, and this will feed forward into the compensation process (for example, if the highest performers are lagging behind in pay compared to their peers, then this will be adjusted).

Calibration is not a perfect science. One analogy is to compare it to security at an airport. Security may catch 80 percent of bad actors, but never all of them. However, having the process also deters incidents because bad actors know they might get caught. When managers know their ratings will be reviewed in the context of the whole organization, they're more likely to be more mindful of being fair and consistent.

Let's step through each of the phases in more detail.

Preparation

After the performance review process is completed, you will likely be invited into the calibration process by HR. There may be some asynchronous preparation first. For example, if you are a director running an area of several hundred people, you may be asked to review any outliers in data ahead of time.

For example, assume that peer feedback and manager assessments use almost identical quantitative statements, with staff rating each statement on a scale of 1 to 5. This means that data can be prepared beforehand for each member of staff, showing their average peer feedback score and their manager assessment score. For staff who have larger discrepancies between the two, you may be asked to review them and find out why. It might look something like this:

Member of staff	Manager rating	Peer feedback average	Number of peers
Alice	4.1	2.3	6
Bob	3.1	4.8	4
Claire	5	3.4	7

In the table, we can see that Alice and Claire have high manager ratings when compared to their peer feedback. Bob is the opposite, with a low manager rating and high peer-feedback ratings. This is worth investigating. As the area's leader, the next steps would be to look at the reviews and feedback in more detail and then arrange follow-up conversations with the managers in question to understand why this is the case and potentially make adjustments if necessary.

Another example of asynchronous preparation is to look at the distribution of ratings per manager and also in aggregate in your organization when compared to other parts of the company. For example, if you had six teams and three different rating categories (negative, neutral, and positive), you might see something like the table on page 240.

Team	Positive (%)	Neutral (%)	Negative (%)
A	80	15	5
B	75	15	10
C	80	15	5
D	85	10	5
E	78	15	7
F	95	5	0
Avg/Dept	79.83	14.83	5.33

Looking across teams A to F, it becomes clear that team F is skewing far more positively than the rest of the other teams and the department as a whole. It has no negative ratings at all and only 5 percent neutral ratings. Now, this may be entirely explainable: perhaps the manager of team F is an exceptional manager with a team of high performers. However, it's worth investigating, and this is a good cue to ask the manager of team F to explain why this is the case. Perhaps they may change their mind.

Your organization may have historical data available on the distribution of ratings across the entire company over time, and these are useful to take into account. It is, of course, a senior executive decision to decide what kind of rating curve is desirable; some organizations press hard on performance and expect a reasonable cohort of the lowest performers to exit the company each year. Other organizations are more lenient and expect a similar cohort to be rated as neutral, with additional support and coaching required for those staff. There's no right or wrong answer here, and you may have zero control over the desired state, but as a senior leader, you need to be able to justify the curve you're aiming for and ensure it aligns with what the company wants.

At most companies, the promotion process runs as a follow-on from the performance cycle. Therefore, going into the calibration, you should know which of your staff is up for promotion in this cycle and also who has recently been promoted. Since assessments are at the level that a member of staff is currently at, you would expect those who are up for promotion to be performing at a high level, and those who have recently been promoted, especially to higher levels of the org chart, may still be finding their feet. This is worth taking into account when reviewing the ratings.

Calibration

Now, with this preparation work done, you are ready for the calibration meetings. Every company will do these differently, but the general procedure is that you will come together with other senior leader peers and will view the positioning of cohorts (or all) staff, including your own. This may be combined with distributions of ratings per manager, per team, and so on. You will then discuss any outliers and make adjustments as necessary.

Here are some of the ways that cohorts may be presented, which may be comprehensive lists or just samples of the entire organization:

- *By level.* This is the most common way of presenting cohorts and is typically done by grouping all staff of the same level together (for example, all engineering managers or all senior engineers). This may be a sample of the entire organization if the company is large.
- *By discipline.* You may have different disciplines within engineering, such as data engineering, front-end engineering, back-end engineering, and so on.
- *By team or wider group.* This gives a picture of an entire area under one manager.
- *By tenure.* How do we rate staff who have been at the company for a long time vs. those who have just joined?
- *By outlier groups.* For example, there may be a cohort of the lowest performers or the highest performers.
- *By typical bias groups.* Is bias being introduced between men and women, remote vs. office, country of residence, or other factors?
- *By promotion cohort.* You would expect this group to be at the high end of the curve and that other senior leaders agree.

Grouping staff together in various cohorts allows you to cross-compare them and bring more context to the ratings. Are all of the lowest performers in one team or discipline, or are they generally the lowest seniority? What does that mean and why? What about the highest performers? Are they *really* the highest performers, or is there a manager who is being too lenient? Calibration meetings are typically a series of questions like this, and the goal is for the group to discuss, debate, and conclude whether they feel that the ratings are fair and consistent.

This, of course, is somewhat subjective. So, it's likely that other data will be available for any staff about whom there are questions, such as their historical performance, their peer feedback and manager assessment, and so on. This is why the preparation phase is so important; it gives everyone the opportunity to come to the meeting with as correct a picture as possible and to make adjustments as necessary.

Let's look at a hypothetical example. If we assume that a company gets managers and peers to rate others by answering questions on a scale of 1 to 5 for each factor of their performance and has done so for many years, then we can compare the current year's ratings to previous years. For example, we might see something like the following diagram:

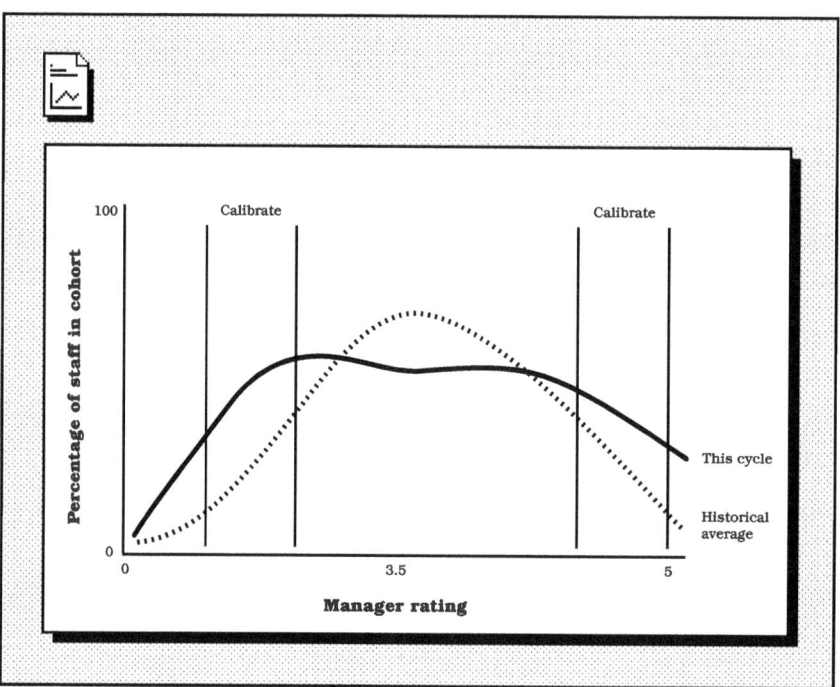

We can see that the general shape of the curve is broadly similar to previous years, but there are some outliers:

- There is an increased number of ratings at the lower end of the scale compared to previous years.

- There is also an increased number of positive ratings.

It seems that ratings have skewed further toward extremes this cycle, and the reduction in ratings in the middle of the curve is further evidence of this.

Therefore, it makes sense to investigate this during calibration sessions. On the diagram, two *slices* of the curve are highlighted: the outlying lowest and highest performers. These slices become cohorts in the calibration discussion that you would be involved in. For example, there could be questions asked such as:

- Why are there more low performers this year? What may have caused this? Is this curve representative of the whole department, or if it is filtered by manager or team, does it look different? If so, why? What is this cohort's historical performance?

- Likewise, why are there more high performers? Can each of the staff in the cohort be explained by the clear impact that they have had in their work? If not, why not?

Remember: the goal of calibration discussion is *not* to change everything so that it fits the curve. Instead, it's to ensure that the curve is representative of the performance of the organization. For example, manager assessments can sometimes be biased by factors external to their teams:

- When companies are not hiring, managers may skew their ratings higher to ensure that their staff are not flagged as a performance issue. They would rather have a full team with a few average performers among them than a smaller team of high performers. Similar behaviors may occur when there is an unstable economic climate, as there is a fear that low ratings may trigger exits that can't be backfilled.

- Conversely, when companies are hiring rapidly, managers may see this as an opportunity to exit staff who they are on the fence about because the prospect of a new hire may be more attractive.

Good calibration processes highlight these behaviors and ensure that staff ratings are as unbiased as possible.

Preparing for Calibration Sessions

If you're new to calibration sessions, then it's a good idea to prepare for them. Ensure you know what the curve looks like for your own organization ahead of time. Are you already aware of outliers?

For your cohort of high performers, ensure that you have access to evidence of why they received their ratings. For example, this could be their self-assessment, manager assessments, peer feedback, or other evidence, such as KPIs and projects they have worked on. This will help you to defend their ratings if necessary.

Similarly, for your lowest performers, ensure that you have access to evidence of why they received their ratings. Know whether this is the first time this has happened or whether it is a pattern over time. If it is the latter, then you should already have an idea of what you want to do as the next steps.

For staff who are up for promotion, ideally, have their promotion packet to hand. The idea is that they should be moving toward

> **Preparing for Calibration Sessions**
>
> the right of the curve in a cohort of their peers, and the following promotion process, therefore, should be self-evident.
>
> Most importantly, be actively engaged. Calibration is best when everyone acts with a longtermist view of building a better, fairer, less biased rating system over time. Sometimes, this means that you will have to make adjustments to your own ratings. It's not your job to fight them doggedly to the end; instead, it's your job to ensure that the system is fair and consistent.

Actions

After calibration sessions have happened, there may be a number of next steps that you will have to follow up on:

- *You may need to discuss their ratings with your managers.* This goes in both directions: you may have staff who have been rated too harshly when compared to others in similar cohorts or too leniently. As such, you will need to follow up with managers directly, dig in, and explain what the calibration process has highlighted.

- *You may investigate managers being too lenient or too harsh.* Similar to the first point, this may or may not mean changing ratings, but it can be useful to highlight this to these managers and make them aware. Ensure there is evidence either way.

- *You will get a clear signal on promotion or compensation processes to come.* Those getting promoted and those performing the highest should be in line for the biggest reward, and you can ensure that you are aligned with this and can advocate for them.

Debugging Common Performance Management Issues

Before we close out the chapter, let's look at some common issues you may encounter. Regardless of your seniority, there will be recurring themes that you will have to deal with when it comes to performance management.

Your Lowest Performer Is the Performance Bar You Accept

We began this chapter by talking about the performance bar: the ever-increasing power curve that represents how your organization is learning and improving over time. You are responsible for where this bar is set, and you are responsible for ensuring that it is continually raised. With that in mind, it's important to remember that despite your best intentions, *your lowest performer is the bar that you are willing to accept.*

Often, without bad intentions, you may let some members of staff become exceptions to your performance bar. Perhaps you like them as a person, or they have a good history with the company, or they are liked by everyone regardless of their output. However, the reality is this: if they're not performing, then you have a responsibility to ensure that these staff are *not* given a pass. If you do, then you are signifying to the rest of your organization that this is where the performance bar lies. This is not fair to your highest performers—they want to be rewarded for their efforts by working with others who are invested, motivated, and doing a great job.

If you have people who aren't performing, regardless of how well-liked they are or how long they have been at the company, then it is your responsibility to ensure it is absolutely clear they are not making the cut and need to improve. Resentment will build around your special cases, and the blame will lie with you for not taking action.

The most respectful thing that you can do for someone who is not performing is to *tell them.* Consider practicing *radical candor [Sco17]*: this is where you combine *challenging someone directly* on a behavior while also *caring personally* about them. Look, sometimes people don't even *know* they're performing badly! Letting them know they're not performing is an act of kindness; it is an open invitation for them to get better.

Current Performance Is Not Historical Performance

Following on, it's important to remember that *current performance is not historical performance.* This is a common trap that managers fall into, especially with staff who have been at the company for a long time.

Just because someone built something incredible two years ago, it doesn't mean it gets them a free pass during this cycle. Performance is always judged empirically within the bounds of the current cycle, and if a member of staff hasn't performed well, what they did last year or the year before is irrelevant.

The capabilities of the organization are always increasing, and so should the capabilities of each member of staff. Being above the bar in the past does not mean that you are above the bar now; each cycle is a clean slate. Words like "tenure" mean nothing when it comes to performance management—it's all about what you have done *now*.

It is important to note that this bias can work in *reverse*, and you need to ensure that you are giving staff who have had a poor past performance the *chance at a clean slate each cycle*. Ensure that you and your managers are not holding grudges against staff who have had a bad cycle in the past—if they have improved, then they should be rewarded for it.

Brilliant Jerks Are Not Worth It

You can insert your engineering stereotype here yourself, so we will save ourselves the trouble. No matter how brilliant someone is, if they are a jerk, then over time, they are not worth it. Brilliant jerks produce output in the short term, but they are a net negative in the long term. They are a net negative because they are a drain on everyone else.

From small papercuts in daily interactions to when those papercuts blow up into wider escalations, there are always others on planet Earth who are able to get a job done *and* be reasonable people. Hire them instead. The amount of time and brain cycles spent on creating exceptions, mitigations, specific working practices, special arrangements, and so on, just because one person lacks the self-awareness to realize that they are not pleasant to be around, is a great shame. This should be channeled into making the organization and what it produces better for *everyone* instead.

No matter how brilliant a jerk is, you need to make it clear that their behavior is unacceptable and that if they don't improve, there's only one way that this can go. The more senior you get, the more that interpersonal quibbles become a major time drain compared to the things that you should *really* be spending your time on. Nip it in the bud.

The Ever-Inflating Job Titles

As one would expect, your best-performing staff are always eyeing up promotion. Progression is good, new titles are cool, and it is good for one's resume. However, it's important to remember that *job titles are not a reward*. They are an indicator of the level of impact that an individual is having on the organization.

Your career tracks should make it crystal clear what the expectations are for each level and what the bar is for promotion. However, it's also important to flag that:

- *Some promotions are a big leap and will not be available for everyone.* Typically, the largest leaps come between senior engineer and staff engineer, which is a promotion into a *leadership* position. An organization will only need so many leadership positions at a given time. The same is also true of all roles on the management track; if the organizational need is not there, you don't need another director or an engineering manager with two direct reports.

- *Some positions are terminal, and that's okay.* The higher you go, the more likely it is that you won't go any higher. This is self-evident in management roles since you need to have enough people to manage. However, it doesn't work if you have a company with more principal engineers than senior engineers. Not everyone can architect the system rather than build it.

Keeping job title inflation under control is extremely important. Not only is it a one-way door that is hard to reverse, but it also diminishes the value of the title itself. In smaller companies, giving bigger titles is an easy way out if you can't pay as much as the big companies, but it comes with serious ramifications: job titles can start to lose their meaning.

One way of working with your HR team to prevent this is to remove upper bounds on pay for each position. For example, it could be possible for a high-impact senior engineer to earn more than people at levels above them if they are truly excellent at their role. This is a good way of ensuring that people are not promoted just for the sake of it and that the bar for promotion is kept high.

Being Held Hostage

Sometimes, your best performers can have their quirks too: they might continually kick up a fuss for more money, higher performance ratings, promotions, or threaten to leave if they can't get their own way.

There are numerous issues with this:

- *It encourages behavior that is not in the best interest of the whole organization.* If you continually appease those who are loudest with their demands, then you are not rewarding those who are quietly getting on with their work and producing equally great output—you are introducing bias.

- *It attempts to shift decision-making power from you to them.* The performance and reward system is there to ensure impartial fairness for everyone. Subverting it is harmful to others.

- *Their behavior is actually poor performance!* You need to coach this behavior *out* of them, not reward it.

- *Creating exceptions is a slippery slope.* If you give in to one person's demands, then you are setting a precedent that you will have to follow for others. With time, you will run out of ways of hiding the fact that you are giving in to demands, and it becomes increasingly difficult to walk your decisions back.

If you find yourself being held hostage, then you need to keep your emotions at bay and deal with the facts. Take pay for an example: if the facts show they are in indeed paid unfairly, you fix it. However, if they are not, then you need to be direct and open with them about both the *facts* and the *effects*. In the pay situation, this would mean:

- *Stating the facts.* Get as much detail as is reasonable to show that they are paid fairly compared to their peers. This could be compensation data showing ranges or percentiles. Make it completely self-evident that they do not actually have a case.

- *Being candid about the effect of their actions.* If there is no issue with their pay after looking at the data, then they need to understand that issuing you ultimatums is not good performance; it's poor performance. This is the catch: if they want to be paid more, then they need to perform better, not worse, as they are doing now.

- *Be clear that perhaps they will never be satisfied.* If they want to double their pay because of an offer elsewhere and it is impossible for you to match, then you need to just tell them that. If they are not satisfied with the facts, then it's on them to make a decision on whether to stay or go.

Never be held hostage by what someone wants to the detriment of everyone else. Your performance system, combined with calibration, should aim to produce output that is as unbiased as possible. Similar to brilliant jerks getting a pass, you shouldn't let your highest performers try to bend the system to work better for them than for everyone else. If they are truly high performers, then they will get what they want through the system. If they don't, then it's on them to step up their game or to leave.

When You Disagree with One of Your Managers

Another common dilemma is when there is an individual you feel is underperforming, but their manager disagrees and believes they're doing well. This is tricky because you're aware that you may not have all of the context, and you don't want to undermine the manager's judgment. In the best case, you might just be wrong. In the worst case, a manager is protecting an underperformer from any consequences. Since you have a responsibility to ensure that the performance bar is fairly implemented and continually raised, if there are bad smells, you need to investigate them.

To elevate the discussion beyond a battle of opinions, you need to gather data. If you have a performance cycle coming up, then you can use this as an opportunity to generate evidence. For example, you can increase the number of requests for peer feedback that the individual gets, ensuring that it comes from a wide and unbiased cohort of peers. Then, you can see if this peer feedback aligns with your or the manager's assessment.

If you are not near a performance cycle, then you can still gather more evidence. You can use skip-level meetings to get a better understanding of what it is like to work with the individual, ensuring that you are approaching the situation with tact. You can gently probe by asking people what it is like to work with other individuals on their team, what they think of their output and collaboration, and so on, perhaps asking for examples of each at their best and in areas where they could improve.

When you have a more cohesive picture, you can then have a more informed discussion. Generally speaking, data is the best way to resolve these kinds of disputes—it's hard to argue with the facts. If you do think they are being given an easy ride, then you need to be direct with the manager about it. It's not about undermining them but about ensuring that the performance bar is being enforced fairly and consistently.

Let's Get Strategic

We've taken a ride along the power curve of performance management and focused on some of the unique activities that you will be involved in as a senior leader. You should find yourself more prepared for what is expected of you and more aware of the common pitfalls that you will need to avoid. You should also be in a good position to help an organization design a performance management system that works for them.

Here's what we covered:

- *We took a tour of performance management as a whole,* looking at how larger organizations typically do it. We also showed how performance is a power curve that keeps getting higher over time as your organization learns and improves and how you are responsible for setting the bar.

- *Next, we looked at the performance management of senior staff* and how to build a complete picture of their impact. We expanded on this to look more broadly at how you could design a performance framework for a whole company by switching out measurement against KPIs for measurement against competencies.

- *Then, we focused on the calibration process,* which is how large organizations attempt to ensure performance management is fair and consistent across the entire org chart. We looked at how to prepare for calibration sessions and how to take action afterward. Senior leadership may be the first time that you are deeply involved in the calibration of staff against one another, so now you are prepared for it.

- *Finally, we looked at some common performance management issues and how to debug them,* including how to deal with brilliant jerks, being held hostage, job title inflation, and more.

This marks the end of the second part of the book. We're going to go up a level into the strategic parts of senior leadership next, starting with how to build a strategy: what it is, why it's important, and most importantly, how do you do it? We'll see you there.

Part III

Strategy, Planning, and Execution

Now, we will spend some time on top of the pyramid. This section is all about strategic activities that go on at the upper echelons of companies.

First, we'll look at how to create and execute an engineering strategy. Then, we'll dig into the fiscal, marketing, and product cycles that companies loop through.

Next, it's all about money. Where does it come from? Where does it go? How can you use it to your best advantage? And what about when there are boom and bust cycles in the market?

We'll close out by looking inward at your career. Where are you going? How can you get there? And what could you be missing?

CHAPTER 11

Strategy 101

Today hasn't been the best day. You've spent the last two hours in an emergency meeting because the company's biggest customer has just cancelled their contract. Microsoft has just launched a new product that seems to do *exactly* the same thing as yours, but it costs half as much. Your CEO, Corie, is panicked. Your CTO, John, is trying to help come up with a plan.

"How did we not see this coming?" she asks. "What are we going to do?"

"They only launched it yesterday, Corie," John replies. "We didn't have any warning. They must have been working on that deal while they were still preparing to launch it."

Corie stares at the floor. "We need a new strategy," she says. "We need to make it absolutely clear why our product is better, different, and worth the extra money. If we lose another customer tomorrow and then another the next, we're going to be in serious trouble by the end of the year."

"Okay," says John. "But what is our current strategy? What were we trying to achieve?"

"That's the problem," says Corie. "We never really had one. We just built this product and *boom*—we got really lucky. Right place, right time. We've been building from our gut instinct, and it's worked amazingly…until now."

"So how do we come up with a strategy?" you say.

"We need to make a plan of everything that we're going to do this year that is going to make us the obvious choice," says John.

"But that's not a strategy," says Corie. "That's a plan."

"But you can't have a strategy without a plan," says John. "How can you know what you're going to do if you don't know what you're trying to achieve?"

"Yeah, but you need to know what you want to achieve before you can make a plan," says Corie. "Otherwise, you're just making a list of things to do. That's what we've done up until now, and it's not working."

John grunts in agreement while nodding.

"Okay, I guess I'll ask the same thing again," you say. "How do we come up with a strategy?"

Corie picks up her pen and stands by the whiteboard.

"Let's grab some food and coffee from next door," she says. "We're going to be in here for a while."

"I'm going to get one of their cakes," says John.

"That's a plan again, John," says Corie. "Not a strategy."

At the beginning of the book, we touched upon The Three Levels of Warfare, on page 9. These three levels, which are derived from military command structure, map similarly to different levels of an organization. The top level of the pyramid is the strategic level, where the overall goals of the organization are set.

When done well, the strategy of an organization should be the root of everything it does. It should be the guidance individual teams use to make decisions about what to do and, more importantly, what *not* to do next. It should help the company confidently choose where to invest money, time, and effort.

The more senior you become, the more involved you will be in setting the strategy of your organization. But what actually *is* a strategy? How do you create one? And how do you know if it's working? These are the questions that we're going to answer in this chapter.

We want to challenge the idea that strategy is complex and difficult to understand. Sure, it may be challenging to get it right for your company, but the concept itself is straightforward once you pin it down. We will also spend a majority of this chapter going through concrete examples to make strategy concepts more tangible, understandable, and interesting.

Here's what we're going to cover:

- *What is a strategy?* We'll define what a strategy is and what it isn't—notably, how it is *not* planning. We'll also look at some examples of strategies from real companies that led to successful actions and outcomes.

- *Next, we'll focus on engineering strategies* since this is more likely to be the level that *you* will be involved in creating. We'll see how engineering strategy fits into the overall company strategy, how it complements the product strategy and other strategies, and how it can be used to help make decisions about what to do next.

- *Finally, we will go through a worked example of creating an engineering strategy* for a fictional company. We will see how to take the overall company strategy and translate it into an engineering strategy and see how this can be used to focus teams, generate ideas, and measure progress.

And with that, let's get started.

What on Earth Is a Strategy, Anyway?

The term "strategy" gets a bad rap. It can easily be filed away as a clichéd business buzzword alongside "synergy" and "paradigm shift." However, strategy is a real thing, and as you become more senior, it will increasingly be your responsibility to create and communicate it.

So what is a strategy? Let's start by consulting some definitions from some reputable sources:

- Strategy is the initiative that a company pursues to create value for the organization and its stakeholders and gain a competitive advantage in the market.[1]

- A business strategy outlines the specific ways in which an organization plans to position itself, achieve its short-term and long-term goals, and grow over a period of time. It draws on other important business resources, such as the organization's mission, vision, and values, to help chart its direction forward and deliver on its objectives.[2]

These are good definitions but lack specifics and are a bit hand-wavy. What does the dictionary say?

- Strategy (noun): A detailed plan for achieving success in situations such as war, politics, business, industry, or sport, or the skill of planning for such situations.[3]

---

1. https://online.hbs.edu/blog/post/what-is-business-strategy
2. https://online.york.ac.uk/what-is-a-business-strategy/
3. https://dictionary.cambridge.org/dictionary/english/strategy

- A plan, scheme, or course of action designed to achieve a particular objective, esp. a long-term or overall aim.[4]

Okay, hang on a second. Hold up. No wonder people get confused about what a strategy is. Is a strategy a specific set of initiatives? Is it a detailed plan? And what's all this about mission, vision, and values? Let's try to clear this up.

A Strategy Is Not a Plan

The first thing to understand is that *a strategy is not a plan, and vice versa*. Planning is a *management* activity that is mapped to the operational layer, whereas strategy is a *leadership* activity. They are different things.

According to Professor Roger Martin, a strategy is an *integrative set of choices that positions you on a playing field of your choice in a way that you win*.[5] Things like building features, opening a new office, or hiring a new team are *not* strategies. They are plans. They are what you consequently do with your resources to achieve your strategy.

Professor Martin outlines that leaders often get sucked into making plans rather than strategies because they are easier to create:

- Strategy is about gaining and satisfying customers, which are *external* to your organization: this is hard to predict and control, and you do not control revenues. This is an uncomfortable place to be.

- Planning is about *internal* resources and costs, which you do control, and *you* are the customer. This is comfortable by comparison.

Making a plan without a strategy and executing on it perfectly may not lead to success. Sure, you've satisfied yourself by getting the plan done, but have you actually secured the long-term success of the company? How would you even know?

What Are Some Examples of Strategies?

Understanding what a good strategy is becomes easier when you look at some examples. The first example is from Professor Martin: Southwest Airlines.[6] They aimed for a specific *outcome*: to be the lowest-cost airline in the United States in a way that wasn't much more costly for people to use for travel than Greyhound buses. This was their strategy, and this is how they accomplished it:

---

4. https://www.oed.com/dictionary/strategy_n?tab=factsheet#20537476
5. https://www.youtube.com/watch?v=iuYlGRnC7J8
6. https://www.southwest.com

- *Not flying hub and spoke.* They only flew point to point, which meant that they didn't have to pay for expensive airport slots to have their planes sit on the ground for hours at a time.
- *Flying only one type of plane.* This meant that they could train their pilots and mechanics on one model and could buy parts for repairs in bulk, which is cheaper.
- *Flying only one class.* This meant that they could turn the planes around faster, and they didn't have to pay for the extra weight of first-class seats and facilities.
- *Flying only to secondary airports.* This meant that they didn't have to pay for premium airport slots.
- *Only allowing booking online.* This eradicated the need for call centers and travel agents.

These were the *choices* that Southwest Airlines made in order to achieve their strategy. They were the *how*. The *what* was the strategy itself: to be the lowest-cost airline in the United States. In fact, Southwest is an example of a great strategy: it is clear, concise, and is quite literally a single sentence. However, the choices and plans that derive from it are numerous and force some innovative thinking.

Another real world example is from Tesla.[7] Their strategy is to "accelerate the world's transition to sustainable energy." Note that this isn't about selling cars. It's about the *outcome*. This is a grand vision, but we can begin to piece together the choices and plans they have made to work toward it:

- *Build electric cars.* This is the obvious one. They are the most visible part of the company, and they are the most obvious way to reduce the world's reliance on fossil fuels. The innovation required to produce the cars is also reusable elsewhere: battery technology can be re-appropriated for other products.
- *Focus on controlling the entire supply chain.* They build their own batteries, and they are building their own charging network. This means that they can control the quality and the cost, and they can innovate faster.
- *Market directly to consumers.* They don't have franchised dealerships, which means they can control the customer experience and the price. You can buy a car on their website with a credit card. Additionally, servicing

---

7. https://www.tesla.com/en_gb/about

is done by Tesla directly, which means they, again, own the experience and the cost.

- *Start at the top end of the market.* They began by building a high-end car, the Roadster, which was expensive and exclusive. This allowed them to build a brand and a reputation and to generate revenue to fund the next steps.

- *Continually move down the market.* They then moved to the Model S, then the Model X, then the Model 3, each becoming more affordable and more accessible to the mass market and each with a larger production run.

- *Use revenues to expand into other areas that are in line with their broader strategy.* They are now building solar panels and batteries for homes and trucks.

> ### Your Turn: Research Some Strategies
>
> Put aside 15 minutes to research some companies that you admire. They can be any kind of company; you don't have to limit yourself to technology.
>
> - What is their strategy? What is the outcome that they are trying to achieve?
> - How does this translate into the choices they have made over the years? How do you think some of the more recent products and services that they have launched fit into their strategy?
>
> If you're struggling to find some companies to research, then try the following: Airbnb, Nike, Amazon, Netflix, and Whole Foods.

Engineering Strategy: Your Piece of the Puzzle

With a good understanding of what a broad company strategy is, we can now zoom in on the engineering strategy. This is the strategy that you are most likely to be involved in creating or owning outright as you become more senior.

The engineering strategy forms a subset of the overall company strategy and is the primary strategy that the engineering department uses to make decisions about what to do and, most importantly, what *not* to do. Often, it is the case that companies neither have an explicit engineering strategy nor is it communicated or documented well.[8] You can change this. However, before we get started and dive into the details, it is important to understand the audience for which the strategy exists and why that can make it hard to create.

---

8. https://lethain.com/eng-strategies/

As an engineering leader, you sit in the middle of two quite different worlds:

- *For those above and around you in the org chart, you represent a department that can often be difficult to understand.* Because of the highly technical nature of engineering work, it can be hard for nontechnical people (and, let's face it, even technical people) to understand what engineering is doing at any given time and why. This is often a source of frustration when it comes to prioritization, resourcing, trade-offs, technical debt, and so on.

- *Below you in the org chart are engineers who want to understand the bigger picture.* Your engineers and the other disciplines that they closely collaborate with (such as product management and design) want to understand how to make the right decisions and trade-offs and how best to contribute to the company's success.

These two groups approach the engineering strategy from two different angles. Senior executives and nontechnical people want to understand what engineering is doing and why and to understand how it assigns time, staff, and money. They want to understand how this complex machine is oriented and what the inputs and outputs of the black box are.

Engineers, on the other hand, are much more focused on the details of how that happens. For example, they want to understand how they should be thinking about the trade-offs between quality and speed, key KPIs to hit, how to tackle technical debt, how they should trade off building vs. buying, and how the department deals with conflicting priorities.

This is a difficult balance to strike, and it is often the case that engineering strategies are either too high level and don't provide enough detail, thus, engineers themselves don't find them useful, or they're too detailed and technical, and nontechnical people don't understand them. You need to write your engineering strategy in a way that is accessible to both groups. The combination of what satiates the needs of both groups is what makes a good engineering strategy, as per the diagram on page 260.

Senior stakeholders and nonengineers want to read your engineering strategy and understand these things:

- What are the key initiatives that engineering is working on?

- How do these ladder up to the company strategy, and what effect has this had on resourcing and prioritization?

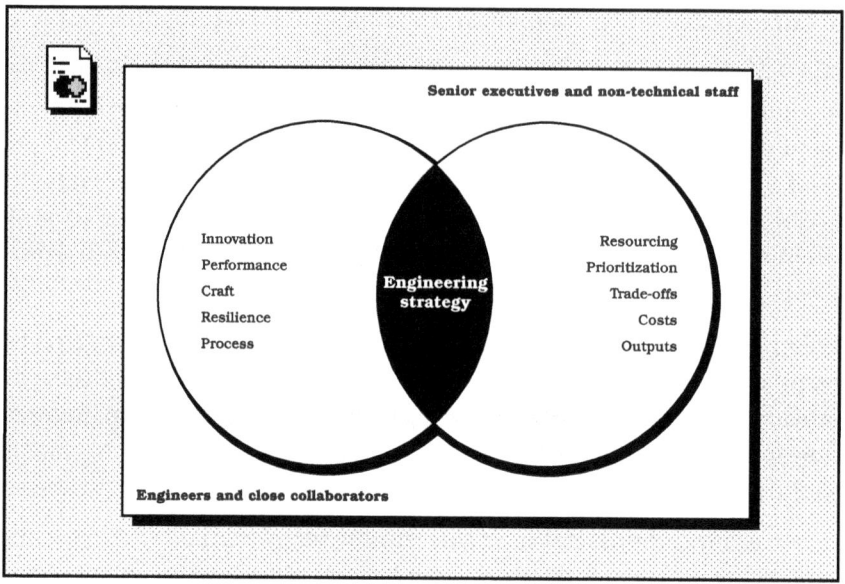

- As a result of making those choices, what trade-offs are engineering comfortable with, and what are they not doing?
- How are they thinking about costs, and what are the key metrics or outputs that will be the result of this strategy being a success?

Engineers and their close collaborators want to read your engineering strategy and understand these things:

- What are the key innovations that we are investing in, that is, what technical bets are we making and investing the majority of our time in?
- How are we thinking about the performance of our software, and what are the key metrics that we are tracking? Do these need to improve, and if so, how are we going to do that?
- What tools, skills, and techniques will we use to get better at our craft of engineering? How will we improve the speed and quality of our work?
- How are we thinking about the resiliency of our systems, and what do we need to do to improve them, if anything?
- What key processes make the department run? How do we deal with blockers, prioritization conflicts, escalations, and so on? How do we make decisions quickly?

Although these are quite different needs, there is also a lot of overlap. The first set of bullet points, which are aimed at senior executives and nontechnical people, act as the *framing* around the second set of bullet points. As such, when written and constructed well, your engineers will find all of it pertinent and actionable, while everyone else will be able to get what they need.

Let's Build an Engineering Strategy Together

We are going to take the approach of building out an engineering strategy from scratch together, starting with a company strategy and working our way down. We'll see how to take the overall company strategy and translate it into an engineering strategy, and then we'll see how this can be used to focus teams, generate ideas, and measure progress.

We'll do this by working through a fictional example. We'll start by setting the scene, and then we'll work through the process of creating an engineering strategy for a company that is in need of a turnaround. We'll see how to take the overall company strategy and translate it into an engineering strategy that works for those that are above, below, and around you in the org chart.

Setting the Scene

You've just started a new job as the CTO of a company called BookATrip that's in need of a turnaround. The company is a vacation booking website that is facing increasing competition from competitors, which is noticeable from revenue and usage beginning to flatline after nearly a decade of growth. This turnaround has also been prompted by the arrival of a new CEO who has experience scaling numerous start-ups to either acquisition or IPO.

Despite the company having been around for a long time and having experienced significant growth, there has been an underinvestment in technology and user experience. As such, compared to other websites, it feels slow and clunky. The mobile experience is poor, and there is no dedicated mobile application. However, due to its marketing presence and the fact that it has been around for a long time, it still has a significant user base, and from a price perspective for bookings, it is still one of the most competitive in the market because of its long-standing relationships with hotels and airlines.

You have spent the last week with the CEO and the rest of the leadership team, and you have been working with them to understand the current state of the website, both from hearing their observations and in getting answers to questions that you have. The leadership team has also agreed that a refresh of the company's strategy is needed. After much deliberation with highly paid consultants, the new strategy is as follows:

> **BookATrip's New Strategy**
> *by: Executive leadership team, BookATrip.com*
>
> We are the fastest and easiest way for anyone to book a much-needed vacation. Whether you're planning a trip months in advance or you're booking a last-minute getaway in your lunch break, we will help you find the perfect trip for you, your friends, and your family.
>
> *Click, click, BookATrip.*

The final tagline holds specific importance: as the new company slogan, it emphasizes the need for anyone to be able to book a trip within three actions for most workflows. This is a drastically different experience than the current website, which can take up to ten frustrating and slow actions to complete just a single hotel booking.

Given this, the leadership team has agreed that:

- The website needs a complete overhaul to be fast, easy to use, and modern, incorporating workflows that are designed to be completed in three actions or less.

- A dedicated mobile application needs to be built; there is currently none.

- The experience needs to become more personalized and intelligent to help recommend trips and destinations to users and to help them find the best deals. The company has a decade of data on users and their bookings, but it is not being used to make the experience better.

The leadership team has decided to significantly invest in growing the UX team and the data team in order to make all of this happen. They are now looking to you to come up with an engineering strategy that will enable this change.

Doing Your Research

With this in mind, you get your senior engineering team together to understand the current state of the website. Here's what you learn:

- *The website is built using a technology stack that is over a decade old.* It is slow, and it is hard to make changes to it. The engineering team doesn't like working with it, and it has been a source of frustration and attrition for some time.

- *The website is slow, and it is slow in a multitude of ways.* Some of the key issues are the speed of page loads (the worst offenders having a Lighthouse score of less than 50),[9] the speed of search, which has a P50 of 5 seconds, and the general speed is unusable for users in Asia and South America, despite having a global user base and localized versions of the website. Support tickets for failed booking requests have been increasing over the last year.

After spending time planning with your senior team, you come up with the following key initiatives for the coming year:

- *A complete overhaul of the website using modern technologies and a modern design.* This will be driven by the UX overhaul that will be taking place. This will run in parallel to the existing website and will be launched when it is ready.

- *A mobile application will be built from scratch and will be launched at the same time as the new website.* Re-use of code is key here.

- *A data team will be built to start making use of the data that the company has.* This will be a mix of data scientists and data engineers, and they will be tasked with making the website more personalized and more intelligent. Making that data accessible to them is also a key part of this initiative.

- *Infrastructure improvements will be made to the website to make it faster*, which can be used in both the new and old websites. This includes a better search experience driven by new search technology, a new caching layer, and a strategy to push more static data out to the edge globally for speed.

You get all of this verbally agreed upon by the CEO, and you begin work on writing your engineering strategy. This engineering strategy is reproduced in full in the next section. After the strategy, we will step through it and break it down into its constituent parts to create a template that you can use for your own strategy needs.

Example: BookATrip's Engineering Strategy

Our company is beginning a period of transformation: we are going to become the fastest and easiest booking website on the Internet. We are beginning this journey by realizing that this requires us to take some big steps over the course of the next year. We are going to be investing in the following key initiatives in tandem with a major upskilling of our teams:

---

9. https://developer.chrome.com/docs/lighthouse/performance/performance-scoring

- *A complete overhaul of the website.* We will be launching the biggest user-facing changes that the company has seen in a decade. This will be a complete overhaul using modern technologies that will result in an experience that is fast, easy to use, and one that our customers will love. This will be driven by the UX team, and we will be dedicating around 25 percent of our engineering resources to this initiative.

- *Launching our mobile app.* For the first time, we will be launching a dedicated mobile application. This will be built from scratch and will be a key part of our new strategy to find and retain customers across all platforms. We will also be dedicating around 25 percent of our resources to this initiative.

- *Significantly upgrading our infrastructure.* The state of the art in storage, search, and resiliency has moved on significantly in the last few years. We will be dedicating around 35 percent of our engineering resources to overhaul search, retrieval, and caching to make our website faster, more reliable, and more accessible to users no matter where they are in the world. All upgrades will work with the existing website and the new website and mobile application when it launches.

- *Keeping the lights on.* We will be dedicating around 15 percent of our resources to keeping the existing website running and making small improvements to it. We will aggressively prioritize building the future experience, but we will ensure that the current experience gets no worse than it is today and that we continue to fix bugs and respond to our users.

We will be measuring the success of these initiatives in the following ways:

- *Page load time.* We will be aiming for a Lighthouse score of 85 across all of our key pages and a P50 page load time of 250ms or less. We will be measuring this across all of our key regions, and we will be aiming for a consistent experience across the world. Currently, our worst page load times are in Asia and South America, with some experiences taking over 10 seconds to load. This is unacceptable.

- *Search speed.* We will be aiming for a P50 search time of 100ms or less for all user journeys. Search is a key part of our future experience, and we will likely need to build a new search index rather than make improvements to the existing one.

- *Uptime and error rates.* We will be getting serious about the availability of our website and aiming for a 99.99 percent uptime and 0.1 percent error rates across all of our key regions. Last year, we only achieved

97.5 percent uptime, and we had 3 percent error rates. This turns customers away. In addition to committing to these new targets, we will also be measuring the number of support tickets that we receive for failed booking requests, and we will be aiming to reduce this by 50 percent over the next year. Also, we will implement a new internal process for reporting and responding to outages and errors, which will result in a public-facing status page for our users and an internal mailing list for post-mortems and learning.

- *Mobile application downloads and ratings.* Once launched, we will be aiming for 1 million downloads in the first three months and a 4.2-star rating or higher across all app stores. We will also be measuring the number of bookings that are made through the mobile application, and we will be aiming for 50 percent of our bookings to be made through the mobile application within the first year of launch.

In order to get here, we will be making some changes to our teams and our processes.

- *We are doubling our UX team.* We will be hiring 15 new people to work on the new website and mobile application. Chris will be leading this initiative, and he will be reporting directly to me. We will be hiring a mix of product designers and user researchers in order to make the new website a reality.

- *We are building a data team.* We will hire a new head of data who will spearhead our initiative to liberate the data that we have to make our booking experiences more personalized and intelligent. These insights will feed back into better search results, better recommendations, and better deals for our users. Our goals for the first year are to build the team, make the data that we have more accessible by investing in a new data warehouse, and to plan and begin executing on the first set of data-driven features.

- *Our infrastructure team will be hiring a principal engineer.* We are already in the process of interviewing for this role. This person will be responsible for the overall architecture of our new system, bridging the data warehouse, search indexes, and the new website and mobile application. They will focus on performance, reliability, and security and will spearhead the new infrastructure initiatives that we are planning.

We are excited about getting started here. However, we must realize that in order to make significant changes, we need to change the way that we work. We need to be able to move quickly by making fast decisions, and we need to be able to pivot and change our minds if they are not working in a transparent and open way.

- *All project approvals will be made by directors and then by me.* In order to keep focus, we will limit the number of projects that we work on at any one time. We will be using a new process to approve projects, the details of which will be communicated to you in the coming weeks. Every single project will have a clear owner and will be signed off by our director layer and then by me. This will ensure we're working on the right things and we're not working on too many things at once.

- *All projects will have a clear set of KPIs, entry, and exit criteria.* As we move through the year, each team will become owners of their own KPIs. We will be setting these KPIs together, and we will begin by enforcing this rigor in our work. No projects will be approved unless they are clear about the current state of the world, where they're trying to get to, and how they will know when they have arrived. We appreciate this will be new for many of you, and we will be working with you to make this a success.

- *There'll be weekly senior leadership office hours for escalations and decisions.* Engineering leadership are available every Tuesday and Thursday afternoon to help unblock you and keep us moving forward. Anyone can book a slot, and we will be there to help you make decisions and get the resources that you need.

- *We expect every team to write an update on their work every two weeks.* The work we do is the heartbeat of our organization, and the rest of the company thrives on the amazing work that we are doing. We will be introducing a new process for writing updates that should take teams no longer than 15 minutes to write and 5 minutes for others to read. We will share links, demos, and other artifacts that we are working on with the rest of the company. This will invite connections, feedback, and ideas and will help us to stay aligned and focused on our goals.

- *We will be moving to a new process for post-mortems and learning.* We have been plagued by incidents and outages over the last year, and we need to get better at learning from them. Every outage will have a post-mortem, and the resulting write-ups will be sent to the whole company.

- *With everything new that we build, we will be focusing on boring, reliable, and open source software.* There are too many thorns in our side from legacy or proprietary software. For all new infrastructure and software we build, we'll be choosing software and frameworks that are globally adopted, battle-tested, and have a strong community around them. We will contribute back to these projects where we can. Additionally, we will choose technologies that allow us to move quickly and re-use code across the website and mobile application. For example, React Native allows us to build for both iOS and Android at the same time.

We are excited about the year ahead, and we know that it is going to be challenging. However, we are going to achieve some amazing things, and you are going to be proud that you were part of BookATrip during this time. Let's do this.

Breaking Down the Strategy

Whew, I hope you're feeling pretty motivated after that! Let's break down the strategy into its constituent parts and see how you can use this as a template for your own engineering strategy.

As we go through this breakdown, remember the two groups we're aiming to satisfy: 1) senior executives and nontechnical people and 2) engineers and their close collaborators. The former group will be interested in resourcing, prioritization, trade-offs, costs, and outputs, and the latter will be interested in the details of innovation, performance, craft, resiliency, and processes.

We'll break our strategy down into four parts:

- *Initiatives*: What are we hoping to achieve and why?
- *Success metrics*: How will we know if we have been successful?
- *Investments in teams and technology*: What are we changing in the department in order to achieve this?
- *Processes and ways of working*: How are we going to work differently to get there?

Let's look at each of these in turn.

The Initiatives

The strategy begins by *framing the time period* in which it is written: the company is beginning a period of transformation. This is a clear and concise way of setting the scene for what comes next.

It then goes on to list the *key initiatives* that the engineering team will be working on over the next year. These are the *what* and detail to all audiences what success means this year. In our example, it is a complete overhaul of the website, launching a mobile application, significantly upgrading infrastructure, and doing so while keeping the lights on for the existing website.

When writing your own strategy, make it so that the busiest executive can stop reading after this point and be crystal clear on what the engineering team is doing.

The Success Metrics

Next, the strategy outlines the *success metrics* the engineering team will be using to prove these initiatives are successful and the software being produced is of high quality. These are the *how*.

Specifically, for our example, the success metrics are page load time, search speed, uptime and error rates, and mobile application downloads and ratings. These are all clear, measurable, and transparent. In the descriptions, we jump one layer down in the specifics, notably, the current state of the system and where we want to get it to. These are measured through industry-standard scores, uptime, error rates, and app store ratings.

Success metrics serve both audiences in different ways. For senior executives and nontechnical people, they're still written in an accessible way and, importantly, they show your engineering department's success is measurable and transparent. For engineers and their close collaborators, they form the top-level KPIs teams will be working toward, and, in turn, they become the basis for projects and KPIs teams will be setting for themselves. You can imagine that each individual team would own a slice of the challenges above and form their roadmap around them.

Investments in Teams and Technology

The next section of the strategy shows what is changing in the department in order to achieve everything listed. In our example, the focus is around *investments in people*, notably, expanding the UX team, building a data team, and hiring a principal engineer for infrastructure.

This is reasonable for a period of change that requires new people and new skills to be brought in. However, you could imagine that in a company during a period of stability, this section could be more about investing money into training, global expansion, new tools or technologies, or in physical or cloud infrastructure. It's worth noting that the latter would likely follow from our example strategy, but we need the people first to create that roadmap!

Again, both audiences are served by this section. Nonengineers would understand that it is a period of change and growth for engineering and that they should expect a focus on hiring, onboarding, and ramping up. Engineers and their close collaborators get a heads-up that they are going to be working with a bunch of new people and already know what they are going to be working on.

Processes and Ways of Working

The final section of the strategy outlines the *processes and ways of working* that the engineering team will be using to make these initiatives a success. These are included because they are notably different from the current state of the department, and they also inject some of the new culture that you wish to see as a leader: you want to move fast, make decisions quickly, and be hands-on in ensuring that everyone is focused on the highest-impact work while being open and available to help unblock people. Similarly, you are putting your stake in the ground with regard to the kinds of technologies that you want to see used in the department.

Even though this section is inward-looking, there are still takeaways for nonengineers. In addition to the cultural changes, they will also see that the engineering team is taking a more rigorous approach to reducing, broadcasting, and learning from incidents and outages and that they are also starting a process of regularly sharing their work with the rest of the company. Engineers will see these as new ways of working, and nonengineers will see this as a new level of transparency and openness. It's a win-win.

> **Your Turn: Write an Engineering Strategy**
>
> No matter how big your current team is or how much you are currently responsible for, take 30 minutes to write an engineering strategy for the next year.
>
> - Do your prework by talking to your team. What are the key initiatives that you are working on? What are the success metrics that you are aiming for? What investments are you making in your team and technology? What processes and ways of working are you changing, if any?
>
> - Use the template that we have just gone through, and make sure that what you write is accessible to both nontechnical people and engineers.
>
> - Once you've written it, share it with your team and get feedback. What do they think? What did you learn by going through this exercise?

Note that the strategy that we wrote *was not a plan*. It was a set of choices that BookATrip is making to set themselves up to succeed, but it doesn't go into the details of how they are going to do it. For that part, it'll be over to your teams.

Cycling Through the Year

That concludes our deep dive into strategy. Although the term is often thrown around as a buzzword, it is a *real thing* that you are expected to create and communicate as you become more senior.

Here's what we looked at in this chapter:

- *First, we defined what a strategy is and what it isn't.* We saw that it is not planning and that it is a set of choices that positions you on a playing field of your choice in a way that you win. We also looked at some examples of strategies from real companies that shaped their success.

- *Next, we looked at engineering strategies specifically* and how they exist to serve two different audiences: 1) senior executives and non-technical people and 2) engineers and their close collaborators.

- *Finally, we went through a worked example of creating an engineering strategy* for a fictional company called BookATrip. We saw how to take the overall company strategy and translate it into an engineering strategy, and we saw how this can be used to focus teams, generate ideas, and measure progress. We concluded with a short exercise to write your own engineering strategy.

In the next chapter, we'll go a layer down and look at the cadences and cycles that companies go through and how they use them to plan, execute, and measure their strategies. We'll see how you can use these cycles to make sure that your engineering strategy is being executed and how you can use them to make sure that you are making the right decisions about what to do next.

CHAPTER 12

Company Cycles

Ben is listening in on the sales kickoff event with you this morning. You thought it would be a good idea to start exposing him more to how other parts of the company work. Each quarter, the sales team gets together to walk through how they did in the previous quarter and cover what their targets are for the coming one.

Oh, and there's *plenty* of hype.

It's the first time that Ben has seen most of the sales team in one place, and he is struck by the sheer size of the team.

"Man, when you've got your head in projects and code, you forget just how many people it takes to sell this thing," he says. "I mean, I knew it was a lot, but this is a *lot*."

"I know, right?" you say.

The chief revenue officer (CRO) is speaking.

"We've had an amazing Q1. Strong results that we project are going to grow and accrue some serious ARR in H2. And you know what we're all about here: ARR is KING!"

The room cheers. "ARR! ARR! ARR!"

Ben turns to you. "What's ARR?"

"Annual recurring revenue," you say. "It's what we make from our subscriptions." Ben looks puzzled. "You didn't know that?" you ask.

"Come on, I write code," Ben says.

"Yeah, but someone's gotta pay you to write it," you say, laughing.

Back to the stage.

"We are approaching the end of the fiscal year. And you know what that means—our customers want to *use* their budgets before they *lose* them. We're going to see a *lot* of deals closing in the next few weeks. Let's WIN BIG so we go into H2 with a BANG!"

Ben turns to you again. "I'm sorry, but how is the year closing when it's only March?"

"End of the fiscal year," you say. "Since we're headquartered in the U.K., the company fiscal year ends in March. That's the end of calendar Q1 for us in the U.S."

Ben is confused. "What? Why?"

"The tax year begins in April in the U.K.," you say. Ben shrugs, turning his head back to the stage. The CRO is getting visibly excited.

"And get this: we have some incredible news thanks to how efficient you're all being. Our CAC is down BIG, and our LTV is up even BIGGER. We're going to be able to invest MORE in marketing and sales, and we are going to keep… WINNING!"

Ben gets his phone out and starts typing "cack" into his search bar. The dictionary says it's British slang for "excrement." He looks at you again, puzzled.

"Erm, what's cack?" asks Ben.

"It's *CAC*," you say. "It's an acronym—customer acquisition cost. It's how much we spend collectively on sales, marketing, and so on to get a new customer through the door. The lower it is, the better."

Ben gets back on his phone to search for "LTV." He scrolls through the results. "Long-term value? Loan-to-value? Lifetime value? Is it the brand of fruity vodka being advertised at the top of the search results?"

Ben puts his phone back in his pocket. He taps you on the arm. "Hang on, what's H2 again?"

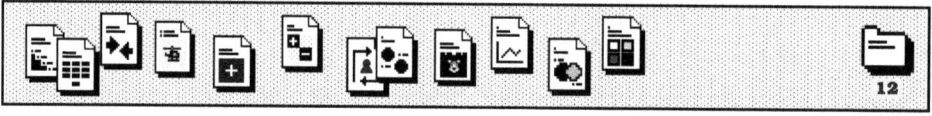

Engineering is a world of its own, with its own language and way of doing things. By now, you probably take for granted the fact that you understand what a sprint is or what CI/CD means. And you probably don't think twice about pairing, garbage collection, pointers, or any of the other things that are part of your day-to-day.

However, as you get more senior, you will run face first into the fact that the rest of the business has its own schedule, language, and way of doing things. And it's not just the language that's different; the way that the rest of the business *operates* is different too.

In the engineering department, you may be used to fluidly working on the product, releasing things when they're done, and iterating on them as you go. Yet, the rest of the business is often working to a different beat. They have their *own* cycles covering how they plan and execute and how they communicate with the outside world.

Being able to understand the world outside engineering and interface with it is critical to your success as a senior leader. It's not just about being able to *communicate* with the rest of the business; it's about developing *empathy, understanding, and alignment* through a symbiotic relationship.

Great engineering leaders are able to ensure that, despite the company wanting to have two big splash marketing events every year, the product is still being delivered continuously at the same time. They are able to help sales land that deal that they've been working on for months in a way that doesn't set fire to the existing roadmap.

Over the next two chapters, we're going to study our interfaces and inputs with other parts of the company. We're going to begin with two that are closely linked: marketing and sales. Here's what we'll cover:

- *First, we'll look at the calendar and see how the year is broken up into cycles that serve as the rhythm of the business.* We'll explore how, with time, engineering culture has evolved to be more continuous, effectively eroding traditional calendar cycles and how other parts of the business are still very much tied to them.

- *With this in mind, we'll look deeper at how you can forge a strong bond with sales by understanding their cycles and how they succeed.* We'll cover how best to drive down uncertainty, keep a roadmap up to date, and how to be a good partner.

- *Next, we'll turn to the marketing team and see how they operate.* We'll discuss how to support what appear to be big bang launches, while behind the scenes, they are *actually* continuous delivery.

- *Finally, we'll troubleshoot common problems that arise between your department and theirs.* These problems will be common themes that you'll wind up dealing with as a senior leader, and we'll give you some tools and techniques to help you navigate them.

Being a successful engineering leader isn't always about being the best at engineering. It's about being the best at *leading*. And leading means steering engineering while focusing *equal* attention on helping the rest of the company succeed, too.

Let's get going.

The Calendar Is Dead, Long Live the Calendar

We could hypothesize that the utopian ideal of software engineering would be similar to a craftsperson in their workshop. Each day, they would enter the workshop and hone their skills, creating tools and products at their own pace. No meetings, no interruptions, just quiet, considered, mindful creation. It's done when it's done, and it's done well.

We know that the reality can be quite different. Since building and selling software requires a diverse cast of humans, from marketers to salespeople to customer support, the utopian ideal is reserved for only a small number of programmers—those who write code for a hobby and perhaps some who have managed to monetize niche pieces of software that only require themselves to build them.

Given this distance between the reality and the utopian ideal, various methodologies have molded the reality into something a little bit more manageable. Given how much of a nightmare waterfall development has proven to be,[1] our development methodologies have moved toward small, iterative cycles that allow us to experiment, learn, iterate, and pivot as needed. Software gets delivered continuously, deployed at any time of the day or week, and there are no more big bang launches and subsequent catastrophes. This is obviously a good thing.

However, this way of thinking has increased the conceptual distance between engineering and everyone else. There is an obvious cultural mismatch between a salesperson who wants to know all of the key shipping dates for features so they can talk to a prospect vs. a selection of engineering teams named after rare marmosets working within two-week sprints named after comic book characters. Knowing that smart search will arrive sometime in the future, maybe around Wolverine or Magneto, is no help to anybody.

Even though engineering has been marching to the beat of its own drum for a while, especially within institutions that follow capital-A Agile fervently, as a senior leader, you need to ensure that your department does *not* become

---

1. https://en.wikipedia.org/wiki/Waterfall_model

allergic to the calendars and schedules that the rest of the company operates on. The frameworks that engineering uses to help itself should *always* translate to projects and dates that make sense to everybody else.

Whatever framework engineering works within, whether estimating in noodles or iterating in boats, it should translate to real commitments for which the rest of the company can hold you accountable. The frameworks are for *you* to work within, not for the rest of the company to understand.

Different Departments, Different Cycles

The majority of humans use the Gregorian calendar: January to December. Companies also use dates, but dates do not form the natural cycles that departments use to plan, execute, reflect, and then do that all over again.

Typically, you will find that other departments chop the year up into four quarters, with the shorthand Q1, Q2, Q3, and Q4. Generally speaking, the dates are defined as follows:

- *Q1*: Starting in January and ending in March
- *Q2*: Starting in April and ending in June
- *Q3*: Starting in July and ending in September
- *Q4*: Starting in October and ending in December

You may also see the shorthand H1 and H2, which refer to the first (Q1 and Q2) and second half of the year (Q3 and Q4), respectively.

Other departments hang their cycles off these quarters. The most prominent of these is the sales team, who use quarters to plan their sales targets and to measure their performance. If you have worked closely with sales before, then you will have experienced the pressure that comes with the *end* of the quarter and the ensuing mad scramble to get signatures on dotted lines. Staff work long days and weekends to hit their targets. Companies often set up end-of-quarter support in the form of "deal desks," which are multidisciplinary squads that help sales close, such as legal and finance, and priority access to the executive team. You may also be expected to be part of these deal desks in order to guide related engineering questions, concerns, and commitments.

Your finance team also organizes themselves around these quarters. If you work for a public company, then you'll be familiar with the earnings calls that happen at the end of each quarter. These calls are where the company reports its financial performance to the public, giving an overview of how the company has performed and what the outlook is for the future. This has a direct impact on stock price, employee morale, and any stock-based compensation.

Your marketing team may organize themselves differently. Although they may report internally in quarters, their yearly milestones are usually pegged to events such as product launches, trade shows, and conferences. The exact timing of these events depends on the industry. For example, technology companies that acquire and deliver on government contracts may have a completely different marketing schedule than those that serve the consumer market through traditional advertising.

As such, a company's calendar is a complex tapestry of events, milestones, and targets that are all interconnected. A simplified version of this is shown in the following diagram:

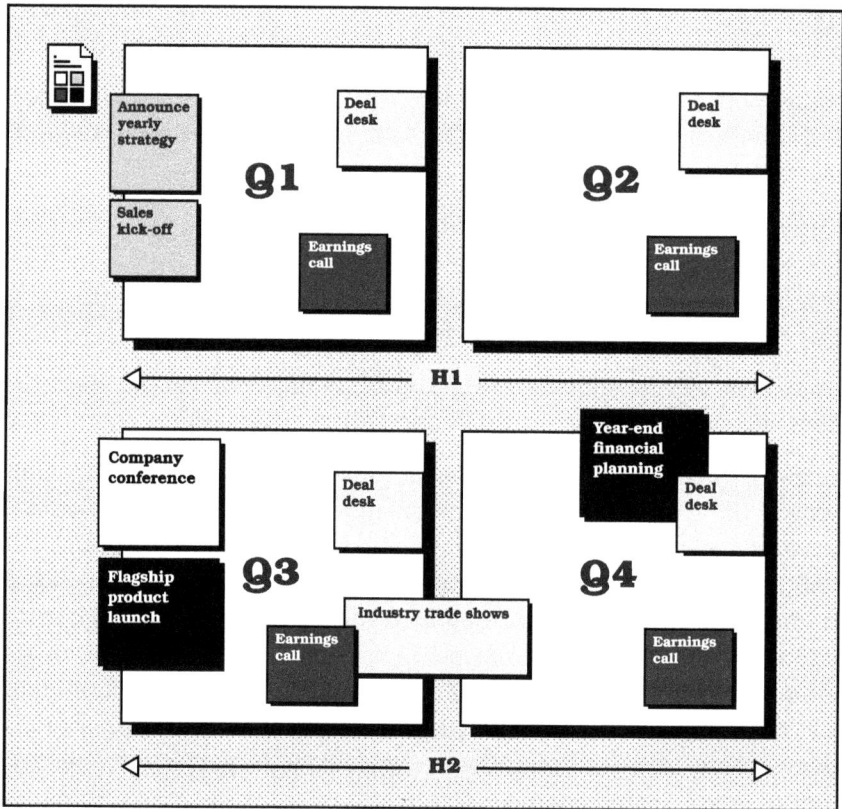

If the example yearly cycle in the calendar was that of *your* company, what does this mean for *you* as a senior engineering leader?

- *You need to develop an understanding of the cycles of the rest of the business to see how you can best align your time, attention, and team to them.* This is not just about understanding the dates but understanding the *context* of what is happening at those times. For example, if you are aware of the sales cycle, you'll know why it's important to keep your roadmap up to date and visible to the rest of the business and to make yourself available when needed.

- *You need to deliver continuously but also be able to support "big bang" unveilings and launches.* The best of both worlds is possible, and we'll dig into how to do this shortly.

- *You need to communicate with the rest of the business in a way that makes sense to them.* It is your responsibility to translate the work that your team is doing into a language that the rest of the business can understand. This is because your work feeds the marketing narrative, the sales pitch, and the financial outlook of the company.

- *You'll need to raise your awareness of financial cycles.* Research and development is one of the most expensive parts of a company, and you control a lot of that budget. You should both be able to understand and justify your spend and also have predictions and forecasts that enable you to plan accordingly for differing financial situations in the future.

This final point, covering how to think about money, will be a chapter in its own right: Chapter 13, Money Makes the World Go Round, on page 295. However, we'll cover everything else in this chapter.

Sales: Can't Live with Them, Can't Live Without Them

Not all software sells itself. In fact, most of it doesn't. For 99 percent of companies, "build it and they will come" is a recipe for having no users. And, even if you *do* work for one of the lucky few companies that have a product that grows seemingly on its own, you may still have salespeople striking data partnerships, selling the ability to advertise on the platform, or upselling premium or enterprise features.

For any large corporation where you would likely find yourself in a senior position, it's likely the sales team is a *significant* driving force in the company. After all, selling a software solution to a large enterprise is a complex process that requires a lot of people, time, and effort. Getting a deal over the line involves building a relationship with the customer, understanding their needs, and then working with them to build a solution they're willing to invest in.

It's not uncommon for a sales cycle to last for months or even *years* in some industries. As such, there are a number of things that you need to be on top of as a senior engineering leader to ensure that your team is able to support the sales team effectively:

- *You need to generate certainty about the future.* Sales teams aren't just selling what is available now as a singular product; they are selling a future proposition that improves over time: more features, functionality, and integrations. You have the job of communicating what is coming and when, and how it will help the customer. This is not just about having a roadmap, but it is also about being able to communicate the *uncertainty and opportunity* that comes with it.

- *You need to be available to support the sales team when they need you.* The larger the deal, the larger the amount of potential engineering support that is required. This spans providing information for requests for proposals (RFPs) to being available to answer technical questions to having clear guarantees around your SLAs and support. It may be the case that a deal could hinge on a feature that is not yet available, and you need to be able to communicate the likelihood of it being delivered in time.

- *You need to give the sales team the flexibility to respond to urgent asks.* As pure as you may wish your product development to be, there'll be times when a left-field request comes in from a customer that could make or break a deal. And those could be really big deals. You need to ride the line of being able to deliver on these asks but not compromise the platform in the process.

Let's dig in.

Removing Uncertainty: The Tip of the Iceberg

Sometimes, we think of great engineering leadership as being about the ability to deliver on time, but it's actually about *managing and reducing uncertainty*.

Why is that? Well, we spend a lot of time working on things that nobody else knows exists. A seemingly simple act of serving up a photostream with infinite scroll may require global infrastructure, aggressive caching, and data being mirrored at the edges of a content delivery network (CDN).

There seems to be an inverse correlation between the *delight* of a user experience and the *challenge* of the implementation in software at scale. This is because in order for the tip of the iceberg to be visible and beautiful, it has to be supported by the 90 percent of it that exists underwater. This is the part that others aren't able to see, and it's why people find it so hard to understand what we do, as shown in the diagram on page 279.

The bigger the scale, the bigger the iceberg. The better the design, the simpler it appears to everyone else. Great software design fools the world into thinking the underwater part of the iceberg doesn't exist. But it does. And it's hard.

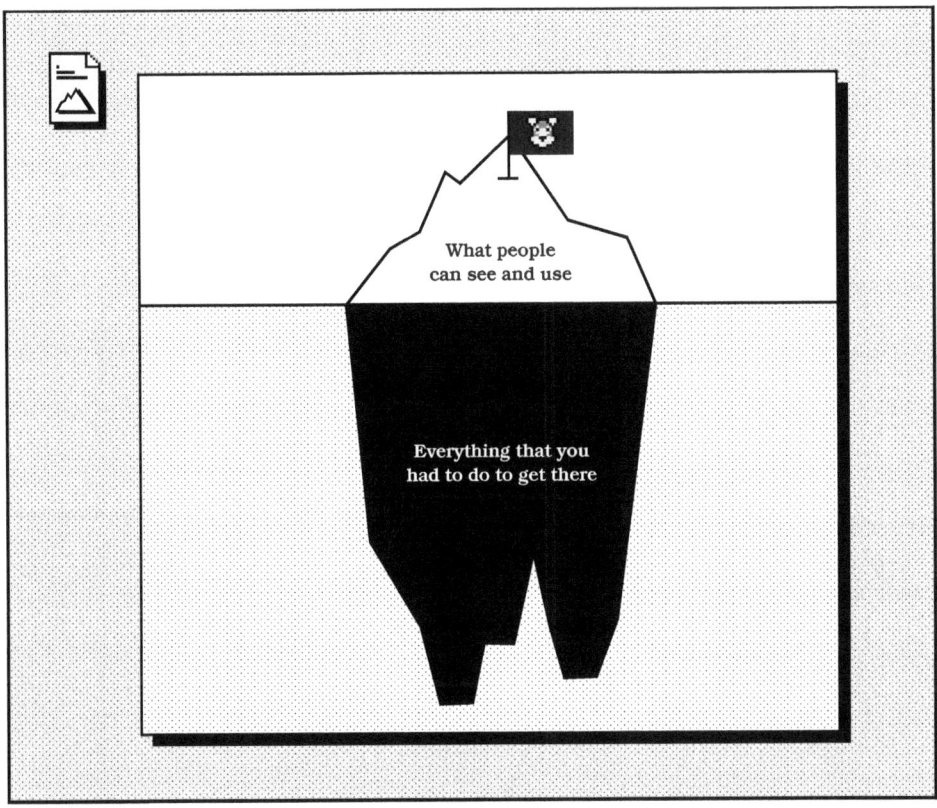

You know the feeling: your design looks so incredibly simple, but the work to bring it to life is immense. And what's worse is that others don't understand why your estimates are so large, if you can even come up with reasonable estimates at all. So, it's no surprise that teams find this challenging to navigate: when working with other parts of the business, you need to shift the mindset *away from dates and toward reducing uncertainty.*

You need to coach this mindset across your whole organization.

When you're staring a huge, challenging project in the face, don't align your team around just getting it done. Instead, *align your team around continually reducing uncertainty.*

You reduce uncertainty until the software exists. You reduce uncertainty by the act of doing: prototyping, designing, writing code, and shipping. Each of these actions serves to reduce the uncertainty about what is left to build. When you have zero uncertainty, the feature has shipped. Until then, when you have uncertainty, you aggressively work on reducing it by taking positive action. By *doing*.

This means you prioritize the most uncertain parts of your project first and focus your efforts on getting answers. Answers fall into two broad categories: that it is possible, as proved by code, or that it's not possible, but yields another avenue to try. You repeat this process until you're done or until you think it's best to stop. An example of how this plays out is shown in the following diagram:

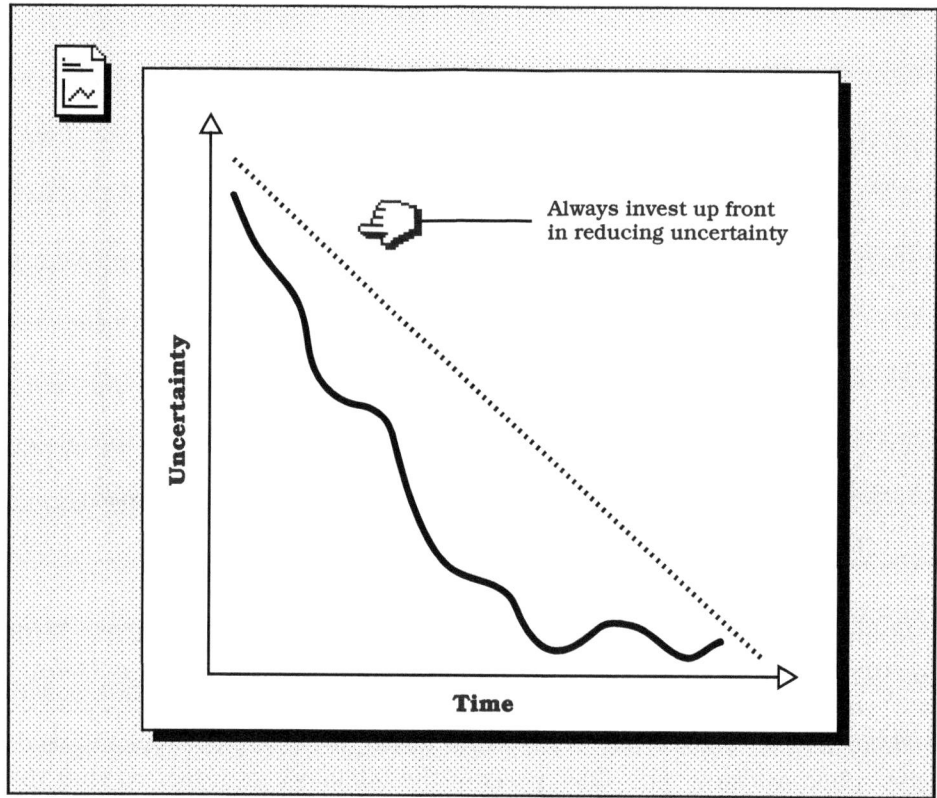

Focusing on reducing uncertainty builds momentum and trust both inside and outside of the team. You can reduce uncertainty by making these things a part of each of your projects:

- *Defining metrics up front.* What does success look like? How will you measure it? What are the key performance indicators that you are trying to move?

- *Prototyping.* What is the smallest amount of throwaway code you can write to prove something is possible or not possible? Similarly, can you build a UX prototype to prove a design is feasible? You can even prototype architecture; can you do back-of-the-envelope calculations to prove a certain approach is feasible and is going to work at scale for cost and throughput?

- *Technical design.* Can you write a design document that outlines the approach that you are going to take so that it can be critiqued and improved before anything hits the codebase?

Think about ways in which you can incorporate these steps into how your department does projects, and you will go faster. You will also be able to communicate more effectively with the rest of the business because you can *taper down uncertainty*.

Structuring a Roadmap Based on Uncertainty

Given that uncertainty decreases as you move through a project, you can structure your roadmap to reflect this. Thinking of the cycles of a business, we can be:

- *Certain about what's coming in the next month.* If it's coming out in the next four weeks, it's probably almost done.

- *Fairly certain about what's coming in the next quarter.* If it's coming out in the next three months, it's probably well underway, at least in terms of prototyping, thinking, and designing.

- *Less certain about what's coming in the next half of the year.* If it's coming out in the next six months, it's probably in the early stages of being thought about; perhaps there are some proposals.

- *Even less certain about what's coming in the next year.* Unless you work in hardware, next year is a very long way away. You can have some ideas, but they are likely to be strategic at this point.

This is a good way to think about how to structure your roadmap. You can be specific with dates for the next month, but as you move further out, you *decrease in granularity as uncertainty increases*. You then keep this roadmap up to date and visible to the rest of the business.

Some may say the production of the roadmap is a product responsibility. However, that doesn't mean they create it in isolation. The best roadmaps are created in *collaboration* with engineering, product, UX, and all other roles in the multifecta. Lean in, and feel ownership over it. It's your team that's going to be delivering on it, after all. Plus, you'll want to advocate for engineering-led initiatives that improve the quality of the software and the speed of delivery.

This example roadmap, as shown in the table on page 282, gives you an idea of what this could look like. This is simplified for brevity, but it should give you an idea of how uncertainty can be communicated by changing the granularity of the dates.

Feature	Stage	Date	Initiative
Third-party auth support	Rollout	2024-03-01	Enhance security
Dashboard Picker	Build	2024-04-15	Reduce top frustrations
Mobile app 1.0	Build	Q2	Expand into mobile
PDF reports	Build	Q2	Reduce common frustrations
Email onboarding flow	Build	Q2	Reduce common frustrations
Multilingual support	Prototype	Q3	Reduce common frustrations
New storage architecture	Prototype	H2	Instant reporting
Charting system V2.0	Design	2025	Instant reporting

Your roadmap may contain far more detail than we can fit into the width of the pages of this book, but it should *at least* contain the columns shown:

- *Feature*: What exactly is the feature that you are building? This should be clear and understandable to the rest of the business. Ideally, the feature should also be a link to your project tracking system so that people can see the details.

- *Stage*: What stage is the feature at? Your mileage may vary, but example stages are shown. The key is that your projects move through stages that reduce uncertainty as they go.

- *Date*: When is the feature expected to be delivered? This should be as specific as possible, given the current uncertainty. As you move further out, the dates should become less specific. This is why that blockbuster movie that you're looking forward to is always "coming soon," then "coming this summer," and then *finally* it has a date, which is next month.

- *Initiative*: Back in Chapter 11, Strategy 101, on page 253, we gave examples of writing an engineering strategy. Every one of your projects should tie to one of the key initiatives you have outlined in that strategy, and there should be a link to the relevant part of the strategy document here, too.

Additional columns that you may want to consider adding are:

- *Owner*: Who is the person or team responsible for delivering this feature? How can they be contacted?

- *Latest update*: What is the latest update on this feature? This could be a link to a document or a summary of the latest progress.

- *Latest demo*: If there is a usable mock-up, prototype, or video demo of the feature, then this could be linked here.

- *Dependencies*: If there are any dependencies that are blocking this feature, then you could link them here, too.

You should decide on a cadence you and your team will keep up to date with the latest projections. The length of the cadence is up to you, but the more often, the better. You should also decide how you'll communicate major updates of the roadmap to the rest of the business. This could be a monthly or quarterly summary, or it could be a live document updated in real time.

Either way, good roadmap hygiene is a boon for sales. Remember: large enterprise deals are not just selling the existing software. They are the beginning of a long-term relationship, and the customer is *buying into the future*. The more that you can communicate about what that future holds, the more you can reduce uncertainty, and the more your sales team can shine on the front line.

A common frustration expressed by engineers is that they are continually answering internal questions about upcoming features. What are we working on? When is it ready? What does it do? This isn't a sign of an annoying sales team but a sign that the rest of the business is not getting enough out of the information that you are providing. Fixing that problem is on you, not them.

> ### Your Turn: RFP Quickfire Round
>
> Before we move on to the next section, let's pretend a big RFP just landed in your email inbox from a salesperson working on a potentially huge deal with a large enterprise. They need a response to these questions in the next hour. Do you have them to give?
>
> - What is your uptime guarantee? What was your uptime for the last three months?
> - List your compliance certifications and attestations, including when they were last audited and when they are next due for renewal.
> - Detail the last three major incidents that you had and what you did to resolve them.
> - Outline where your data is hosted and what your data retention policy is. Explain how you action requests for data deletion by users.
> - Give an overview of your architecture and how you ensure that it is secure. List key vendors that you are dependent on and how you would handle a failure of one of them.
> - Detail your disaster recovery plan and how often you test it.
>
> If you don't already have these answers in documents that are shared with your commercial teams, then that's another way you can be a great partner: take ownership of making the common answers to engineering questions available for RFPs.

Marketing: Big Bangs Without the Bang

Sales gets the signatures that bring in the money, but marketing ensures that the sales team has a steady stream of leads to work with in the first place. Marketing itself has a wide scope and can encompass everything from product marketing to demand generation to brand marketing to events to content to PR to analyst relations and more.

Abstracting that complexity away, marketing is about getting the right message about your software to the right people at the right time. How exactly that happens will depend on your company and what kinds of products you are selling. Some companies, like Apple, have a culture of secrecy and unveil surprise launches at special events, whereas others prefer to continually drip-feed features and updates to the market over time.

The key thing to understand here is that, regardless of how marketing engages with the market, *you* need to ensure that marketing and engineering are aligned. Much like with sales, you need to ensure that you are *reducing uncertainty and delivering based on an up-to-date roadmap*. This is because marketing will be using your roadmap to plan their campaigns. And depending on the size of those launches, they may be planning them *months* in advance.

This interplay between marketing launches and engineering delivery is why the video game industry suffers from *crunch*: the period of time before a game is released when the team works long hours to get it over the line and ready for launch. Within the levers of scope, resources, and time, video games often have the least wiggle room to play with.

While you may not be working in the videogame industry, you'll still have to navigate this pressure. You'll have to deal with the fact marketing will want to plan launches that attract attention and generate leads, but you'll want to avoid the crunch and the stress that comes with it. But how do you do this?

"Big bang" launches are the most risky kind of launch. Imagine if, for every large, marketable feature that you built that had a significant marketing campaign, you had to:

- Ship it to production as the marketing launch went out so that it was hidden from users beforehand.

- Enable it for all users immediately.

- Deal with the fact that this is happening for the first time (is it going to work?) right as the whole world is watching (I hope it doesn't break!).

If you've ever done this before, you'll know how sweaty it is. Abstracting *this* situation away, we can see that in addition to giving your marketers predictability through a clear roadmap that progresses by reducing uncertainty, they also want *complete certainty and control* as to when a feature is going to be available.

The dichotomy of this situation is that, from an engineering standpoint, you want to deliver continuously and iteratively, testing new features with real load and traffic, but from a marketing standpoint, you want to be able to plan and execute a big bang launch. When deciding how your department is going to run, you need to be able to balance these two competing forces.

Feature Flags: The Best of Both Worlds

If your software isn't able to already, you need to add a layer of feature flags, or toggles, that allow you to show and hide features in real time without the need to deploy new code. This will allow you to deliver continuously, but you can hide the feature from users until a marketing launch goes out. Then you just flick the switch, and it's there. Hey presto.

There are a multitude of reasons that you'll want to coach your teams to work with feature flags:

- *You can deliver continuously.* By being able to ship into production at any time, you prevent long-lived branches hanging around that continually need rebasing until a feature is launched.

- *You can deliver new functionality way ahead of time.* Not only does this allow you to use the feature internally and test it in production, but it also decouples the need to deploy from the need to launch.

- *You can route real traffic to the feature without users knowing.* For example, if you were building a new search index, you could both populate, update, and query the new index behind the scenes. For example, you could route all search queries to it in parallel but not show the results. The rubber only hits the road in production, after all.

- *You prevent the need for a multitude of intermediate testing environments.* Instead of needing to maintain several staging environments with increasingly larger datasets that are *like* production, you can instead test in production *directly* and then roll out the feature when you are ready. This is far simpler.

- *Rollbacks are easy.* If something goes wrong, you can just turn the feature off.

- *Marketing, sales, and anyone else can see new features in action.* By enabling your feature flags for internal users, staff can see what is coming and how it works. This allows marketers to use the product they are building campaigns for and for sales to be able to show it to prospects.

For some organizations, this is a significant shift in how they work. However, as an engineering leader, you should ensure that your team has the tools and the processes to build high-quality software that is rigorously battle-tested but without the user needing to be the guinea pig.

What's more, a feature flag system can be used for more than just marketing launches. In fact, it can support the following:

- *A/B testing.* You can use your feature flags to define cohorts of users that see different versions of the same feature, thus allowing A/B testing.

- *Beta programs.* Some users may want to opt in to using new features before they're generally available, especially if you have an engaged user base. You can build beta programs on top of collections of feature flags.

- *Early access and developer previews.* If you have a developer audience, you can give them early access to new features or API endpoints. Not only is this practical for them to get a heads-up on upcoming functionality that may require changes in their integrations, but it also gives marketing the ability to build a community of developers that form an *essential* part of the periphery of the company.

Don't leave the relationship with sales and marketing to chance. Be proactive and use it as an opportunity to improve your practices in your teams. Build an interactive roadmap that links to your strategy and progress, and make engineering a process of *reducing uncertainty* rather than hitting deadlines. Do all of this in the open to give sales teams what they need to excel at their own jobs. This makes pivots and failures far less painful, and it also makes the rest of the business far more confident in your ability to deliver. Use feature flags and toggles to deliver continuously and to support big bang launches that actually aren't big bangs at all.

Looking back at the beginning of the chapter, you can see much of the company operates on rigid calendar cycles: end-of-quarter sales crunch and deal desks, fixed marketing launches, and earnings calls. If you're working for a technology company, underpinning the success of all these is *your team's output*. By making your strategy, roadmap, and progress visible and interactive and by decoupling delivery from launch, engineering really can be a smooth and continuous process that enables and empowers the company to excel.

Two Worlds Collide: Troubleshooting and Solutions

As you well know, there are always thorns in your side. In fact, sometimes there are whole rose bushes. We are going to round out this chapter by covering some of the common problems that you will face at the intersection of engineering and the rest of the business, and we'll give you some tools and techniques to help you navigate them.

Mis-selling: The Tail Wagging the Dog

One of the most common frustrations is when salespeople sell things that don't exist. Perhaps they sign a deal with a large enterprise client that agrees that an integration will be available for their own login provider, or they agree to having a feature that is not yet available. Let's be straight: this shouldn't happen. But, guess what? It does.

> **Well, You're Building It Now**
>
> One of your engineering managers has come to you with a problem. A salesperson has told them that they urgently need to build a new feature that is not currently in the product, and it needs to be ready for next month when ACMECorp onboards.
>
> It turns out the landmark sales deal recently celebrated was contingent on this feature being available, but something has clearly gone wrong. It isn't even on the roadmap.

Why does this happen? Sometimes, it's down to miscommunication around what's on the roadmap and what isn't. Sometimes, it's down to sales just wanting to get the deal over the line and not consulting with product and engineering first. Sometimes, it's just poor practice. Regardless of the reason, it's a problem that you need to solve since it causes panic, disrupts your planning, and erodes trust between departments. Here are some things that you can do:

- *Understand how this happens in the first place.* Meet with sales leadership and understand how they are selling. Are they clear on what the roadmap is? Have you provided it in a format like we discussed earlier? Do they know the process for requesting urgent features that don't exist? Is there one? What incentives do they have in place that drive this behavior?

- *Build better connections at the periphery and at the top of sales.* If you are able to build better connections with the sales team, then you can build bidirectional empathy—both what it means for them when the product is lacking and what it means for you when they sell things that don't exist.

Regular communication brings feedback from the periphery to you, which you can action. See if you can build a symbiotic relationship, much like you would with your manager. Consider setting up regular meetings with the head of sales to discuss the roadmap and the current deal pipeline.

- *Set aside resource allocation for these surprises.* In the spirit of being prepared regardless, if you build a buffer into your capacity planning for these surprises, then you can have easier choices when it comes to replanning and reallocating. Even better, if your teams know that sometimes a quick priority switch will secure a key deal, then it can be a morale boost for them to be able to help out.

- *Make it clear what suffers as a result of reprioritization.* Whenever this happens, make it completely transparent as to what other work gets pushed back. Include it in your roadmap, make an announcement, and ensure that *everyone* knows. Not only is this important to keep the rest of the company updated, but it also helps broadcast that this isn't work that can be done secretly behind the scenes: there is likely a cost on other features and initiatives that *other* deals need too. It's all a trade-off, and you can expose that trade-off to everyone.

Ideally, selling features that don't exist will only happen rarely, or when it does, it has senior leadership sign-off first. If it is an endemic problem, and leadership won't resolve it or take it seriously, then it might be the sign of a deeper cultural problem that you may not be able to fix.

No Feature, No Deal

If mis-selling is the *worst* case scenario, then the slightly-less-worse situation is being held hostage by a deal that is contingent on a feature that is not yet available. Companies with poor relationships between sales and engineering can create situations where engineering is put under pressure to reprioritize in order to deliver something that could potentially close a deal, even if there isn't complete certainty that the deal will close.

This One Thing Will Change Everything

You've opened your email to read a message from the head of sales, which also copies in the CEO.

They explain that one of the biggest potential deals of the quarter won't happen unless the product supports detailed customer account permissions. They want you to get it shipped ahead of their meeting with the client in two weeks.

The beauty of software is that it can be written once and then used by thousands, millions, or billions of people. The perfect roadmap is one that is built on the needs of the market at large and says "no" to niche requests far more than it says "yes."

There'll always be potential customers who won't buy your product because it doesn't have a niche feature they *alone* need. The key strategic choice here is working out what the feature set is that continually improves the product for the many, not the few, and either broadens or deepens the potential market, both now and in the future. Everything else is not worth building. Or perhaps this is where you should think about how to make your product extensible so that customers and developers can build their own integrations and apps—then you can focus on the core product.

There is a serious cost to making a series of little hacks and niche features again and again. It dilutes your core vision, clutters your roadmap, and makes your product confusing. And it's in your court as a leader to push back; over time, it is death by a thousand papercuts.

In a previous startup that I worked for through to acquisition, in order to get a deal over the line in the early days, sales held engineering hostage over a nuance in how charts were displayed. A particular customer wouldn't sign their deal unless the data in our charts was rendered to their exact specification, despite that not being how the product worked for everyone else.

This hack resulted in tens of places in the code that had a function call that overrode the output of charting calls and formatted it as the customer wanted if we knew it was them making the request. As time passed, these forks in the code had many years of additional development layered on top, and the code had to be continually maintained and tested. It was a nightmare. It felt like you had to build some features twice. After that customer left us, we never had time to clean up the mess.

See whether your executive leadership wants to build a platform for the future by making the hard decisions now or whether there will be harder decisions to make later because they are avoiding it. It's a great test of leadership.

Full-On Feature Factory Grind

If you're feeling like your department is a feature factory,[2] that is, you are expected to use all your capacity to continually produce new features, leaving no space to pay down technical debt, improve resiliency and scalability, or

---

2. https://cutle.fish/blog/12-signs-youre-working-in-a-feature-factory

improve developer efficiency, then you need to realize that the buck stops with *you* as a senior leader.

> **What Is Engineering Even Doing?**
>
> You've just been in a meeting with the head of product, and they are frustrated at the pace of delivery in engineering. They feel that the roadmap is too thin compared to what competitors are shipping and the size of the department.
>
> They want to see more features, and they want to see them faster. In the heat of the moment, you were unable to articulate a good answer to this accusation, and now you're not sure what to do.

It is your responsibility to allocate your engineering resources appropriately. And guess who the person is who understands the pain of not investing in resiliency, scalability, and clearing down technical debt the most? You! Similar to how in Chapter 3, Time: Observed, Spent, and Allocated, on page 55 we discussed reserving some of your own capacity, you need to ensure that the same is true of *your teams*. You need to be investing in a *platform* that can support the features that you need now and into the future.

There are some approaches that you can take to do this:

- *Teach the rest of the business that speed and stability are features.* Nobody likes using buggy or slow software. If you can build speed and resiliency into your engineering strategy, then you can use this to inform and educate the rest of the company as to what benefits nonfeature work brings.

- *Work within your multifecta to earmark an acceptable percentage of time spent on engineering-led initiatives.* This could be 10 percent or even 50 percent when there are big rocks to move. Either way, the allocation should be agreed upon, present and visible in the roadmap, regularly reviewed, and tracked in an understandable way, with measurements. Every piece of engineering-led work should *still* make the product better: that caching layer will make page load speeds faster, or that new architecture will make the product faster for users outside of the United States. Speed is a feature.

- *Be clear about the cost of not doing this work.* For example, do you foresee that page load speeds will atrophy over the coming years with the current growth of the user base? Spread that narrative. Remember, as a senior engineering leader, it's on *you* to be able to communicate the value of the work your team is doing, not to hide it out of plain sight. Doing the latter reinforces the stereotype that engineers will just "go off and do their own thing" when they are not working on features. Sell the story instead.

- *Publicly celebrate the wins that you achieve.* As engineering-led work lands, celebrate it in the same way that you celebrate new features going live: give it the same internal airtime and attention. Record videos of the experience before and after the work was done. Show the before and after metrics. This builds a culture of performance improvements as a first-class citizen *alongside* new features rather than a second-class citizen underneath them.

Remember, They're Smart Too

Something that can broaden the void between engineering and other parts of the business is a culture of engineering thinking that a lot of what they do is not understandable to others. This stereotype isn't only damaging, but it's also not true. Sure, it might be the case somebody in sales or marketing couldn't fire up their code editor and ship something to production today, but that doesn't mean they can't understand it's important to spend time bringing another availability zone online in a different continent for speed or rebuilding the logic around payments will make the product less prone to errors that frustrate users.

> **Why Can't You Just Explain It?**
>
> One of the product marketing leads has come to you because they are struggling to work with one of your teams. Getting them to clearly explain the user impact of this year's scalability improvements is going nowhere despite it being a headline item in the latest marketing splash. Each interaction with your team either makes her feel stupid or makes the engineers defensive about her probing for details that will make sense to customers.
>
> She's frustrated, and it's now time for you to help her fix this broken communication.

Richard Feynman once said that if you can't explain something simply, then you don't understand it well enough. This is a good rule of thumb to live by. Your teams should be fully able to give explanations of what they are doing to nontechnical people. After all, everything that engineering does is in service of making the product better.

If there's a pervasive culture of engineering thinking that they are smarter than the rest of the business or that the business can't understand them, you should fix that immediately. Here's how you can do that:

- *Be clear that this is unacceptable.* This is a culture problem, and it's on you to resolve it. Absolutely everything your teams are doing, even if it is the most complex and esoteric technical problem, should always be framed in how it makes the product better, more stable, or how it makes engineers able to go faster. That's how the roadmap should be framed, and it's how your engineers should be able to talk about their work.

- *Help your teams understand that being more visible and understandable buys them more time to do engineering work.* Hiding engineering work from the company invites increased scrutiny. Working on it in the open, in a way that others can understand what is going on, actually *increases* trust in a way that compounds over time, further unlocking the amount of time you can spend on engineering-led initiatives. Once other parts of the business can see all the work you're doing to make things better, safer, faster, and more stable, they will celebrate it and want more of it.

- *Be clear that the rest of the business is incredibly smart, too.* It's unlikely one of your engineers could land an enterprise deal, launch a marketing campaign, or de-escalate a complex customer account problem. A great company is a collection of specialists that master a part of the whole. Engineering is no different. Everyone needs everyone else—it's a team sport. And to reiterate the previous point, if people don't understand what you're doing, then it's your fault. Fix it.

Dollars, Pound, Euros, and Yen

That brings us to the end of this chapter—a two-parter that deals with other parts of the business. Here's what we've covered:

- *We've looked at the calendar and seen how the year is broken up into cycles that serve as the rhythm of the business.* We've explored how, with time, engineering culture has evolved to be more continuous, effectively eroding traditional calendar cycles and how other parts of the business are still very much tied to them.

- *We looked at how to build a better relationship with sales by focusing on reducing uncertainty rather than hitting deadlines.* In addition to this, we covered how to structure a roadmap that uses granularity of dates to communicate this uncertainty.

- *Then, building on this, we saw how to support marketing launches while still delivering continuously.* We covered how to use feature flags and toggles to keep engineering streamlined and support big bang launches that actually aren't big bangs at all.

- *Finally, we troubleshot some common problems that arise between other parts of the business and engineering.* Notably, how to handle mis-selling, being held hostage over features, escaping the feature factory grind, and avoiding an engineering culture that is difficult to interrogate.

In the next chapter, we will move on to money. As you become more senior, you will be expected to handle large budgets, and you will need to be able to justify your spends and forecast your future needs. Do you build or buy? Hire or outsource? What is the difference between capital and operational expenditure? We'll cover all of this and more.

CHAPTER 13

Money Makes the World Go Round

It's late Tuesday afternoon. You're attending a meeting with the CFO, along with all of the other directors.

"Okay, so if you all check your inboxes right now, you'll each have a detailed breakdown of your area's spend for the last twelve months. I want you all to take a look at it and then provide a forecast for the next twelve months, highlighting any key areas of spend that you think are going to change."

You open your inbox, locate the email, and click on the attachment. Your spreadsheet application whirrs to life, and you're presented with a bewildering array of columns, rows, and numbers. You're not sure where to start.

"When do you need this done by?" asks one of the other attendees.

"By the end of the week," replies the CFO. "I need to get the budget finalized and signed off by the board by the end of the month."

You feel a mild panic as you realize you're on vacation on Friday, giving you a grand total of 48 hours to wrap your head around this. You scan the columns from left to right. Capex, opex, amortization, depreciation, and a whole host of other terms that haven't been part of your daily vocabulary.

You look at the bottom of the sheet where the totals are. Your department spent $10 million last year on cloud compute alone? But how? Is that normal? And how can it be that the enterprise version of that ticket-tracking software costs more than a house?

"I've got to run to another meeting," says the CFO. "If you have any questions, my team can help you with the details. To help put things into perspective, there's another sheet in there that shows some top line numbers for the company, similar to what we report to the board. That way, you can compare and contrast your area's spend with the company's overall P&L. Back in a bit."

You keep staring at the original sheet. Are these numbers good? Bad? Normal? Hmm. You click across to the sheet that was just mentioned and see a whole new set of numbers and terms that you aren't sure about. What does EBITDA mean? What's the difference between a cost center and a profit center? And what is an LTV:CAC ratio?

Some of the other people in the room are already furiously typing away, and you're not sure whether you want to be searching the Internet for what this all means in front of your peers.

"Just gotta take a quick call," you say, slipping out of the room. You find a quiet corner and open a new tab. You type "company finance 101" into the search bar and hit return...

Back in Chapter 11, Strategy 101, on page 253, we worked through the basics of strategy and how as a senior leader, you will be expected to define, communicate, and execute a strategy for the engineering department. Often, when we think about the execution of this strategy, we think about the people, the technology, and the processes that we need to put in place. But there's another crucial part of the puzzle that we need to consider: *money*.

As the title of this chapter suggests, money makes the world go round. For your company, it keeps the servers running, your people compensated, and allows you to invest in the long-term future by creating new products and services. One key indicator of becoming more senior and trusted, regardless of your exact position in the org chart, is being responsible for more of the company's budget. After all, money is the power to make things happen.

Front-line teams often have their budgets abstracted away from them: each person in their team is a headcount rather than a raw dollar amount, and the costs of running their code and infrastructure are hidden behind services or centralized teams. They often have little agency in how they spend their money. They're users of somebody else's budget rather than the owners. They rarely make a decision that has a significant impact on the company's bottom line.

As you move to more strategic positions, the kinds of decisions that you're able to make with money become broader, more impactful, and more ambiguous. Directors, VPs, and above may need to make decisions about how to spend millions of dollars, and those decisions can have a *huge* impact on the company's future.

As such, it's important to equip yourself with a functional understanding of how money works in a company, what that means specifically for engineering, and how to make decisions that are both financially sound and strategically aligned. That's what this chapter is all about.

Here's what we're going to be covering:

- *We'll begin with Finance 101*, where we'll cover the basics of company finance and typical financial business jargon that you may be encountering for the first time. We'll compare and contrast the different modes of operation that companies can use to fund themselves and understand the implications of each. We'll also cover the difference between cost centers and profit centers and how engineering may be one or the other depending on the company.

- *Next, we'll move on to managing a large budget.* We'll dig into the common areas that will require your attention in engineering and manifest as the levers that you can pull to make a difference.

- *Finally, we'll cover some common dilemmas you'll face around handling money.* Should you build or buy? Should you hire or contract? How much should you spend?

There's lots to get through. Have you got your checkbook ready? Let's get started.

Finance 101: The Basics of Company Finance

Let's imagine a company as a black box with an input and an output:

- *The input is money.* This can come from the sale of the products or services, or it can come from investors, lines of credit, and so on.

- *The output is the products or services that the company creates.* This could be software, hardware, consulting, or anything else.

Similar to how a factory turns low-value raw materials into high-value products that are worth more than the sum of their parts, a company turns money into products and services that are (usually) sold for more money than it costs to make them. This is the essence of a *flywheel*: a healthy company takes capital and then turns it into *more* capital. In engineering, a spinning flywheel serves to stabilize the output of a mechanical motor but, most importantly, to store excess energy, which can be *fed back into the system* if there is a drop in power. An example diagram is shown on page 298.

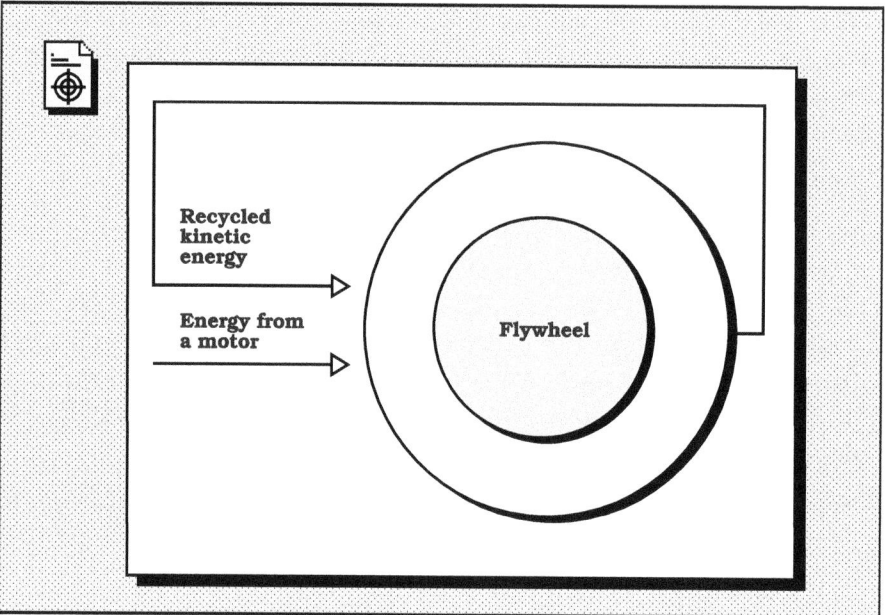

Each department in the company is a subsystem of this black box, and each has its own input and output. The executive team, enabled by the finance team, will take the overall company strategy and then decide how to allocate the input money across the different departments to maximize the output. In technology companies, research and development spend, which engineering is part of, is often one of the most significant line items in the budget.

When money comes into the company, either through revenue or funding, and is allocated and spent, it generally falls into one of two categories: *capital expenditure* (capex) or *operating expenditure* (opex).

- *Capex* is the money that is spent on the acquisition of assets. It includes purchases of property, physical servers, and so on. These have a longer-term focus.

- *Opex* is the money that is spent on running the business. This includes salaries, rent, cloud compute, and so on. It's the money that is spent to keep the lights on and the business running: it has a short-term focus since decisions can be altered quickly.

The distinction between capex and opex is important because it affects how money is accounted for. Whereas opex is typically accounted for immediately (for example, salaries cost money as soon as they are paid), capex is typically accounted for over time (for example, a server is accounted for over the course of its useful life). The value of an asset is typically depreciated over time in a process called *amortization*. There are tax implications in how capex and opex are accounted for, but that's beyond the scope of this book.

You may also come across the term *EBITDA*. This stands for *earnings before interest, taxes, depreciation, and amortization*. It's a measure of a company's operating performance, and it's often used to compare the performance of different companies. It's a measure of the company's ability to generate profit from its operations, and it's often used as a proxy for the company's ability to generate cash. The higher the EBITDA, the better the company is doing.

Getting back to our flywheel:

- *Revenue* is the money that comes from the sale of products and services. This is the primary way that companies fund themselves: it's the main input into the flywheel.

- *Profit* is the money that is left over after all the costs of running the business are accounted for. This also feeds back into the flywheel.

We often talk about the top line and the bottom line of a company. The *top line* is the revenue, and the *bottom line* is the profit. The difference between the two is the cost of running the business, and the goal of the company is to *maximize* the difference between the two; this makes the flywheel spin faster. This is illustrated in the following diagram:

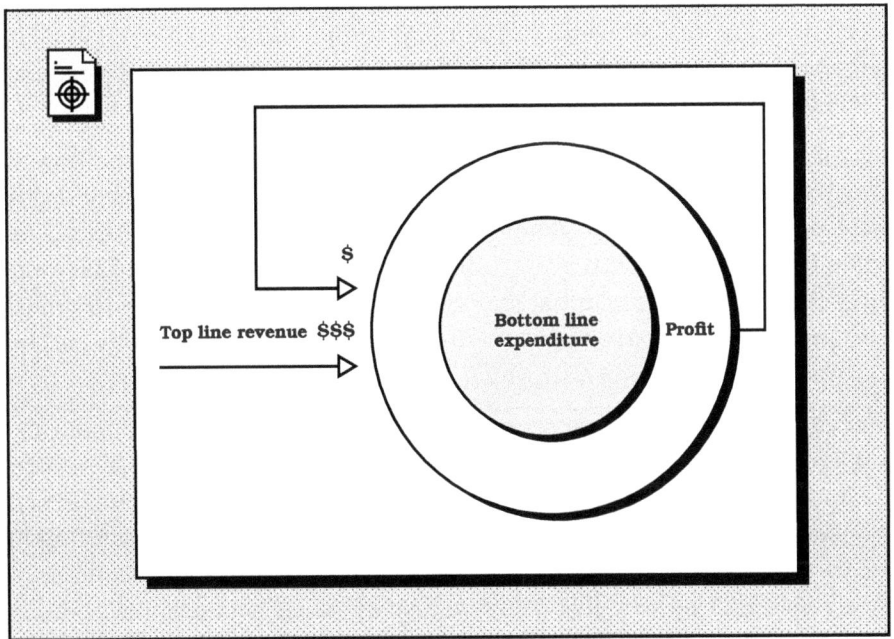

You can increase the top line by selling more or by selling at a higher price. You can increase the bottom line by reducing costs or by increasing the efficiency of the business. Engineering can have a significant impact on both of these, and we'll cover that in more detail when we discuss managing a large budget later in this chapter.

Modes of Operation: Bootstrapping, Venture Capital, and More

Large companies already have their flywheel spinning, but how do startups get going? There are a few different modes of operation that companies can use to fund themselves:

- *Bootstrapping* is where the company funds itself from its own revenue with no external investment. This allows the company to maintain control and ownership, but it can be slow and difficult to get going. There's no big injection of cash to get things moving.

- *Venture capital* is where the company raises money from investors in exchange for equity. This allows the company to grow quickly, but it comes with the expectation of a return on investment from the investors.

- *Angel investment* is where the company raises money from individuals in exchange for equity. This is similar to venture capital but usually occurs at a much earlier stage and with smaller amounts of money.

- *Debt financing* is where the company raises money from loans. This allows the company to grow without giving up equity, but it's often not available to early-stage companies; after all, there is no guarantee that the company will be able to pay the loan back.

Each of these modes of operation has different implications for how the company is run and how money is spent. This has important second-order effects on engineering. For example, a company that is bootstrapped may need to be more frugal with its spending, whereas a company that has raised a large round of venture capital may be able to spend more freely in order to grow quickly. Being aware of the mode of operation of your company can help you understand the context in which you are making decisions.

For example, if you have taken a senior role at a startup that has just raised a large round of venture capital, and you are tasked with creating the strategy for your infrastructure, then it may make sense to utilize that capital in order to go fast: go all-in on cloud and use managed services, rather than building your own infrastructure. This allows you to move quickly and focus on the product instead. However, if you were at an early-stage bootstrapped company, then the forced frugality may mean that having your own servers in a colocation facility is far cheaper and leaves more money for other things.

Cost Centers and Profit Centers

A *cost center* is a department that costs money to run but does not directly generate revenue. An example of this is the HR department; it supports the rest of the business. A *profit center*, on the other hand, is a department that generates revenue. An example of this is the sales department; it brings in money.

Interestingly, and depending on the company, engineering can be either a cost center or a profit center, or both.[1] It can even vary from team to team. For example, take X, formerly known as Twitter:

- The team that builds the search infrastructure is a *cost center*: it costs money to run, but it doesn't directly generate revenue. Despite how well it works, an increase in usage of the search feature doesn't bring in more money.

- On the other hand, the team that builds the ad platform is a *profit center*: it generates revenue directly. An increase in usage of the ad platform brings in more money.

However, even though some teams are cost centers and some are profit centers at X, engineering as a whole is a *profit center* because the company's primary product is software. Without the engineering team, there would be no product to sell. This is in contrast to, say, a company like an insurance company, where the engineering team is a *cost center* because the primary product is insurance, and the engineering team is a support function to the rest of the business.

If engineering is a profit center, then it means you'll have greater flexibility in how you spend your budget. You can make an argument to invest in people, hardware, and compute because it will directly lead to more top-line revenue, spinning the flywheel faster. You can also work on efficiencies in order to increase the bottom line, such as reducing the cost of running the infrastructure. If you are part of an engineering department that is considered to be a cost center, then you may only be able to make choices that affect the latter: it's a far trickier place to be. After all, if you are a cost center, then you are a *cost* to the business, and the goal is to reduce that cost as much as possible.

---

1. https://newsletter.pragmaticengineer.com/p/profit-centers-cost-centers

> **Your Turn: Are You a Cost Center or a Profit Center?**
>
> Consider cost centers and profit centers and think about the following:
>
> - Is your department as a whole a cost center or a profit center?
>
> - What about the individual teams within your department? Are they all profit centers or cost centers, or is there a mix? What about the teams that are part of your own organization?
>
> - What would need to be true for any team that is a cost center to become a profit center? Is it even possible?
>
> - Look across the rest of the business at other departments. How would you classify them? What are the implications of this for how they spend their budget?

SaaS Jargon Busting: Acronym Soup

Finance, like engineering, is full of a bunch of jargon and acronyms. This is especially true in technology companies that sell software as a service (SaaS), which is a subscription-based model. Even companies that don't sell SaaS as a primary product often use SaaS for additional services, such as premium content, features, or add-ons.

SaaS has become so prevalent because it allows companies to have a predictable revenue stream through these subscriptions. Rather than having to build a product, sell it, and then hope that next year customers will buy the newest version, the SaaS model instead has customers pay a monthly or yearly fee for access to the product, and then that product is continuously updated and improved. Generally speaking, this is a win-win for both the company and the customer. Long gone are the days when you'd need to buy a new version of Microsoft Office for $299 every year; instead, you pay $9.99 a month, and you get the latest versions as they come out.

Many new startups are SaaS companies, and because of the predictable revenue stream, they have added a layer of metrics on top of the traditional finance metrics that're incredibly useful for measuring the health of a company.

Here are some of the key terms that you may encounter:

- *MRR* stands for *monthly recurring revenue*. This is the amount of money that the company makes from subscriptions each month.

- *ARR* stands for *annual recurring revenue*. This is the amount of money that the company makes from subscriptions each year.

- *LTV* stands for *lifetime value*. This is the amount of money that the company makes from a customer over the entire time that they are a customer: it's the sum of all subscription money that they pay.

- *CAC* stands for *customer acquisition cost*. This is the amount of money that the company spends to acquire a customer. If a customer signs up for a free trial and converts to a paid customer, then the CAC is virtually free. Signing an enterprise customer, on the other hand, may require a lot of sales and marketing effort, and so the CAC is high.

- *LTV:CAC* is the ratio of the lifetime value of a customer to the customer acquisition cost. This is a key metric for SaaS companies: if the LTV:CAC ratio is high, then it means that the company is making more money from customers than it costs to acquire them—a sign of a healthy flywheel.

- *Churn* is the rate at which customers stop paying for the product. This is a key metric for SaaS companies. If the churn rate is high, then it means that the company is losing customers faster than it is acquiring them, and the flywheel is slowing down.

It therefore follows that a perfect SaaS company would have zero CAC and zero churn, leading to an infinite LTV:CAC ratio. This is rarely the case, but it's a useful mental model to have in mind. High churn is like a leaky bucket: you can keep pouring new revenue in, but if it's all pouring out the bottom, then you're not making any progress.

Generally speaking, a good LTV:CAC ratio is considered to be 3:1 or higher.[2] For every dollar you spend acquiring a customer, you make three dollars back. If you're achieving more than this, then it's a sign you could throw *more* money at acquiring customers and grow *even faster* since you have a good product-market fit—you're stashing too much cash, so spend it to get more!

Thinking back to our flywheel model, the LTV:CAC ratio is a measure of how well the company is turning money back into more money. High churn eats away at the top line, and high CAC eats away at the bottom line.

Do You Need to Make a Profit?

Eventually, yes. However, if you follow the news, you may have noticed that many technology companies are not profitable. This is especially true of fast-growing companies that are backed by venture capital rather than being bootstrapped. In startup land, the goal is often to grow rapidly in order to

---

2. https://blog.hubspot.com/service/ltv-cac-ratio

capture as much of the market as possible and use the money from investors to fund this growth, even if it means being in the red.

This is why it's important to understand the difference between the *top line* and the *bottom line*. A company can grow rapidly and still be losing money, but if the top line is growing *faster* than the bottom line, then it's a sign that the company is on the right track. With time and some small tweaks in spending, it'll all iron out. This is why you often hear about companies that are "burning cash" but are still considered to be successful—they are investing in *growth*, rather than profit. Being in the red here is a sign of health through growth, whereas in a more traditional business, it would be a sign of trouble. We'll look at this in more detail in the next chapter, where we'll cover the boom and bust cycles of the tech industry.

In a venture capital-backed company, the flywheel receives nitrous oxide in the same way a souped-up car does: the cash feeding the flywheel doesn't have to come from earned revenue. Instead, it shortcuts the wait by using a big heap of cash up front in exchange for some equity in the company. This is shown in the following diagram. The cash investment spins the wheel far faster than it could manage without it, allowing it to gain enough *momentum* to fuel the growth needed to keep it spinning on its own in the future when the right time to make a profit comes.

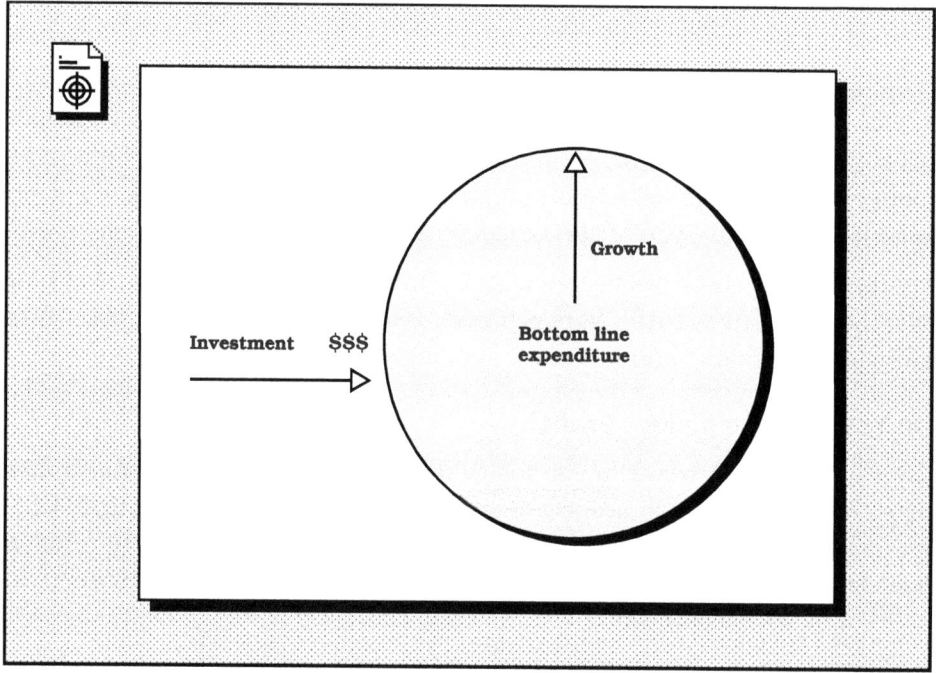

If this nitrous injection works out, then when the company goes public or gets acquired, the investors get their money back and then some. To carry on the souped-up car analogy, the nitrous injection gives a temporary burst of speed that can help it win the race. However, if the money runs out and the flywheel isn't producing enough revenue to keep itself going, then the company goes under. In this scenario, the car's engine gets blown out because it is unable to cope.

Usually, venture capital funds are structured so that they invest in a portfolio of companies, knowing that many will fail, but the ones that succeed will more than make up for it, often bringing a return that is ten or a hundredfold what they put in. And, importantly, bankruptcy laws are structured so that the company can fail without taking everyone else down with it. It's the beauty of limited liability and possibly one of the most important inventions in capitalism.

When it comes to running your organization effectively, it's critical to understand the financial mode of your company. If you are part of a rocket ship that is growing rapidly and is funded by plentiful venture capital, then spending *lots* might be exactly what you need to do to be successful, even if it means that you are not profitable (yet).

Managing a Large Budget: Levers and Dials

So, with the basics under our belt, what exactly will you find in your engineering budget? What are the common areas that will require your attention, and what are the levers that you can pull to make a difference?

If we think about the kinds of costs that engineering departments typically have, they can be broken down into a few key areas:

- *People*, which is one of the largest costs for most engineering departments. This includes salaries, benefits, insurance, and so forth.

- *Infrastructure*, which includes the cost of running servers, databases, and so on. This can be in the cloud, or it can be on-premises.

- *Software and Hardware*, which includes the cost of work computers, licenses, support contracts, and so on. Software may be open source, or it can be proprietary.

- *Temporary services*, which includes the cost of contractors, consultants, and other temporary supporting casts. This can be for specific projects, or it can be for ongoing support.

You will be expected to manage these costs in a way that is both financially sound and also strategically aligned with the culture and mode of operation of your company. After all, at some of the world's largest technology companies such as Apple, Amazon, and Meta, R&D spending is in the tens of billions of dollars.[3] In terms of the flywheel model, you will need to understand the best way to manage your bottom line in order to maximize the top-line growth.

Let's step through each of these areas. For each, we will look at some "rule of thumb" models that you can track alongside finance that will help you understand your spend and see whether you are on the right track.

People

You can't have an engineering department without engineers, so a large portion of your budget will be spent on people. People are *opex*: you don't own them. You pay them to do a job. Now, you may or may not view your people budget primarily as a raw dollar number; it may instead be provided as a total headcount since that's an easier abstraction to work with when interfacing with the finance team. After all, not everyone has exactly the same salary, benefits, pension contributions, and so on. That can vary across seniority, location, method of compensation (cash, stocks), and so on.

If you are working with a headcount number, then you should work with the finance team to understand whether every headcount is essentially equal. You could use one of these "slots" to hire a junior engineer or a senior engineer, the idea being that, in aggregate, it all evens out. In terms of how your headcount is allocated, you have to solve a multivariate optimization problem around allocation. These are some of the criteria:

- *Alignment with strategy*: You need to ensure you have the right people in the right places to execute on your product and engineering strategy. Do you have the right people, with the right skills, in the right places? If not, what is the delta between the ideal and the actual, and how do you close it?

- *Alignment with increasing the power curve of capabilities*: Back in Chapter 10, Performance Management: Raising the Bar, on page 223, we discussed how the power curve of your organization should be increasing over time. Do you have the right composition of people and teams to ensure that everyone is skilling up? This can manifest as the ratio of junior to senior engineers in general and within teams and the ratio of generalists to specialists.

---

3. https://www.statista.com/statistics/265645/ranking-of-the-20-companies-with-the-highest-spending-on-research-and-development/

- *Alignment with the mode of operation*: If you are a bootstrapped company, then you may need to be more frugal with your hiring, which may mean that you need to hire fewer senior people and focus on coaching and mentorship. If you have lots of cash in the bank, then you may be able to skew more senior and experienced in your ratios to get impactful people in the door quickly.

As such, in order to manage your people budget effectively, you need to understand the composition of your teams, the skills that they have, and the skills that they need. If it isn't already provided to you, then you should create and maintain a spreadsheet that shows this information for each person in your department:

- Their *role*, including their specialization, for example, back-end engineer, front-end engineer, and so on

- Their *seniority*, for example, junior, mid-level, senior, or their numerical level if you have a leveling system

- Their *team*, and depending on the size of your organization, their group or division

- Their *project assignment*, to whichever level of granularity is appropriate for you

- Their *location*, if you are globally distributed, including their time zone

You may want to record other information if you wish. However, the idea is that by keeping this information up to date, you can easily filter and chart the composition of your teams individually and as a whole to understand whether your balance of roles, skills, and seniority is in line with your strategy and mode of operation. If you keep a history of this information, such as creating a new sheet for each quarter, then you can also track how your composition is changing over time. Being able to do this is often not easy in even the most sophisticated HR systems that typically only track the *current* state.

Having a system like this also makes it easier whenever there are resourcing discussions. If another team is asking around for three more back-end engineers, then you can quickly reason to see whether you can help or whether it would disrupt your own strategy and roadmap and by how much. It never pays to artificially withhold your people as it decreases trust and makes it harder for *you* to get help when you need it.

With this implemented, you can use your spreadsheet to track the current state of your organization vs. your ideal state as per your strategy (for example, you may currently have a pressing need for mobile engineers, as the delta between your staffing and strategy is too high), which you can then use as a basis for your reviews and asks of the finance team.

From experience, keeping a spreadsheet like this up to date is critical, as you know you can trust yourself to understand the state of your organization. HR systems can suffer from a lack of granularity or data input issues, and sometimes, finance systems can be even *worse*. Holding the system of truth for what your ideal state is, who you have, and where they are is a key part of being in control of the people budget; applying the lever of money only works if you know where to apply it.

> **Your Turn: Create Your People Index**
>
> If you haven't already, create a spreadsheet that shows, for each person in your department, their role, seniority, team, project assignment, and location.
>
> - What is your distribution of roles and seniority? Is it what you expect, or is there a delta between the ideal and the actual?
>
> - Which of your teams are the most and least balanced in terms of roles and seniority? What is the impact of this on the team's performance?
>
> - How does your distribution of roles and seniority align with your strategy and mode of operation? Are there any changes that you need to make?
>
> - Keep this spreadsheet up to date every quarter, and track how your composition is changing over time. What are the trends that you see?

Rule of Thumb: Revenue per Employee

Given that it can be difficult to understand the exact contribution of each employee to the top line, a useful rule of thumb is to track the *revenue per employee*. This is simply the total revenue of the company divided by the number of employees. If you manage a portfolio of products with different revenue streams, you can calculate this per engineer per product. The idea is that over time, you want to see this number increase—it's a sign that your company is becoming more efficient and effective. Maintenance aside, engineering is *additive*—you build a feature, and it is there indefinitely, sold to many customers. An example chart of a good state over time is shown on page 309.

A healthy revenue-per-employee curve is a sign you're getting more out of your people and you're able to grow the top line more rapidly than the bottom line. This is a sign of a healthy flywheel. Ensure you track this over time. You

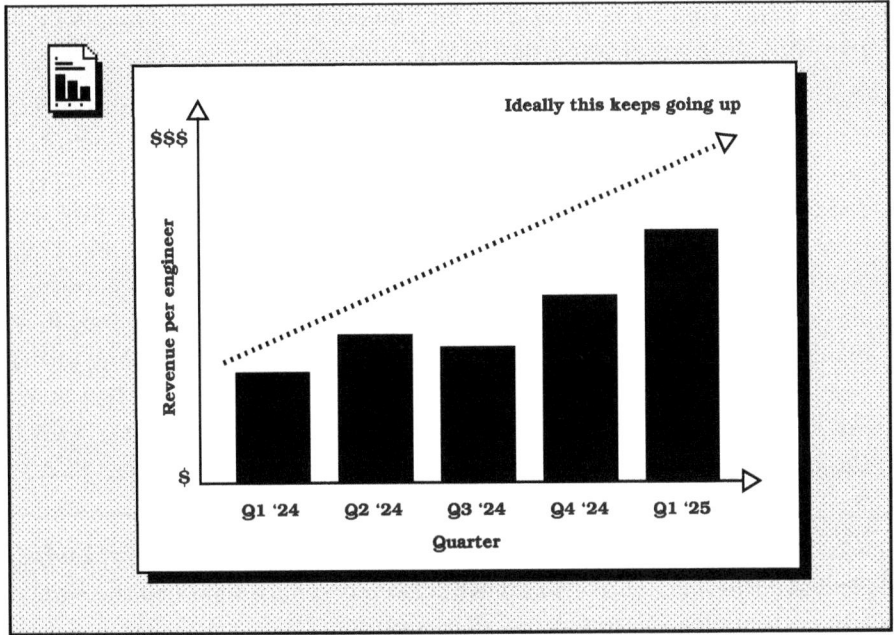

can then reason about what a comfortable number for your company is, which allows you to reason about top and bottom-line trade-offs.

As an example of high operational efficiency, the revenue per employee at a company like Apple or Meta is in the millions of dollars, as seen in example data from 2022.[4] Start-ups and smaller companies will have a lower number, but the same rings true: over the long term, you want to see this number increase.

If you've ever wondered why companies that're *not* in dire straights (in other words, they have large cash reserves) lay off people, it is often a preemptive measure to keep this number high as a protection against future downturns.

Infrastructure

The next largest cost for most engineering departments is infrastructure. This includes the cost of running or leasing servers to run all of the software that you use and build. This can be in the cloud, or it can be on-premises. If you are running in the cloud, then this is *opex*. The same is true if you are leasing servers in a colocation facility. If you own your own servers, then this is *capex*.

Depending on whether you are dealing with capex or opex, you may notice differences in the way that the costs are accounted for:

---

4. https://www.statista.com/statistics/217489/revenue-per-employee-of-selected-tech-companies/

- *Opex* infrastructure is accounted for immediately. You are typically billed monthly. An annual projection is that number times twelve.

- *Capex* infrastructure, for example, owning servers, is an upfront cost: you buy the servers and then use them, with the additional costs being any incurred data center costs such as power and cooling. However, in order to help with accounting, capex infrastructure is typically amortized over time: the cost of the server is spread out over its useful life. This is typically three to five years, but it can be longer or shorter depending on the specifics of the server and how long you are willing to run it. For example, sometimes old servers get removed from the front line and are used for less computationally demanding operations. This is why you may see a line item in your budget for "depreciation" or "amortization," showing the cost of the servers spread out over time in the same way that you would with a loan.

The way that you spend on infrastructure is part of your strategy, and being able to have the finance team and other executives understand the implications of your choices is important. For example:

- *If you are running in the cloud, then you are paying for the convenience of not having to manage your own servers.* This can be a good trade-off if you are a small company or if you are growing rapidly and need to be able to scale up and down quickly. However, it can be more expensive in the long run, and you may want to consider moving to your own servers if you are at a certain scale or want to keep your bottom line under tighter control.

- *If you are running your own servers, then you are incurring additional costs in manpower and the time taken to manage them.* This can be a good trade-off if you are a large company or if you have specific requirements that the cloud can't meet. However, it can make you go slower than competitors may be able to go in the cloud and also expose you to needing to hire specialists to manage the infrastructure. Having worked with sysadmins who needed to drive to the data center at 3 a.m. to replace a failed RAID array, you'll want to choose this route carefully.

Depending on the mode of operation of your company, you may want to make different choices. For example, if you are bootstrapped, then running or leasing your own servers can be far cheaper. However, if you have investors who are expecting rapid growth, then being able to ten times your infrastructure in a few clicks can be an incredible advantage worth paying for.

Fundamentally, there is no right answer here: it's a trade-off between cost, control, and speed. You will be expected to make the best decision for your company.

> **Your Turn: Do Your Engineers Know What They Spend?**
>
> Often, engineers are not aware of how much they are spending on infrastructure.
>
> - For any of your given teams, do you or your engineers know how much they cost the company in terms of infrastructure spend? Which is your most expensive team or service? Why is that?
> - If they don't know, is it easy for them to find out? Does this data exist in a dashboard or a report that they can access?
> - Consider how your organization could better expose this information to your engineers. Could your infrastructure team, if you have one, generate a monthly report, or could it be built into an internal dashboard?
> - If your engineers knew how much they were spending, do you think it would change their approach to how they think about their work? Would it encourage more performance and cost optimization projects to be undertaken?

Rule of Thumb: Infrastructure Spend as a Percentage of Revenue

Similar to contrasting the revenue per employee, you can also track the *infrastructure spend as a percentage of revenue*. This is the total infrastructure spend divided by the total revenue. The idea is that over time, you want to see this number decrease—it's a sign that your company is becoming more efficient and effective. An example chart is shown on page 312.

If your chart looks similar to this one, then you're doing well. Again, this is a sign of a healthy flywheel. You can see how it's important to track capex as amortization over time since it allows you to model your infrastructure spend similarly to cloud opex and to plot the two on the same chart if needed.

Software and Hardware

You can't build everything yourself. It's almost impossible to run a modern engineering department without using third-party software and without each employee having a computer. Hardware is *capex*. From licenses for GitHub, to IDEs, project management tools, and so on, in large companies, the software budget can be significant. Software is measured as *opex*.

The long-term goal is *not* to decrease these costs to zero. Preventing your engineers from using the tools that they need to be productive is a false

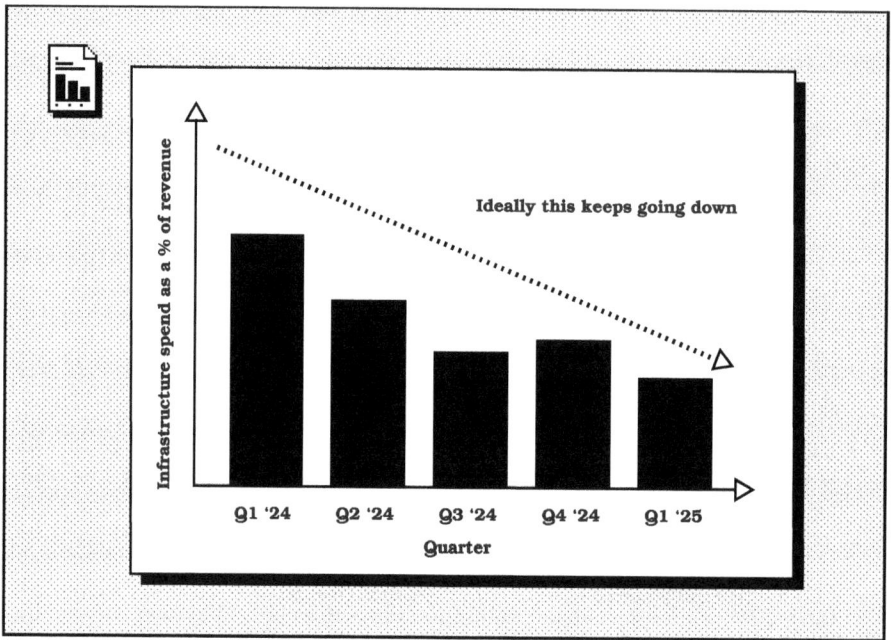

economy. However, it will be on you to recommend and make decisions about what software to use and to ensure that the costs are in line with the value that you are getting from the software.

Broadly, there are two categories:

- *Essentials*, which are almost impossible to operate without. This includes computers for each employee, operating systems, IDEs, and so on. You can't really cut costs here, but you can make sure that you are picking the best value for money that also aligns with what your engineers want.

- *Productivity gains*, which covers spending money so that you don't have to build and maintain something yourself. This includes hosting your code in GitHub, using Actions and Copilot, using Jira for project management, and so on. Yes, you can potentially build these things yourself, but doing so would be a distraction from your core business. Spending money here will not make your top-line revenue go up; it will just make the bottom line better.

The good news is that most engineers want to focus on growing the top line by building cool new things, so you will never have to argue with *them* about spending money on software. However, sometimes this can be a point of contention with the finance team, who may not understand the value of the software that you are using. That enterprise license may be quite expensive.

Rule of Thumb: Software and Hardware Spend as a Percentage of Revenue

In order to understand the value of the software and hardware that you are using, you can do pretty much the same thing as you did with the infrastructure: track the *software and hardware spend as a percentage of revenue*. The idea is that you'll want this to go down over time as well.

As an additional rule of thumb, you can estimate the cost of building and maintaining the software yourself. For example, if that GitHub license is expensive in the eyes of the finance team, then you can make the argument that it would cost you a whole engineering team a year to build and maintain something equivalent yourself, hence that license is a good deal in comparison.

Temporary Services

Finally, you may need to hire temporary services, such as contractors, consultants, and so on. This is a way to get additional capacity or expertise without having to hire full-time employees. This is counted as *opex*.

Typically speaking, well-known technology companies prefer to hire full-time employees rather than contractors. Usually, this is because full-time employees are more invested in the company for the long term, and they are more likely to be aligned with the company's culture and strategy. Compensation is also normalized across all staff, and larger companies also use stock-based compensation, which is not normal for contractors. There are times when you may still need to hire contractors, such as:

- *To fill a gap*: If you have a specific project that needs a specific skill you don't have, then it may be easier to hire a contractor than to hire a full-time employee. This is especially true if the skill is rare or in high demand.

- *To keep the core team focused*: If you have a specific one-off project that needs to be done or categories of tasks that are a distraction from the core business, then it may be easier to hire contractors temporarily to do this work.

- *To scale up quickly*: If you are growing rapidly, then it may be easier to hire contractors temporarily to get some package of work done quickly rather than to hire full-time employees. However, this is quite rare and may happen more often in supporting functions rather than engineering.

While it's less common to pad out your engineering department with contractors, it's more common to hire contractors who have specific knowledge to consult on a project. For example, if you are considering choosing and migrating to a new database or search index, you can dramatically reduce the risk of the project and the time taken in design and prototyping by hiring a contractor who is an expert. Many popular open source projects spin out companies that offer consulting and support contracts from the maintainers themselves; getting the right input at the right time can shave months or years off your project.

Getting the right balance of permanent and temporary staff, including their seniority, location, and skills, is a key part of how you manage your people budget, and it may not be entirely your own choice. Different companies have existing cultures and norms around hiring contractors, and you will need to work within those constraints or work to change them. It requires a different set of skills to manage contractors than it does to manage full-time employees, and you will need to balance the short-term needs of projects with the long-term needs of talent development and retention in your organization.

Rule of Thumb: The Cost of Distraction from the Top Line

With that in mind, the rule of thumb for pitching that you need to hire contractors is to estimate the cost of *not* using them. Using that example of migrating to a new search index, you could estimate the amount of time that it may take your team to research and prototype until the right solution is found, along with contingency time for when things (inevitably) go wrong. You could also put a monetary value on the risk of the project: if it goes wrong, how much money could you lose because of outages or poor performance of the system?

Assuming a contractor with specific knowledge can progress the project faster and with dramatically less uncertainty, consider the following: without them, what is the delta in engineering cost that has been taken up trying to figure out what the contractor could tell them immediately? With that in mind, you can then make the argument that the cost of the contractor is a good deal.

Common Dilemmas: Patterns to Follow

You will find that there are recurring themes in the discussions and decisions that you will have to make around money. We'll close out the chapter by covering some of these to help you understand the trade-offs that you may have to make. Remember: there is no right answer since the context of your organization, strategy, and company as a whole will dictate the best choice.

Build vs. Buy

This is a classic dilemma in engineering: should you build something yourself, or should you buy it from a third party? For example, let's say that you don't currently have a feature flag system, and you are considering building one. However, you are also aware that there are existing third-party feature flag systems for which you could pay a subscription instead.

Let's look at the trade-offs:

- *Building it yourself* gives you control over the feature flag system, and it means that you can build it to your exact specifications. However, it will take time and effort to build, and it will also take time and effort to maintain. You don't *explicitly* decrease the bottom line by spending money on a new service, but there is an *implicit* cost in taking engineers away from building new features and increasing the top line.
- *Buying it from a third party* means that you can get a feature flag system up and running quickly, and you can likely also get support and continual updates as they work on it. However, it costs money, you are locked into their system, and you may not be able to get it to do exactly what you want.

The decision that you make will depend on the specifics of your company and your strategy. If you are bootstrapped, then you may want to build it yourself in order to save money. If you have a lot of free cash, then you may want to buy it from a third party in order to focus more of your time and effort on growing the top line instead.

Generally speaking, for most of us, the rule of thumb is that you should buy it from a third party if it's *not* part of your core business and vice versa. Top-line focus always wins over bottom-line efficiency. However, when you do so, you should always have a plan for what you would do if the third party went out of business or if they changed their pricing to be unaffordable.

However, if you are already scaled, it may be easier to build your own since you have the resources to do so, and you can fully control access, security, and decrease your dependency on third parties. Building things yourself could even be part of your long-term strategy. For example, Google famously built most of its own tooling in-house over the years, and that has been a key part of its success; in fact, it's now sold back to you and me in the form of Google Cloud. However, do remember that most of us aren't Google.

Dealing with Vendors: Never Trust the Book Price

Regardless of your size and budget, you'll always be buying *something* and dealing with vendors. This could be your cloud hosting, your software licenses, your hardware, and so on. The book price is the price that the vendor lists, and it's *almost always* negotiable. In fact, book prices tend to be more negotiable the larger the deal is—the vendor would rather have a large deal at a lower price than no deal at all.

Use this to your advantage when you are negotiating pricing and contracts:

- *Always negotiate*: This bit is simple: you can often get a better deal by asking for one. This is especially true if you are a large company or if you are buying a large quantity. After all, they want your business.

- *Consider contract length*: The longer the contract, the better the deal. This is because the vendor can rely on your business for a longer period of time, which results in predictable spend for you and predictable income for them. Keep in mind, however, that the longer the contract, the more locked in you are. You will have to reason about the trade-off between the two.

- *Consider volume*: The more you buy, the better the deal. Economies of scale are real, and you can take advantage of them by buying more. Are you considering refreshing the laptop fleet for your entire company? You can get a better deal if you buy them all at once rather than in dribs and drabs. Use this to your advantage.

- *Consider competition*: If you are buying something that has multiple vendors, then you can use this to your advantage. Always shop around if you can, and use the quotes that you get from one vendor to negotiate with another. This is especially true if you are buying something that is a commodity.

Always, always, always ask whether there is a discount. It costs nothing to do so, and the worst thing is that they say no. See whether you can get sweeteners, such as additional support, training, or other services. You could save 20 percent off your budget's bottom line by just asking. So why not ask?

Top Line vs. Bottom Line: The Eternal Struggle

All of the dilemmas that you will face around handling your budget will come down to the trade-off between the top line and the bottom line. After all, you are trying to make your flywheel spin faster. But how much time should you be spending on making your department cost less vs. making your department make more money?

The first thing to understand is that the *only* way that you grow your top line is by building the unique proposition that your company is offering. The more time and effort you spend building your product, the better it will be and the more revenue it will bring in. This is what you should optimize for first: get the most people building the most product that you can.

However, the second-order effect here is that you will need some amount of supporting software, hardware, and services in order to do this. How much you need and how much you spend on them is a trade-off between the top line and the bottom line. You can spend more on supporting services and software in order to have more people building more product faster, but you will also be spending more money. Is that bad?

How much money you have to spend entirely depends on the mode of operation of your company. If you are flush with venture capital, you can spend more freely to have more people building product in order to find product-market fit. If you are bootstrapped, you won't have the luxury of spending as much and may have to do more in-house or use less fully featured tools to get the job done.

The following diagram shows an example of how you'll need to think about the trade-off between the top line and the bottom line at different stages of your company's growth:

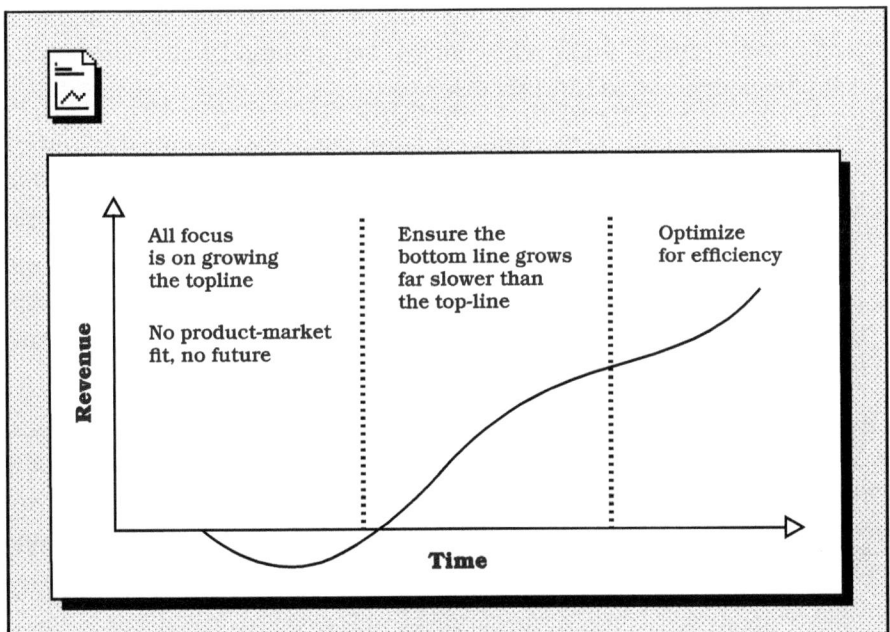

It's all an eternal struggle between the top line and the bottom line. You control the levers, and you know the context. But, if you use the rules of thumb that we've covered in this chapter, then you're in a pretty good place to make the right decisions for your company. You should track the following:

- *Revenue per employee*: You want this to go up over time.

- *Infrastructure spend as a percentage of revenue*: You want this to go down over time.

- *Software and hardware spend as a percentage of revenue*: You also want this to go down over time.

- *The cost of distraction from the top line*: You want this to be as low as reasonably possible for the phase that you are in.

If you can have all of these rules of thumb going in the right direction, then you're doing a good job of managing your budget. You're making the flywheel spin faster under the constraints that you have.

Good Times and Bad Times Ahead

With some simple models and rules of thumb, the daunting task of managing a large budget can be made more manageable. Here's what we've covered in this chapter:

- We covered the *basics of company finance* including the flywheel model, the difference between the top line and the bottom line, a whole host of jargon, cost centers and profit centers, and the modes of operation that companies can use to fund themselves.

- Then, we moved on to *managing a large budget* where we dug into the common areas that will require your attention in engineering and manifest as the levers that you can pull to make a difference.

- Finally, we covered *some common dilemmas you'll face around handling money*, recapping our rules of thumb and how they can be used to make the right decisions. There's no right answer—only you have the context for your unique situation.

In the next chapter, we'll stay close to the theme of money, but we'll zoom out and focus on macroeconomic trends and the boom and bust cycles of the tech industry. This is important to understand, as over the course of your career, it will have a significant impact on the jobs that you have, the companies that you work for, and how you show up as a leader.

CHAPTER 14

Boom and Bust

While catching up on the morning's communication, you notice a direct message from Tara.

```
[11:13] <tara> there's some rumors flying around, can we chat?
```

You seek more context.

```
[09:04] <you> of course. what rumors are we talking about?
[09:05] <tara> layoffs. next week, apparently
[09:06] <you> I haven't heard anything about that. where is it coming from?
[09:07] <tara> a number of people now, and it's leaking online too
```

You start a video call.

Bing!

Tara's face appears on your screen.

"Hey, Tara. What's going on?"

"Hey, I just wanted to give you a heads up, really. I've heard from a few people now that there are going to be layoffs next week. I don't know how many, or who, but it's been going around for a few days now."

"I hear you. Are you okay? I appreciate you letting me know, but as you also know, we can't really do anything about it. And even if I did know, I wouldn't be able to tell you, if you know what I mean."

"I know, I know. It's just been driving me crazy. I've been trying to keep my head down and do my work, but it's hard to focus when you know something like this might be coming. We've just remortgaged the house, and I honestly don't know what we'd do if I lost my job."

"I understand. I'm sorry that you're dealing with this. The best you can do is keep distracted, and hopefully, it'll all blow over. Rumors fly all the time, and most of the time, they're just that—rumors. I'm always here if you need to chat, though. Just do me one favor?"

"Sure, what's that?"

"Keep it to yourself. The last thing we need is for the whole team to be distracted by this. See if you can help keep everyone focused on their work. And look, we're still hiring, aren't we? We just had some new folks join us last week. Why would we be hiring if we were going to lay people off?"

"Of course. Thanks for listening. I'll chat to you later."

"Take care."

The call ends. You continue to sift through your messages, but your mind is elsewhere. Come to think of it, you've not really heard directly from leadership in a while. *Is* there something going on?

No, no, you tell yourself. Forget about it. You've got work to do. On to the next email…

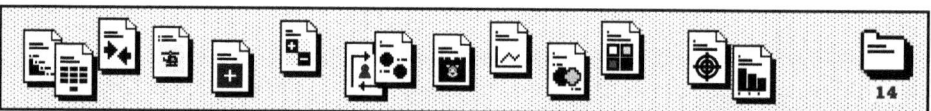

If you've been working in the tech industry for a while, you'll know that it's prone to boom and bust cycles. One minute, you're reading in the news that a company has just raised half a billion dollars in funding and is hiring thousands of people, and the next minute, you're reading that another is laying off 25 percent of its workforce and closing its offices. To the outside observer, technology can be a volatile industry: the pay and perks are good, but you need to learn how to ride the rollercoaster that comes along with it.

As a senior leader, you are going to find yourself among the pendulum swing of these cycles. You'll need to adapt your strategy, leadership style, and tactics to be successful. In this chapter, we're going to focus on the boom and bust cycles of the tech industry and how you can lead your team through them. Here's what we are going to cover:

- *We will build on what we learned about money* in the previous chapter to understand the phenomenon of boom and bust cycles: why they happen, how they link to macroeconomic factors, and what they may mean for you in terms of your role and the different acts of your career.

- *Then, we will categorize the operations of a company along a scale, from peacetime to wartime.* Both peacetime and wartime have different characteristics and effects on company operations and how you will be expected to lead your organization. We'll cover what these are.

- *Finally, we will focus on both peacetime and wartime leadership individually* and what you can do to be successful in each. We'll see what you can control, what you can't, and how you can best position yourself regardless.

This will then set us up for the final chapter of the book, which is all about your own ongoing career in senior leadership. You will have to put into practice your leadership, be able to ride the rollercoaster of boom and bust cycles in the industry, and also understand how your ultimate destination may require *more* than just working hard in the place that you are.

What we're trying to say is that we're in the homestretch now. Let's get going.

Spend! Invest! Grow! Crash! Burn! Rebuild!

In the previous chapter, we touched upon the *flywheel model* of company finances. To recap: within the engine of each company is a flywheel model that takes money as input, produces products and services, and then sells those products and services to make *more* money. In an ideal world, a healthy amount of profit is generated that then feeds *back* into the flywheel to make it spin faster and faster.

However, exactly how that flywheel is fed depends on the *mode of operation* that the company is in. These modes of operation range from bootstrapped startups to publicly traded companies, and each mode has its own unique characteristics in the macroeconomic environment surrounding it.

So, why is it that we see reported in the news so many technology companies going through boom and bust cycles? Why are they sometimes used as a barometer of the economy as a whole? And why are they so subject to the boom and bust that we are going to talk about in this chapter?

The answer lies in the unique characteristics of how the technology industry operates. Consider this: there are few industries where an idea can so quickly become tangible capital. A thought can become software that can become a product that can become a company that can become a billion-dollar asset. Money from nothing. No mining, no factories, no supply chains. Just a computer and an internet connection.

Since technology companies are built on the back of innovation, innovation is inherently *risky*. The vast majority of new products and services fail, and even those that succeed can take a long time to become profitable. This means that many technology companies often need to raise large amounts of money to fund their operations as they scale, typically in the form of investments: angel, seed, and venture capital. This money is then used to fund the rapid development of the product or service and to attempt to grow the company as quickly as possible before competitors can catch up.

Growing as quickly as possible is typically the primary way for ideas to be successful in the long term. The technology industry is characterized by network effects, where the value of a product or service increases as more people use it. This means that the first company to reach a critical mass of users can often dominate a market, and the second company to reach that critical mass can struggle to compete.

As such, going back to our flywheel model, if you have a good idea, the faster you can feed money into it, the faster it will spin, the more it will grow to generate more money, and the more likely it is to be successful.

There are two typical outcomes from here:

- *If the company is successful, it will continue to grow rapidly to a point where it can either be acquired by a larger company or go public.* This gives the investors a return on their investment, and the company has successfully scaled quickly and then stabilized as one of the market leaders.

- *If the company is not successful, it will run out of money and be forced to either tread water, downsize, or close.* This experiment at accelerating growth has failed, and the company is forced to retrench and rebuild via a pivot or even shutter its doors.

We could categorize the activity in the first bullet point as the "boom" and the second bullet point as the "bust." The boom is characterized by rapid growth, hiring, and investment, and the bust is characterized by layoffs, downsizing, and closures. For investors, bust isn't always bad. Typically, they are investing in a portfolio of companies, and they *expect* that some of them will fail. For employees, however, it is a different story.

An even spread of boom and bust at any given time would be ideal, but the reality is that the industry is prone to cycles with correlated activity among many companies. One year, it's hiring season, and candidates are in high demand, fielding increasingly eye-watering offers from multiple places. The next year, it's the complete opposite: layoffs are happening left, right, and center, and the market is flooded with people unable to find work. What on earth is going on? Can you somehow predict when these cycles are going to happen, and what can you do to prepare for them?

ZIRP, QE, and the Tech Industry

The technology industry is acutely affected by macroeconomic factors, which you can read about in-depth in a four-part newsletter by Gergely Orosz.[1] When we talk about these factors, we're talking about things like interest rates, inflation, and whether or not the government is printing money. These factors can have a big impact on the technology industry and can often be the cause of boom and bust cycles.

Now, we're not going to go into a deep dive into macroeconomics here, and we defer readers to Orosz's newsletter, but let's briefly see how some of these factors can affect the technology industry. For example, when there is a financial crisis like the subprime mortgage bubble that happened in 2008,[2] the government will often lower interest rates and undertake quantitative easing to try and stimulate the economy again.

But what are these things, and why do they matter? Let's break them down:

- *Low interest rates*: When interest rates are low, it's cheap to borrow money. However, when interest rates are low, it's hard to get a good return on traditional investments like bonds. This means that investors are more likely to put their money into riskier investments like technology companies. So, low interest rates can lead to a boom in the technology industry. This is what happened after the 2008 financial crisis and also during the COVID-19 pandemic.

- *Low inflation*: As a result of low interest rates, inflation is also low. This means that the cost of living may shrink or hold stable, and people are more likely to have more spending money for things like technology products and services. Clearly, that's good for business.

- *Quantitative easing (QE)*: This is when the government generates money to stimulate the economy, for example, by using it to buy assets like government bonds, increasing the total amount of money in circulation. This can eventually lead to inflation, which is clearly bad, but in the short term, it means more cheap money for investors to borrow and use to seek greater returns.

So, it follows that in these zero-interest rate periods (ZIRP), the conditions are prime for investment in technology companies, fueling their growth. This is the *boom* period where it seems like there is an endless supply of money to expand product lines, hire, and grow.

---

1. https://newsletter.pragmaticengineer.com/p/zirp
2. https://en.wikipedia.org/wiki/2007%E2%80%932008_financial_crisis

However, when the economy starts to recover, the key macroeconomic factors will start to change:

- *High inflation*: Prices will start to rise as a result of increased demand. This means that the cost of living goes up, and consequently, people will have less money to spend on things like technology products and services. That means less input to the flywheel.

- *High interest rates*: These are put in place by central banks and governments to try and control inflation. When interest rates are high, it's expensive to borrow money, reducing the amount of money available for spending, thus slowing down the rate of inflation. The result is that when it is more expensive to borrow money, there is less money to invest in technology companies, further drying up the input to their flywheels.

- *The end of QE*: As the economy recovers, the government tightens the money supply to prevent inflation from getting out of control. Again, there is less money available for investment to obvious effect.

These periods are where technology companies can struggle. The money that was once flowing freely has dried up, and the cost of borrowing money has increased. If a high-growth company needs another round of investment to keep feeding its flywheel, it may find that the money is no longer there, and instead, they have to pivot to cutting costs to survive.

There have been numerous cycles with characteristics like this, ranging from the dot-com bubble of the late 1990s[3] to the aforementioned subprime mortgage bubble of 2008 and, most recently, the COVID-19 pandemic.[4]

When the pandemic happened, effectively shutting down the global economy, central banks and governments responded with unprecedented levels of stimulus to keep the economy afloat. These stimulus measures were similar to the ones mentioned, ZIRP and QE, and even included direct payments to citizens in the form of stimulus checks. With technology companies shifting to remote work and the need for digital services increasing, we saw this macroeconomic environment fueling a boom in the technology industry.

Using crowdsourced layoff statistics from layoffs.fyi,[5] we can see the ZIRP period that covered the worst part of the pandemic and the subsequent recovery period. The data is shown in the diagram on page 325.

---

3. https://en.wikipedia.org/wiki/Dot-com_bubble
4. https://en.wikipedia.org/wiki/COVID-19_pandemic
5. https://layoffs.fyi/

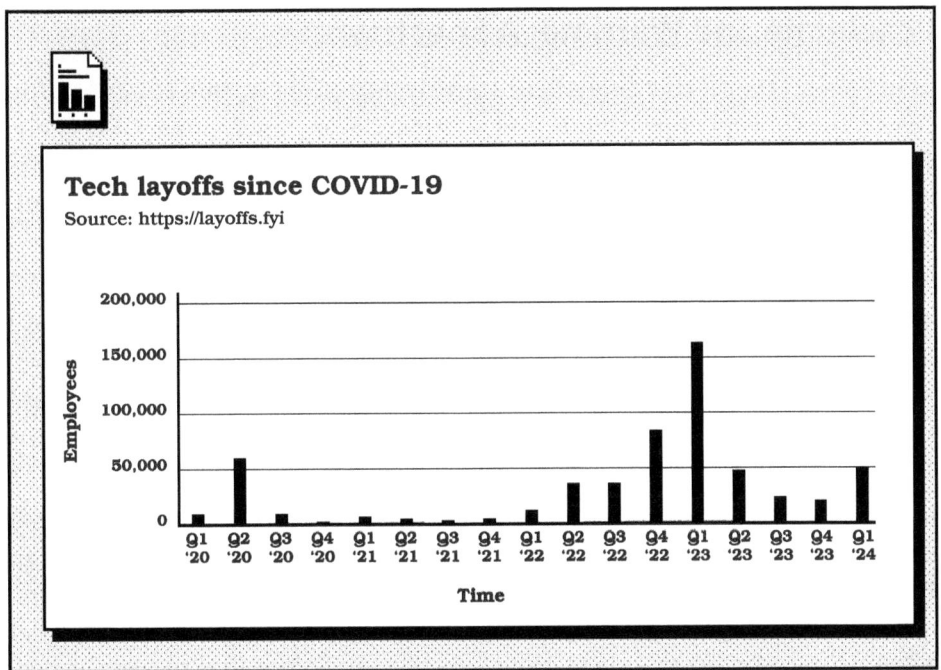

From Q3 2020, which is when the macroeconomic stimulus measures started to take effect, we see a sharp decline in the number of layoffs across the technology industry. This was the boom period where companies were seeing revenue growth from surging demand for their services and also had access to cheap capital to fuel their growth.

Forecasts of future growth and revenue from this "new normal" showed it was time to hire, grow, raise money, and *fast*. However, as the world came out of the worst of the pandemic during 2022 and the macroeconomic factors started to change to high inflation and interest rates, future growth forecasts were now highly uncertain. This was the bust period where companies pivoted to cut costs and save money, which meant that hundreds of thousands of people lost their jobs from 2022 to 2024.

It's likely we will see future cycles like this, caused by as-yet-unknown macroeconomic black swans.[6] Given that they're going to happen and you will likely have no control over them, as a senior leader, you need to learn to operate in both boom and bust periods and understand how to lead your team through them.

---

6. https://en.wikipedia.org/wiki/Black_swan_theory

Peacetime and Wartime: A Spectrum

In his book, *The Hard Thing About Hard Things [Hor14]*, Ben Horowitz discusses the concept of peacetime and wartime CEOs. A peacetime CEO is one who is focused on the growth and expansion of the company. His example is Eric Schmidt, who presided over a multiyear period of record growth and expansion at Google. They went far beyond just being a search engine and expanded into maps, wearables, and even self-driving cars.

A wartime CEO is one who is focused on survival, cutting costs, and rebuilding the company to fit a new environment. His example is Andy Grove, who led Intel through a period of intense competition and market change. They had to pivot from being a memory chip company to a microprocessor company while fighting off serious competition from Japanese firms.

In each case, conditions external to the company dictate what kind of strategy is required and how the people in charge need to be able to adapt to them. Peacetime operations line up with boom periods, and wartime operations line up with bust periods. As a senior leader yourself, it's important to understand where your company stands at any given time and what that means for how you should be leading your organization.

In fact, we can plot peacetime and wartime on a spectrum, with peacetime at one end and wartime at the other. In the middle is a steady state, where the company is neither dramatically growing nor shrinking but is stable, and leadership believes that the current strategy is working. You can see this spectrum in the diagram on page 327.

We can see each of these modes has unique characteristics. On the left side of the diagram, in peacetime, a company is within a boom period, and either through investment or revenue growth, the company is expanding, hiring, and growing. As such, it invests as much cash as possible in growing the top line with the expectation that the bottom line will follow later. This comes through hiring people, expanding product lines, and entering new markets. Additionally, an increased appetite for risk results in trying new things, such as launching entirely new products that may be only loosely related to the core offering. Since peacetime companies are trying to attract the best talent, it often results in an increased focus on high-quality culture, perks, and benefits to attract and retain employees.

In the middle of the diagram is the steady state, where the company is neither growing nor shrinking. This is where headcount and expenses are kept stable,

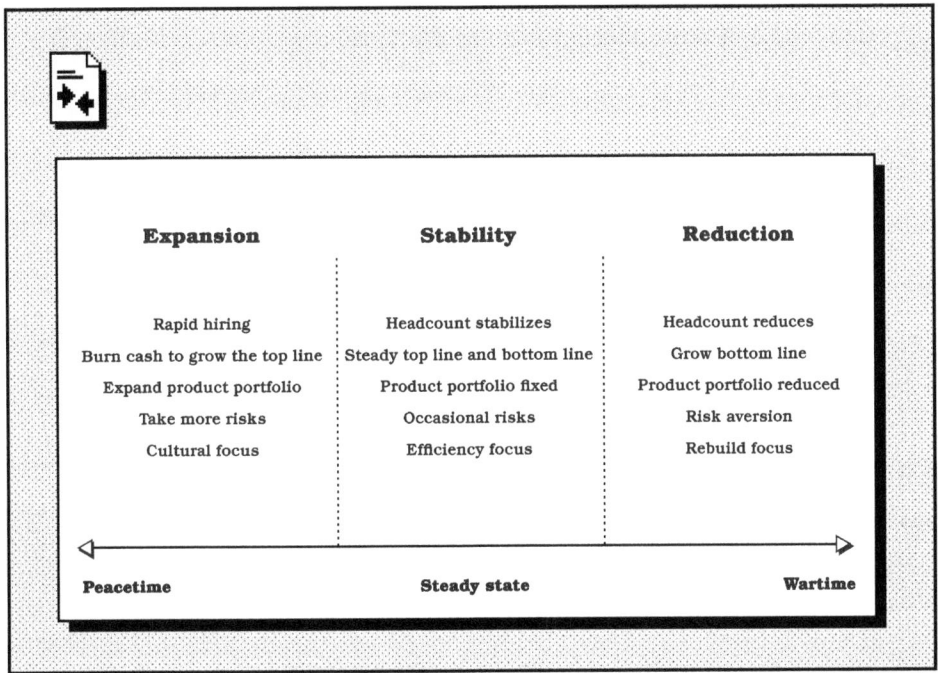

and the company is focused on executing the current strategy. The overall goal is to keep the flywheel spinning at a steady rate, thus resulting in a focus on efficiency: how can we do things better, faster, and cheaper without compromising the quality of the output?

The right side of the diagram is wartime, where the company is in a bust period, either due to a lack of investment or a decline in revenue. This means either protecting the company at all costs or mitigating its decline so that it can be rebuilt later. As such, headcount and expenses are cut to help the bottom line through layoffs, office closures, sunsetting products, and reducing marketing spend. Companies here are extremely risk averse—getting the balance sheet in order is the top priority.

Earlier in your career, it's unlikely that you will ever have had to change your strategy or tactics to fit either peacetime or wartime. As a less senior engineer or leader, you are typically focused on executing tactics that have been given to you. However, your senior leaders at the time would have been navigating these extremes to generate those tactics, and now it's your turn to understand what *you* should do in each that is *different* from the steady state. We'll look at each of these in turn, starting with peacetime.

> **Your Turn: Are You in Peacetime or Wartime?**
>
> Looking at the spectrum in the diagram, consider the following questions.
>
> - Where would you place your company? Is it in peacetime, wartime, or somewhere in the middle?
>
> - What characteristics of your company make you think that it is placed where you think it is?
>
> - Given your assessment, do you think that you are operating in the right way? What would you change?

Concentric Circles of Trust

Before we go any further, it is worth highlighting that during peacetime and wartime, the plans that you must make and the subsequent actions that you must take are at varying levels of confidentiality. Even positive news, such as wanting to hire a significant number of people, needs to be handled with care before you know exactly how many people you are going to hire and where they are going to be placed. Incomplete information can lead to rumors, and rumors can lead to a lack of focus and productivity.

As such, it helps to keep in mind a model of *concentric circles of trust*. The diagram on page 329 is a visual representation:

Let's step through the circles in turn, starting at the center:

- *Confidential*: This is the most sensitive information that you have, and until your strategy and tactics are finalized, this information should be limited to the smallest amount of people possible. This information causes *harm* if it is communicated in an incomplete state. The most obvious example here is wartime layoffs: you do *not* want this information to leak before you are ready to execute it. This is the kind of information where at a public company, you may have to sign a nondisclosure agreement (NDA) to even know about it.

- *Sensitive*: This is information that could cause *distraction* but would not cause harm if it were to leak. Although it is not secret, it's best not to over-broadcast it. For example, if you are planning to move from a data center to the cloud, this is an investigation that you would want to keep within a small task force of people until you are sure about what you want to do. This is because the implications of such a move could be

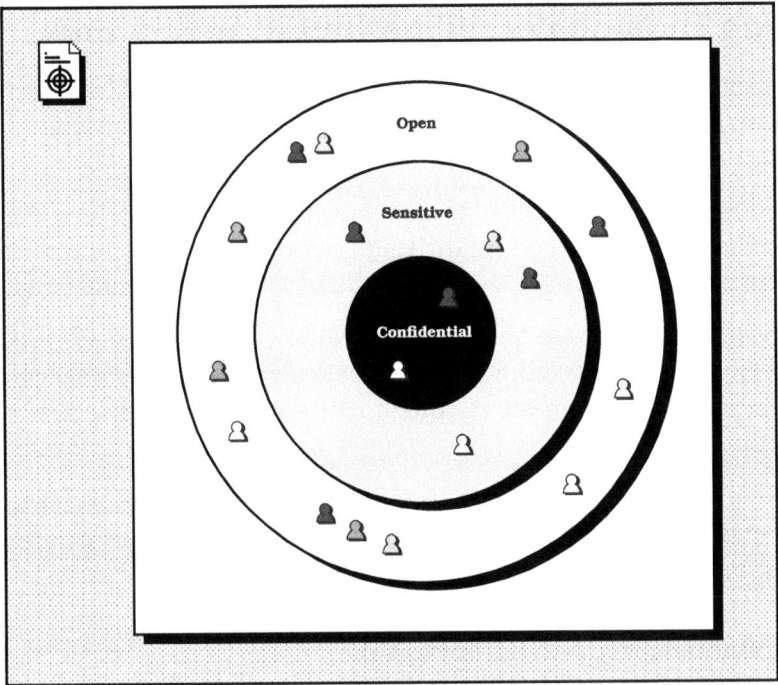

significant for your infrastructure team. It may mean that they need to learn new skills or pivot to a new way of working. Also, engineers may get distracted by the worry of needing to deploy on new environments and what that may entail.

- *Open*: This is information that is not sensitive and can be shared, even when incomplete, with the wider team. In fact, it is beneficial to do so. For example, your engineering strategy fits into this category. You may not have all of the details worked out, but that's fine; it's on everyone to help you figure it out, and they will appreciate your openness in sharing it with them.

The closer the information is to the center, the more careful you need to be when communicating it when it's time to do so. Typically, the most confidential information is shared when *completely final*, and even already executed (in other words, layoffs seemingly happen out of the blue along with numerous prewritten and prerecorded announcements), whereas the most open information is continually available in draft form for feedback and iteration.

Keep this in mind as we go through the rest of the activities in peacetime and wartime. We'll mark underneath each of them where they fit in the concentric circles of trust.

Leading Through Peacetime: Invest, Spend, Grow

In peacetime, growth is the agenda. This means that you will be asked to lead your team in such a way as to help the company grow as quickly as possible. For you, this usually means:

- *Organizing your department to hire, onboard, and ramp up new employees quickly.* This means getting the right processes in place to hire the best talent and then reducing the time it takes for them to become productive.

- *Allocating resources to brand new products.* While your main product or service is growing, you may also be tasked with spinning out teams that build entirely new products, which can mean introducing new ways of working.

- *Taking part in due diligence for acquisitions.* Depending on the size of your company, you may be asked to help evaluate potential acquisitions and then integrate them into your organization.

Hiring, Onboarding, and Ramping Up

During peacetime, expect a significant increase in hiring. Therefore, you need to ensure that if recruitment is feeding you a firehose of candidates, you have the processes to quickly evaluate them and make a decision. We dedicate an entire chapter to hiring in *the first book [Sta20]*, so if you lack a good hiring process to begin with, we recommend you start there.

> **Expansion Plans Are Sensitive**
>
>  Since your hiring plan may mean some areas will receive investment and others may not, ensure that you keep initial planning among your leaders so that they are able to prepare their teams for the changes that are coming.

Hiring, especially during rapid growth, can quickly eat up a significant amount of your organization's time. The key is to ensure that you are spending the least time with candidates as possible, especially at the beginning of the hiring funnel and that you are making decisions quickly. This means that you need to have a good idea of what you are looking for in a candidate and that you are able to evaluate them quickly against that criteria. You can see a diagram on page 331 of the hiring funnel.

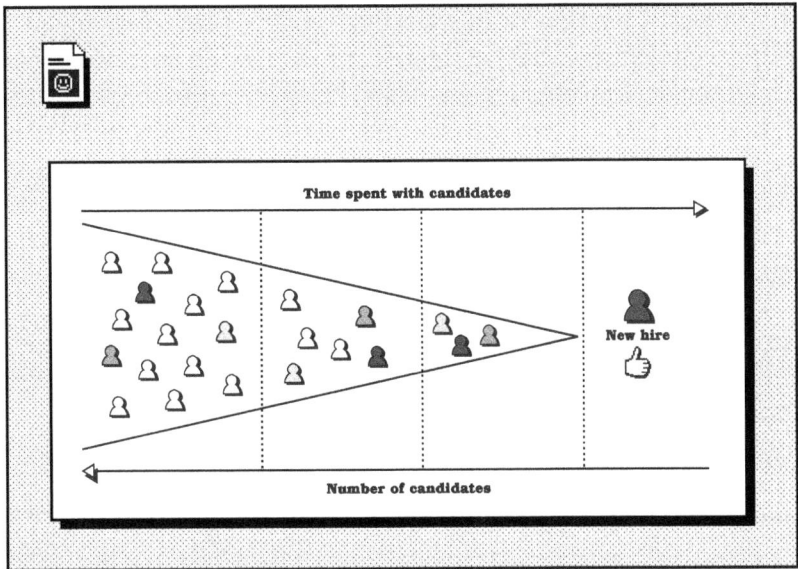

In order to keep some order and predictability for your staff, you should consider:

- *Getting as many engineers trained in interviewing as possible.* This will help spread the load and also ensure that you are getting a diverse set of opinions on each candidate.
- *Automating booking and scheduling of interviews.* For example, get each of your engineers to block out several afternoons a week for interviews and then have a system that automatically schedules candidates into those slots. This eliminates the back and forth that can happen and gives candidates a poor experience.
- *Working with your recruiting team to ensure they can perform both effective sourcing and screening.* This means they are able to find the right candidates and then evaluate them against the criteria you have set out. You may want to spend dedicated time pairing with them on this: sit down together, review resumes, search for candidates on LinkedIn, and then evaluate them together. What tools, experience, technologies, and companies are signals of a good candidate? What are the red flags?
- *Dedicating your time to outreach.* During macroeconomic boom periods, it can be hard to find good candidates, as they are often already employed or are already being bombarded by messages from recruiters. Blocking out time each week to find the best candidates yourself and messaging them personally can have a high hit rate as it makes you stand out.

And what about after they're hired? Once you've gotten candidates in the door, you need to ensure that they can be productive as soon as possible. No matter how senior someone is, they will be entirely new to the context of your company. Hence, when they arrive, they will be a *net-negative contributor* because they need more support from others than they are able to give back. Going from net-negative to *net-positive* is the goal of onboarding, and you want to make the speed of your contribution curve as steep as possible. You can see an example of that contribution curve here:

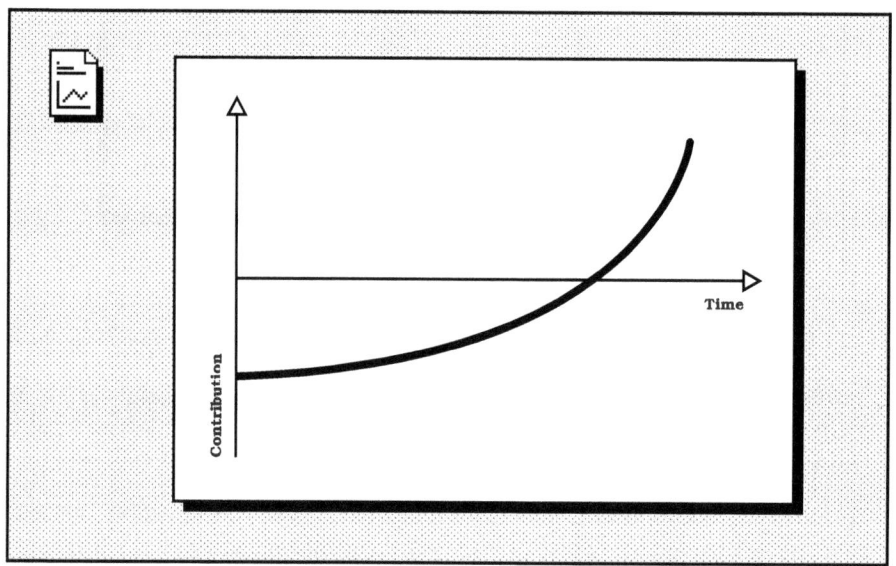

The amount of time it takes for someone to progress along that curve is a function of your onboarding process. So, how do you improve that process? Well, the best way to understand what it's like to join the company and ramp up is to do it yourself. Get a fresh computer from the IT team, and then go through the onboarding process and development environment setup as if you were a new hire. Trust me, there will be a *lot* of things to fix. Then, turn that backlog of fixes and improvements into a project that you can delegate to one of your teams. If you haven't hired many people for a long time, you may be surprised at how completely broken the process is, and it may take weeks of work to make it seamless again.

If it's broken, fix it; accelerating staff along the contribution curve as quickly as possible is key to new hires being uniformly productive, as opposed to your organizational productivity grinding to a halt as each new hire encounters problems that need fixing that then suck time away from your engineers. If you are hiring a significant amount of people, you may want to consider *permanently* dedicating a team to onboarding throughout the peacetime period so that you can organize and scale the process. For example, have new hires always start at the same time each month and form a cohort that goes through the process together. This way, you can ensure that you are always improving the process and that you are always getting feedback on how to make it better.

One of the benefits of peacetime and the available capital is that you can both increase the efficiency of your engineers and the attractiveness of your company to new hires by spending on the best computers, tools, and services that engineers want. Skimping cents on the dollar and not giving engineers access to fast computers, AI tools like GitHub Copilot, and the ability to move quickly by spending on services like AWS or GCP can be a false economy. The best engineers will go to the companies that give them the best tools to do their job. If using tools like Copilot increases the productivity of your engineers by 10 percent, then it's a no-brainer to spend the money on it. Hiring 10 percent more engineers is a far more expensive alternative. If you have the capital, deploy it.

> **Your Turn: Start from Scratch**
>
> How long does it actually take to be productive as a new hire in your organization? Get a new computer from IT, and then go through the onboarding process and development environment setup as if you were a new hire.
>
> - Did all of the documentation and tools that you needed exist? If not, what was missing? Did the documentation even exist in the first place?
> - Was the process painful or pleasant? What made it feel that way? If it was painful, do you think it's worth delegating the fixes to one or more of your teams? If it was pleasant, can you duplicate that experience elsewhere?
> - How long did it take you to be productive? How could you have made that process faster?
> - What would an ideal experience look like, where a new hire is able to commit code to production on their first day? How far away are you from that ideal?

Incubating New Products

Another common peacetime activity is the company wanting to spin out new products or services. If you are an established company, making progress on a new product can be difficult. The ways of working required to build a new product are often very different from the ways of working required to maintain an existing one.

If you're facing this challenge, there's an entire book waiting for you: *The Innovator's Dilemma [Chr11]* by Clayton Christensen. In it, he discusses how companies can be so focused on their existing products that they miss out on new opportunities. This oversight is exactly what makes startups so dangerous to established companies: they are able to focus on the new product without the baggage of the old one.

As such, if you are tasked with spinning out a new product, you need to ensure that you are able to do so in a way that gives the team the autonomy and freedom to prototype, build, and iterate quickly:

- *Establish them as a separate team from the rest of the department.* Let them choose their own ways of working and their own tools, and even consider treating them as a separate *company* with their own budget and P&L. Letting them operate independently will allow them to move quickly and make decisions without having to go through the bureaucracy of the rest of the company.

- *Staff the team with engineers who have the mindset for this.* It may mean that your best engineers on the existing product are not the best engineers for the new product. Who do you have that is able to work quickly, iterate fast, and take risks? These are the people that you want on the new team.

- *Ensure that there are clear tripwires for success and failure.* Don't let the team work on the new product indefinitely: set clear goals for what success and failure look like. If they are not meeting these goals, then it may be time to pivot or shut down the project. All outcomes are valuable, and failing fast should be encouraged.

> **New Product Plans Are Sensitive**
>
>  Since spinning up new products requires potentially reprioritizing existing work to free up staff to work on them, ensure that you have your plans finalized before you start communicating them to the wider team.

Depending on the size of your company, peacetime may mean incubating multiple new products at any given time. Regardless, the same holds true: unpin them from the existing ways of working, staff them with the right people, and do whatever you can to ensure that the only blockers they face are outside of your incumbent organization.

> **Your Turn: A New Startup Inside Your Company**
>
> Imagine that tomorrow your company is spinning out an entirely new product which is going to be staffed by engineers from your department.
>
> - Have you done this before? Did it work well or not? If it didn't work, why?
> - Do you have a subset of your engineers that you think would be a good fit for this new team? What characteristics do they have that make you think that?
> - How much resistance do you think that they would face from the rest of the department if they were to operate independently? What if they wanted to use a completely different technology stack?
> - If the answer to this question was that they would face a lot of resistance, how do you think you could communicate this initiative to the rest of the department in a way that would make them more accepting of it? How would you frame it?

Mergers and Acquisitions (M&A)

Peacetime companies looking to grow quickly may look to buy other companies, either to expand their product portfolio or to have a chance to acquire a team with a great track record. The level of involvement you'll have in this process will depend on your seniority and the trust you have built up with your leadership team. If you want to dive deeper into what the process of M&A looks like as a whole, then we recommend the article "Engineering in Mergers and Acquisitions" by Will Larson.[7] If you want to go even deeper than that, there is a whole chapter in Elad Gil's *High Growth Handbook* [Gil18].

> **M&A Is Confidential**
>
> It should go without saying that M&A activity is highly confidential and should only be discussed with the smallest group of people possible. You may want everyone involved to sign an NDA.

If you are new to being involved in M&A, then remember that most of it comes to *nothing*. This is the reason, confidentiality aside, that the staff involved in M&A are often a small and trusted circle. The truth is that most M&A deals fall through, either through the due diligence process or because the two companies are not able to agree on terms or even because a bidding war happens at the end of the process and someone else wins. As such, you should

---

7. https://lethain.com/engineering-in-mergers-and-acquisition/

be prepared for the fact that most of the work that you do will not result in a deal. This does not mean that you should take it any less seriously; it just means that you need to hold multiple parallel futures in your mind at any given time. What would the organization look like if we bought this company, and what would it look like if we didn't? You have to resist the urge to fixate on one outcome.

The *due diligence* process is where you are likely to be involved, even if you were not part of the strategic side of the deal. This is where you will be asked to evaluate the technical capabilities of the company that you are looking to buy and to ensure that they are a good fit for your organization. Generally speaking, you want to break this due diligence process down into constituent parts:

- *Technical due diligence*: This is where you will be looking at the codebase, the architecture, and the technical capabilities of the company that you are looking to buy. You will want to ensure that they are using best practices, that they are able to scale, and that, if the product is being kept, there are options to integrate or coexist with your existing systems and products. This part also covers whether their product actually exists or not (seriously) and works how they say it does.

- *Talent assessment*: For each of the engineers that you are looking to bring on board as part of the deal, you want to ensure that they are going to be successful. Generally speaking, you will want to bring each engineer through the standard interview process that you use for external candidates, ensuring that the confidentiality of the deal is respected, and then make a decision based on their performance.

- *Organizational fit*: Assuming that all of the engineers come on board, who are they going to report to and why? There are usually two main options chosen here, depending on whether the acquired company continues to run its own product or whether the acquisition is just about bringing the team across. If they are coming as a whole company, product and all, it can make sense to initially keep them together as a separate business unit, with the acquired CEO reporting in to a suitable executive in your company. This is a reasonable holding pattern while an integration plan is worked out. If they are being acquired without their product, then it can make sense to integrate them into your existing team while maintaining as much of their existing structure as possible (for example, their CTO becomes a suitably leveled manager in your organization).

If deals happen, then you need to not overlook the effect on your current team. Even though M&A is a gigantic vote of confidence in your company and market position, and despite that vote of confidence extending to you and your own organization because *you* get more people and products, M&A can be unsettling to existing staff. This is because they may see the new company as an existential threat to their own capabilities, as a loss of control over parts of their roadmap, or that their company has secretly acquired another because they are failing in some way.

All of this is very rarely true, so it is your job as a leader to communicate repeatedly the strategic reason that this piece of M&A is happening and the value it adds: it is a way of adding more strength, diverse ideas, increasing domain knowledge, and fundamentally, it brings more capability to their team. Have your new additions treated like any new engineer: onboard them the same way, pair them up with buddies for knowledge sharing and mentoring, and make them feel at home.

Leading Through Wartime: Cut, Save, Rebuild

The opposite of peacetime is wartime. In wartime, your company is focused primarily on survival. There could be a number of reasons for this: revenue may be stagnating or falling, the company may have been unable to raise another round of funding on good terms, or the macroeconomic environment may have changed suddenly after a period of growth (the previous 2022–2024 COVID-19 example). Regardless of the reason, wartime is about cutting costs, saving money, and rebuilding the company to fit a new environment.

Even though wartime is a time of crisis, it is also a time of opportunity where great leaders are forged. It is likely that you are going to go through numerous wartime periods in your career, and it is important to frame them as opportunities for you to grow and develop as a leader. It will stretch you in ways that you never thought possible, and whether the company survives or not, you will come out of it a better person. Embrace the challenge.

Reforecasting, Restrategizing, and Reorganizing

Given that wartime is about survival, the first thing that you need to do is consider whether your current strategy is still valid. Depending on the seriousness of the downturn that you are facing, you may need to effectively delete all of the plans that you have made and start again. This isn't a sign of failure, it's a sign of strength. Leaders who doggedly stick to a plan that they made during a time of growth or stability will more likely fail than those who are able to pivot quickly when the environment changes.

> **Wartime Reorganization Can Be Confidential**
>
> Wartime reorganization requires clear messaging since it represents a culture shift in the organization. Depending on the severity, this activity is either sensitive or confidential. As a package of separate units of work, round them up to the highest level of confidentiality before execution.

The first thing, therefore, is to understand what is happening. There are a number of drivers that could be causing your company existential risk, and you need to understand what they are. They could be:

- *Significantly missing revenue targets*: Your product isn't selling as well as it was expected to, so there isn't as much money feeding into the flywheel in the future as you thought there was going to be.

- *Inability to raise another round of funding*: As startups grow and scale, they often assume that they will pass through a number of increasingly sized funding rounds on the way to an exit. Macroeconomic conditions can change the ability to raise the next round as expected, and this can be a significant problem if the company is not yet profitable.

- *Significant increase in costs*: Dynamics in the market can drive up the cost of doing business. During periods of high inflation, a rise in prices can put pressure on the bottom line, from hosting to salaries to office leases.

- *Failure to achieve product-market fit*: Generally a more common problem in startups, the company may have been unable to create a product that a predictable number of customers are willing to pay for. This means the company is burning cash without a clear path to profitability and needs to pivot to a new product or market.

The exact reason or reasons that you and your company face will be unique to your situation. The more you are able to know about what is happening, the more you are able to make a plan to deal with it. Talk to your peers, the executive team, and especially your finance leaders to understand the ramifications of the wartime situation and what that could mean for your department in terms of a reforecasted budget for the coming year. If you are not getting this information, then you *must* press for it to be made available to you as soon as possible. You can't act without it.

Every wartime financial reforecast will rebalance the company flywheel based on the new reality that is being faced. This means modeling out the new revenue and cost structure and then mapping that to the current headcount and expenses to see what the difference is between the two. This difference is the amount that you will need to cut or find in order to survive.

The first time that you experience a situation like this can be incredibly stressful. You may have never had to cut costs before, and you may be worried about the effect that it will have on your product and your team. It is your job to act as the mitigation function between the new reality for your company and your team, and before you do so, you need to make a draft of a new plan that has enough information for you to be able to communicate it effectively with the smallest circle needed to progress it.

The challenge with this situation is that you cannot be transparent with the entire organization immediately. The key is to have *just enough* plan to be able to communicate the situation to your immediate team and then be able to lead them through the next phase. In order to do so, you will likely need to work with your most trusted peers and staff in order to come up with potential scenarios and then decide on the best course of action.

We are going to work through a fictional example of a wartime scenario in the next section to give you an idea of how you might approach it and in what order you might want to tackle the mitigation plan. Situations like this are challenging, stressful, and often involve long hours, late nights, and difficult decisions. We present the following scenario in a matter-of-fact way in order to keep the focus on the process, but it by no means reduces the emotional gravity of these situations in real life.

Enumerating the Options

Let's imagine that a global financial crisis has led to high inflation, high interest rates, an increase in costs, and a decrease in consumer spending. Since you serve a consumer market, your executives are predicting that your revenue will stagnate or fall in the coming year rather than grow by 25 percent as was previously forecast. The finance team has modeled a number of scenarios, and they are recommending that the company cut costs by 25 percent in order to survive. The CEO has told each department head to come up with a plan to save this amount of money. What do you do?

First, you need to understand what the options are. There are a number of ways that you can cut costs, and each of them has different implications for your team:

- *Freezing hiring*: This is the most common way to cut costs, and is a surefire way to reclaim budgeted money. In your budget, this finds you 10 percent of the way to your target, but it also means that you are going to have to do more with less. You can work with your engineering leaders to come up with a plan here. You classify this as *confidential* in the concentric circles of trust, since it can cause panic.

- *Auditing software and services*: You look through what your team is using and note that there are numerous paid services that you could live without, which accumulated during the peacetime period. This finds you another 5 percent of the way to your target. You can work with your IT team to do this and also to recommend free or open source alternatives. You classify this as *sensitive* since it's fairly normal to audit your software costs, but you don't want to cause worry.

- *Negotiating hard with vendors*: You have been a customer with your cloud hosting provider since the start-up was founded, and you have not renegotiated your contract in years. You reckon that with help from your executive team, you could likely get a 10 percent discount on your bill, which will get you another 5 percent of the way to your target. You will work with the finance partnerships team to do this. You also classify this as *sensitive*.

- *It isn't immediately obvious where the remaining savings are going to come from*: This is where you decide that you are going to have to escalate back to the executive team with some options and a recommendation before you can move forward. You will do this alone. You classify this as *confidential* until you know what the plan is.

You feel that if you are able to do this, including coming up with a solution to the final bullet point, you should be able to continue developing and supporting your current products.

This generates four actions, following each bullet in turn. The first is straightforward and requires no further planning: hiring will just stop. For the next two, you call a meeting with the leaders of both IT and procurement to say you're going to be working with them to help cut costs and you'll need their help to do so. You ask them to come up with a plan that will save the money you need, and given this is sensitive information, to keep their work within the smallest group possible.

For the final bullet point, you go back to the executive team to have them help you make a decision. You realize that you effectively only have a small number of options here:

- *Having your money savings target reduced*: Here, you convince them to give you a pass on that remaining 5 percent, then continue as normal and hope that the company can either find more savings elsewhere or that the revenue forecast is proven wrong with time.

- *Seeing whether product trade-offs could save money*: For example, you know that the cost of compute is a significant part of your budget and that you could save money by having data refresh daily rather than hourly, saving on spot instances. There are likely many other trade-offs here, such as reducing the number of backups and read replicas in your databases. You don't know exactly how much this would save yet, and it would likely not be all of the 5 percent, but you want to see whether they feel it is worth investigating.

- *Layoffs*: You know that this is an option, but you would rather it wasn't. Like the previous option, you don't make any plans here yet, but you want to get a sense of whether this is on the table or not. After all, it's typically the last resort, but it would find the money that you need.

You meet with the executive team and present these options, and then they ask you to sign an NDA. Your final option, layoffs, is actually happening regardless. It turns out you weren't in the confidential circle of trust for this information until now. You need to cut 15 percent of your team in addition to the other savings that you have found.

Layoffs: The Worst Part Comes First

Layoffs are the worst part of wartime. They are the most stressful, the most emotional, and the most difficult part of leading a team. Leading a large organization, you will not be alone—you will have support from HR, finance, and the executive team. However, it is likely that the decision of exactly *who* to lay off will be yours, and you will need to ensure that when asked to provide a list of names, you are able to do so in such a way that:

- *Maximizes the chances of the department and company surviving*: This means that the remaining team has the highest possible chance of being able to execute the new plan that you have come up with.

- *Retains the best talent*: This follows from the first point, as you are going to have to do more with less.

- *Complies with labor laws*: This is a given and will require you to work with HR, finance, and legal, but many factors such as tenure, geography, and role will need to be considered in who makes the final list.

Given that you are an experienced leader, we will not enumerate the entire process of layoffs. It's likely you've been through them before on both sides of the table. They suck hard. You'll be supported in the process, but ultimately, you'll expected to communicate some or all of the news to your team.

Layoffs Are Confidential

 If you work for a public company, expect to sign an NDA if you are involved in planning or executing layoffs. This is some of the most sensitive information that you will handle.

The key is this: nobody should know about layoffs until they are happening. Many technology companies have come under scrutiny for layoffs that seemingly happened out of the blue, with employees logging on in the morning to see an email that either they were safe or they have been made redundant, alongside numerous prewritten and prerecorded announcements. Such scrutiny has come from the fact the company wasn't transparent about the situation beforehand or people weren't given the opportunity to prepare.

However, here's the question: *what other way can you do this?* In my opinion, any other way is even *more* heavily flawed. If you tell people that layoffs are coming, then you will have mass distraction and panic, and you may even have an exodus of your best talent before you start removing your worst. If you offer voluntary layoffs, then you may get people leaving that you'd rather keep on for the benefit of the company. If you do it in waves, then you will have a constant state of distraction and low morale. One and done, in my opinion, is always the best way. As a leader, you want the pain to be over quickly so that you can focus on rebuilding.

At larger companies, communications from the CEO and the executive team are often done publicly as well as internally when layoffs happen. These companies have a responsibility to their shareholders and the market to be transparent about what is happening. You can see examples of what these announcements look like in Meta's announcement from 2022,[8] Airbnb's announcement from 2020,[9] and Google's announcement from 2023.[10]

Layoff announcements, like any major announcement during wartime that communicates that the world is changing, are a *line in the sand.* You will likely have to communicate in this way often as a senior leader, so let's see how it's done.

---

8. https://about.fb.com/news/2022/11/mark-zuckerberg-layoff-message-to-employees/
9. https://news.airbnb.com/a-message-from-co-founder-and-ceo-brian-chesky/
10. https://blog.google/inside-google/message-ceo/january-update/

A Line in the Sand

As wartime unfolds, you need to control the narrative and the morale of your team. Whether you're facing layoffs or just challenging circumstances, you have a responsibility to make crystal clear what is happening and where you are going next.

> **Broadcasting Your Line in the Sand Is Open Information**
>
> This is the beginning of the rebuilding process and is open information. You should be as clear as possible about what has happened and what is going to happen next.

For the narrative, you need to be as clear as possible that there was a world prior to this wartime period that is no longer the case, and you are collectively facing a new reality.

A line in the sand is the culmination of all your activities inside the inner rings of the concentric circles of trust. It involves taking that sensitive and confidential information and bringing it into the *open* with clarity. Be as clear as possible about what this line is, what came before it, and what this means for the future. You'll notice many formal wartime communications are written in this way, and you can see an example of what this might look like here:

An Important Message to Everyone
by: Executive Leadership Team, ACMECorp

Team, today we are facing a new reality. The company and the environment that we operate in are not the same as the ones from the previous few years. The world has changed significantly. The recent global financial crisis has meant that our customers are spending less and that it is much harder to ensure that we are able to grow as we have done in the past. Additionally, the next funding round is not going to be as easy as we thought it was going to be.

Today, we said goodbye to some of our colleagues. We thank each of them for their hard work and dedication to the company, and we wish them all the best in their future endeavors. Each has been offered generous severance and outplacement services to ensure that they are able to find a new role as quickly as possible.

Despite the challenges that we are facing, we are still in a strong position. We have a great product, so much that we want to build, and most importantly, we have you. Every single one of you is vital to the future of this company, and we are going to need to work together to ensure that we prosper in this new environment.

As we regroup, we must face the reality that we are going to need to do more with less. Look around at your team, your roadmap, and your priorities. Say no to anything that is not essential. We must all wipe the slate clean and then build in this new reality. We are here to support you as you do this.

Everyone is invited to an all-hands meeting later today where we will discuss the future of the company, and we will be available for any questions that you may have. Check your inboxes for the invite and the submission form for questions.

Thank you for being part of this team. We are going to get through this together.

Once you have broadcast your line in the sand, then you need to start *rebuilding communication*. This is increasingly less formal and is about ensuring that your team is able to move forward in the new environment.

There are a number of ways in which you can help your team onward through periods of uncertainty:

- *Increase your broadcast communication to your team*: Consider writing a weekly update highlighting the progress that you are making through difficult periods or recording regular videos to celebrate all of the positive work that is being done despite the challenging circumstances. This will help to keep your team focused on the positive rather than the negative.

- *Increase the number of check-ins you have with your team*: This also includes skip-level meetings, where you meet with the team members of your direct reports (and beyond). Even if you *are* working on confidential plans, by being available to talk and to listen, you can help alleviate some of the stress that your team is feeling.

- *Increase the opportunity for Q&A at all-hands meetings*: During any period of worry or change, you should always give people the opportunity to ask questions, including anonymously. For example, you could circulate a Google Form before your meetings and then answer the questions that you receive.

- *Work on shaping the current circumstances as a challenge*: This is a time for you to show your leadership skills. You can help your team see the current situation as a challenge that they can rise to and overcome rather than as a threat to their livelihood. You will know your team and what motivates them, and you can use this to help them see the current situation in a positive light.

- *Encourage your team to resist overworking and take appropriate time off*: Any stressful period is made worse by no ability to rest and recharge. Encourage your team to take time off, including leading by example where you can.

So, remember the pattern as you progress through the next wartime period that requires a major pivot: make your plan confidentially, execute it with a line in the sand, and then rebuild in the open.

So, Where Are You Going?

We've reached the end of our whirlwind tour of peacetime and wartime. This means that we're almost at the end of the book! There's just one more chapter to go, and don't worry—it's going to be future-facing and positive.

Here's what we've covered in this one:

- *Building on top of what we learned about money* in the previous chapter, we looked at boom and bust cycles in the economy and how they can affect you, your company, and your career.

- *We then categorized possible operational states of a company along a scale from peacetime to wartime, with a steady state in the middle.* We looked at the characteristics of each and how they can affect your leadership. Given the length of your career, it is likely that you will experience both of the extremes multiple times.

- *Then, we looked at peacetime and wartime in turn* and what some of the activities are that you may be leading in each. We looked at hiring, onboarding, ramping up in peacetime, and layoffs and rebuilding after "line in the sand" moments in wartime.

We'll close out this book by spending time introspecting on your leadership journey so far and then looking at what the future may hold for you. We'll see that if you want to continue to grow as a leader, you need to be able to accept and embrace the fact that the path ahead may not be as much of a straight line as you may have thought. However, there is still a model that you can follow to ensure that you are writing a career narrative that you are proud of.

CHAPTER 15

Tarzan Swings from Vine to Vine

You are searching through your inbox to find a summary of a meeting you had last week. By chance, you stumble across the confirmation email that you got when you formally accepted your current director of engineering role the day after Lisa told you the news of her own promotion.

You notice the date. Wow, has it already been six months? The time has absolutely *flown* by. You've been so busy that you've barely had time to think about what you're doing each day, let alone where you are going in the future.

You remember back to when you were promoted to engineering manager for the first time. Before it happened, you had worked on a career plan with your manager, and you were absolutely *certain* about what you wanted to do next. You read books, took online courses, watched conference talks, and fully immersed yourself in the world of management. When it happened, you were ready. It's almost as if you *made* it happen.

Since then, you've always been curious about the big next step—getting into the role that you're in now. This time was different, though—it occurred out of the blue. It just happened. You made director without even formally applying. No career plan, no guidance, and no training. It seemed like it was just the next logical step. So you took it. But should you have?

You second guess yourself—was it the *right* thing to do? Should you have instead challenged yourself more by going to a different company rather than staying where you already were? Is this going to look worse on your resume in the long run? But then again, you've been at this company for so long that you know the ins and outs of everything. *Surely* that's a good thing, right?

You are distracted by new messages rolling in as you stare across the room and think. You dip your laptop screen down to ignore them for the time being.

Where are you right now in the grand journey of your career? And what actually comes next for you? Should you stay in this role for another few years and see whether there are any opportunities for you to move up to VP? Or do you need to go somewhere else to get that experience first?

And is this really *it* for the rest of your working life? Just climbing the management ladder indefinitely until you're eventually at the top? Is that what success means for you? Or is it something else?

How are you meant to work out the answers to these questions? Honestly, you've been so busy you haven't even thought about it.

But maybe it's time to start.

Well, you've made it to the end of the book. This is the final chapter before we part ways. But before we do, we are going to be thinking all about you: where you are right now, where you want to go, and how you can get there.

If you've arrived here after reading the rest of the book first, then, other than wishing you congratulations, I hope that you have noticed that senior leadership is less about following prescriptive advice and more about understanding the context of your situation and making the best decisions you can with the information you have and the tools and frameworks that you've learned. There really is no *right* answer to any given situation.

This can often throw new leaders off. Every situation that they face is unique when they factor in their context, people, and company. As such, they have to learn that their ongoing success is about developing a strategy for where they want to go and then defining the operations and tactics that will get them there. As they grow in seniority, they'll begin to pattern-match aspects of situations that they've seen before, mapping them into new contexts.

I am not an expert in your career. But I've been around enough to begin to see some of those patterns, and this chapter is about *your own* strategy for getting where you want to go. We'll look at some tools and frameworks that you can use to help you understand where you are, where you want to go, and how you can get there.

Here's what we're going to cover:

- *We'll begin by considering how your career from now is rarely ever a straight line.* In fact, trying to make it one might do you more harm than good.

- *Then, we'll introduce the Tarzan method.* Rather than focusing on climbing the ladder, you should consider what it means to swing playfully from vine to vine, traversing the jungle. You'll never know what you might discover along the way.

- *If we're swinging, then what is our trajectory?* We'll explore some heuristics that you can use to help you work out where you want to go. These heuristics are scope and impact and whether you are at a point in your career where you want to be earning or learning.

- *Finally, we'll wrap up with an exercise.* If you can write a strategy for your department, then you can write one for your career, too. We'll then think about how that strategy could unlock the tactics that you can take right now to start seeing the next vine swings that you could take.

Okay! Pen and paper at the ready for this one. It's time to think about *you*. This is the fun part. Let's begin.

The Fallacy of the Straight Line

If you read the first book in this series, you may remember that the final chapter was a career development exercise that asked you to think about where you were, where you wanted to go, and how you could get there. However, given that the first book was aimed at new managers or those who were aspiring to be managers, the scope of that exercise was reasonably narrow: it was about developing the skills needed to manage a single team and then working out how to either do it for the first time or do it better than you were already doing it.

Since this book has traversed a far broader landscape, and since you could be at any point on that map, we're going to be thinking about a far broader set of questions. After all, you could be an existing or aspiring engineering manager, a director, a VP, or even a CTO. You could be in a start-up, a scale-up, or a large enterprise at *any* of those levels. You could be in a company that is growing rapidly or one that is in decline, or you could be freshly promoted or looking for a new role.

Only you know where you are and where you want to go. However, it's worth noting that *up* isn't the only destination worth visiting.

Something that often throws mid-level leaders off is the idea that they need to doggedly progress in a straight line. We can see this in the diagram on page 350 by mapping it to one of the first diagrams that we encountered in this book.

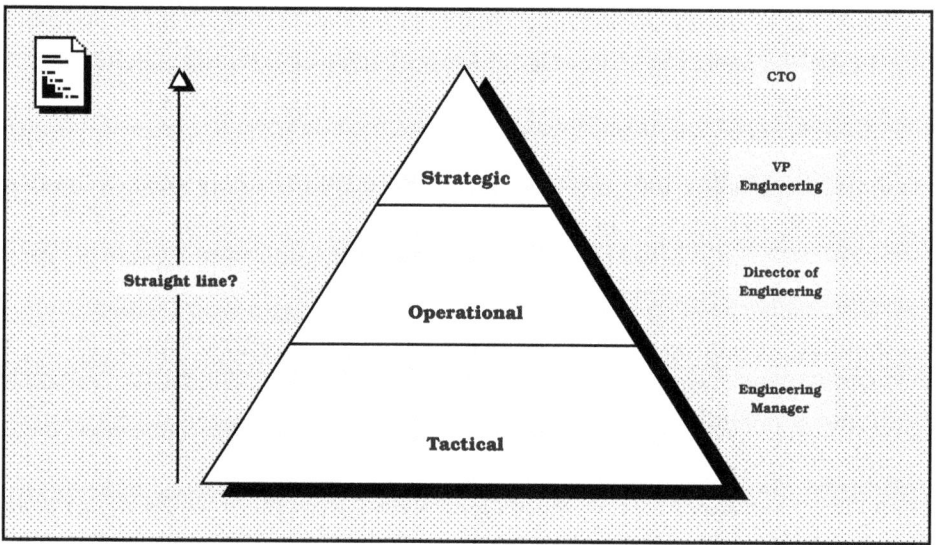

Sometimes, people believe that the game is about going from engineering manager to director to VP to CTO as quickly as possible, or else they have failed in their quest. However, careers are long. This narrow focus on getting everything yesterday can be incredibly damaging to their mental health and their career. This quest for self-actualization through becoming CTO before the age of 30 can often lead to burnout, disillusionment, and a sense of failure. It may also lead to a lack of focus on the things that actually matter, such as building a portfolio of skills and experiences that will make you a better leader in the long run.

And get this: the path to increasingly senior roles is *not something that you have complete control over*. The upper echelons of leadership, which include senior individual contributor roles, are a function of the skills of the person that is doing them, but most importantly, the fact that the given company *needs someone to do that role*.

Sometimes, they just don't.

If you work for a small agency, it will likely never get to the scale where it will need middle management, let alone a CTO or principal engineer. If you work for a large enterprise, it may have a rigid structure that doesn't allow for the kind of lateral moves that you need to make to get to the top. You could wait your whole life for a promotion there. If you work for a company that is in decline, it may not have the resources to promote you, even if you are the best person for the job; in fact, they may be trying to flatten the organization to reflect an upcoming period of austerity.

It's not you, it's *them*.

This is why it's so important to focus on what you can control and *let go* of what you can't. And it's also important to loosen your expectations of where exactly your career may end up and, instead, focus on the *journey* that you are on right now, with a mindful eye on your general direction toward a future that makes you happy and developing a portfolio of skills and experiences that makes you a better leader.

And it turns out that there is an analogy that we can use to help us think about this: the Tarzan method.

The Tarzan Method

New York City-based filmmaker Casey Neistat once answered a question about his career progression with a neat analogy.[1] It fits in well with having a more exploratory, playful, and joyful approach to your career. In the video, to answer the question, he pulls out a big roll of paper from the wall, lays it across his table, and then proceeds to draw something similar to this diagram:

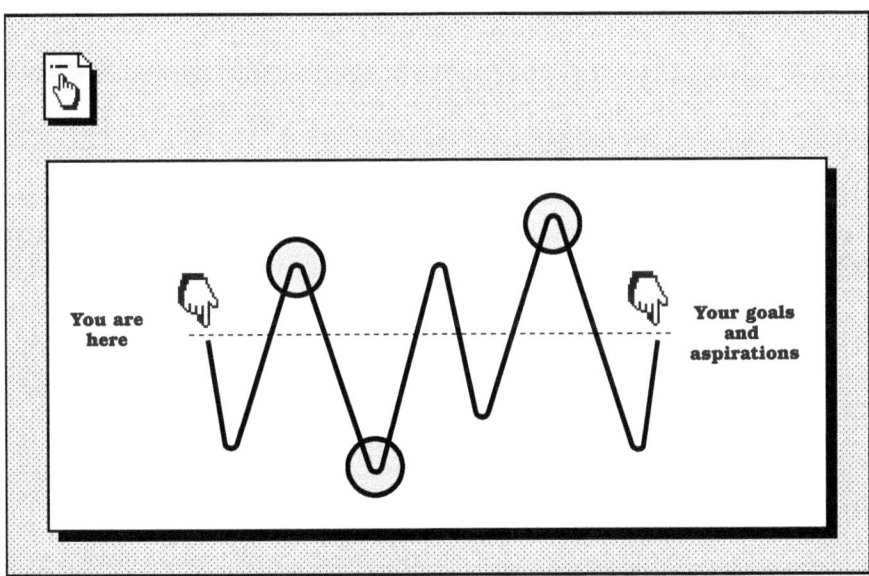

On the left-hand side of the diagram is where you are right now in your career. On the right-hand side of the diagram are your current goals and aspirations, whatever they may be. The dotted line that connects the two is an idealized optimal shortest path that you could take to get from where you are to where you want to be.

---

1. https://youtu.be/7HF4peQxeXA?si=tN6s9_wpj9g2LBll

However, the problem is that this direct path may not be possible, and it may not even exist. If your dream is to be the CTO of the biggest technology company in the world in twenty years' time, which is a grand, respectable dream, then how do you even plan for that? It's highly likely that this company doesn't even exist yet, and the skills that you need to get there may be in a field that hasn't even been invented yet.

Instead, you should think about your career like Tarzan swinging through the jungle. Tarzan starts at one tree and knows that he has an ultimate destination, but the path to get there isn't immediately clear. There are hundreds of different trees that he could swing to. He doesn't know which one is the right one at any given time. He just has to trust his instincts and his general sense of direction and then progress to the next vine, and then the next, and then the next. In the diagram, these vine swings are represented by the up-and-down line that eventually connects you to your goals.

As you swing from vine to vine, those leaps will take you along a path that is *unique to you*. Your first swing may take you off-course when you measure yourself against the dotted straight line, but it may *also* take you to a place that you never even knew existed. The same is true for the next swing and the one after that. These new and unknown places are marked on the diagram as circles at the peaks and troughs of the swings. They may even be the most important places that you visit on your journey.

And here's the neat thing: it's likely at these outward swings of each vine that you discover what *really* matters to you. And what matters to you may change over time. You may find that you love a particular type of work, a particular type of company, or a particular technology. You may find yourself trying a role that you hadn't originally considered, trying out working remotely, or moving to a different country. You may find that you love smaller start-ups rather than big enterprises or perhaps the other way around. Who knows what you might find? That's the beauty of the Tarzan method.

The Trajectory of Your Swing

The Tarzan method is a great way to think about your career progression metaphorically, but it doesn't give you a lot of *practical* advice on how to actually get from one vine to the next. For that, we need to think about the trajectory of your swing. Some heuristics can help here.

We have repeatedly referred to the concepts of scope and impact throughout this book. This will be our first heuristic. As a refresher:

- *Scope* is the breadth of your responsibility. It covers the size of the team that you manage, the size of the budget that you control, the number of projects that you are responsible for, and the number of people that you influence. It is the size of the sandbox that you play in.

- *Impact* is the depth of your responsibility. It covers the result of the work you produce, the output of your team, and the effectiveness of the decisions you make. It is the quality of the sandcastles that you build.

If you are thinking about your leadership career as a series of vine swings, then you can think about each swing as a progression in either scope or impact or both. Ideally, when you zoom out at any point in your career, you can step back and observe that both have been trending upward over time.

In fact, we can plot the interplay between scope and impact as a quadrant:

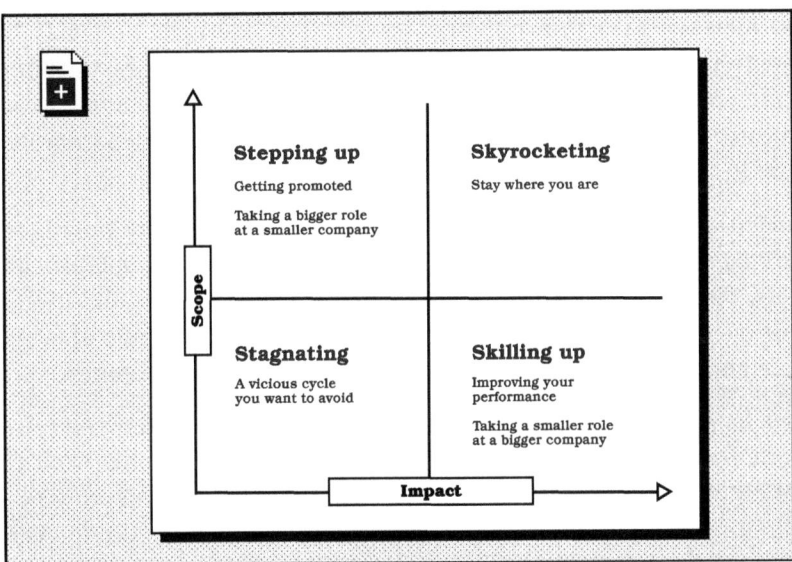

On the x-axis, we have impact, and on the y-axis, we have scope. Given your own internal measurement of your current scope and impact, you can work out which quadrant applies to you in your current situation and then think about which of them should guide you in your next vine swing.

Each part of the quadrant begins with the letter S, and they are, starting at the bottom left and progressing clockwise:

- *Stagnating*: You have low impact and low scope compared to where you want to be. You are likely in a role that is not challenging or satisfying you, and you are not making the impact that you want to make. Staying in this zone is not good in the long run. For you, it means that you are going to grow continually more dissatisfied with your work. It also becomes a vicious cycle: the less satisfied you are, the less you are likely to do good work and the fewer opportunities that you are likely to get. You need to move out of this zone as soon as possible.

- *Stepping up*: You are in a period where you are primarily focused on increasing your scope so that it can lead to a larger impact in the future. This can happen by taking on more responsibility, such as by getting promoted or by taking a vine swing to a different, often smaller, company offering a bigger role than you currently have. You commonly see this happen when someone moves from a bigger company to a smaller company for a more senior role, such as a director of engineering at a public company moving to a smaller private company as a VP of engineering.

- *Skyrocketing*: This is where you are in a role that is offering you a continued increase in *both* scope and impact. For example, you may be in a leadership role in a start-up that is growing extremely fast around you. When you're in this position, the best move is to stay where you are and continue to grow with the company. This is the most desirable position to be in, but it is also the most rare.

- *Skilling up*: This typically follows a *stepping-up* period where you're primarily working on improving your performance and impact through learning new skills. This can be done by doubling down where you are and investing in your own personal development or by taking a smaller role at a bigger or more challenging company that'll push you to learn new things.

The key to progressing in your career is to continually move around this quadrant between the top left and the bottom right, hoping that you get periods of time in the top right. The more that you can do this, the more that you will grow in your career. And, it goes without saying, you don't want to be in the bottom left for too long.

Earn, Learn, or Quit

Another heuristic that can be useful to guide you between each vine swing in your career is the interplay between increasing your skills and increasing your compensation. Y Combinator CEO Garry Tan suggests that when you are surveying the trees around you and working out whether to move or stay put, then consider that "at every job, you should either learn or earn. Either is fine. Both are best. But if it's neither, quit."[2]

---

2. https://www.youtube.com/watch?v=eLelgy5zRv4

Earn, learn, or quit is pithy and easy to remember. It's worth keeping the phrase in mind as you pass through milestones at work, such as anniversaries, team changes, manager changes, the end of large projects, and so on. Are you learning? Are you earning? And if you're not, what are you going to do about it?

Learning and earning, mixed with the right amount of good timing and opportunity, have a symbiotic relationship:

- *The more you learn, the more you increase your earning potential.* Experience pays, and it can open doors for you in terms of bigger roles and opportunities down the line.
- *The more you earn, the more you increase the chance of being able to take a financial risk for more learning.* For example, once you have a certain amount of money to make yourself financially stable, taking a pay cut to have a more senior position than your current one at a start-up or scale-up becomes more palatable for yourself and your family.

Since this is a symbiotic relationship, it forms a cycle similar to the ones that we have seen before in this book:

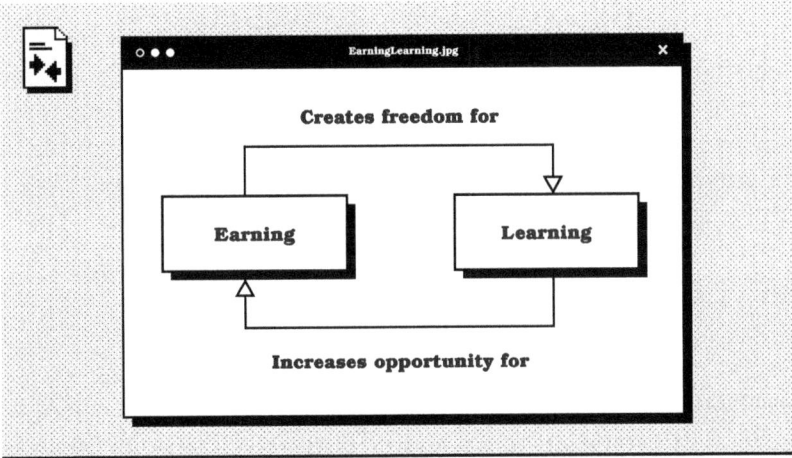

So when surveying the next vine swing available to you, remember that it's an optimization problem where the unique variable, and the *only* person that can solve it, is *you*.

Are you learning? Are you earning? And what do those terms mean to you specifically? Do you have a particular role you're aiming for? Over what time frame and what size of company? Are you trying to earn a certain amount of money? Do you want to guarantee a steady, predictable monthly income, or could you take a bet on a big payday in the future for less money right now?

The symbiotic cycle of earning and learning is a pattern you often see in the resumes of the most senior folks at notable companies. This is because one is far less likely to go all the way from the bottom to the top of the career ladder by staying at the same place; to do so, you have to stay in the top-right quadrant for a long time, and the probability of that happening is low.

If you are an engineering manager right now, or even a director, as much as you wish you could become VP at your current company, if there already is a good VP in place and the company is unlikely to grow much in the coming years, you're probably not going to get that role. Sorry for the bad news, but that's just the way it is.

Consider this: typically, the amount of org chart growth required to need a *net-new* VP is huge. And who's to say that they wouldn't hire externally? And if money is a major motivator for you, getting a gigantic compensation package while working for a small local business probably isn't going to happen, no matter how well you perform. Instead, it is far more sensible to switch up jobs via a vine swing when you start to hit ceilings of earning or learning.

Again: *go where the chance to get what you want is higher since not everything is under your control.*

Growth is very rarely a straight line; it's a swing from vine to vine. And when choosing that next vine swing, think about what the next role should be delivering to you. How much do you want to earn? What do you want to learn? How can you increase your scope and impact? And how can you make sure that you are not stagnating?

Only you have the answer.

Putting It All Together

With everything in mind, let's wrap up this book by doing an exercise together. This exercise is designed to help you think about where you are right now, where you want to go, and what you need to do to take that first vine swing. It works best if you actually follow along with it, so grab a pen and paper, either physical or digital, and let's get started.

Writing Your Strategy

It's time to think about the strategy of your *career*. Back in Chapter 11, Strategy 101, on page 253, we went through an exercise of writing an *engineering* strategy for the first time. If you remember, it started with a vision that then translated into a direction of travel. In that chapter, this was BookATrip's new strategy:

> **BookATrip's New Strategy**
> *by: Executive leadership team, BookATrip.com*
>
> We are the fastest and easiest way for anyone to book a much-needed vacation. Whether you're planning a trip months in advance, or you're booking a last-minute getaway in your lunch break, we will help you find the perfect trip for you, your friends, and your family.
>
> *Click, click, BookATrip.*

Now, since it's unlikely that your own career goal is to be the fastest and easiest way for anyone to book a much-needed vacation, it's time to spend some time thinking about what *your* strategy is for where you want to go.

Set yourself a time frame of five to ten years, and then answer the following questions:

- *What kind of role might you see yourself in if you could achieve everything you wanted?* Are you aiming to be the CTO of an up-and-coming start-up? Or are you looking to work for a publicly traded company as a VP of engineering?

- *What kind of environment do you want to work in?* Do you see yourself living in a particular location? Do you want to work for a company that is remote-first? Do you want to work for a company that is growing rapidly or one that is more stable?

- *What sort of products or services is the company creating?* Are you interested in working in a particular industry, such as healthcare or finance? Do you want to work on a particular type of product, such as a consumer-facing app or a B2B SaaS product?

- *What kind of people do you want to work with?* Do you see yourself primarily as a mentor, bringing up the next generation of leaders? Or do you see yourself surrounded by peers who are at the top of their game, pushing you to be better?

- *What kind of impact do you want to have?* Do you want to be responsible for a large team of engineers with a large budget? Or does that not matter to you, so you would rather be responsible for getting your hands dirty with a small team of hackers that are doing cutting-edge work?

- *Most importantly, what does all of this mean for other aspects of your life?* Visualize a hypothetical day from this place. When you wake up in the morning, where are you, and who are you surrounded by? What do you see when you look out of the window? How do you get to and from your work? How do you spend your evenings? Be as detailed as you can as you visualize this day.

Make some notes on each of these questions, and then write them up into a high-level strategy for yourself. For example, it might look something like this:

> **My Career Strategy**
> *by: My current self*
>
> My strategy is to become a VP of engineering at a large, publicly traded company that is creating software that helps connect people together to improve their lives. The products that the company creates should be ethically and morally sound through making a positive impact on how the world communicates. Our software will be used by a significant proportion of the global population; the work we do will make a ding in the universe. When people ask what I do, I will be proud to tell them that I build this software.
>
> I see myself living in London with my partner and my children, in a house with a small garden and a view of the city. I will split my time between working in the office and working from home so that I am always available for my family. I will never miss breakfast, dinner, or bedtime with my children. I will earn enough money so that my partner has the opportunity to retrain in a new career that they love. He has spent too long away from doing what he is truly passionate about.
>
> The size of my department will be at least several hundred engineers. This will give us the opportunity to incubate new ideas and products as well as build our core offerings; we will be able to spin up little start-ups from within the department, giving us the best of both worlds from my career so far. When I come to work, I want to continually feel like the dumbest person in the room; each day will be an opportunity to learn.
>
> I will be surrounded by a team of peers who are at the top of their game, pushing me to be better. Although our team works hard together, we maintain a healthy work-life balance; we're efficient and effective, but we're not working 80-hour weeks. I want to help drive this culture in all of our industry through our success.
>
> I will be known in the industry as a leader who is technically skilled, visionary, and empathetic. I will be a mentor to the next generation of leaders, and I will be a role model for those who are underrepresented in the industry. I will have a monthly column in a well-known industry publication, and I will be a regular speaker at conferences.
>
> Most importantly, my life and work will feel like a game; I will be having fun, I will be challenged, and I will be making a difference. Long gone are the days of stress, anxiety, and burnout; every time I have my morning coffee, I will feel proud and excited about the day ahead.

Now, it's your turn to write your own strategy. Take as long as you need, and come back here when you're done.

The Next Vine Swing

How was that exercise for you? Did it just fall out of your head, or did you have to ruminate on it for a while? Either way, we're glad that you did it.

With your strategy in mind, it's time to think about the next vine swing that you need to take to get there. In order to leave ourselves open to pleasant surprises, let's not fixate on the entire dotted line to get to the end goal. Instead, let's start by looking around at where we are.

Look back at the quadrant of scope and impact, and consider the following:

- *Where are you right now in the quadrant?* Are you stagnating, stepping up, skyrocketing, or skilling up?
- *How long have you been in this quadrant?* Are you riding on several years of success and growth, or are you feeling yourself drifting toward stagnation?
- *Is there a route to the top-right quadrant from where you are right now?* Is that route possible at your current company, or do you know deep down you need to move on to get there?
- *With this in mind, consider the strategy that you wrote down earlier.* What could you start doing tactically to identify the next vine swing that you need to take?

Also, consider the earn, learn, or quit heuristic:

- *At this moment, are you learning, earning, or both?* If not, what might that mean for you tactically?
- *What sort of opportunity would tempt you if it arrived tomorrow?* Would you be looking to do something new or learn additional skills next, or would you ramp up the intensity of your current work in order to earn more money?

Make some notes on each of these questions, and then consider some tactics to help identify your next vine swing. Your tactics should cover a period of months rather than years and should be specific and achievable. For example, it might look something like this:

> **My Career Tactics**
> by: My current self
>
> With my strategy in mind, my tactics for the coming months are going to be:
>
> - *Have a career conversation with my manager.* I need to understand what potential next steps there are for me at my current company. I know that we don't have a VP of Engineering role, nor do we build software that aligns with my overall strategy, but if I discuss it, will they, in time, be able to work with me to create a role that does?
> - *Reconnect with key people in my network.* I know I've been bad recently at keeping in touch with people that I've worked with in the past. I will take some time each evening to send a message to the folks I enjoyed working with the most and see what they're up to: where

they are, what they're working on, and whether they know of any opportunities that might be interesting to me.

- *Contact with some executive recruiters.* Since many of the most interesting roles are headhunted for rather than advertised, I will reconnect with the executive recruiters that I've worked with in the past and see what they have on their books. I will also share the kind of role that I'm looking for with them so they can keep me in mind in the future.

- *See which companies are graduating from accelerators like Y Combinator.* I know that these companies are likely to be looking for senior engineering talent if they are beginning to see success. I'll investigate what these companies are doing and building, and I'll reach out to a few of them if their mission aligns with mine.

Go ahead and think about what you could do in the next few months that might present a number of different vine swings for you to take. Consider where those vine swings could take you, in terms of scope and impact, earning or learning, and what new and unknown places you might find yourself in.

It's healthy to refresh your tactics every few months so that you give yourself many opportunities to get exposed to routes through the jungle that you may not have considered before. And remember, you don't have to take every vine swing that you see; just having optionality is often enough to keep you feeling in control and on track toward the strategy that you have set for yourself. After all, it only takes one conversation to send you skyrocketing to a place you've always dreamed of.

As with every journey, it begins with a single step. Or should that be swing? Don't be afraid to take it.

Once Again, It's Been a Pleasure

And with that, we come to the end of this book. Before we say goodbye, let's review what we've covered in this chapter:

- *We began by exploring how your career is rarely ever a straight line.* In fact, thinking that your career should be the fastest possible elevator ride to the top of the strategic pyramid can be harmful in the long run. The unknown is where the magic can happen.

- *Then, we introduced the Tarzan method.* This is a way of thinking about your career as a series of vine swings where you're continually moving from one vine to the next. This method is a great way to think about your career progression metaphorically and help you stay open to new and exciting opportunities.

- *We then looked at the trajectory of your swing.* We introduced the concepts of scope and impact and how you can use them to plot your growth over time. We introduced the quadrants of stagnating, stepping up, skyrocketing, and skilling up, and also the heuristic of earning, learning, or quitting.

- *Finally, we wrapped up with an exercise.* We asked you to write a strategy for your career and then think about the tactics that could reveal the next vine swing that you need to take. It's worth refreshing your tactics every few months so that you increase your chances of getting exposed to routes through the jungle that you may not have considered before.

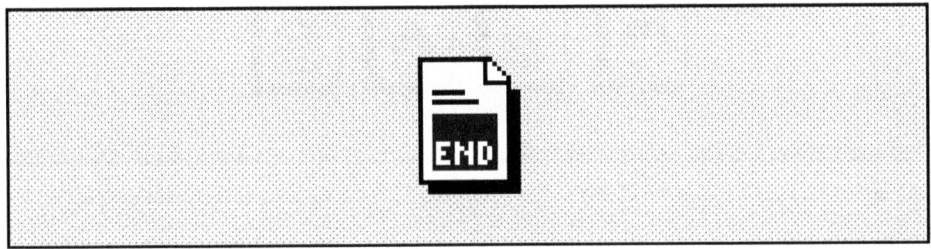

Come to think about it, perhaps *this book* has been one of your tactics for working out what comes next for you. If it has, then I hope that we've filled your mind with new tools and frameworks that you can use right away to help you grow in your career.

After all, what we need in our industry is more intelligent, empathetic, and visionary leaders. These are leaders who are passionate about their craft, always learning, and always pushing themselves to be better in service of their teams. These are leaders just like *you*.

So, with that, all that is left is to thank you for going on this journey together with me. Having the opportunity to write this book has been a privilege. Words have hit the page early in the morning, late at night, during weekends, at home in the countryside in Cumbria, while traveling on trains and planes, and in London, Toronto, and New York. Writing is *thinking* after all, and I am always grateful to have such a fantastic audience to think with.

As this big project comes to a close, another one is beginning. There's a little clue coming right up. But in the meantime, I hope that you'll pick up these pages again and, as such, we will meet again very soon.

I'll sign this book off the same way that I signed off the first one: *you've got this.*

Trust me, you really have.

Bibliography

[Car12]   James P. Carse. *Finite and Infinite Games*. The Free Press, New York, NY, 2012.

[Chr11]   Clayton Christensen. *The Innovator's Dilemma: The Revolutionary Book That Will Change the Way You Do Business*. Harvard University Press, Boston, MA, 2011.

[Cir06]   Francesco Cirillo. *The Pomodoro Technique*. Portfolio Hardcover, USA, 2006.

[Cov94]   Stephen R. Covey. *The 7 Habits of Highly Effective People*. The Free Press, New York, NY, 1994.

[Dow14]   Myles Downey. *Effective Modern Coaching*. LID Publishing, London, UK, 2014.

[GHJV95] Erich Gamma, Richard Helm, Ralph Johnson, and John Vlissides. *Design Patterns: Elements of Reusable Object-Oriented Software*. Addison-Wesley, Boston, MA, 1995.

[Gil18]   Elad Gil. *High Growth Handbook: Scaling Startups From 10 to 10,000 People*. Stripe Press, San Francisco, California, 2018.

[Gro95]   Andy Grove. *High Output Management*. Vintage Books, New York, NY, 1995.

[Gup17]   Kapil Gupta. *A Master's Secret Whisper: For those who abhor the noise and seek The Truth about life and living*. Self-published, https://www.kapilguptamd.com/books/, 2017.

[Har15]   Yuval Noah Harari. *Sapiens: A Brief History of Humankind*. Vintage Books, New York, NY, 2015.

[Hel20]   Heidi Helfand. *Dynamic Reteaming: The Art and Wisdom of Changing Teams*. O'Reilly & Associates, Inc., Sebastopol, CA, 2020.

[Hil15]   Napoleon Hill. *Think And Grow Rich! The Original Version, Restored and Revised.* The Mindpower Press, USA, 2015.

[Hor14]   Ben Horowitz. *The Hard Thing About Hard Things: Building a Business When There Are No Easy Answers.* Harper Business, New York, NY, 2014.

[Hug23]   Clare Hughes Johnson. *Scaling People: Tactics for Management and Company Building.* Stripe Press, San Francisco, California, 2023.

[KM15]   Rich Karlgaard and Michael S. Malone. *Team Genius: The New Science of High-Performing Organizations.* Harper Business, New York, NY, 2015.

[Lar21]   Will Larson. *Staff Engineer: Leadership beyond the management track.* Self-published, https://lethain.gumroad.com/l/staff-engineer, 2021.

[Mac15]   William MacAskill. *What We Owe the Future.* Basic Books, New York, NY, 2015.

[Rei22]   Tanya Reilly. *The Staff Engineer's Path: A guide for individual contributors navigating growth and change.* O'Reilly & Associates, Inc., Sebastopol, CA, 2022.

[Sco17]   Kim Scott. *Radical Candor: Be a Kick-Ass Boss Without Losing Your Humanity.* St. Martin's Press, New York, NY, 2017.

[SP19]   Matthew Skelton and Manuel Pais. *Team Topologies: Organizing Business and Technology Teams for Fast Flow.* IT Revolution Press, Portland, Oregon, 2019.

[Sta20]   James Stanier. *Become an Effective Software Engineering Manager: How to Be the Leader Your Development Team Needs.* The Pragmatic Bookshelf, Dallas, TX, 2020.

[Sta22]   James Stanier. *Effective Remote Work: For Yourself, Your Team, and Your Company.* The Pragmatic Bookshelf, Dallas, TX, 2022.

[Urb23]   Tim Urban. *What's Our Problem? A Self-Help Book For Societies.* Wait But Why, USA, 2023.

Index

DIGITS

1:1s, *see* one to one meetings
360 feedback, 229, 232, 235

A

A/B testing, 286
accountability
  communication and, 203
  deadlines and, 203
  delegation and, 97
  demonstration of leadership and, 105
  holacracy, 29
  operational level and, 11
  org charts and, 28, 49
  senior engineering managers and, 14
  strategic level and, 13
  time management and, 75–76
  trifectas and, 180–182
accountability partners, 75–76
achieved level of KPIs, 232
acquisitions and due diligence, 330, 335–337
actions
  additive and subtractive actions and relationship with your manager, 161–162
  in calibration process, 238, 244
  in coaching with GROW model, 94
  meetings and, 86, 101
  performance assessments and, 234

ADRs (Architecture Decision Records), 211
agendas
  documentation of, 201
  one to one meetings, 101, 108
  strategies for, 85, 87
  trifecta office hours and syncs, 182
Airbnb, 342
alignment, trifectas and, 180
all-hands meetings
  defined, 217
  post-layoffs, 344
  town hall scenario and, 84
  when to have, 84
allies
  defined, 175, 186
  identifying and building, 188
  utilizing, 186–189
amortization, 299, 310–311
anemones, 160
angel investment, defined, 300
announcements
  as communication artifacts, 213, 215, 219
  layoffs, 342–344
annual recurring revenue (ARR), 302
approvals
  approval information as communication artifact, 216
  trifectas and, 181, 183

architect archetype, 123–129, 131
Architecture Decision Records (ADRs), 211
area technical lead, in org charts, 35–36
ARR (annual recurring revenue), 302
assignment, senior individual contributor archetypes and, 124
assistants, executive, 73
asynchronous communication, 196–198
authority, escalations and, 166, 181
automation and peer group projects, 149
autonomy
  brag docs and, 102
  delegation and, 97
  new product development and, 334

B

best practices, codifying, 149
beta programs, 286
bias, calibration and, 237, 241
bidirectional empathy, 288
big bang launches, 284
black swans, 325
blockers
  ally relationships and, 188
  trifectas and, 178, 180–181

board, strategic leadership communication and, 221
book price, 315
boom and bust cycles, 320–345
    concentric circles of trust and, 328–329, 343
    layoffs, 322, 324, 327, 341–344
    peacetime strategies, 321, 326–328, 330–337
    reasons for, 320–325
    reforecasts and reorganizations, 337–344
    wartime strategies, 321, 326–328, 337–344
bootstrapping
    building vs. buying dilemma, 315
    defined, 300
    top line vs. bottom line dilemma, 317
bottom line
    defined, 299
    growth and, 304
    vs. top line dilemma, 316
brag docs, 102–103, 229, 231, 235
brain, second, 207–209
brainstorming, 87
budgets
    building vs. buying, 314
    common dilemmas, 314–318
    as communication artifacts, 220
    infrastructure and, 305, 309–311, 318
    people and, 305–309
    revenue per employee, 308, 318
    software and hardware, 305, 311, 318
    strategies for, 305–314
    temporary services, 305, 313–314
    vendors, negotiating with, 315, 340
    VP role and accountability for, 13
Buffer, 29
business cycles, *see* cycles, business
business reviews, 221

C

C-suite executives
    in career track overview, 6
    engineering strategies and, 258–261, 267–269
    Eye of Sauron and, 165, 169
    home team and, 136
    in org charts, 35
CAC (customer acquisition cost), 303
cadences
    brag docs and, 102
    deadlines and, 204
    defined, 74
    project updates, 213
    strategic level communication and, 220
    time management and, 74–76
calendars
    blocking time in, 77–80
    business cycles and, 273–277
    continuous development and, 273, 277
    executive assistants and, 73
    focus blocks, 80–83
    managing meetings, 83–86
    quarters, defined, 275
    resetting, 86
    software for, 79
    time management and, 73, 76–89
    unallocated time and, 78
calibration process, 224, 226, 233, 237–244
candor, radical, 245
capacity
    balancing input and output, 68
    energy and, 65–67, 73
    feature factories and, 289
    framing work with games, 112
    loneliness and, 136
    planning for surprises, 288, 290
    saying no and, 72
    time management and, 64–69, 78
capex (capital expenditure)
    defined, 298
    hardware budget and, 311
    infrastructure budget and, 309, 311
    vs. opex, 298
career progression
    career track, defined, 6
    career track, overview, 5–14
    competencies and, 16–17
    earn, learn, or quit heuristic, 354–356, 359
    fallacy of straight line, 349–351
    heuristics for, 352–356, 359
    job titles, 5–14, 246
    manager in training position, 32
    one to one meetings and, 101
    opportunities for, 17, 350, 356
    randomness in, xiii
    scope and impact, 5–6, 8, 10–11, 14, 19, 353, 357, 359
    strategies for, 347–356
    strategy exercise, 356–360
    thinking about, xi–xvi, 347, 356–360
    warfare levels and, 9–14
Carse, James, 109
chairs, meeting, 86
chat
    as communication artifacts, 213, 215, 219
    escalations and, 167
    vs. meetings, 84, 87
    peer relations, 148
    trifectas and, 182
chief executive officer (CEO), Eye of Sauron and, 165, 169
chief technology officer, *see* CTO (chief technology officer)
Christensen, Clayton, 334
churn, 303
circles, 29
Cirillo, Francesco, 81
cloud computing, infrastructure budget and, 309–311
clownfish, 160

coaching
 ally relationships and, 189
 defined, 93
 vs. directing, 93–96
 escalations and, 168
 Eye of Sauron and, 169–170
 following interests mode, 94–96
 framing work with games, 112–114
 GROW model, 94–96, 101
 leadership development, 106
 performance management and, 231–236
code
 code health and peer group projects, 150
 as communication artifacts, 210
 speed and stability as feature, 290
 technical due diligence and, 336
cohorts, calibration process, 238, 241–244
collaboration
 org charts and, 29
 polarity model, 139–146
 roadmap responsibility, 281
 team topologies and, 44
 time management and, 63
commit messages, 211
communication
 additive and subtractive actions and relationship with your manager, 162
 artifacts, importance of, 193
 artifacts, one-to-many relationships and, 198–201
 artifacts, producing, 193, 209–221
 asynchronous/synchronous, 196–198, 200
 business cycles and, 271–274, 277
 cadences, 75
 competencies and, 17
 Conway's Law, 41

culture of engineering and, 291–292
decision-making and, 201
discoverability and, 213, 216
Dunbar's Number, 42
executive assistants and, 74
Eye of Sauron and, 169–170
importance of, 192, 195
learning and organizational communication, 192
line in the sand, 343–344
manager as single point of contact antipattern, 147–148
meeting needs and, 83, 87
on layoffs, 342–344
on mergers and acquisitions, 337
on reorganizations, 338
one to one meetings and, 98
org charts and communication flow, 41–52
paper triangle, 204–205, 208
patterns of, 193, 195–204
percentage of time spent on, 192
permanence and, 198, 200
progress as fueled by, 194–195
propagation of information upwards, 210
recommendations, asking for, 203, 206
with sales team about features, 287
saying no and, 73
team topologies and, 44–45
time management and, 75, 200, 203–204
trifectas and, 178, 182
trust and, 42, 216, 328–329, 343
unpleasant surprises and, 171
writing artifacts and note-taking, 207–209
writing as leadership, 204–209
compensation
 calibration and, 238, 244

career progression and, 8, 354–356, 359
 performance management and, 226
 promotions and, 247
 scheduling and, 226
competencies
 career progression and, 16–17
 competency grid, 17
 defined, 16
 impact and, 17
 performance management and, 236
 talent assessment in due diligence, 336
competition
 tragedy of the commons and, 139
 vendor contract negotiation and, 316
compliance team, multifectas and, 184
complicated subsystem teams in team topologies, 43, 50
concentric circles of trust, 328–329, 343
confidentiality
 concentric circles of trust, 328
 hiring freezes, 340
 layoffs and, 328, 342
 mergers and acquisitions information, 335
 one to one meetings, 100
 reorganizations, 338
conflict
 competency in conflict resolution, 17
 escalations and, 166
 manager as single point of contact antipattern, 148
 polarity model and, 140–145
 with your manager, 156–158, 161–162
containers, projects, 212
context
 brag docs and, 103
 business cycles and calendar, 277
 in Eisenhower Matrix, 70–72, 78
 focus blocks and, 81

framing work with games, 112
time management and, 70–72, 78
continuous development
business calendar and, 273, 277
with feature flags, 285–286
contracting exercise, 99, 161
contractors, when to use, 313–314
contracts, vendor, 315, 340
contribution curve, 332
control
delegation and, 105, 164
org charts and span of control, 37–41
span of control and org charts, 30–36
Conway, Melvin E., 41
Conway's Law, 41
Copilot, 333
costs
cost centers vs. profit centers, 301–302
cost-cutting options, 339
reforecasts and reorganizations, 338
Covey, Stephen, 69
COVID-19 pandemic
boom and bust cycles, 323–325
layoffs, 31, 324
span of control and, 31
craft lead, in org charts, 36
cross-disciplinary relationships, 173–190
allies, 175, 186–189
business cycles and calendar, 273–277
common issues, 273, 287–292
culture of engineering and, 291–292
marketing team, 273, 276, 284–286, 291–292
multifectas, 175, 184–185, 281
sales team, 184, 273, 275, 277–284, 286–292
trifectas, 174, 176–184
crunch, 284
CTO (chief technology officer)
in career track overview, 6

in org charts, 35
vs. VP of engineering, 12, 36
culture of engineering, 291–292
customer acquisition cost (CAC), 303
customer success team, multifectas and, 184
customers
ally relationships and, 188
customer acquisition cost (CAC), 303
lifetime value (LTV), 303
cycles, business
boom and bust, 320–345
calendar and, 273–277
communication and, 271–274, 277

D

dashboards, 216, 219
deadlines, time management and, 74, 203–204
deal desks, 275
debt financing, defined, 300
decision-making
additive and subtractive actions, 162
communication and, 201
defined, 201
Eye of Sauron and, 169
one-way vs. two-way doors, 201
relationship with your manager and, 158, 162
role of manager in, 89
rule of three and, 176
short-sightedness and, 57
deep work
calendar management for, 78
technical council and, 130
defined level of KPIs, 232
delegation
basics of, 96–98
control and, 105, 164
Eye of Sauron and, 169–170
framing work with games, 112
relationship with your manager and, 164–165

right-hand engineer and, 127
saying no and, 73
spectrum diagram, 97
swamp and, 108
delivery dates, in roadmaps, 282
demos, 282
dependencies, in roadmaps, 282
depreciation, 299, 310
design
design documents as communication artifacts, 212
iceberg model, 278
patterns of, 195
removing uncertainty and, 278–284
developer experience surveys, 150
developer relations, multifectas and, 184
developers, see individual contributors
direct reports, see one to one meetings
directing vs. coaching, 93–96
directly responsible individuals (DRIs), identifying, 150
director of engineering
in career track overview, 6, 14
in competency grid, 17
as operational level, 11
in org charts, 34
relationship to VP of engineering, 34
senior individual contributor archetypes and, 127
as terminal position, 34
disciplines, calibration cohorts and, 241, see also cross-disciplinary relationships
discoverability, communication and, 213, 216
distinguished engineer, in career track overview, 8
division of labor, 25
documentation
importance of, 200
mission and vision statements, 219

strategies for, 212
time management and, 200
types of, 211
DRIs (directly responsible individuals), identifying, 150
due diligence for mergers and acquisitions, 330, 335–337
Dunbar, Robin, 42
Dunbar's Number, 42
duplication
avoiding with org charts, 29
communication and, 193

E
earn, learn, or quit heuristic, 354–356, 359
earnings calls, 275
EBITDA, 299
effort, trade-offs in trifectas, 177
Eisenhower Matrix, 69–73, 78, 82
Eisenhower, Dwight D., 69
email
executive assistants and, 74
focus blocks and, 81
vs. meetings, 85
empathy, bidirectional, 288
employees, *see also* hiring; individual contributors; people; senior executives
contribution curve, 332
revenue per employee, 308, 318
enabling teams in team topologies, 43, 50
energy, time management and, 65–67, 73, 78
"Engineering in Mergers and Acquisitions", 335
engineering manager
in career track overview, 6
in competency grid, 17
in org charts, 32
senior individual contributor archetypes and, 125
as tactical level, 10
engineering strategies
audiences and, 258–261, 267–269

building example, 261–269
understanding, 255, 258–261
engineers, *see* individual contributors
entry criteria, framing work with games, 110–113
equity, startup financing modes, 300, 304
escalations
decision-making and one-way doors, 202
defined, 165
example, 167
Eye of Sauron and, 169
org charts and, 28
relationship with your manager and, 165–168
strategies for, 165–168
trifectas and, 178, 180–181
Evans, Julia, 104
exceeded level of KPIs, 232
executive assistants, 73
exercises
accountability, 77
additive and subtractive actions, 162
allies, 189
boom and bust cycles, 328, 333, 335
brag docs, 104
calendar management, 80
capacity, 67, 69
career progression, 15, 19–20, 356–360
coaching, 96
communication, 199, 209, 221
competency grids, 19
cost centers vs. profit centers, 302
cross-disciplinary relationships, 178, 183, 189
Eisenhower Matrix, 72
engineering strategies, 269
finances, 302, 308, 311
framing work with games, 113, 117
infrastructure budget, 311
longtermism, 62
new product development, 335

onboarding, 333
org charts, 36, 51
people index spreadsheet, 308
performance management, 228
polarity model and peers, 142
relationship with your manager and, 158
request for proposals (RFPs), 283
scope and impact, 20
second brain, 209
senior individual contributor archetypes, 125
strategic level thinking, 258
team topologies, 44, 51
time management, 62, 67, 69, 72, 77, 80, 87
trifectas, 178, 183
exit criteria, framing work with games, 110–113, 117
experience, competencies and, 16
expertise, relationship with your manager and, 156
Eye of Sauron, 165, 169–170

F
facilitation, team topologies and, 44
failure, new product development and, 334
feature flags, 285–286
features
feature factories, 289
feature flags, 285–286
leadership development and, 106
marketing team realtions and, 285–286
in roadmaps, 282, 287
sales team relations and, 287–291
speed and stability as, 290
feedback
360 feedback, 229, 232, 235
brag docs and, 102
contracting exercise, 100
leadership development and, 106
one to one meetings, 100–101

finance team, business cycles and calendar, 275
finances, *see also* boom and bust cycles
    basics of, 297–305
    business cycles and calendar, 275
    common dilemmas, 314–318
    cost centers vs. profit centers, 301–302
    definitions, 297–305
    earnings calls, 275
    modes of operation, 300, 307, 317
    reforecasts and reorganizations, 337–344
    SaaS and, 302
    strategies for, 305–314
    vendors, negotiating with, 315, 340
    VP role and accountability for, 13
finite games, 109–117
firings, calibration process and, 240, 243, *see also* layoffs
first team, 136
flags
    as communication artifacts, 220
    feature flags, 285–286
flow, 78
flywheel
    boom and bust cycles, 321, 324, 326
    budget strategies, 305–314
    finance basics, 297–305
    reforecasts and reorganizations, 338
    top line vs. bottom line dilemma, 316
focus
    focus blocks, 80–83
    senior individual contributor archetypes and, 124
forecasts, as communication artifacts, 220
framing
    engineering strategies and, 261
    swamp and absence of, 107
    work with games, 107, 109–117

freezes, hiring, 340
future, focus on, 13, *see also* longtermism

G

games
    framing work with, 107, 109–117
    peer relations and, 147
gatekeeping, avoiding, xii
General Electric, 225
Gil, Elad, 335
GitHub, 211, 333
global maxima, relationship with your manager and, 156
goals
    accountability partners, 75
    brag docs, 102
    in coaching with GROW model, 94
    focus blocks, 80
    mastermind groups, 76
    new product development and, 334
    performance improvement plans (PIPs), 235
    time management and cadences, 75
    time management and tracking organizational, 62
Google, 326, 342
group syncs, 87
Grove, Andy, 87, 186, 229, 326
GROW model, coaching with, 94–96, 101
growth
    boom and bust cycles, 322
    mergers and acquisitions, 330, 335–337
    peacetime and wartime strategies, 326–328, 330–337
    redundancy antipattern and, 38
    span of control and, 38
    top line vs. bottom line and, 304

H

hardware
    budget strategies and, 305, 311, 318
    onboarding and, 333
headcount, *see also* hiring; layoffs
    budget strategies, 306
    VP role and accountability for, 13
health metrics as communication artifacts, 214, 217
High Growth Handbook, 335
Hill, Napoleon, 76
hiring
    boom cycle strategies, 330–333
    calibration process and, 243
    freezes, 340
    hiring funnel, 330
    longtermism and, 61
    net-negative/net-positive contributors and, 332
    onboarding and, 330, 332, 337
    outreach, 331
    performance management and attracting talent, 227
    recruiting and, 330
    scheduling and, 330
holacracy, 29
home team, 136
Horowitz, Ben, 326
hostage situations and performance management, 247

I

iceberg model of design, 278
impact
    career progression, 5–6, 8, 14, 19
    career progression and, 353, 357
    defined, 14, 353
    scope and competencies, 17
impedance mismatch and relationship with your manager, 164–165
importance, in Eisenhower Matrix, 70–72
improvisation, as unnecessary, xii

Index • 371

incident logs, as communication artifacts, 214, 217
individual contributors
  career track overview, 6–8, 120–123
  career track positions, 32–33, 35–36, 119
  coaching, 96
  competencies and, 16–17
  cross-organization connections and, 131–132
  delegation and, 105
  developer experience surveys, 150
  engineering strategies and, 258–261, 267–269
  leadership by, 103–107, 120, 131, 229
  managers as, 12, 31
  managing senior contributors as similar to managing managers, 103–107, 229
  matching senior individual contributors with managers, 125–129
  in org charts, 28, 32–36, 122, 125–129
  self-selection of teams, 40
  senior individual contributor archetypes, 123–129, 131–132
  senior individual contributors as technical council, 129–132
  senior individual contributors, utilizing, 120–133
infinite games, 109, 113–117, 147
inflation, boom and bust cycles and, 323
influence and competencies, 17
information
  additive and subtractive actions and relationship with your manager, 162
  allies and, 188
  communication artifacts and one-to-many relationships, 198–201
  concentric circles of trust and, 328–329, 343
  escalations and, 166
  Eye of Sauron and, 170
  ownership of system of truth and, 219
  propagation of information upwards, 210
  role of manager, 87
  unpleasant surprises and, 171
  writing as second brain and, 207–209
infrastructure, budget strategies and, 305, 309–311, 318
initiatives
  engineering strategies, 267, 282
  in roadmaps, 282
The Innovator's Dilemma, 334
input, time management and, 68–69
integration plans, mergers and acquisitions, 336
interest rates, boom and bust cycles and, 323
interests, following interests mode of coaching, 94–96
Internal Tech Emails newsletter, 198
interviews
  talent assessment in due diligence, 336
  training in, 331
investment, org charts and levels of, 28
investors, strategic leadership communication and, 221
iron triangle, *see* rule of three
isolation
  allies and, 186, 189
  lack of peer group and, 135–137

J

jerks, 246
job titles, 5–14, 246
journals, 208

K

Key Performance Indicators (KPIs)
  as communication artifacts, 213, 217, 220
  defined, 213
  in engineering strategies, 268
  levels of, 232
  performance management of senior staff, 230, 232, 235
  reducing uncertainty and, 280
knowledge graphs, 207
KPIs, *see* Key Performance Indicators (KPIs)

L

labor, division of, 25
Larson, Will, 123, 335
launches, 284
layoffs
  boom and bust cycles, 322, 324, 327, 341–344
  calibration process and, 240, 243
  communication, 342–344
  confidentiality and, 328, 342
  COVID-19 pandemic and, 31, 324
  revenue per employee and, 309
  span of control and, 31
  strategies for, 341–344
  voluntary, 342
leadership
  concentric circles of trust and, 328–329, 343
  cross-organization connections and, 131–132
  demonstration of, 105
  developing, 106, 131
  first and second order effects, 140
  of managers as similar to that of individual contributors, 103–107, 229
  performance management of senior staff and, 228–237
  as personal, xiv, 156
  senior individual contributors and, 106, 126, 131
  as writing, 204–209
learning
  career progression and, 354–356, 359
  organizational communication and, 192
  performance management and, 225

legal team, multifectas and, 184
levels.fyi, 14
lifetime value (LTV), 303
line in the sand and layoffs, 343–344
local maxima, relationship with your manager and, 156
logs, as communication artifacts, 214, 217
Logseq, 207
longtermism
 cadences and, 75
 calibration process and, 244
 defined, 58
 focus blocks and, 81
 framing work with games, 109
 multifectas and, 185
 peer relations and, 147
 performance management and, 225
 relationship with your manager and, 156
 saying no and, 72
 strategic level and, 59–62
 time management and, 57–62
 vs. tragedy of the commons, 138
LTV (lifetime value), 303
LTV:CAC ratio, 303
lunch, 78

M

macroeconomics, boom and bust cycles, 323–325
management
 fundamentals of, 93–103
 gatekeeping and improvisation as unnecessary, xii
 lack of training in, xii, 5
 shift from single-team to multiple teams, 4
management of self
 competition for manager's attention, 146
 self-sufficiency and, 146, 156
 understanding own management needs, 162–165
 your manager as single point of contact antipattern, 147–148
management, span of, see span of control
manager in training, in org charts, 32
manager, your, see your manager
managerless companies, 29
managing managers
 brag docs, 102–103, 229, 231, 235
 challenges of, 92
 coaching vs. directing, 93–96
 delegation, basics of, 96–98
 framing work with games, 107, 109–117
 management fundamentals, 93–103
 managing senior individual contributors as similar to, 103–107, 229
 one to one meetings, basics of, 98–101
 operational level and, 11
 org charts and, 33, 35
 performance management of senior staff, 224, 228–237
 shift to senior management and, 5
many-to-many relationships
 communication and, 198
 design and, 196, 198
marketing team
 business cycles and calendar, 273, 276, 284–286
 culture of engineering and, 291–292
 launches and, 284
 multifectas and, 184
 roadmaps and, 284
Martin, Robert, 256
mastermind groups, 76
McCallum, Daniel, 26
Medium, 29
meetings, see also one to one meetings
 agendas, 85, 87, 101, 108, 201
 auto-declining, 79
 calendar and, 78, 86
 vs. chat, 84, 87
 communication artifacts and, 214, 217, 220
 vs. email, 85
 meeting hygiene, 85, 100
 operational level, 217
 peer relations, 142–146, 148
 polarity model and peers, 142–146
 post-layoffs, 344
 resetting recurring, 86
 strategic level, 220
 tactical level, 214
 time management and, 63, 83–86, 99, 101
 trifectas and, 182
 when to have, 83–85, 87
mentorship, 16, 189, 236
mergers and due diligence, 330, 335–337
Meta, 342
metrics
 as communication artifacts, 213, 216, 220
 for engineering strategies, 267
 performance management of senior staff and, 230, 232, 235
 reducing uncertainty and, 280
mission, 219
modes of operation
 defined, 37
 financing models, 300, 307, 315, 317
 span of control and, 37
monthly recurring revenue (MRR), 302
multifectas
 defined, 175, 184
 resource allocation and, 290
 roadmap responsibility, 281
 vs. trifectas, 185
 utilizing, 184–185

N

NDAs (nondisclosure agreements), 328, 335, 342
negative feedback, 233–234
Neistat, Casey, 351

net-negative/positive contributors, 332
neutral feedback, 233–234
New York and Erie Railroad, 26
no, saying, 72
non-management employees, *see* individual contributors
nondisclosure agreements (NDAs), 328, 335, 342
nontechnical people, *see also* cross-disciplinary relationships; marketing team; sales team
    culture of engineering and, 291–292
    engineering strategies and, 258–261, 267–269
note-taking
    brag docs and, 103
    communication and documentation, 201
    journals, 208
    meetings, 86
    writing as second brain, 207–209
nothing, focus blocks and, 82
Notion, 207
nudging, role of manager, 89

O

Obsidian, 207
office hours, 182, 217
onboarding, 330, 332, 337
one to one meetings
    basics of, 98–101
    coaching in, 96, 99, 101
    contracting exercise for, 99
    frequency of, 99
    status updates and, 87, 101, 108
    time management and, 87, 99, 101
one-to-many relationships
    communication and, 198–201
    design and, 196, 198
one-to-one relationships
    communication and, 198
    design and, 196, 198
one-way doors in decision-making, 201
open information, concentric circles of trust, 329

operation, modes of, *see* modes of operation
operational health metrics, as communication artifacts, 214, 217
operational level
    career progression and, 9, 11
    communication artifacts and, 193, 214–218
    defined, 9
    Dunbar's Number and, 42
    framing work with games, 109, 115
    org charts and, 34
    senior individual contributor archetypes and, 128
opex (operating expenditure)
    vs. capex, 298
    defined, 298
    infrastructure budget and, 309
    software budget and, 311
    temporary services and, 313
opinions, strong opinions, loosely held, 170, 206
options, in coaching with GROW model, 94
org charts
    antipatterns, 36–41
    communication flow, 41–52
    defined, 26
    designing, 41–52
    Dunbar's Number and, 42
    history of, 26
    importance of, 24
    operational level and, 34
    refactoring example, 46–52
    reviewing, 40
    senior individual contributors, 28, 32–36, 122, 125–129
    shapes, 30–36
    span of control, 30–41
    strategic level and, 35
    tactical level and, 32–34
    topologies, 43–52
    trifectas vs. reporting lines, 180
    uses, 24, 27

organizational charts, *see* org charts
organizational fit, 336
Orosz, Gergely, 323
outcomes, meetings and, 85
outlier groups, calibration cohorts and, 241
output
    measuring performance of senior staff, 229–234
    time management and, 68–69
outreach, 331
ownership
    brag docs and, 102
    coaching and, 94
    communication artifacts, 214, 219, 221
    delegation and, 97
    leadership of managers vs. senior individual contributors, 106–107
    refactoring org chart example, 49, 51
    in roadmaps, 282
    swamp and, 108
    of system of truth, 219
    tragedy of the commons and, 137

P

Pais, Manuel, 43
paper triangle, 204–205, 208
Parkinson's Law, 74, 203–204
pay, *see* compensation
peacetime, boom and bust cycles, 321, 326–328, 330–337
peers
    additive and subtractive actions and relationship with your manager, 162
    communication and synchronousness, 197
    escalations and, 167
    lack of peer group, 135–137
    manager as single point of contact antipattern and, 147–148
    tragedy of the commons and, 137–139
    tragedy of the commons, countering with polarity model, 139–146

people, *see also* C-suite executives; hiring; individual contributors; layoffs; non-technical people; your manager
   budget strategies and, 305–309
   contribution curve, 332
   people index spreadsheet, 307
   revenue per employee, 308, 318
   in span of control, 30
   talent assessment in due diligence, 336
   temporary services, 313–314
   time spent of managing, 62

performance
   defining, 226
   individual vs. group performance, 147
   peer relations and, 146
   power curve, 227, 306

performance improvement plans (PIPs), 224, 226, 234

performance management
   360 feedback, 229, 232, 235
   basics of, 224–228
   brag docs and, 102
   calibration process, 224, 226, 233, 237–244
   coaching and, 231–236
   common issues in, 224, 244–249
   company performance and, 226
   conflicts over, 248
   current vs. historical performance, 245
   elements of, 226
   fairness and, 226, 237–244
   hostage situations, 247
   jerks, 246
   job title inflation and, 246
   longtermism and, 225
   measuring output, 229–234
   power curve, 227
   raising bar of performance, 225, 235, 244
   review components, 226
   scheduling, 224, 226
   self-assessment, 229–232, 234–235
   of senior staff, 224, 228–237
   terminal positions and, 247
   training in, 224
   writing assessments, 230, 234

periphery, utilizing allies and, 186–189
Peter Principle, 157
Peter, Laurence J., 157
Peter's plateau, 157
PIPs, *see* performance improvement plans (PIPs)
plans vs. strategies, 256
platform teams in team topologies, 43
polarity model, 139–146
Pomodoro technique, 81
positive feedback, 233–234

post-mortems
   as communication artifacts, 214, 217
   unpleasant surprises and, 171

power curve
   budget strategies and, 306
   performance management and, 227

principal engineer
   career track overview, 8
   as right-hand engineer, 127

problem solving
   escalations and, 166
   tools vs. prescription approach to, 159
   writing and, 205

processes, engineering strategies and, 267, 269

product team
   multifectas and, 184
   roadmap responsibility, 281
   trifectas and, 176–184

production environment health and peer group projects, 150

productivity, hardware and software budget and, 312

products
   boom cycle strategies, 330, 333–335
   focus blocks and, 82
   launches, 284
   new product development, 333–335
   product health and peer group projects, 150
   product-market fit, 338
   reforecasts and reorganizations, 338
   simplicity trade-offs, 177
   technical due diligence and, 336

profit
   defined, 299
   EBITDA as measure of, 299
   profit centers vs. costs centers, 301–302
   startups and, 303–305
   top line vs. bottom line, 299, 304, 316

progressed level of KPIs, 232
progression.fyi, 17
projects, as communication artifacts, 212, 216, 219

promotions
   calibration process and, 240–241, 243–244
   compensation and, 247
   limited numbers of, 247

prototyping, 279–280, 282

Q

qualitative level of performance management
   360 Feedback, 233
   self-assessments, 231

quantitative easing (QE), 323

quantitative level of performance management
   360 Feedback, 233
   self-assessments, 231

quarters, defined, 275
questions, coaching and, 94
quitting, career progression and, 354–356, 359

R

radical candor, 245
random walk, career progression as, xiii
ratings, calibration process and, 237–244

reading, focus blocks and, 82
reality, in coaching with GROW model, 94
recommendations, asking for, 203, 206
recruiting, boom cycle strategies, 330, *see also* hiring
redundancy antipattern, 37–39
reforecasts, 337–341
relationships, *see* cross-disciplinary relationships; peers; your manager
reliability
  longtermism and, 61
  reliability projects, 106
reorganizations, 337–344
Reporting to Peter principle, 157
request for proposals (RFPs), 278, 283
resilience, longtermism and, 61
resources
  allocation for surprises, 288
  boom cycle strategies, 330, 333–335
  capacity planning, 288, 290
  rule of three and, 175, 203
  tragedy of the commons and, 138–139
responsibility, *see also* accountability; scope
  abdication of, 97
  career progression and, 353
  delegation and, 97
  individual contributors career progression, 6, 8
  management career progression, 5, 8
  in multifectas, 184
  org charts and, 28
  senior engineering managers, 14
  in trifectas, 176
retrospectives, 170–171
revenue
  defined, 299
  infrastructure spending as percentage of, 311, 318

per employee, 308, 318
reforecasts and reorganizations, 338
SaaS jargon, 302
software and hardware spending as percentage of, 313, 318
reviews
  business reviews and strategic communication, 221
  technical council and, 130
RFPs (request for proposals), 278, 283
right-hand engineer
  career progression, 35, 119
  cross-organization connections and, 131
  in org charts, 35
  right-hand archetype, 123–129, 131–132
risk
  boom and bust cycles, 321, 323, 326
  learning and career progression, 355
roadmaps
  architect archetype and, 126
  components of, 282
  examples, 281
  finite and infinite games and, 114
  marketing and, 284
  reducing uncertainty in, 281–283
  responsibility for, 281
  sales and, 283, 287
  technical council and, 130
  trifectas and, 177, 181
Roam Research, 207
role model, manager as, 89
roll-up dashboards, 216
rollbacks, 285
rule of three, 175, 203
rules, framing work with games, 110–113

S

SaaS (software as a service), financial jargon, 302
salary, *see* compensation

sales team
  business cycles and calendar, 273, 275, 277–284
  culture of engineering and, 291–292
  deal desks, 275
  multifectas and, 184
  removing uncertainty and, 278–284, 286
  roadmaps and, 283, 287
  trouble shooting common issues, 287–292
saying no and time management, 72
scaling
  longtermism and, 61
  technical due diligence and, 336
  temporary services and, 313
Scaling People, 228
Schmidt, Eric, 326
scope
  career progression and, 5–6, 8, 10, 14, 19, 353, 357, 359
  defined, 14, 353
  impact and, 17
  operational level and, 11
  Parkinson's Law, 203
  rule of three and, 175, 203
  tactical level and, 10
  trade-offs in trifectas, 177
second brain, 207–209
security team, multifectas and, 184
self-assessments
  KPIs and, 232
  levels of, 231
  performance management and, 229–232, 234–235
self-selection of teams, 40
self-sufficiency, 146, 156
senior director of engineering, in career track overview, 14
senior engineering manager
  in career track overview, 6, 14
  in org charts, 33, 35
  senior individual contributor archetypes and, 126
  VPs of engineering and, 35

senior staff engineer
    career track overview, 8
    as right-hand engineer, 127
    as terminal position, 126
seniority
    calibration cohorts and, 241
    in people index spreadsheet, 307
    span of control and, 31
sensitive information
    concentric circles of trust, 329
    hiring plans, 330
    new product development, 334
    reorganizations, 338
    software audits and cost cutting, 340
servers, budget management, 309–311
Shopify, 87
silos
    avoiding with org charts, 29
    cross-organization connections and, 131
singleton pattern, 195
Skelton, Matthew, 43
skills, *see also* competencies
    overlap in individual contributor and management career tracks, 7
    skilling up in career progression quadrant, 353, 359
skyrocketing, in career progression quadrant, 353, 359
software
    audits and cost cutting, 340
    budget strategies and, 305, 311, 318
    calendar, 79
    onboarding and, 333
software as a service (SaaS), financial jargon, 302
solver archetype, 123–129, 131
Southwest Airlines, 256
span of control
    defined, 30
    growth and, 38

manager in training position, 33
modes of operation and, 37
org charts and, 30–41
reviewing, 40
Staff Engineer, 121, 123
The Staff Engineer's Path, 121
staff meetings, 87
stage, in roadmaps, 282
stagnating, in career progression quadrant, 353, 359
stakeholders
    multifectas as stakeholder groups, 184–185
    trifectas and communication with, 178
stand-ups, 87
standards, technical council and, 130
startups
    boom and bust cycles, 321
    funding models, 300, 307, 317
    profit and, 303–305
    revenue per employee, 309
status updates
    one to one meetings and, 87, 101, 108
    project updates as communication artifacts, 212, 216
stepping up, in career progression quadrant, 353, 359
strategic level
    budget strategies, 306
    career progression and, 9, 12
    career strategy exercise, 356–360
    communication artifacts and, 193, 218–221
    communication on mergers and acquisitions, 337
    defined, 9
    Dunbar's Number and, 42
    framing work with games, 109, 115
    importance of, 254
    longtermism and, 59–62
    org charts and, 35

polarity model and peers, 142, 144
reforecasts and reorganizations, 337–344
senior individual contributor archetypes and, 128
time spent on, 63
trifectas and strategic alignment, 177
strategies
    basics of, 253–270
    defined, 255
    examples of, 256
    importance of, 254
    vs. plans, 256
strategies, engineering, *see* engineering strategies
stream-aligned teams in team topologies, 43, 49
strong opinions, loosely held, 170, 206
subjective level of self-assessments, 231
success, measuring
    engineering strategies, 267
    new product development, 334
    operational level and, 11
    reducing uncertainty and, 280
    tactical level and, 11
succession planning, longtermism and, 61
support team, multifectas and, 184
surprises
    planning for, 288, 290
    resource allocation for, 288
    unpleasant surprises and relationship with your manager, 165, 170
swamp, 107
symbiosis
    allies and, 188
    earning and learning, 355
    relationship with your manager and, 158, 160–162
synchronous communication, 196–198
syncs
    disadvantages of, 87

operational leadership communication and, 218
strategic leadership communication and, 221
trifectas and, 182

T

tactical level
  career progression and, 9–10
  communication artifacts and, 193, 210–214
  defined, 9
  Dunbar's Number and, 42
  framing work with games, 109, 115
  org charts and, 32–34
  senior individual contributor archetypes and, 128
talent assessment in due diligence, 336
talking points, polarity model and peers, 142
Tan, Garry, 354
targets, role of managers vs. senior individual contributors, 106–107
Tarzan strategy for career progression, 347–356
team members, *see* individual contributors
teams
  calibration cohorts and, 241
  as cost centers vs. profit centers, 301–302
  escalations and, 166
  home team, 136
  investments in and engineering strategies, 267
  mergers and acquisitions, effect on, 337
  new product development, 334
  in people index spreadsheet, 307
  post-layoffs, 344
  self-selection and, 40
  team topologies, 43–52
tech lead archetype, 123–129, 131
technical constraints, tradeoffs in trifectas, 177
technical council, 129–132

technical debt, 59, 61, 130
technical due diligence, 336
technical knowledge, competencies and, 16
technical lead
  cross-organization connections and, 131
  in org charts, 32–33, 35–36
  tech lead archetype, 123–129, 131
technology and communication, 194, 196
temporary services, budget strategies and, 305, 313–314
terminal positions
  director of engineering as, 34
  performance management and, 247
  senior staff engineer as, 126
Tesla, 257
testing, 285
three, rule of, 175, 203
time management
  accountability and, 75–76
  activities outside area of responsibility, 63
  antipatterns, 64
  audits, 67, 69, 87
  balancing input and output, 68–69
  blocking time, 77–80
  cadences, 74–76
  calendars and, 73, 76–89
  capacity and, 64–69, 78
  challenges of, 56
  communication and, 75, 200, 203–204
  deadlines, 74, 203–204
  documentation and, 200
  Eisenhower Matrix, 69–73, 78, 82
  energy and, 65–67
  executive assistants, 73
  flow chart, 63
  focus blocks, 80–83
  hiring and, 330
  longtermism and, 57–62
  meetings, 63, 83–87, 99, 101
  Parkinson's Law, 74
  Pomodoro technique, 81
  rule of three and, 175, 203

saying no and, 72
tasks needing to be included, 62
time as resource for the organization, 62–64
tools and techniques, 69–76
unallocated time, 64, 78
tools
  vs. prescriptions, 158
  strategic level decisions and, 219
top line
  vs. bottom line dilemma, 316
  cost of distraction from, 314, 318
  defined, 299
  growth and, 304
topologies, team, 43–52
town hall meetings, 84, 220
traffic light system, 212
tragedy of the commons
  countering with polarity model, 139–146
  defined, 138
  vs. longtermism, 138
  opportunities for fixing, 149–150
  reasons for, 137–139
trifectas
  defined, 174, 176
  vs. multifectas, 185
  utilizing, 176–184
triple constraint, *see* rule of three
trust
  allies and, 188
  communication and, 42, 216, 328–329, 343
  concentric circles of, 328–329, 343
  delivery opportunities, 149–150
  Dunbar's Number and, 42
  escalations and, 166–167
  meetings and, 83, 87, 98
  one to one meetings and, 98
  peer group and, 138, 142, 145, 148–150
  people as a resource and, 307
  polarity model and, 142, 145

reducing uncertainty and, 280
right-hand engineer and, 127
visibility and, 292
truth
  ownership of system of, 219
  radical candor, 245
two-way doors in decision-making, 201

U

uncertainty, removing, 278–284, 286
updates
  one to one meetings, 87, 101, 108
  project updates as communication artifacts, 213, 216
  in roadmaps, 282
  vs. syncs, 87
Urban, Tim, 194
urgency, in Eisenhower Matrix, 70–72
user education, trade-offs in trifectas, 177
user needs, trade-offs in trifectas, 177
UX team
  multifectas and, 184
  roadmap responsibility, 281
  trifectas and, 176–184

V

values
  longtermism and, 59
  polarity model and peers, 141–146
  relationship with your manager and, 158
Valve, 30
vendors, negotiating with, 315, 340
venture capital
  defined, 300
  profits and, 303–305
  top line vs. bottom line dilemma, 317
visibility
  cross-disciplinary relationships, 292
  trifectas and, 179
  trust and, 292
vision
  defined, 219
  longtermism and, 61
  strategic level communication and, 219
VP of engineering
  in career track overview, 6
  in competency grid, 17
  vs. CTO, 12, 36
  in org charts, 35
  relationship to director of engineering, 34
  senior individual contributor archetypes and, 127
  strategic level and, 12

W

warfare
  boom and bust cycle strategies, 321, 326–328, 337–344
  career progression levels, 9–14
  communication artifacts and, 193, 210–221
waterfall development, 274
What's Our Problem?, 194
wingspan, *see* span of control
work processes, engineering strategies and, 267, 269
Workflow Builder, 213
wrap-up in coaching with GROW model, 94
writing
  artifacts and note-taking, 207–209
  commit messages, 211
  design documents, 212
  editing, 205
  leadership as, 204–209
  paper triangle, 204–205, 208
  performance assessments, 230, 234
  as thinking, xi, 205, 361

X

X, 301
X-as-a-service, team topologies and, 44, 50

Y

your manager
  additive and subtractive actions and, 161–162
  competition for manager's attention, 146
  conflict with, 156–158, 161–162
  disappointment with, 156–158, 162
  escalation and, 165–168
  Eye of Sauron and, 165, 169–170
  global vs. local maxima, 156
  meetings with peers and, 148
  relationship with, 153–172
  single point of contact antipattern, 147–148
  symbiotic relationship with, 158, 160–162
  tools vs. prescriptions for, 158
  tragedy of the commons, 138–139
  understanding your management needs, 162–165
  unpleasant surprises and, 165, 170
  when things go wrong and, 165–171
your mananger, managing upwards, 13

Z

Zappos, 29
zero-interest rate periods (ZIRP), 323

Thank you!

We hope you enjoyed this book and that you're already thinking about what you want to learn next. To help make that decision easier, we're offering you this gift.

Head on over to https://pragprog.com right now, and use the coupon code BUYANOTHER2024 to save 30% on your next ebook. Offer is void where prohibited or restricted. This offer does not apply to any edition of *The Pragmatic Programmer* ebook.

And if you'd like to share your own expertise with the world, why not propose a writing idea to us? After all, many of our best authors started off as our readers, just like you. With up to a 50% royalty, world-class editorial services, and a name you trust, there's nothing to lose. Visit https://pragprog.com/become-an-author/ today to learn more and to get started.

Thank you for your continued support. We hope to hear from you again soon!

The Pragmatic Bookshelf

Become an Effective Software Engineering Manager

Software startups make global headlines every day. As technology companies succeed and grow, so do their engineering departments. In your career, you'll may suddenly get the opportunity to lead teams: to become a manager. But this is often uncharted territory. How do you decide whether this career move is right for you? And if you do, what do you need to learn to succeed? Where do you start? How do you know that you're doing it right? What does "it" even mean? And isn't management a dirty word? This book will share the secrets you need to know to manage engineers successfully.

James Stanier
(396 pages) ISBN: 9781680507249. $45.95
https://pragprog.com/book/jsengman

Effective Remote Work

The office isn't as essential as it used to be. Flexible working hours and distributed teams are replacing decades of on-site, open-plan office culture. Wherever you work from nowadays, your colleagues are likely to be somewhere else. No more whiteboards. No more water coolers. And certainly no Ping-Pong. So how can you organize yourself, ship software, communicate, and be impactful as part of a globally distributed workforce? We'll show you how. It's time to adopt a brand-new mindset. Remote working is here to stay. Come and join us.

James Stanier
(348 pages) ISBN: 9781680509229. $47.95
https://pragprog.com/book/jsrw

Competing with Unicorns

Today's tech unicorns develop software differently. They've developed a way of working that lets them scale like an enterprise while working like a startup. These techniques can be learned. This book takes you behind the scenes and shows you how companies like Google, Facebook, and Spotify do it. Leverage their insights, so your teams can work better together, ship higher-quality product faster, innovate more quickly, and compete with the unicorns.

Jonathan Rasmusson
(138 pages) ISBN: 9781680507232. $26.95
https://pragprog.com/book/jragile

The Agile Samurai

Here are three simple truths about software development:

1. You can't gather all the requirements up front. 2. The requirements you do gather will change. 3. There is always more to do than time and money will allow

Those are the facts of life. But you can deal with those facts (and more) by becoming a fierce software-delivery professional, capable of dispatching the most dire of software projects and the toughest delivery schedules with ease and grace.

Jonathan Rasmusson
(264 pages) ISBN: 9781934356586. $34.95
https://pragprog.com/book/jtrap

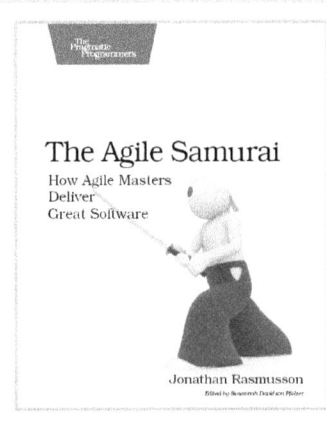

Software Estimation Without Guessing

Developers hate estimation, and most managers fear disappointment with the results, but there is hope for both. You'll have to give up some widely held misconceptions: let go of the notion that "an estimate is an estimate," and estimate for your particular need. Realize that estimates have a limited shelf-life, and re-estimate frequently as needed. When reality differs from your estimate, don't lament; mine that disappointment for the gold that can be the longer-term jackpot. We'll show you how.

George Dinwiddie
(246 pages) ISBN: 9781680506983. $29.95
https://pragprog.com/book/gdestimate

Real-World Kanban

Your team is stressed; priorities are unclear. You're not sure what your teammates are working on, and management isn't helping. If your team is struggling with any of these symptoms, these four case studies will guide you to project success. See how Kanban was used to significantly improve time to market and to create a shared focus across marketing, IT, and operations. Each case study comes with illustrations of the Kanban board and diagrams and graphs to help you see behind the scenes.

Mattias Skarin
(138 pages) ISBN: 9781680500776. $28
https://pragprog.com/book/mskanban

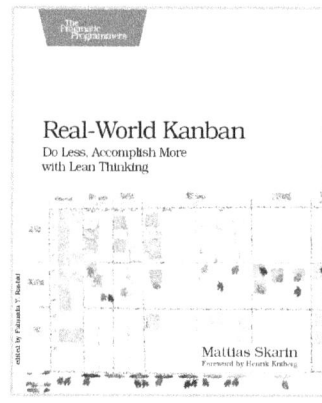

Lean from the Trenches

You know the Agile and Lean development buzzwords, you've read the books. But when systems need a serious overhaul, you need to see how it works in real life, with real situations and people. *Lean from the Trenches* is all about actual practice. Every key point is illustrated with a photo or diagram, and anecdotes bring you inside the project as you discover why and how one organization modernized its workplace in record time.

Henrik Kniberg
(178 pages) ISBN: 9781934356852. $30
https://pragprog.com/book/hklean

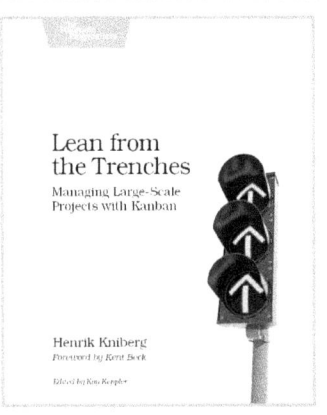

The Nature of Software Development

You need to get value from your software project. You need it "free, now, and perfect." We can't get you there, but we can help you get to "cheaper, sooner, and better." This book leads you from the desire for value down to the specific activities that help good Agile projects deliver better software sooner, and at a lower cost. Using simple sketches and a few words, the author invites you to follow his path of learning and understanding from a half century of software development and from his engagement with Agile methods from their very beginning.

Ron Jeffries
(176 pages) ISBN: 9781941222379. $24
https://pragprog.com/book/rjnsd

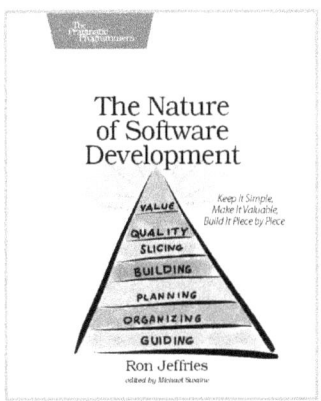

The Pragmatic Bookshelf

The Pragmatic Bookshelf features books written by professional developers for professional developers. The titles continue the well-known Pragmatic Programmer style and continue to garner awards and rave reviews. As development gets more and more difficult, the Pragmatic Programmers will be there with more titles and products to help you stay on top of your game.

Visit Us Online

This Book's Home Page
https://pragprog.com/book/jsenglb
Source code from this book, errata, and other resources. Come give us feedback, too!

Keep Up-to-Date
https://pragprog.com
Join our announcement mailing list (low volume) or follow us on Twitter @pragprog for new titles, sales, coupons, hot tips, and more.

New and Noteworthy
https://pragprog.com/news
Check out the latest Pragmatic developments, new titles, and other offerings.

Save on the ebook

Save on the ebook versions of this title. Owning the paper version of this book entitles you to purchase the electronic versions at a terrific discount.

PDFs are great for carrying around on your laptop—they are hyperlinked, have color, and are fully searchable. Most titles are also available for the iPhone and iPod touch, Amazon Kindle, and other popular e-book readers.

Send a copy of your receipt to support@pragprog.com and we'll provide you with a discount coupon.

Contact Us

Online Orders:	*https://pragprog.com/catalog*
Customer Service:	*support@pragprog.com*
International Rights:	*translations@pragprog.com*
Academic Use:	*academic@pragprog.com*
Write for Us:	*http://write-for-us.pragprog.com*

www.ingramcontent.com/pod-product-compliance
Ingram Content Group UK Ltd.
Pitfield, Milton Keynes, MK11 3LW, UK
UKHW050454150426
5217IPUK00025B/1682